THE OLD FRENCH EPIC

THE OLD
FRENCH EPIC

BY

JESSIE CROSLAND

HASKELL HOUSE PUBLISHERS Ltd.

Publishers of Scarce Scholarly Books

NEW YORK. N. Y. 10012

1971

First Published 1951

HASKELL HOUSE PUBLISHERS Ltd.
Publishers of Scarce Scholarly Books
280 LAFAYETTE STREET
NEW YORK. N. Y. 10012

Library of Congress Catalog Card Number: 73-117589

Standard Book Number 8383-1022-2

Printed in the United States of America

INTRODUCTION

THE object of this study is not to break a lance in support of any of the conflicting theories which have been put forward as to the date, the origin or the historical accuracy of the Old French national epic, though these questions will have to be considered in the course of the work, but to give a plain, unvarnished account of this remarkable 'genre', this outburst of epic poems during the eleventh and twelfth centuries which is quite unparalleled in the history of French literature. It has been estimated that some eighty to a hundred epic poems were produced, mostly in the twelfth century. The poems were, of course, of very unequal value, but the importance of this phenomenal output cannot be overlooked. They appeared 'not (as) single spies but in battalions'—the history of each outstanding hero developed into a cycle of poems which revolved round the original hero and furnished him with ancestors and descendants. The cyclic manuscripts containing these poems may contain as many as twenty-seven 'chansons' which form a kind of continued story in which the same characters appear and reappear—sometimes after they have been killed off in a previous chapter. The 'jongleurs' themselves were responsible for these collections and in some cases have added a few lines to one poem in order to form a connecting link with the next in the series, thus ensuring continuity. There is much that is decadent in character in the later ones and more still that is purely conventional, but, strange to say, fresh shoots of this 'floraison épique' appeared in other lands long after it had passed its prime in the land of its birth. The present work is an attempt to view this phenomenon against its historical background, to examine the soil from which it sprang, to indicate the unique character and beauty of its most noble exponents and to trace the development of certain ideals of thought and conduct which run through it. The poems have a value to-day not only from the place they occupy in literary history and a certain alluring quality which constantly draws the reader on, but they are extremely important as representing the best and the worst in the epoch which produced them. They present a picture of feudal society with its combination of idealism and brutality, its extremes of loyalty and treachery, such as no chronicle of the time can give. It is frankly admitted that in consideration of such a vast and complex subject much will be unavoidably omitted both in respect of the 'chansons' themselves, and the many incidental questions which have arisen in connection with them. The greatest attention has naturally been paid to the most justly famous of these epic poems and, as far as can be ascertained, to the earliest in date. This includes of course the *Chanson de Roland*, certain outstanding poems of the cycle of *Guillaume d'Orange*, and that of the 'revolted barons' (of which the best known is *Raoul de Cambrai*), bearing in mind that, although for the sake of convenience this classification has been retained, there is much that is common to all these poems as they had their roots in the same soil and are expressions of the same spirit.

A word must be said about possible discrepancies in the spelling of proper names which will almost inevitably have crept into the text. It has been difficult to be consistent in the use of Anglo-Norman and Old French forms (e.g. Willame and Guillaume, Gurmund and Gormont); of names ending in d or t (e.g. Renaud and Renaut, Girard and Girart) and the declension of proper names, with s or z in the nominative, has added to the difficulty. The indulgence of the reader must be craved if this lack of consistency has become too obvious.

Sincere thanks are due to the librarian and other members of the staff of Westfield College for the help and encouragement they have given me in a work which is the fruit of long devotion to a very fascinating subject.

J. C.

CONTENTS

LIST OF ABBREVIATIONS

C.F.M.A. — Classiques Français du Moyen Age.
E.E.T.S. — Early English Text Society.
A.P.F. — Anciens Poètes de la France.
S.A.T.F. — Société des Anciens Textes Français.
R.D.R. — Romans des Douze Pairs.

THE OLD FRENCH EPIC

CHAPTER I

THE BACKGROUND OF THE OLD
FRENCH EPIC

A. *HISTORICAL*

So much has been written and so many theories have been put
forward on the subject of the origins and the date of both the Old
French epic poems and the 'genre' to which they belong, that it is
difficult in the welter of opinions to find any fixed point from which
we may proceed to unfold their history. The views are widely
divergent, ranging from the earlier school of thought which held
that these poems had their roots in the distant past and were composed
of an agglomeration of shorter poems sung by contemporaries of the
heroes themselves, perhaps actually on the field of battle, to the less
romantic view that the poems, in a form not unlike their present one,
are of much later date and that they are due to the collaboration of
monks and jongleurs, brought together by the mass-movements of
pilgrims along the famous pilgrimage routes of the Middle Ages and
incited to poetic production by the hope of gain. This view has
received many hard knocks in its turn and the pendulum has swung
partially back again—but it still hovers rather uncertainly and refuses
to be stabilized at any one definite point. There is so much room
for conjecture where there is a paucity of reliable documents, and the
search for origins is such an alluring one that the question ends by
becoming a sort of will-o'-the-wisp. One of the great difficulties lies
in the fact that few of these so-called *chansons-de-geste* have come
down to us in their original form. The very name is hard to define.
The word 'gesta' originally meant 'deeds', actions accomplished,
things done. From this evolved the sense of 'history' or record
relating the deeds (e.g. 'gesta Francorum,' 'geste des Français', etc.)
and eventually that of 'family', lineage—in other words, 'those who
accomplished the deeds'. So, too, the poems themselves probably
evolved and changed in the process. The evidence that heroic poems
in some shape or form existed already as early as the first quarter of

the eleventh century is too considerable to be overlooked. It would make this chapter too long to sift all the evidence for the existence of ancient poems celebrating heroes, or to mention all the allusions to be found in chronicles of the period to 'vulgaria carmina, etc.' which obviously must have existed and been handed down from one generation to another. But one thing is certain: all the more notable figures of whom we have historical evidence and who form the centres of the later cycles—Charlemagne himself, Louis, his son, Roland (died at Roncevaux in 778), William of Orange (died in 803), Raoul de Cambrai (died in 943)—belong to the Carolingian epoch, i.e. roughly the ninth and tenth centuries. Other heroes, mentioned in some of the poems themselves—Chlodoveu, Floövent, Pepin 'le petit poigneür'—go back even further, but the references to these heroes are somewhat suspect and must be discounted as proof positive of the existence of songs celebrating them, although the possibility cannot be ruled out. In any case the ninth and tenth centuries, which saw the decay and break up of the Carolingian empire, the growth of feudalism and the expansion of the ecclesiastical power, form an unmistakable background for the events and ideas which we find portrayed in the earlier epic poems, before the more romantic ideas of chivalry and love had begun to invade the poetry of France. It is noteworthy and in accordance with fact as furnished by chronicles of the ninth century, how soon Charlemagne had developed into a legendary figure. Nowhere in the Old French epic is he seen active and at the height of his glory, and rarely as a very heroic figure. In the *Pèlerinage de Charlemagne*, a poem which bears certain marks of an early date, he plays an almost comic part. Even in the *Chanson de Roland*, where he is seen at his noblest, he is at times a testy old gentleman who rates his knights, bursts into tears at frequent intervals, and has to be supported in weak moments, both morally and physically. So, although it has been suggested that in its earliest form the *Chanson de Roland* was a product of the revolution against the dynastic change which placed Hugh Capet on the throne and was written 'avec le souci de flétrir les traîtres de 987',[1] if one reads the poem with an unbiassed mind, there is little to justify this opinion. It is noticeable how impersonal the expressions of loyalty often are: 'Ben devuns ci estre pur nostre rei' or 'Pur nostre rei devum nus ben murir', or words to that effect are repeated almost like a refrain. The idea of royalty was respected even after kings had

[1] See Mireaux (E... .e): *La Chanson de Roland et l'histoire*, 1945.

become weak and corrupt and the strength of this feeling can be detected in all the *chansons-de-geste*, including those in which the king plays a sorry rôle. But other factors are equally evident. During these two centuries we can trace the rise of the turbulent barons, of the dukes and the counts who play such a large part in the epic legends. We may read of their ambitions, their hostility towards a weak king, their quarrels amongst themselves in any page of Flodoard or Richer whose chronicles give us such a valuable picture of those times. Here we find, in fact, the ideal setting for our earlier *chansons*. The poems are imbued with both the nobler ideas of feudalism, with its loyalties to lord and peer and with its evils. The ingratitude or injustice of a sovereign, the discontent caused by the method of bestowing fiefs, the generally unsettled state of society largely caused by devastating raids of heathen of all descriptions, the superstitious beliefs in miracles and portents encouraged by the Church—all these features of the times, so amply testified to in the chronicles, are reflected in the earliest epic poems in the vulgar tongue. Another prevalent idea to which the contemporary writers bear witness forces itself on our attention. All through their writings runs the proof of the importance attached to birth during the Carolingian epoch. On one occasion a man of obscure birth volunteered to act as the king's standard-bearer when all the barons were wounded. He apologizes almost abjectly for suggesting such a thing. 'Ego ex mediocribus, regis agaso (=palefrenier), si majorum honori non derogobar, signum regium per hostium acies efferam.'[1] Much more serious and far-reaching was the case in which a king lost the support of all his feudal lords and was within an inch of losing his throne by extending his favour to a man of humble birth[2] and allowing him to sit on his council. Many are the echoes of this strong feeling in Old French literature of which the aristocratic nature is well known. Charlemagne, giving advice to his son in the *Couronnement de Louis*, warns him solemnly against seeking advice from a 'vilain' or even a magistrate's son. Birth is the one criterion, as can be seen in the evolution of meaning in words such as *gentil* and *franc* and in the prominence given to words such as *lignage* and *geste* in the *chansons-de-geste*. In the later romances, where there is often a weighing up of *nature* versus *nourriture* (= heredity *v.* environment) it is always *nature* which tips the scale. But noble birth involved noble qualities and any injustice on the part of a king was greatly to be deplored. Among the instruc-

---

[1] Richer, Bk. I, Ch. ix.
[2] *obsuris parentibus.* Ibid., I, 15.

tions given to the young King Louis in the poem just mentioned is included a warning against injustice:

> Ne orfe enfant por retolir son fié
> Ne veve feme tolir quatre deniers (ll. 178-9).

Guillaume in the *Chançun de Willame* claims that he has never been guilty of such an act of injustice. On the contrary:

> Apres le pere jo'n oi le fiz si chier,
> que unc la mere ne laissai corecier (ll. 1576-7).

This inexcusable injustice on the part of a weak king forms the pivot on which the whole lurid poem of *Raoul de Cambrai* revolves. How much such an action on the part of the king was criticized in the tenth century we may learn from the account in Richer's Chronicle (IV, lxxv) of the indignation felt when Eudes, Comte de Chartres, was unlawfully deprived of his stronghold by the will of his king. 'Do you not think', says his ambassador, 'that the Divinity itself is offended when on the death of the father an orphan son is deprived of his patrimony?' 'That must be so,' is the reply, 'and not only that, but it is a great discouragement for good men ("honorum desperatio").' Here we have the theme of the Old French poem in a nutshell. To the same realm of feudal customs and ideas belongs the insistence on the twofold relationship of 'auxilium' and 'consilium'. We may judge of the hold which this relationship had over minds in the tenth century even in non-military matters by the constant reference to this mutual source of strength in the letters of the learned Gerbert. 'O amicorum fidissime,' he exclaims in a letter to a friend,[1] 'ne deseras amicum consilio et auxilio', and he refers to it again and again. This fundamental idea runs all through the Old French epic. Even the emperor in the *Chanson de Roland*, though in full knowledge of what is right, cannot act without the advice of his barons. If any decision has to be made he summons his knights 'pur sun conseill finer'. In the *Chançun de Willame* (most unjustly relegated by a recent critic[2] to the repertoire of a 'gedankenloser Spielmann niederer Art'), Vivien, the ill-fated nephew of Guillame d'Orange, valiantly refuses to risk the lives of men who do not legally owe him allegiance and 'auxilium'. All the earlier *chansons-de-geste* abound in such allusions showing how deeply imbued they are with the feudal idea of loyalty to one's lord and one's peer. In *Raoul de Cambrai* it is long before the woefully wronged Bernier throws off his allegiance to his liege-lord

---

[1] Circ. Anno 983. Cf. G..rbert: *Lettres* 983-97. Ed. J. Havet, 1889.
[2] Curtius: 'Ueber die altfranzösische Epik,' *Ztsch. für romanische Philologie*, Bd. LXIV, 1944.

and defies him openly. How loyal the knights are to each other and
what noble ideas of friendship inspire these companions-in-arms!
Oliver calls to Roland 'sun ami et sun per' to keep close to him in the
battle,[1] and the enigmatic Gualter del Hum recalls pathetically that
he was ever Roland's companion in courage and knew no fear when
in his company.[2] How completely different the spirit of these earlier
epics is from that of the later romantic epic need hardly be pointed
out. It is obvious that the setting in which they are placed is an
essentially different one. The literature of a period reflects certain
current ideas and tendencies. The Old French epic poems reflect
what was 'in the air' at a period clearly distinguished from that
reflected in the romances of (say) Chrétien de Troyes in the second
half of the twelfth century, or even of the so-called 'romans imités
de l'antiquité' of a somewhat earlier date. In these latter a new
conception of love and of the relations between the sexes had already
crept in. A sort of revolution in ideas had taken place. The religious
element, so prominent in the earlier poems, is almost completely
absent from the romances. The Church as such no longer has the
same grip over men's minds. An occasional formal reference to God,
a visit to a hermit when life has been rendered hard by sinful conduct,
is the most that we find in Chrétien and his followers. The religious
background seems to have completely changed. The inspired army
has been replaced by the individual knight; the Church with its
hierarchy of priests and monks by the solitary hermit who does not
figure in the earliest *chansons-de-geste* and but rarely in the Carolingian chronicles. The knight of the romances is willing to fight for
his own (or his lady's) honour in an adventure, but has no desire to
die for his religion or his country. His enemy is another individual
knight, whereas in the earlier poems the combat is between the
armies of the true faith and massed hordes of the heathen—be they
Norman, Huns, or Saracens only slightly disguised under the name
of pagans. In any case, those not killed in battle must be converted to
Christianity and baptized at the earliest opportunity. The first
poly-baptism described in Richer's Chronicle[3] is interesting as it
shows the doubt felt by the archbishop and the priests as to the proper
procedure in this unaccustomed rite. A synod had to be specially
convoked, both God and the pope had to be consulted as to the
appropriate method and only then could the ceremony take place.
In the *Chanson de Roland*, however, the event is treated as quite
normal, and we are told of 100,000 being baptized at once in the

[1] *Chanson de Roland*, l. 1975.   [2] Ibid., ll. 2046, 2049.   [3] Anno 921.

B

'baptisterie', only the Queen Bramimunde being reserved for less impersonal treatment by the susceptible emperor. From the date of Charlemagne's campaign against the Saxons and his crude methods of conversion,[1] the attitude towards the unbelievers was crystallized. There is merit in killing a heathen, even after his baptism, if fear had been the cause of it or if danger would result from his remaining alive. Both these ideas crop up again in the Old French poems. In the *Chanson de Roland* the archbishop chooses out the most villainous-looking heathen to slay, and after his death he is discovered by Charlemagne with 400 dead and dying around him ! In the *Chançun de Willame*, Gui, the precocious young nephew of Guillaume, treacherously slays a heathen when he is on the ground for fear of the mischief he might still perform if left alive, and is applauded by his uncle for the action. There may be an occasional fine pagan or even a handsome one, but for the most part they are repulsive and treacherous and only fit to be exterminated. Incursions by the heathen were very frequent during the Carolingian period—whether of the Avars under their *Kagan*, or the Northmen under their warlike dukes, or the Saracens under their fanatical leaders. The countryside was ravaged, the cities burned, the inhabitants murdered, and rich booty, sometimes including the holy relics, carried off. Any one of these incursions could have been in the author's mind when the *Chançun de Willame* received its earliest form. The incursion of King Déramez against the coast of France sounds a familiar note:

> Les marches guastet les aluez vait esprendre,
> les veirs cors sainz trait par force del regne.

This might be the echo of any of the savage raids on the coast which made it necessary to transfer the relics and move further inland, involving at times a change of capital. On rare occasions the struggle between two armies might be decided by a single combat (*singulare certamen* or *monomachia duorum*). The belief in the *judicium Dei* to decide a battle or uphold the honour of an accused person is found even amongst the savage Lombards, although one enlightened emperor expressed some doubt as to its validity in all cases. No such doubts troubled the authors of the Old French epics where famous battles between Roland and Fernagu and other notable heroes became traditional. But the fact of defeat or disaster in the French poems was not always a proof that God had deserted the righteous any more than it was in the chronicles. Indeed, the hero of defeat was perhaps

---

[1] The Bible or the sword—equalling in ruthlessness the methods of Mahomet.

the best loved hero of all, as we may have seen from the popularity of a Roland and a Vivien, the two ill-fated nephews of two famous men. It was rare for the fighters to feel themselves forgotten of God as did Vivien's army in the *Chançun de Willame* ('Deus nus ad ubliez'). The inevitability of death is generally accepted, and it is not to be deplored if it overtakes those fighting for a good cause. Robert, Duke of Celtic Gaul, encouraged his men in their fight against the pirates in 921 to care little for death which may come at any time to any of us when fighting for fatherland, life and liberty. Earlier still, King Eudes, in a furious battle against the Northmen in 892, encouraged his soldiers with the words 'decus pro patria mori, egregiumque pro christianorum defensione corpora morti dare'. This is, indeed, a prose version of what we find expressed so often in verse by the French poets. Roland, too, exhorts his men to die fighting and not to flee, for certain death awaits them:

> Pramis nus est, fin prendrum aitant,
> Ultre cest jurn ne serum plus vivant (ll. 1518–19).

Doubtless the assurance of a seat amongst the 'Innocenz' in holy Paradise would be a solace in view of death just as the promise of the 'martyrii palmam' and the 'coronam caram' had been to a previous generation. To ask for respite from death was an ignoble petition. Vivien in the *Chançun de Willame* repents immediately of having prayed for 'respit de mort' in view of the fact that even God did not spare Himself, and twice over he asks his men scornfully if they want to die in their beds.[1] Only in a few cases was it granted to the happy warrior to have concrete certainty that his soul would go straight to Paradise. Roland, in a symbolic gesture, was allowed actually to hand his glove to God, but this is an isolated example. The support and solace of the Church, however, was available for all who died in true repentance, and during the ninth and tenth centuries, if we may trust the chronicles, the favour or disfavour of heaven was manifested in unmistakable ways. Not only the monastic annals, but the histories of Paulus Diaconus, Flodoard and Richer abound in records of signs and portents which show which way the wind is blowing. Eclipses, comets, earthquakes, tempests all happen with amazing frequency. Visions and dreams abound, and the death of any important person is almost always foretold by a portent or a disaster of some sort. The

---

[1] The prayer of Vivien in his extremity rings true though most of the prayers in the Old French poems are of a formal character. Such expressions as *Dieu vrai paterne* and *Seinte Marie genetrice* take us straight to the litany or to well-known passages in the Latin hymn-writers.

death of King Raoul in January 936 was preceded by a number of
'presages funestes'—armies of fire in the sky, flames of blood, and a
terrible pestilence. Before the death of the Bishop of Tours in 943 a
luminous globe was seen flashing through the sky. These are but two
examples out of many. It is small wonder then that, arising out of
such a soil, Charlemagne in the *Chanson de Roland* should see visions
and dream dreams, and that Roland's death should be preceded by
an earthquake, and a tempest accompanied by thunderbolts and
terrifying lightning, or that the superstitious should think that the end
of the world was upon them.[1] The famous prophecies of Raoul
Glaber, writing in the eleventh century, may have been something in
the nature of an *Old Moore's Almanack*, but there is no doubt but that
there was a certain apprehension of the year 1000 in some pious
people's minds. The events of the second half of the tenth century,
the unsettled state of things generally, the change of dynasty with its
accompanying disorders, in fact, the *acerba tempora*, for which,
according to Gerbert (later Pope Sylvester II), the only remedy was
a philosophic mind, all these things turned men's minds inevitably to
the thought of the end of a disastrous age and to the hope of a better
one to follow. This is the background which explains the hopeless,
almost nostalgic state of feeling we find expressed in the earliest Old
French epic. 'O God,' says Charlemagne (aged 200 years or more),
when called to make fresh exertions, 'how wearisome is my life.'
Even more pitiful is the discouragement of Guillaume (aged 150 years
and more) after his defeat, when he laments to his wife: 'I am old
and feeble; I shall never bear arms again. My honour in this life is
finished.'

B. LITERARY

The Gerbert just mentioned (Gerbertus or Girbertus) was director
of studies ('scolasticus') at the Cathedral School of Rheims from 972
to 982. His learning and skill were such that even during his lifetime
he was suspected of a certain intercourse with the devil, a suspicion
which developed freely during the later Middle Ages. He was far
too exceptional a man to be taken as typical of his age but, though
he himself was an isolated example, the instruction which emanated
from him must have had wide dissemination, as we know that
students flocked to his classes from all parts in ever increasing numbers.[2] His reputation was so great that his name was widely known

---

[1] 'La fin del siecle ki nus est en present' (l. 1435).
[2] Cf. Richer: Bk. III, ch. 55

not only through all parts of Gaul ('per Gallias') and among the peoples of Germany, but also on the other side of the Alps, where his fame spread as far as Tuscany and to the shores of the Adriatic. The cathedral school at Rheims was justly celebrated in those days, and doubtless became a model for other schools throughout the country. Gerbert's curriculum of studies therefore presents some interest for the period which constitutes the background of the Old French epic.

The future pope was first and foremost a philosopher, very famous for his logic ('in logica clarissimus habebatur'), his dialectic, and his exposition of Aristotle. Following his courses on these subjects he wished to proceed to the study of rhetoric but found that it was impossible for his students to attain to a knowledge of oratory unless they were familiar with the writings of the poets. He therefore put his students through a course of literature. He read and commentated ('legit itaque et docuit') Virgil, Statius, and Terence (poetas), Juvenal, Persius, and Horace (satiricos), and Lucan (historiographum).[1] Only after he had familiarized his students with these authors could he pass on to instruction in rhetoric, the subject most highly esteemed in those times. Virgil the poet and Lucan the poet-historian are the two authors that most concern us here. Amongst those pupils of Gerbert who came from their own homes in France, Germany, or Italy, it would be strange indeed if no potential poet was inspired to do for his own country what Virgil had done for his. The theme of patriotism, of obligations to one's faith and one's family, the belief that the contest is between a superior race directed by divine providence and inferior races governed by inferior deities would have been enough in itself to be a source of inspiration in those troublous times. But add to this a much-admired technique, an orderly and symmetrical arrangement, descriptions of single combats by heroes mentioned by name, insults heaped upon the fallen foes, laments for the dead and other technical devices, and we have a clear source of inspiration for the poet trying out a similar theme in a nascent and as yet imperfect language. There is hardly a rhetorical device (except perhaps that of the lengthy similes) which we do not find in the Old French national epic. Many of these tricks of style, such as hyperbole, apostrophe, rhetorical questions, etc.,[2] are common to all primitive poetry and are almost inseparable from the epic form. Descriptions

---

[1] Ibid., III. 47.
[2] Seventeen of which have been classified, defined and named by German scholarship. Cf. Curtius, *loc. cit.*

of landscapes would be perfectly natural, not to say indispensable in a
long poem. The brief juxtaposition of mountains and valleys, so
much favoured by the author of the *Chanson de Roland* who refers
again and again to 'les vals et les munz', especially in the antithesis
'Halt sunt les pui et les vallees tenebreuses', is such a natural figure of
speech that it seems a little unnecessary to describe it as 'eine ver-
witterte Schrumpfungsform antiker Landschafts-Ekphrasis'.[1] But the
fact remains that the technique of the earliest Old French epic poems,
as well as their subject matter ('la grande bataille'), do reflect much
of the character of the Latin authors most favoured in the ninth and
tenth centuries. The *Pharsalia* of Lucan, studied in the schools with
as much zeal as Virgil's poem and greatly beloved in the later Middle
Ages, is rich in romantic descriptions, portents, dreams, and witch-
craft. It could hardly fail to be a source of inspiration to the potential
poets of a period in which the copying of manuscripts flourished, by
virtue both of its subject matter, its pathos, and its characterization.
The moral content, too, was not without its effect. For both Virgil
and Lucan the virtue of 'temperantia' outshines almost all others.
'Servare modum',[2] so difficult especially when fortune smiles ('rebus
secundis'); to believe oneself born not for oneself alone but for the
whole world,[3] what marvellous ideas for the pupils of Gerbert to
carry away with them and make their own. It is not surprising that
we find the idea of *mesure*, or its opposite *démesure*, so prominent in
the Old French epic legends, side by side with the idea that the hero
lives not for himself alone, but for his family, his country, his religion,
and his king, in fact for the whole world. One would search in vain
for any direct imitation or conscious verbal borrowing from the
Latin poets, but these are the models which were available to any
poet of that time who had enjoyed an average 'clerical' education,
and it becomes more and more patent that the epic poems of the
eleventh and twelfth centuries were the work, not of an indefinite
mass of individuals known as 'the people', but of individual authors
of a considerable amount of culture. The medieval or late Latin
poems, on the other hand, or at any rate those which have come
down to us, were not of a kind to become sources of inspiration to
the new generation of poets who wrote in the vulgar tongue. They
smack so much of the classroom, they are so artificial in character,

---

[1] The expression *les vals et les munts* means no more than the English 'up hill and down dale'
even simply 'up and down'.
[2] *Æneid* X, 502; Lucan: *Pharsalia* II, 381.
[3] 'Nec sibi sed toti genitum se credere mundo.' Ibid., II, 383.

giving the sort of impression of prize poems, that they cannot be seriously considered as forerunners of the *chansons-de-geste*. They are padded with imitations of the classics and stilted in style, even wl ere the subject matter is heroic in character; it would need a stretch cf imagination to suppose that they served as models to our poets. We can only rejoice that their style did not become a more lasting fashion. The passage in the poem in Latin hexameters of the so-called Poeta Saxo (ninth century), which mentions the defeat at Roncevaux in 778 and speaks of 'vulgaria carmina' celebrating the heroes and their ancestors, is only an amplification of a reference in Eginhard's *Vita Caroli Magni*[1] to 'barbara et antiquissima carmina quibus veterum regum actus et bella canebantur'. These 'carmina' would presumably have been in German and do not concern us here. The Poeta Saxo's work itself cannot be considered as a heroic epic. It is a metrical paraphrase of Annals and Eginhard's *Vita* and adds nothing to the background we are endeavouring to sketch. Nor is the poem of Ermoldus Nigellus (ninth century), *In honorem Ludowici*, very much more fruitful. This poem is a rather fulsome panegyric of Louis the Pious written in the hope of winning back the Emperor's favour. It is stuffed with reminiscences of Virgil, Ovid, and later Latin poets. Neither of these poems can be considered as genuine heroic epic. The obscurity of style, coupled with their artificial rhetorical devices and lack of naturalness, marks them out as the work of scholars interested in giving proof of their own scholarship. They are poles apart from the simplicity and straightforwardness of style that we find in the *Chanson de Roland*, which is the least 'popular' in style of any of the Old French epic poems. The same may be said of another ninth-century poem which is not a mere panegyric and has a more heroic subject. This is the poem entitled *Bella parisiacae urbis*, written by Abbo in the year 897 and describing the siege of Paris by the Normans in 885-7. Here we find all the epic 'motifs' of love of one's country, pious belief, etc., but the subject matter is so hopelessly obscured by the fantastic artificiality of the style that we are almost reminded of the *trobar clus* of the troubadours in the twelfth century. The work begins characteristically:

> Urbs mandata fuit Karolo nobis basileo
> Imperio cujus regitur totus prope Kosmos

and throughout the poem Greek words, obscure words, heathen deities and ideas occur with such frequency that the author himself

---

[1] Cap. 29.

was obliged to add glosses to elucidate his contorted and intentionally perplexing style. Here again we are disappointed if we hope to find a model for the *chansons-de-geste*, although the author has a good tale to adorn. Nor can anything concrete be adduced for the pre-history of the *chansons-de-geste* from another elusive document known under the title of the *Fragment de la Haye*, a curious and unique fragment of Latin prose preserved in the Bibliothèque Royale at the Hague. The text has been variously dated from the ninth to the twelfth century—so uncertain is the dating of these medieval Latin texts. It is generally accepted that the fragment is a prose version of a poem in Latin hexameters and is an example of an 'exercice d'écoliers'. If the latest date (twelfth century) be accepted for the fragment it obviously cannot find a place in our background. But there is much that points to an earlier date even if we do not accept the view that it proves the existence of a literary tradition and may be the reproduction of an Old French poem of the tenth or early eleventh century. The fragment describes in turgid style a siege in which 'Carolus imperator' and various heroes with names familiar to us from the Old French epic poems (chiefly those of the Guillaume cycle) take part. Even the heathen Borel with his troop of sons (*unum e natis Borel*), a mysterious figure often mentioned casually in the early *chansons*, finds his place in the description. But the style is artificial, the reminiscences of classical authors are numerous, the introduction of classical mythology—Mars, Gradivus, Bellona, Orcus, Tonans (=God) and constant references to Fortune—abound side by side with references to the Deity in a way that does not seem to point to an original in the vulgar tongue. These characteristics and other technical devices are, however, so typical of the late Latin epic of the tenth century that we cannot entirely ignore a document with a knowledge of the Old French heroes even though it be a mere 'exercice d'écoliers'—perhaps even a rather clever parody. One can well imagine a schoolboy writing an impudent imitation of Virgil or Lucan about the Emperor Charles:

Carolus imperator ut fortis, fixus pietate Tonantis, quam semper sciebat presentem largamque, . . . semperque tollit lumina ad sidera, soluta manantiore lacrimarum, humectatque genas, etc.

The fragment remains an intriguing one showing certain affinities with the early Old French poems and bringing the Emperor Charles into the same picture as the heroes of the Guillaume cycle in a way we rarely find in the early *chansons* with the exception of the *Pèlerinage de Charlemagne*, which also partakes rather of the nature of a parody. In the wake of these turgid, artificial works of late Latin, redolent of the midnight oil, obscure, affected and lacking in human feelings, the earliest poems in the vulgar tongue must have come like a breath of fresh air haling the spring of a new epoch.

There is, however, one poem which is in a different category from those to which we have briefly alluded and which does present many analogies with the Old French poems. The so-called *Waltharius* or *Vita Waltharii manu fortis* is as obscure as to its origin as it is to its date. Little reliance can be placed on the ascription of the poem by Ekkehard IV in the *Casus Scti Galli*[1] to his predecessor Ekkehard I of the monastery of St. Gallen as the former is notorious for his inaccuracies. If we could trust his dates the poem would have to be placed somewhere in the second half of the tenth century. Actually an even earlier date has been generally accepted and recent research would place it away back in the ninth century. It has been claimed by both French and Germans as a national product. The names of some of the characters—Hagen and Gunther—are well known in German legends and, if Ekkehard can be trusted, it originated in a German cloister. An awkward passage in the prologue which precedes the work in some of the manuscripts mentions a certain Geraldus, 'peccator fragilis', whose connection with the poem is rather vague but who is very unlikely to have been the author. Whatever its source, it was known in both 'romance' and German-speaking lands; the hero is an Aquitanian (later transplanted into Spain), and a certain confusion arose in legends attributed to him and to Guillaume d'Orange, perhaps on account of a likeness between them and their belligerent careers. In any case the question of origins does not concern us here as Latin was the common language for written records and histories and all forms of 'book-epic' in those days. What does concern us is that the *Waltharius* undoubtedly presents some striking analogies with the Old French epics. The story is of the escape of two hostages from the court of Attila (a theme very reminiscent of a chapter of Gregory of Tours' 'Historia Francorum'), and it revolves round one character built on heroic lines and identified by his attribute of 'manu fortis' just as Guillaume d'Orange was later by his sobriquet of 'fiere-brace'. The actual characters bear no striking resemblance to those of later epics—indeed, the only feminine character provides us with a contrast rather

---

[1] Ch. lxxx.

than a parallel. One could hardly imagine it being stated of the stout-hearted wife of Guillaume that:

Ipsa metu perculsa sonum prompsit muliebrum (l. 892).

It is the form and arrangement of the poem which strike such a familiar note to those acquainted with the French epic poems. Naturally the ordinary epic technique is there—Virgilian phrases, apostrophes, antitheses, insulting epithets of the combatants who are all distinguished by name. But besides this we find a division into sections of varying length, rather like the 'laisses' in the Old French epic and the mixture of direct and indirect speech so common to all these poems. The opening lines (as in the *Chanson de Roland*) are quite simple and essential to the story:

Attila rex quodam tulit illud tempore regnum, etc.

The main part of the poem consists of a series of single combats between the hero and his adversaries, each of whom is named and briefly characterized in a way exactly corresponding to that in the *Chanson de Roland*. There is not much religion in the poem, but the vision-'motif' is here and, strangely enough, the ominous dream of Hagen before the battle is almost identical with one of the visions of Charlemagne in the *Chanson de Roland*. As in the other medieval Latin epics, we find the mixture of heathen and Christian ideas. Orcus, Erebus, the Parcae, Phoebus, all play their part. But the Christian element predominates. When Walther has committed the sin of pride he immediately falls on his knees and prays for forgiveness—on another occasion he makes the sign of the cross; he interpolates 'volente Deo' when expressing a wish for the future, he addresses God as 'Dominum benignum . . . qui peccantes non vult sed perdere culpas'. When he has killed all his adversaries he places each of their heads on its appropriate trunk, prostrates himself, and prays that he may meet them again in paradise, an action even more touching than that of Roland in fetching and ranging the bodies of his twelve peers before the archbishop, as in the latter case they were his friends and not his enemies.

The method of describing the series of combats, too, is very similar in the two poems—the spear, the sword, the triple hauberk, the blow which cleaves the helmet, the body, and the horse's back. The vocabulary employed is often nearly related to that of the vernacular, and one or two set phrases are of special interest. To describe the outstanding valour of a hero the author exclaims:

Quisquis ei congressus erat, mox tartara vidit,

an exact parallel to a favourite description, particularly frequent in the Guillaume cycle, which appears with many variations in the second half-line:

cui il consuit, n'a pas de mort garant.

Another customary device of the Old French poets when describing a furious battle scene is to exclaim in admiration: 'If only you had seen, etc.' or 'Then you might have seen . . .'

La veïssiez fier estor esbaudir!

This, too, we find in the *Waltharius*:

Hic vero metienda virum tum bella videres!

These examples do not exhaust the affinities that can be traced between the *Waltharius* and our French poems. They may be small points but there is too much, both in details and in the subject and framework of the Latin poem to dismiss its claim to being, in many respects a predecessor of the epic poems in the vulgar tongues. Walther, like many a hero of the latter legends, was reputed to have ended his life as a hermit. This may have been a later addition as a holy ending was often found the best method of disposing of turbulent heroes. Doubtless here the 'Lives of the Saints' and the writings of the early fathers provided many models for this excellent way of employing the last lap of an active life. But it was the last lap only—for in those chaotic days when bishops fought and monks were despised it was the deeds of warriors which interested the public for whom the epic legends were destined, far more than the lives of the gentle saints who healed head-ache and stomach-ache, made friends with the beasts and suffered such horrible persecutions from man. The warlike Frank preferred the pugilist to the priest as hero of their epics. It is interesting to recall that even in the Old Saxon poem *Der Heliand*, which is a kind of *Gesta Christi*, the hero Christ is represented as a feudal lord surrounded by his twelve barons, and the scene in which Peter cut off the high priest's servant's ear is described with evident relish and with much unnecessary effusion of blood.

The love for epic poetry seems to have persisted through all those centuries which are commonly lumped together as 'The Dark Ages'. It emerges out of the darkness in various forms, religious, legendary, panegyrical. But the Old French epic poems have quite a special character of their own. They are not purely historical, nor are they purely legendary. They are not panegyrics of saints or kings. They contain many deep truths: they embody much of the wisdom of the ages which is expressed sometimes in proverbs, sometimes in reflections of the authors, but more often in the characters themselves. These characters are as yet little touched by the somewhat artificial influence of the refined courts. The portents, dreams and miraculous happenings are serious, biblical ones such as we find in the books of Daniel and Hezekiah—not yet the marvels, living or automatic, which the later romances derived from sources opened to them by the Crusades. Indeed, it cannot be insisted upon too much. Just as the history of the tenth and eleventh centuries, their social customs and their institutions give us the historical setting of the Old French epic, so, too, the annals and chronicles of the period furnished an inexhaustible store of semi-historical, semi-legendary occurrences which were at the disposal of the first authors of epic poems in the vulgar tongue. It is more than possible that certain anecdotes, certain details were stored in the minds of the French poets, as well as the general impression of the period of which they sung. Paulus Diaconus tells a delightful story of the little boy Grimoald who was in danger of being left to the mercy of the invading pagan army because he was too small to gallop on a full-sized horse. He pleads to be allowed to try and, mounted on a charger with neither reins nor saddle, follows his fleeing brothers. He is overtaken, alas, by the Saracens, but whilst they pause before killing him, the quick-witted youth seizes a stick and cleaves his captor through the skull. This causes the author to quote an apt line from Virgil's description of the bees in the *Georgics* in which he describes the wit of those tiny creatures: 'Ingentes animos angusto in pectore versant'.[1]

It is impossible to read the description of the final defeat of the heathen in the *Chançun de Willame* without recalling this episode. Gui, the young nephew of Guillaume, has followed the army (against his uncle's wishes) on a huge horse. His feet cannot reach the stirrups and he has to ride bare-back. But his final act is to give a coup-de-grace to a fallen pagan and justify himself for the action in such a way as to make his uncle remark:

> Cors as d'enfant mais raison as de ber (=baron
> =grown man).

Possibly the horse described by both Flodoard and Richer as 'validissum' at the age of 100 years and over suggested to the author of the *Chanson de Roland* the name of 'veillantif' for his famous steed. But it would be futile here to collect details, even though they exist in considerable number, as they would merely obscure the broader issues which form the subject of this chapter.

[1] *Georgics* IV, 83.

CHAPTER II

THE EPIC CYCLES AND THE *GESTE DU ROI*

THE Old French epic poems, or *chansons-de-geste* as they will be called from henceforth, can be conveniently, if not always accurately, distributed into three main groups, or 'cycles', according to their subject matter and the outstanding hero, or type of hero, about whom they are grouped. These three cycles, or 'gestes' are (1) that of the king or emperor, namely Charlemagne; (2) that of Doon de Mayence from whom are descended all the large family of traitors even including such noble figures as Renaut de Montauban and his brothers; (3) that of Garin de Montglane, the ancestor of the famous Guillaume d'Orange, and all his numerous family. The first and third of these groups which centre round Charlemagne and Guillaume respectively are fairly well-defined. The second includes all the numerous poems celebrating the exploits of unruly barons, and it will be simpler if the three groups are spoken of in the following pages as (1) the 'cycle du roi', (2) the 'cycle de Guillaume d'Orange', and (3) the 'cycle des barons révoltés' or 'feudal cycle', even though epic heroes of this group were not precisely in the mind of the medieval poet when he drew up his classification. The division into groups is, of course, artificial and of relatively late origin. It was neither necessary nor possible at the date when the first epic poems were composed. But as these poems increased in numbers and the heroes, we may suppose, became popular, some sort of grouping became almost inevitable. If we take as an example the cycle of Guillaume d'Orange, which gives us the best sample of this kind of cyclic formation revolving round a central figure, or figures, we are introduced to two heroes, Guillaume and his nephew Vivien, both full of interest and dramatic possibilities and, perhaps, most appealing of all, full of tragedy. It is therefore not surprising that Guillaume once having been 'launched', people asked for more—(there are many examples of this in modern literature—e.g. Sherlock Holmes)—and the 'jongleurs' hastened to meet the request by supplying details of his youthful escapades, his manner of obtaining a fief, his old age, and finally his death. The cycle of Guillaume is an exceptionally complete one, as we may follow him almost from the cradle to the grave. Some of the heroes died young and were spared the cares of matrimony and the despondency

The Old French Epic

of old age. This was the case with a Roland and a Vivien. But the exploits of their youth—the 'enfances' as they were rather attractively called, could still be sung. Moreover, the biblical taste for genealogies developed during the period which produced the *chansons-de-geste*—fostered, perhaps, by the annals of the times[1] and the urge to provide a respectable origin for the hero. During no period of French literature was the necessity for being 'bien né' more ingrained in men's minds than in the twelfth and thirteenth centuries. This idea accounts probably for the classification into cycles which we owe to the 'jongleurs' themselves and which acquires some sense when looked at from this point of view. A famous passage in *Girard de Viane*, a poem belonging to the 'feudal cycle', groups the 'chansons' into three *gestes* which are characterized as follows:

> N'ot que iii gestes en France la garnie:
> Dou *Roi de France* est la plus seignorie
> E de richesse et de chevalerie.
> Et l'autre apres (bien est drois que jo die)
> Est de *Doon* a la barbe florie
> *Cel de Maiance* qui tant ot baronie.
> En son lignage ot gent fiere et hardie
> De tote France eüssent seignorie. . . .
> Se il ne fussent plain de tel felonie.
> De cel lignage ou tant ot de boidie
> Fut Ganelons qui, par sa tricherie,
> En grant dolor mist France la garnie
> Don furent mort entre gent paienime
>   Li doze per de France.
> . . . La tierce geste ke moult fist a proisier
> Fu de *Garin de Montglane* le fier.
> De son lignage puis je bien tesmoignier
> Que il n'i ot ne coart ne lainnier
> Ne traïtor ne felon losengier.

It will be seen that, in two cases out of the three, this passage concerns roots, or ancestors. We find the same division in a poem devoted to one of these ancestors, viz. the *Chanson de Doon de Mayence*, so that it was evidently current amongst the 'jongleurs' themselves, who were eventually responsible also for collecting the poems of the biggest group into cyclic manuscripts so as to give a kind of continued story. In the case of the 'geste du roi', however, this was hardly possible. In spite of the fact that Charlemagne became a legendary figure at a very early date, it is noticeable that he did not lend himself much to epic development. Walter Map, writing in the

---

[1] Cf. the expression 'ex patre' = 'sired by' in these documents.

twelfth century, laments that, though Caesar lived in the praises of
Lucan and Æneas in those of Virgil, the godlike nobility of the
Charleses and Pepins was only celebrated in the vulgar rhymes of
mimes, and their characters full of bravery and self-control were still
awaiting the pen.[1] The renaissance of learning, of which Charlemagne
was the promoter, did not appeal much to the popular imagination,
and the figure of the emperor was perhaps too august to be treated
like that of an ordinary man. Whatever the reason may be, the fact
remains that the *Chanson de Roland*, in which Charlemagne appears
in his most regal capacity, is like 'a triton among the minnows' when
compared with the rest of the poems which went to the formation of
this cycle.

In fact, although the thirteenth-century author of *Girart de Viane*
speaks of the 'geste du roi' as being 'la plus seignorie', the royal
cycle, or 'cycle de Charlemagne', can hardly be said to exist. With
the exception of the *Chanson de Roland*, in which the emperor and his
nephew vie with each other as the focal point of interest, and the
Pèlerinage de Charlemagne, which it is difficult to take seriously, there
is hardly a poem of real poetic value in this group. Charlemagne was
too nebulous, too much enveloped in his cloud of glory to furnish a
really sympathetic hero. He was too great to be tied down to one
cycle or one particular set of poems. In the *Fragment de la Haye*,
mentioned in the last chapter, 'Carolus Imperator' urges on his men
by his battle-ardour, but the knights around him are not the twelve
peers who normally form his bodyguard, but heroes bearing the
well-known names of another family, that of Aymeri de Narbonne.
In the *Pèlerinage*, too, we find Ogier of Denmark, Duke Naime,
Turpin and Roland rubbing shoulders with Guillelme d'Orange and
his brothers Bernard, Hernaut and Aïmer in an eclectic group of
'doze pers'. Nor was the emperor furnished with a pedigree or
descendants. True, his mother, the so-called 'Berthe au grand pied',
forms the subject of a thirteenth-century poem which describes how
Berthe, fraudulently deprived of her conjugal rights by her waiting-
maid and banished into the forest, is eventually discovered by the
king when the fraud has been exposed, and the marriage is consummated by the impatient king in the waggon ('grand char') in
which he has made his journey to her hiding place. The infant, who
is born in due time, is christened 'Char-le-magne' to perpetuate the
place of his origin, and becomes the illustrious emperor. Meanwhile
a son of King Pepin's first wife has grown up and wages war on his

---

[1] Cf. *De Nugis Curialium*, Div. V, Prologue i.

young half-brother Charles, and the bastard, disguised under the name of *Mainet*, forms the subject of another poem which has come down to us in a garbled and fragmentary form. Poems like this make us incline to agree with the verdict of Walter Map. These late and unheroic personal poems are unworthy of the great king. It is possible that other poems which have not come down to us celebrated the male ancestors of the emperor. In an interesting passage in the *Chançun de Willame* we hear of 'un jugleür' who is present at the battle and can relate 'de geste les chançuns' (the first known use of this expression), and amongst the songs expressly mentioned are those of

> Chlodoveu le premier rei Francur
> Ki creeit primes en deu nostre seignur[1]

and of

> Pepin le petit poigneür[2]

—presumably *Pepin le bref*, the father of Charlemagne. Poems about Chlodovech (French Clovis) and Pepin may have existed but they have not come down to us, whereas the other heroes mentioned by the 'jongleur'—Floovent (=Chlodovenc), Charlemagne, Girart and 'Olivier le prou' have all been perpetuated in song.[3]

Roland himself is anxious that no 'malvaise cançun' should be sung about him or his men[4] and that no blame should attach to his 'parents' on his account.[5] In a famous passage he refuses to be accompanied on his dangerous mission by too large an army lest he bring disgrace on his kin:

> Deus me cunfunde se la geste en desment.[6]

But the fact remains that the family idea, so prominent in the Guillaume cycle, plays but little part in the 'geste du roi'. The sons of Charlemagne did not lend themselves to epic celebrity. His wife plays no such rôle as that of Guibourg or Hermenjart (respectively

---

[1] *Chanson de Guillaume*, l. 1264 f. Ed. Suchier.

[2] Ibid., 1269 f.

[3] Here it may be objected that the 'juglere' (nom. form) himself is but a fiction of the poet's brain. It was part of the epic technique to introduce a trustworthy source for the events he relates, and we must not take at face value the references to eye-witnesses on the field of battle. And yet who knows whether songs celebrating famous warriors did not accompany the army marching into battle just as, until a fairly recent date, the drums and fifes, or bagpipes played a modern army into action? The soldier-minstrel does not occur for the first time in the Old French epic. The tradition goes back to Tacitus. The poet Angilbert, in his short lyrico-epic poem on the battle of Fontenoy (written *c.* 841), after describing the slaughter of the Franks, who were 'most learned in the art of war' (*proelio doctissimi*), tells us that he was present on the battlefield:
'Angilbertus ego vidi pugnansque cum aliis,
Solus de multis remansi prima frontis acie.'

[4] *Chanson de Roland*, l. 1014.   [5] Ibid., 1063.   [6] Ibid., 788.

wife and mother of Guillaume). Perhaps her legendary character was of a less majestic nature than that of her husband. In the *Chronicon Novaliciense* (tenth century) we read of how she tried by a ruse to penetrate a chapel reserved for the other sex and was stricken down dead in the attempt. Shortly afterwards her royal husband passed that way and, on learning the identity of the corpse he sees lying on the path, remarks unfeelingly: 'Thy feet have carried thee hither, my dear (mi cara), but they will not carry thee back.' In the *Pèlerinage de Charlemagne* she dares to make a derogatory remark to her husband as he struts gloriously to church surrounded by his nobles and very nearly loses her head for her indiscretion. There is nothing in either the *Chanson de Roland* or the *Pèlerinage* that bears any comparison with the clan-idea which dominates the cycle of Guillaume. Curiously enough, in the former poem it is only in connection with the traitor Ganelon that family relations play any part. He sends salutations to his wife, his little son, his 'amis et ses pers'. His uncle holds his stirrup for him, and presumably Pinabel with his thirty relations belonged to his clan. But of his antecedents we hear nothing beyond the fact that he was 'de mult grand parented' (l. 356), and it was left for a later poem to introduce him into the lineage of Doon de Maiance, thus forming a link with the cycle of traitors and rebellious barons. It was obviously impossible to keep the three 'gestes' in closed compartments. Charlemagne and his son Louis play a considerable part in the *Couronnement de Louis* of which, however, the real hero is Guillaume, whose exploits fill the poem. There is a reference to the 'lignage' of the emperor, but it is rather a sad one as Charles is fain to admit, when Guillaume places the crown on the head of his weak son Louis that Guillaume's family has sustained and raised his own:

> Sire Guillelmes, granz merciz en aiez.
> Vostre lignages a le mien essalcié (ll. 148–9).

It is only too clear in this poem that the kith and kin of Guillaume are of nobler build than the feeble scion of the 'geste du roi'. It is the twelve peers—Roland and Oliver, Yve and Yvoire, Gerins and Engeliers, the archbishop and the rest—to whom the pope refers longingly when he returns from a vain attempt to pacify the heathen king by bribes. But to the list of the 'doze pers' he immediately adds the warrior Aymeri and all his numerous family who would have daunted any foe. So here again we see how the cycles intermingle, though it is Guillaume who eventually becomes the hero of the poem.

There are other poems besides the *Couronnement* in which Charles

C

is a sort of starting-point from which the chief actor sets out on his career of glory. In the thirteenth-century poem *Aymeri de Narbonne*, by Bertrand de Bar-sur-Aube, we are told that the army was returning sadly from Spain after the destruction of the rearguard at Roncevaux. The knights are weary and longing for a little ease and recreation. But on their return journey they pass the town of Narbonne which the Saracens have converted into a fortress, and the indefatigable, ever-young Charles looks upon it with covetous eyes and is seized with a desire to wrest it from the hands of the enemy. In spite of the remonstrances of his wise counsellor Naime, he calls upon one knight after the other to go in and win, but is met with blank looks and refusals. 'If I could but be back in my own country,' says Richard of Normandy, 'I would want no castle in Spain.' How much the emperor wishes his nephew Roland and the twelve peers were still alive! At last, however, Ernauz de Biaulande is moved with shame at the idea of letting his sovereign down and suggests that his own son Aymeri might undertake the task. The emperor is delighted at the idea (in spite of the fact that the young Aymeri had once supported his rebellious subject Girart de Viane against himself), and Aymeri is willing, nay eager to rejoice the hearts of his father and his 'fier parenté'. He refuses all gifts offered by the emperor with indignation as he intends to carve out a good inheritance from the 'paiene gent', an intention which furnishes the fundamental idea of the 'Guillaume-cycle'.

So the cycles dovetail again and from this point Aymeri becomes the hero of the poem and Charles fades out of the picture. This proceeding is typical of other 'chansons' in which the protagonist is often one of the feudal barons warring against his own sovereign and which loosely form the cycle of the 'revolted barons'. Leaving aside the *Chanson de Roland*, which must have a chapter to itself, there is, however, another poem in which the Emperor Charles plays a vital part, although his nephew Roland shares the glory with him as he does in the *Chanson de Roland*. We refer to the *Chanson d'Aspremont*, a late twelfth-century poem modelled on the *Chanson de Roland* and supplying us with some details of Roland's youth. It opens, like its model, with Charlemagne surrounded by his barons at Aix and the arrival in their midst of an envoy from the heathen king Agolant, lord of all Africa, who wishes to extend his territory and crown his son Eaumont king of Rome. The natural struggle ensues between the rival kings and their armies. Roland is left behind as too young to join in serious fighting, but escapes from his guard and with one or two companions joins the army. In the course of the battle he saves the life of his uncle Charles, kills Eaumont, and obtains the latter's sword, the world-famed *Durendal*, besides the horn (l'olifant) and the swift horse, Veillantif (6076–8). In addition to the help of Roland and his young comrades in the battle, Charlemagne has a rather unwilling ally in the person of Girart d'Eufrate, one of the unruly barons who believe themselves to have been wronged by the king. Girart swears at first with many oaths that he will not join the army of Charles, the son of the dwarf Pepin, who was so small that you might have played ball with him (l. 1133). He starkly refuses all homage to Charles and advises his barons to do the same. But his good wife ('sa prode feme') Emmeline, to whom he has been married 100 years, reasons with him and at last persuades him to join his forces to those of the emperor, and he sets out with his two nephews Bueve and Claire. In the end it is his help which decides the battle and his nephew Claire, who kills King Agolant. Girart then declares himself quit of any allegiance to the emperor and there is a hint of future trouble between them. Here the mingling of the cycles is obvious. It is not only the young Roland, nephew of the emperor, who wins his spurs, but Claire, the nephew of the defiant Girart, whose prowess is equally well proved.

The *Chanson d'Aspremont* is, as has been said, obviously modelled on the *Chanson de Roland*. The framework is the same—the parallel treatment, the mission of the ambassador, the 'grande bataille' with its single combats and its 'eschielles', its alternations of success and failure, and all the customary technical devices. In some ways the valiant young heathen, Eaumont, corresponds to Roland in the earlier poem—he refuses to sound his horn to summon his father to his aid,

> Que mon lignage ne fu onques mentant (l. 5355).

and he dies gallantly, committing his sword into the care of the one who kills him. The prudent heathen Balan reproaches him for his folly in the words of Oliver:

> Vostre olifant ne degnastes tentir (l. 5446).

There are other passages which show that the author was well acquainted with the earlier 'chansons' and, in spite of one or two interesting episodes, he is extremely conventional both in thought and style. This is true particularly of the second half of the poem, which is largely a mere tedious repetition of battle-scenes. There is the customary advice as to protecting orphans and widows given by the

counsellor Naimes to the emperor and by Duke Girart to his son[1];
the (conventional) warning against trusting a 'vilain' or man of low
degree who has no conception of honour and should stick to his job.[2]
The same conceptions of what constitutes regal behaviour, with
special emphasis on generosity which is 'le royal mestier'.[3] Charlemagne is represented as somewhat in need of support and good
counsel, but still valiant in the fight. He even has to be implored by
his knights not to risk his life in battle. He dares to ignore convention
on one occasion when he makes knights of many men of humble
birth provided they possess courage and loyalty,[4] and there is an
attractive description of him armed and ready for the fray, and
looking like an angel descended from heaven.[5] Girart, too, the
turbulent baron who began by insulting Charles and his ancestry, is
shown to be a 'gentleman' in his behaviour at the end when he pays
honour to the dead King Agolant and has him buried with military
pomp. In this respect, the author tells us 'fist molt Girar que ber',
using almost the identical expression as that used by the author of
Gormont et Isembart on a similar occasion.[6] In language and style and
rhetorical device the *Chanson d'Aspremont* is equally indebted to its
predecessors. The battle scenes are conventionally described, the
prayers and the apostrophes all 'coulent de source', the stock phrases
(*la veïssiez . . .; cui il consuit . . .*' etc.) abound, and St. George,
accompanied by St. Mercure and St. Domin, appear on the battlefield
to help the French 'exalt' Christianity—'Chrestienté tenir et essaucier'.[7]

   The *Chanson d'Aspremont*, conventional and unoriginal though it is,
and only bearing comparison with poems of an earlier date in rare
moments, merits attention because it forms one of the stepping-stones
to a later conception of heroic values—particularly as exemplified in
the character of Roland—which we propose to study in another
chapter. The scene in *Aspremont* is placed in Italy (Aspramonte),
where a remarkable development of the Old French epic subjects was
destined to take place. But it soon shifts back to Spain. The author
of the *Chanson de Roland* in the skilfully turned first stanza—or
'laisse'—so much more attractive in its simplicity than the conventional opening of the 'jongleurs'[8]—had left a cunning loop-hole

---

[1] Cf. *Couronnement de Louis*, etc.
[2] l. 11224.
[3] l. 11185.
[4] l. 7442 f.
[5] l. 4231.
[6] l. 544: 'De ces fist Loowis que pruz'.
[7] l. 9396.
[8] '*Oyez, seignor, , . .*' with their stock phrases about the inferiority of other 'jongleurs' to
themselves.

which constituted almost an invitation to other poets and chroniclers to supply an introduction to his story:

> Carles li reis, nostre emperere magnes,
> Set anz tut pleins ad esté en Espagne.

Seven years in Spain—spent in conquering the country and reducing all its strongholds with the exception of Sarragossa. This, without any details, is all we hear of Charles' activity during those seven years. And what had the restless, ambitious Roland been doing all that time? We get a hint of his activities in the list of places,[1] which he himself claims to have conquered for the emperor, and in the malicious speech of Ganelon[2] when he recounts Roland's misdeeds to his uncle in an attempt to prove his untrustworthiness. He had taken Noples without the emperor's permission, and, after killing all the Saracens, had washed the fields with water to hide all trace of the battle! This reference to an otherwise unknown episode proves that his 'prouesses' or 'enfances' had not been entirely commendable, but it was left to others to fill in the gaps in his history. This was done in various ways. About the middle of the twelfth century—or even somewhat earlier—appeared a curious work in Latin prose which became a source for later authors in search of legendary matter concerning Charlemagne and his nephew. This was the so-called *Chronicle of Turpin* or *Pseudo-Turpin* or *Historia de Vita Caroli Magni et Rotholandi*, the author of which, in a dedicatory epistle, claims to be the archbishop who fought in the battle of Roncevaux, was wounded, but, instead of dying as related in the *Chanson de Roland*, lived to give an eye-witness's account of the battle. This he does in an abridged form in pleasant Latin interspersed with many prayers and pious ejaculations as became a monk of the period. But leading up to the battle and the description of the death of Roland (*passio Rotholandi*), he describes various events and miracles accompanied by moral reflections, which happened during those years (the number of which he has increased to fourteen) that Charlemagne and his army spent in Spain. The two main episodes he describes are the struggle for mastery between Charles and Agolant and the single combat between Roland and Ferracutus. Both of these episodes enjoyed great popularity—as indeed did the rest of the false Turpin's *Chronicle* —in French literature of the period. This is proved by the frequent allusions to it in later poems, more particularly to the fight between Roland and the giant whose name appears as Ferragu or Fernagu in various works of the twelfth and thirteenth centuries.

[1] ll. 198 f.   [2] ll. 1770 f.

Turpin's worl, although completely fabulous, is extremely interesting and instructi . It translates into monkish form, with suitable moralizations and n ovations, the legendary matter which had collected round Cha. agne and Roland. It is but another proof of the inter-relation of chronicles and poems in the twelfth century, the former being more pious in character but just as fabulous, the latter more military and national but hardly less ecclesiastical. The chief points of contact between the *Chronicle* of Turpin and the epic poems concern the *Chanson de Roland* and *Aspremont*. With the latter he has in common the struggle between Charles and Agolant, ending with the latter's death—not at the hands of the youthful Claire, nephew of Girart, but a victim to the sword of Arnoldus de Bellanda (known in French poems as Hernaut de Biaulande). Of Eaumont we hear nothing, but in place of that a single combat between Roland and Ferracutus, the giant of the Saracen army, is described at considerable length. This duel is obviously based on that of David and Goliath in the first book of Samuel (ch. xvii), indeed we are told that the 'gigas Ferracutus' who was sent by the Emir of Babylon to fight Charles, was descended 'de genere Goliad'. Thus, as regards his lineage, he was a worthy antagonist for Roland. He issued forth from the city in the pride of his strength and challenged any of Charles' warriors to come out against him. One by one they came forth and were picked up ignominiously by the heathen and handed over to the Saracen army to be incarcerated. Some of them he even tucked under his arms in pairs—one under each arm—and Ogier himself was carried off as if he had been an uncomplaining sheep ('mitissima ovis'). Charles is dumbfounded at this disgrace, but the youthful Roland now insists on taking up the challenge. They fight, first with swords, then with fists, and then with stones till evening, when Ferracutus requests a truce till next day. Next morning the battle is resumed, again degenerating into an orgy of stone-throwing as the soil of the field abounds in large, round stones (reminiscent of the small round stones with which David killed Goliath). At last Ferracutus calls for a truce again as he is overcome with a desire to sleep. Whilst he sleeps uncomfortably on the ground, Roland, who was a nimble youth (*juvenis alacer*), slips a stone beneath his head for his greater comfort—an act of courtesy which denotes a raising of standards in the art of warfare. When the giant awakes, the two combatants sit side by side and the simple giant, speaking in the Spanish tongue which Roland understands, lets out the secret of his vulnerable spot (the navel) and his doom is sealed. But as they sit he inquires of Roland concerning his origin and—when he knows he is 'de genere Francorum'—concerning his faith. Then follows a long exposition of the Christian faith by Roland in which its mysteries are explained to a very incredulous heathen. The Trinity is illustrated by the tripartite nature of the almond, the cithar, the sun, the wheel, and even by man himself who consists of body, members and soul, and yet is one man. The virgin birth, the idea of which brings a blush to the modest heathen's cheek, is then explained, and the mystery of Christ's death and resurrection. At long last Ferracutus arises from his seat and says he will now continue the battle and the result shall determine which is the true faith and to which nation is due ever-lasting praise or blame. 'So be it,' replies Roland, and the battle begins again, but this time it is short. Roland is overcome for a moment, but calling in his extremity on the Virgin's Son, by the help of God he thrust his sword into the heathen's navel and fled. The horrified Saracens carried their dead leader back into the city, which immediately surrendered to the Franks.

The third major episode contained in this curious chronicle is 'that of the destruction of Charles' rearguard at Roncevaux (Runciavalle) after Marsirius (Marsilie) and Beligandus (Baligant) had taken their false oath at the instigation of the traitor Ganelon. The account of the battle, the sounding of the horn and the death of Roland is a brief but garbled version (interspersed with wordy ejaculations, invocations and prayers) of the noble theme of the *Chanson de Roland*. The main subject of the *Chronicle of Turpin* is thus the same as that of the crusading epic. It is the struggle between the true religion and the false—the Christian faith and the law of Mahomet, just as in the days of Goliath it was between the dogs of Philistines and the Jews. The Franks were God's chosen race and their cause had to triumph in the end. Charles and Agolant dispute and argue as each in turn asserts 'quod magis valet lex nostra quam vostra'. Roland and Ferracutus fight their single combat ('duel judiciaire') to decide the same question. In each case the heathen obviously has to suffer final defeat. But a subtle difference between the approach to the subject can be detected in the *Turpin Chronicle* and that which we find in the *Chanson de Roland*. Charlemagne in the latter work may be emotion-ally weak and in need of support, but he is spiritually upright. He is not only the emperor, the feudal lord, but he is also God's elect who can perform the act of absolution before the battle. In the *Pseudo-Turpin*, however, he is far from being the impeccable saint and hero. His failure to act up to the truth of his baptism has dire results. The heathen King Agolant, who has been baptized and converted, actually abjures his newly-found faith because he notices in Charles' treatment of the poor an absence of the true fruits of baptism ('baptismi opera recta in Carolo non vidit'). Agolant renews the battle and is killed shortly afterwards, thus losing his life and presumably his soul owing to Charles' lack of Christian charity. On another occasion the emperor is guilty of trying to prevent some of his knights who are pre-destined to a martyr's death from obtaining the crown of martyrdom. He is frustrated in this by the divine will. He acts democratically when, in his anxiety to defeat the heathen army, he makes many freed-men and knights from serfs and men of low degree—a symbolic act to which we have already drawn attention in the *Chanson d'Aspremont*. Thus the author bestows blame and praise indiscriminately, but it is noteworthy that he has no word of censure for Roland or his pride. His characters, which are chiefly familiar to us from the *Roland* and the *Aspremont*, are without individuality and, as in the poems of this cycle, women play but a small part in the story. Indeed, the presence of women, both Saracen and those of their own country, has a disastrous effect on the Frankish knights and proves the wisdom of Charles in *Aspremont* in banning their presence from the battlefield.

The long sojourn of Charles in Spain having been thus satisfactorily accounted for, the other main activity of the great king to receive attention from the poets was his war against the Saxons. Of this, too, we have only a rather belated account in the *Chanson des Saisnes* of Jean Bodel. The poem belongs to the end of the twelfth or the beginning of the thirteenth century and shows signs of foreign influences infiltrating themselves into the old heroic epic. The action takes place after the defeat at Roncevaux and the loss of Charles' army. Charles is at Laon (no longer Aix) in a gloomy and despondent mood, when he is threatened by the inroads of the Saxon King Quiteclin (Witekin). His own barons are unwilling to join in battle with him, not only from weariness but on account of provincial jealousies. However, the inevitable battle takes place. Charles kills Quiteclin in single combat but loses many of his own men and dearest relations. The outstanding character, however, in the Old French poem is that of the obnoxious and shameless Queen Sibille, who betrays her husband and her country, seduces Baudouin (brother of Roland), and by her example encourages a horde of ladies (wives of barons) to defy their husbands and invade the army in order to indulge in the 'jeux d'amour'. This preposterous woman shows how far we have travelled from the feminine ideal represented by the chaste Aude in the *Chanson de Roland*—but it exemplifies in very marked fashion the absence in this and the other poems belonging to the so-called 'cycle du roi' of the worthy feminine rôle and influence which is such a marked and attractive characteristic of the *Cycle de Guillaume*.

It is impossible to examine in detail all the poems which are distantly connected with the cycle of Charlemagne. They are mostly of later date and are decadent in character. The two important poems—the *Pèlerinage de Charlemagne* and the *Entrée d'Espagne*, as well as the *Chanson de Roland*, are reserved for treatment in a later chapter.

CHAPTER III

LE CYCLE DE GUILLAUME

OR

CYCLE NARBONNAIS

WE turn with some relief to the Guillaume-cycle. It is so much more compact than that of the king. The question of the identity of the central hero, William of Orange, has been much canvassed, but Bédier in Volume II of his *Légendes Épiques* has reduced the number of sixteen possible prototypes to one tolerably certain one. The William of the Old French epic, if not completely legendary, is probably a somewhat elaborated portrait of William, Count of Toulouse, who fought against the Saracens, founded the monastery of Gellone, and died in 803. It is in this group of poems that the idea of 'family' is so dominant. No disgrace must be brought upon the family. The most crushing taunt that Aymeri, father of Guillaume, can hurl at one of his sons is: 'You do not belong to my family' (N'estes mie de ma geste'). William is the focal point of the cycle and round him all the other characters revolve. He has an immense reputation already in what is probably the earliest poem in our group—the *Chançun de Willame*—a mysterious poem which was discovered in England in the year 1903 and has necessarily caused some modification of views held before that date. The only extant copy of this poem is the work of an Anglo-Norman scribe, and the general style and composition give the impression of its having been written down from memory. Whatever its literary value may be—and there have been widely different views expressed on this subject—the poem is of extraordinary interest and contains certain disconcerting features for some of the theories which have been put forward to account for the sudden outburst of epic poetry in France about the year 1100. Here in a poem which is perhaps contemporary with the *Chanson de Roland* we find already constituted and famous the epic family of Aymeri de Narbonne. True, we do not yet travel so high or so low in the genealogical table as some of the poems of later date: but the *lineage* (the 'lign') is already conspicuous. Guillaume (whose name appears in the Anglo-Norman form of Willame in the manuscript) is the centre of the picture, but it is by no means a case of 'Just William',

30

for we hear of his father Aymeri, his brother Bernard de Bruban, his nephew (on his brother's side) Count Bertran, his two nephews (on his sister's side) Vivien and Gui, another pair of nephews Girart and Guishart (the latter through his wife), and last but not least his incomparable wife Guibourg. Here at the turn of the eleventh century is evidence of a store of epic traditions already existing—not only the heroes of the Narbonne-cycle, but there is a reference to the heathen King Borel and his twelve sons who crop up in various old poems and to whom we have already noted an allusion in *Le Fragment de la Haye*. There is an allusion to Vivien's combat with the heathen Alderufe, one of those famous single combats comparable with that of Roland and Fernagu or Guillaume and Fierabras. Tiedbalt of Bourges and his nephew Esturmi, the villains of the early part of the poem, are obviously well-known characters. The heathen —'cele pute geste'—are thinly-disguised Northmen who have been harrying the coast under their leader Deramed with his 'Sarazine flote', and the battle follows its usual epic course 'uphill and down-dale' with thousands of slain on either side. As in the *Chanson de Roland*, we have the tragic death of a young hero in the early part of the poem followed by the fearful vengeance taken by his uncle in the later part. All the familiar epic devices and formulae are present, the insults to the slain, the apostrophes to sword, shield or horse, the exclamations and repetitions. These latter are indulged in somewhat to excess and yet they are not without their dramatic effect, especially where there is a kind of 'steigerung' in the variant forms. One cannot read the poem without coming to the conclusion that this is not the first of its kind. It is not only that the *jongleur* mentioned in the poem is said to have a regular repertory of 'de geste les chançuns', including songs of Chlodoveu, Flovent, Pepin, Charlemagne, and his nephew Roland, of Girart and 'Olivier le prou', but the whole poem teems with familiar ideas (*compagnonnage*, etc.), symbols (*Monjoie*, etc.), expressions ('*Ki dunc veïst*', etc.), which give the impression of quite a considerable poetic tradition behind it. The characters themselves stand out in true epic grandeur. They are traced by no uncertain hand. Guillaume has already achieved a reputation such that, as his jealous rival remarks, if he merely takes part in a battle the glory all accrues to him. Vivien, in his youthful pride, considers himself his uncle's equal in valour, but not in his wide experience in battle. Guillaume is indeed a 'preux', a 'nonper', a 'proelio doctissimus'—but he is also the hero of defeat. He is pathetic in the extreme when he returns without his army, with no friend (relation) but God, and so

dejected that he wants to give up the struggle. But a good meal and
the encouragement of his wife revive his drooping spirits and he is
once again ready for the fray. His two young nephews, Vivien and
Gui, stand out just as clearly defined. Vivien, whose 'enfances' will
be described again in other poems, notably the *Bataille d'Alischans*
and *Les Enfances Vivien*, has vowed that he will never flee before the
heathen, and in the poem we are discussing he does not break that
vow but dies a hero's death in face of fearful odds. His fate resembles
that of Roland in that his uncle does not arrive in time to help him,
but there is no hint of the hazardous pride and lack of moderation
displayed by the youthful Roland. The pathos of Vivien is less that
of a Greek tragedy where the hero's ὕβρις brings about his fall, but
lies in the touching love and admiration he feels for his uncle Guillaume and his loyalty to his aunt Guiburg who has brought him up.
He has an appealing sensitiveness of conscience too, as is shown by
his prayer when, having in a miserable moment asked God to save
him from death, he repents immediately, full of shame that he has
prayed for 'respit de mort' when God did not spare Himself but died
for us. This prayer stands out from the stereotyped long-drawn-out
liturgical prayers that we often find in these poems. Vivien's young
brother Gui, a boy of fifteen, is another notable personality as he
wishes, with his aunt's connivance, to join the battle contrary to his
uncle's orders. He overcomes the latter's objections by the wisdom
which flows from his mouth and which makes Guillaume remark
several times—

Cors as d'enfant mais raison as de ber[1]

thus becoming the first of a line of successors in French literature who
house big minds in small bodies.

But a most important feature in this rather uncouth and carelessly
constructed poem is the rôle of Guibourg, Guillaume's wife. It has
often been noted that the part played by women in the Old French
epic is small. The conception of love and of the function of women
that characterizes the courtly lyric poetry and the romances of the
twelfth century has not yet invaded the domain of epic poetry,
though it is shortly to do so. The hero of the earliest Old French
epic poems has but little time for amorous adventure. Not for him
is the temptation to dally at home with his newly-wedded wife,
which causes the heart-searchings of the hero of Chrétien de Troyes'
romance, *Yvain*, and the caustic remark of Parolles in Shakespeare's
All's Well that Ends Well that 'a young man married is a man that's

[1] 'You have the body of a child but the sense of a man.'

marred'. Nevertheless, women do play a part in some of the *chansons-de-geste*, and this is one of the characteristics of the Guillaume-cycle which distinguishes it from either of the other two. Charlemagne's wife, as we have seen, plays but a sorry rôle in the legends of the emperor and 'la belle Aude' but an infinitesimal part in the *Chanson de Roland*.

In the cycle of the unruly barons there is little space for love-affairs or feminine solicitude. In *Raoul de Cambrai* the hero's mother curses her son and, though she regrets it immediately after, the curse has gone forth. In the same poem, Bernier, the knight who kills Raoul and is second only in interest to the hero himself, actually tells the maiden who is rash enough to ask him for a kiss that he has no time for love. But in the cycle of Guillaume d'Orange we meet some of the most gallant ladies in French literature. Hermenjart, the wife of Aymeri and mother of his large family, is a worthy type of Roman matron—faithful to her spouse and full of affection for her numerous sons who answer to her love with a due sense of filial duty. She even tries to protect them from the austere treatment of a rather autocratic father, and on one occasion is knocked down for her pains. But the rôle of Hermenjart pales before that of Guibourg, the peer and help-mate of Guillaume himself. Although, according to the story, she is a heathen by birth and has been subjected to baptism and then wedded by the conqueror of her husband (alluded to in the *Chançun de Willame*), she proves absolutely faithful, both to her new religion, her second lord, and her adopted family. She is as anxious as her husband both to 'essaucier chrétienté' and to maintain the high tradition of his 'lignage'—the famous Aymerides. When Guillaume returns completely discouraged after his defeat and weeps and talks in a rather unmanly strain, this noble woman, although heartbroken at the news of her nephew's death, forgets some of her own grief ('partie ubliet de la sue dolur') and seeks to raise her husband's drooping spirits. She shows no sentimental weakness, for she reminds him that he had far better die on the battlefield as his ancestors had done before him than bring disgrace on his family.[1] She lies manfully (though only after having obtained her husband's consent) so as to raise another army for him, feigning a joy which she does not feel, and, having succeeded in this effort, she acts again with fine psychological perception and provides him with an ample repast. When Guillaume has disposed of this Gargantuan meal (consisting of a large loaf, two large cakes, a large brawn, a shoulder of boar, a large roasted

[1] ll. 1328 f.

peacock, and an enormous goblet of wine), without raising his head from the dish or offering a morsel to his wife, Guibourg shakes her head and between laughter and tears remarks: 'By the glorious God of heaven to whom I shall render up my sinful soul at the last day, a man who can make such a meal as this would be a very dangerous neighbour.'

There are few descriptions of actual battle-scenes in this poem, no long-drawn-out single combats, not a hint of pilgrimage-routes (the geography is fantastic), and not a very strongly emphasized faith in God—the main interest of the poem lies in the characters. The human element predominates. Comparing it with the *Chanson de Roland*, the first known poem of the Charlemagne-cycle, there is a notable absence of the deep moral significance which raises that poem from a mere crusading epic to a moral conflict fought out in the human soul. But on the other hand we have Vivien and Guibourg, and the little Gui and the drunken Esturmi, and the war-weary Guillaume who pathetically draws young Gui into a companionship of arms with himself,[1] thus bringing old age and youth together into a delightful friendship (*dui reial compaignun*), as so often happens in real life. The *Roland* carries the war into the enemy's camp—it is a crusading epic, or at all events an epic of conquest, ambition and national pride; the *Chançun de Willame* is an epic of resistance to the invader, of pushing the enemy back from his marauding incursions into 'Terre Certaine', a vague term which the author uses, perhaps wisely, so as to allow himself a certain geographical poetic licence. The *Chanson de Roland* is more homeric in character; his heroes are Virgilian with a certain biblical touch added, and partake of the large dimensions permitted in all classic epics. The *Chançun de Willame*, on the other hand, is more 'jongleresque' in character. The author may not be acquainted with the classics, but he is well-versed in the literature of his time. He knows the tradition about the feeble King Louis who was saved when fleeing in cowardly wise by a faithful member of the Guillaume clan; he emphasizes the unparalleled reputation of Guillaume, his pride therein coupled with his loyalty to a weak king; he enumerates the members of the Guillaume clan, his father Aymeri, his brother Bernard, his nephew Bertrand, etc.; he knows the tradition of the heathen King Borel and his twelve sons; he takes for granted William's crooked nose (curb nez) and the story of Guibourg and her former husband, Tiebaud of Orange. From these and other allusions it is clear that the author was acquainted

---

[1] l. 1676.

with some version of the following poems: The *Couronnement de Louis*, *Aymeri de Narbonne*, *Les Narbonnais*, the *Prise d'Orange*, the *Chanson de Roland*, *Girard de Viane*, and others which we cannot identify. The members of Aymeri's family mentioned in this poem (Bernard and Bertrand Palatinus) and the heathen King Borel and his sons are already known to us from the *Fragment de la Haye*, where, as in the *Chançun de Willame*, Bernard and Bertrand are not cited as uncle and nephew, but appear in close contact in the text. And so the mystery of these ancient documents and poems deepens as we find the epic traditions and family relationships already fixed and formulated in the earliest versions of the legends that we possess.

The first part of the *Chançun de Willame*, which might be described as an *Enfances Vivien*, we meet again in the so-called *Bataille d'Alischans*, which describes Vivien's death, Guillaume's return to Orange and his failure to be recognized by his wife, his initial defeats and eventual victory—due largely to the assistance of the gigantic Rainouart who, at first unrecognized and relegated to the kitchen, is finally identified and duly honoured as the brother of Guibourg. Not that Rainouart was invented by the author of *Aliscans*. He is celebrated already in a continuation of the *Chançun de Willame* of later date than the first part, and became in his turn the centre of a little cycle of his own. His interest lies in the fact that, although he belongs to the 'pute geste Sarasine', he is not wholly unsympathetic. He is a Rabelaisian figure, fights with a huge club instead of a sword, has an enormous appetite, makes himself respected by his courage and brute strength, and ends up, baptized and knighted, as a respectable member of society—in fact, he marries the king's daughter.

We have dealt at some length with the *Chançun de Willame* because of its importance as the earliest known poem of the Guillaume-cycle. But in both this poem and the kindred *Aliscans*, Guillaume is already an elderly and disillusioned man. There are other poems of his immediate cycle which tell of his adventurous youth, his numerous exploits and his manner of procuring a fief and a wife. The most important of these, and indeed of the whole cycle as far as the Guillaume legend is concerned, is the *Couronnement de Louis*. The subject of this poem, which is one of the earliest of the cycle even in its present form, is the support given to Louis, son of Charlemagne, against enemies at home and abroad, by Guillaume Fierebrace or *Guillelme al cort nes*, with whom we are already familiar. We cannot but be struck by Guillaume's steadfast faithfulness to the idea of royalty personified in the feeble King Louis. In spite of the fact that he realizes that his years of early manhood will be spent ('ma jovente user') in serving a king who has lost everyone's respect,[1] nothing turns Guillaume aside from his duty of upholding and helping his rightful lord.[2] It is the most beautiful example of loyalty in action that we find in all these old poems. Guillaume, unlike the king, is poor in lands and possessions, but rich in relations and friends. We will leave his character, as illustrated in the *Couronnement*, for a later chapter, just pointing out the foil provided for it by the picture of the ungrateful pusillanimous king and that of the undignified pope who tries to buy off his enemy with the treasures of his church and induce Guillaume to take up the enemy's challenge by giving him lifelong permission to eat flesh every day of the week and to take as many wives as he has a mind to.[3] It is hardly surprising that Guilliame remarks: 'Never was there such a generous priest!'[4] The composition of the poem is loose—it consists of five more or less independent episodes, but the same idea runs through them all. It is the best account of Guillaume's 'Enfances' that we possess. The hero is still a young man. We hear in one episode that he is either affianced or married to Orable[5] whom he momentarily but shamefully forgets when offered another damsel; his youthful exploits form the subject of the poem, the most noteworthy being the single combat with the giant Corsolt which cost him a piece of his nose. The earlier form of 'curb nez' is replaced by the more picturesque 'curt nez', an epithet that clung to him and has proved the truth of his witty remark when speaking of his disfigurement that the shortening of his nose would prove the lengthening of his reputation.[6] The poem concludes with a terrible indictment of the faithless, ungrateful king:

> En grant barnage fu Loöis entrez:
> Quant il fu riches Guillelme n'en sot gre.

In addition to the events related in the *Couronnement de Louis*, which are an indication of Guillaume's function in life, and those in the *Chançun de Willame* which depict an ageing and disillusioned man, intermediate episodes occur in other poems in which we can picture the warrior at the top of his form. It is true that in the *Charroi de Nîmes* he speaks of himself as having grown grey in the king's service,[7] but the introductory lines make it clear that he has not yet conquered Orange or abducted and converted the wife of its king when the episode of taking Nîmes by means of a 'charroi monté' took place.

---

[1] ll. 2252–3.   [2] l. 2010.   [3] l. 391.
[4] 'One mais nuls clers nen out le cuer si large!' (l. 399).   [5] l. 1433.
[6] ll. 1159–60.   [7] 'Tant t'ai servi que le poil ai chanu' (l. 257).

In the early part of this poem Guillaume recounts much of what is familiar to us from the *Couronnement de Louis*—how he had served King Louis in many different ways, how he had lost a piece of his nose in the battle with Corsolt, how he had saved the king's life as he ran like a beaten hound between the tents, and how in the course of his loyal service he had burdened himself with sin by causing death and sorrow to many a wife and mother. He indignantly refuses the king's offer of fiefs which would mean disinheriting a young son, but finally at his nephew Bertrand's advice, he requests and receives a large territory including Nîmes and Orange at the price of conquering them from the enemy, for, as the king himself remarks, they are not his to give but are still in the hands of the Saracens. The only boon that Guillaume craves from Louis is a promise of help once in seven years. The rest of the poem has no particular connection with other events of Guillaume's life. It is merely a pleasant story of a time-honoured ruse by which Guillaume takes the city and then disposes of the heathen king and many of his entourage by a multiple defenestration. The story is well told. Guillaume, with his two nephews Bertrand and Guielin and a considerable army, leave the royal palace and set out on their journey, not without a touch of nostalgia on the part of Guillaume:

> Vers douce France a son vis restorné.
> Un vant de France lou fiert enmi lou neis,
> Ovre son sain si l'an laist plain antrer.
> Ancontre l'ore se prist a guarmenter:
> 'Hei, ore dolce, qui de France venes,
> Tu ne viens pas devers la Rouge Mer,
> Ans viens de France qui tant fait a loer.'
> . . . De ses beas oilz commenca a plorer
> L'eve l'an cole fil a fil sor lou neis
> Que ses blïaus en estoit arousés . . . (ll. 830-9, 846-8).

This passage, taken from MS. D of the *Charroi*, is typical of Guillaume in sentimental mood. As they approach Nîmes by a carefully described route coinciding with the pilgrimage route to St. Jaques de Compostelle, they meet a peasant leading a rough cart formed by a barrel fixed on wheels and full of salt. This gives the idea to one of the knights that, by constructing a convoy of such vehicles and disguising themselves as merchants, they could gain an entrance to the town and seize it from within. Hence the title of the *Charroi de Nîmes*. The trick succeeds and the town is taken. There are several noticeable features about this poem besides the author's gift of graphic description. The scene opens in Paris, but we are soon trans-

D

ported to the South of France, and the accurate description of the route makes it appear probable that the author had traversed it in person, perhaps in company with other pilgrims. The personage of the peasant leading his ox-waggon with his children playing marbles on the top of the salt introduces a human element, and the truculence of Guillaume when he sees his nephew Bertrand trying to hoist the wheel of the waggon he is leading out of the mud, throws a new light on his character. But one serious theme comes to light in the *Charroi de Nîmes* which runs through other poems of this cycle and that of the revolted barons, and that is the recurrent reference to the injustice and scorn which poverty and misfortune always have to endure. Royalty remains an object of loyalty, but the contemptible character of the king who now sits on the throne of Charlemagne produces an element of social discontent even amongst the highest in the land. The author of *Aliscans* expresses it in almost bitter terms when Louis refuses to help Guillaume in distress:

> Ensi va d'omme ki chiet en povertés.
> J'a n'ert cheris, servis ne honorés. (ll. 2416–7).

We have seen that the *Couronnement* ends on the same note, and in the *Charroi de Nîmes* Guillaume, after recalling all he has done for the king, adds reproachfully:

> Tu es or riche et je sui po proisié (l. 253).

Such scorn for the poor and unfortunate might break through in the court of Charlemagne, but it would be found in the servants of the household, not in the emperor himself. One of the finest passages in the Old French epic is the outcome of indignation for this social injustice. A noble youth in the feudal epic of *Girart de Viane* is refused entrance to the court of Charlemagne by the usher (*huisier*) on account of his shabby appearance and replies indignantly:

> Li cuers n'est pas ne el vair ne el gris
> Einz est el ventre la ou Deus l'a assis.
> Teus est molt riches qui est de cuer faillis
> Et tieus est povres qui est fiers et hardis
> Vasaus de cors et frans hom et gentis (ll. 609 f.)—

words which might well have been uttered by Guillaume himself when scorned and neglected by Charlemagne's unworthy son.

In the *Prise d'Orange*, another poem located in the South of France, we see yet a different aspect of Guillaume's character. This poem shows us Guillaume in love—'Guillaume l'amiable'—and his love-making is as tempestuous as his war-making. He hears from an escaped captive of the beauty of Orable, wife of King Tiebaut of Orange. As he is already suffering from boredom at Nîmes and is thirsting for adventure, he sets out at once for Orange, which he enters in disguise. At the first sight of the beautiful Orable he thinks he is in Paradise, but he is unfortunately recognized by one of the pagans, and a fierce battle ensues between Guillaume, supported by a solitary companion, and a whole army of Saracens under the command of Aragon, who is in charge of the town and the queen, while his father, Tiebaut, is away in Africa. The Frenchmen are captured and imprisoned, but resist with the help of Orable, who has already fallen in love with Guillaume at first sight and expressed a wish to become his wife. They are eventually rescued by the timely arrival of members of Guillaume's family (led by his faithful nephew Bertrand), and Orable is converted and baptized. The marriage takes place at once and her character undergoes a complete change. From being an unfaithful wife and, according to some versions of the legend, a clever and inhuman sorceress, she becomes the faithful, self-sacrificing wife of Guillaume, full of devotion to his family and his cause—though there is a hint, perhaps, in *Aliscans* of her previous history, when Aïmer remarks:

> Je quit Guibors nos veut tos enchanter (l. 4282).

The problems raised by the *Prise d'Orange* are amongst the most complicated that exist in reference to the cycle of Guillaume d'Orange. Here we have a melodramatic poem of third or fourth rank and relatively late date which goes back to the very foundation of the Guillaume legend. It is unlikely that we have it in its original form, but that does not affect the importance of its subject matter. Even if we leave on one side the poem of the *Enfances Guillaume*, which is another version of the same subject, the names of Orange and Tiebaut take us back to the roots of our legend. The battle under the walls of Orange is mentioned in the *Chançun de Willame*, and Vivien actually claims to have killed Tiebaut l'Escler. Guillaume and Guibourg have lived long together in 'la bone cité' as they have also in *Aliscans* where the town of Orange is much in evidence. In the latter poem Tiebaut is not dead but is still in Africa. Such discrepancies are frequent and inevitable in these serial stories. In the *Couronnement* the hero is called Guillaume of Narbonne and Tiebaut is not mentioned, but we hear of Orable. The author of the *Charroi de Nîmes* briefly recapitulates the whole story in two or three lines at the beginning of his poem, and there are further references to Orange, to Tiebaut and his wife Orable. We are back again in the unknown. Why was Guillaume connected with Orange, where he gained a wife and a fief but suffered so many hardships? Who was this King Tiebaut whose name occurs so frequently in the *chansons-de-geste* and to whom there seems to be a reference in the twelfth century *Vita S^{cti} Wilhelmi*, which tells us that the Spaniards 'cum suo Theobaldo' besieged Orange? So persistently does his name recur that one critic has assumed that Guillaume's imaginary fights with a 'sea-captain' (the *esturmant* of the *Chançun*), Theobald, for the possession of Orange formed the subject of the original poem (*Urlied*) of the whole Guillaume-cycle to which he would give the title of '*la chanson de Thibaut l'esturmant*.[1] It is hard to say, but there were certainly many traditional characters that were well known to the audiences of those days which are an unknown quantity to us now. In any case, Tiebaut or Theobaldus is a strange name to be borne by a Saracen king, and as such is unknown to history.

We have now arrived at the last lap in Guillaume's chequered career. In the *Moniage Guillaume*, of which we have two versions dating probably from the second half of the twelfth century, Guillaume becomes a monk. Here we find the monastic tradition adapted to the legendary figure. Guillaume is sad—he has lost his faithful wife Guibourg, he has many sins on his conscience, so he decides, against the entreaties of all his friends at court and elsewhere, to enter a monastery and become a 'preuz' in the sight of God. From this moment his character changed and he became, for a time at any rate, humble and docile, as behoved a man of God. But the leopard cannot change his spots nor the Ethiopian his skin. Some of the rules irked him; the monks disliked him for his voracious appetite and feared him for his strength. So when someone had to go on a dangerous expedition against robbers in a nearby forest, Guillaume was elected for the task, and the monks were in high hopes that he would not return. Guillaume, in accordance with the rules of his order, may carry no weapons, and in reply to his humble questions to the abbot as to how far he should go in handing over his garments if the robbers demand them, he is told that he may refuse his trousers for decency's sake but nothing more. All happened as might be expected. At the refusal of his trousers the robbers began to handle him roughly. Instead of arms he used first his fists and, when these proved inadequate, a thigh torn from his own beast of burden, with which he defeated the robbers. The beast is miraculously healed and

[1] Cf. Becker, 1939.

Guillaume returned in triumph. The monks were horrified at seeing their 'enfant terrible' return and tried to shut him out. But, like Samson, he lifted the gates from their hinges and forced them to sue for mercy. Soon after this he rises even higher in the spiritual sphere, though he leaves his cell yet once more to help his liege-lord Louis, who has, as usual, alienated all his barons. Many other fantastic stories are added to these in the second version of the legend, and Guillaume's character becomes more monastic as time goes on until he dies in odour of sanctity. Now the interesting thing about these absurd tales is that we meet them again in a completely different setting and related to a different hero. In the *Novalese Chronicle*[1] we find every detail of the robber story, trousers and all, attributed to *Waltharius de manu fortis*, the hero of the Latin poem of that name!

And so we find chronicles and poems, poems and chronicles, all dovetailing and overlapping until we sometimes hardly know which we are reading. The *Novalese Chronicle* could as easily be transformed into a *chansons-de-geste* as the *Moniage Guillaume* could be turned into an equally fabulous chronicle. It is useless to ask which derived from which. The dates are difficult to attribute with any certainty to the documents; the episodes may be attached to different heroes; and each served in turn to build up the sort of semi-historical narrative which we find in the more ambitious chronicles of that age.

So much, then, for the quintette of poems which really constitute the poetic life of Guillaume d'Orange—the *Couronnement*, the *Charroi* and the *Prise d'Orange*, the *Chançun* (or *Aliscans*), and finally the *Moniage*—we might almost identify them with the *Quatre Ages de l'homme*:—youth, early middle age, later middle age, and old age, or more accurately with the four seasons: spring, summer, autumn, and winter. But how many questions remain unsolved. The historical Guillaume is as little documented as the historical Roland. The basic Roland is only known to us from the few lines in Eginhard's *Life of Charlemagne*; for Guillaume d'Orange (if we dare to identify him at all—so common is his name) we have only the following facts according to the records: a William made Count of Toulouse in 790; he was defeated in a battle 'super Oliveio' by the Saracens in 793; is mentioned as *Primus signifer* at the siege of Barcellona in 803; became a monk at Aniane in 806. Hardly more than the details of the battle of Roncevaux. But, if we can trust the chronicle, he had a family— father, mother, brothers, sisters, sons, and daughters, and two wives

[1] See Ch. II, p. 21.

(one named Guibourg). Perhaps: therein lies just the difference. He was not 'Just William'.

Guillaume's Brothers

None of the names however mentioned in the chronicle tally with the traditional names in the Old French cycle except Guibourg (Witburgh), Guillaume's wife. Whence comes his father Aymeri 'à la barbe florie' (or Naimeri = Sir Aymeri), and his five interesting brothers: Bernart, *li ainznex*, Hernauz *li rouz*, Bueve, Garin, Aïmer *le chaitif*, who never slept under a roof, and Guibert, the youngest, who would have inherited the fief of Narbonne by the right of ultimogeniture had it not been for a caprice of his father's. None of these has any historical basis (as far as we know) except possibly Aïmer, who may be a reminiscence of a certain Hadhemar,[1] Count of Narbonne, of whom it is reported that, when fighting Charlemagne's battles in Spain and marching through the forests, he had no roof but the sky (*caelo protecto utens*). This is very little to go on, but the references to Aïmer's life of hardships, his imprisonment (hence *le chaitif*), and his determination not to sleep beneath a roof until he has conquered the Saracens, are very persistent and it does not take much to create a legend. It is possible that each of these brothers had a special *chanson* to himself in the 'grand cycle'. At all events, the poem celebrating the youngest son Guibert has been preserved to us and may be taken as a sample of these later poems which filled out the picture of the famous clan. But we must look for a moment at the poem which introduces us to the Aymeri family at home and relates their dispersion to the various scenes of activity with which they are always connected.

Les Narbonnais, as this poem has been called by its editor (Suchier), is the most considerable of a little group of 'chansons' which form a kind of 'petit cycle', or *cycle narbonnais*. The poems treated hitherto are of relatively early date and constitute in themselves a cycle dedicated to the main hero, Guillaume d'Orange. But as time went on Guillaume wore a little threadbare in spite of his vast reputation, and recourse was had to his relations to sustain the public interest. His father, Aymeri, was already known for his capture of Narbonne which formed the subject of a poem, and now, having lived happily with his wife, Hermenjart, for many years in the captured city and produced a numerous family of sons and daughters, his stirring spirit

---

[1] *Vita Hlodowici*—l'Astronome. Cf. *Romania*, t. XXXII (1903)—Suchier.

begins to move afresh. What are six (number varies) great useless sons doing wasting their time in Narbonne and waiting for him to die? They must go forth and win their spurs even though it leaves the ageing parents unprotected in the midst of a Saracen land. The early part of the *Narbonnais*, which is the most interesting, relates the *departement* or distribution of functions by Aymeri amongst his sons. Aymeri's autocratic character and family pride stand out in strong relief, but the maternal solicitude of Hermenjart and the distinctive character of each of the sons are also graphically described. Guillaume himself is somewhat in the background, but 'Hernauz li rouz' (=red-haired) plays many an arrogant prank and draws forth the remark that a gentlemanly, red-haired man is never to be found ('*Que debonaire ne puet on rox trover Tuit sont felon*, etc.'), though it is interesting that Hernauz is the only one to protest when his father strikes his mother. Here, too, we hear of the vow of the hardy Aïmer who swears never to sleep under a roof (unless it be in a Saracen prison) while he is in a heathen land. But the bulk of the poem, which relates the siege of Narbonne during the absence of the young men and its raising by their return each at the head of a troup of followers, is not of great interest although one or two fresh characters are introduced, such as Forré the clever Arab doctor, Claris the converted heathen, and Romant the son of Garin, who undertakes a single combat against the huge, hideous giant Gadifer—a version of the David-Goliath episode which became extremely popular. *Les Narbonnais* has much in common with another poem entitled *Les Enfances Guillaume*, which sometimes follows it in the larger groups of the cyclic manuscripts and which treats of the same basic facts though differing in many details. In the *Enfances Guillaume* references to the love affair between Guillaume and Orable occur. It is noticeable that in the *Narbonnais* there is no allusion either to Tiebaut or Orable, ex-wife of the heathen king, a fact that may point to a more archaic tradition for this poem. Otherwise the author is well versed in the works of his predecessors. Charlemagne is alive and described as being still vigorous in the early part. He constantly regrets his two valiant knights, Roland and Oliver, killed at Roncevaux. When he dies[1] a reference is made to the part played by Guillaume in the *Couronnement* (though here his brothers share the glory with him). In addition to genuine allusions to other poems, various references to later 'chansons' have been interpolated to bring the whole poem into line with others of the cycle. The last few lines, which announce yet

[1] l. 1000.

further attacks on Narbonne, are evidently meant to prepare the way for the *Siège de Barbastre*, which follows the *Narbonnais* in the grouping of manuscripts of the so-called 'petit cycle' and relates the deliverance from prison of Bueve and his two sons, Girart and Gui. The *Siège de Barbastre* is a second- or third-rate, conventional poem of the decadent period containing the hackneyed accounts of Saracen prisons full of dirty water abounding in nasty creatures,[1] of silly love-affairs with Saracen princesses interspersed with battle-scenes, sieges and embassies, and all the usual personnel of the stereotyped descriptions of the period. Bueve, the brother of Guillaume, is the hero of the poem *Bovon de Commarcis*; whereas four other of the sons of Aymeri—Guibert, Guillaume, Bertrand, and Hernaut—are delivered from prison in the *Prise de Cordoue* and Bertrand is provided with a wife. There is, however, one short poem which stands out from this group of vapid 'chansons' devoted to Aymeri's sons. *Guibert d'Andrenas*, which probably also dates from the beginning of the thirteenth century, is an excellent little poem of its kind. Apart from a fraction of it which is a concession to the taste of the period and treats of maidens' dreams and desires, it is a monument to the cohesion and mutuality of the Aymeri family. It opens with a scene very similar to that in the *Narbonnais*, in which Aymeri and his wife Hermenjart are discussing the careers of the various members of the family in their palace at Narbonne. Both have aged considerably since we last met them, and Aymeri is considering seriously to whom he will leave his territory. He runs through the list of his now famous sons: Garins li *poëstis*,[2] Guillelmes li marchis, Aïmers 'li chetis', Bernarz and Hernauz, until he comes to Guibert, the youngest, who, as we know from the *Narbonnais*, unwillingly stayed at home and, as a result of his one escapade, was caught and put on a cross by the Saracens. The character of the individual brothers corresponds exactly to what we have found in other poems: Guillaume has an enormous reputation,[3] but he is tired and has no desire for further conquests though he does not expect ever to lead a quiet life[4]; Hernauz is 'li felon roux' and Aïmer is the 'chetif' who is far away in Spain. Aymeri is again the heavy father who suddenly decides that his youngest son shall also go and carve himself out a kingdom 'entre la jent savaje'. Hermenjart is dismayed; Guibert himself is extremely rude and tells his father he is a fuddled dreamer who is only fit to

---

[1] E.g. vers coëz = tailed worms, l. 3203, etc.
[2] = the powerful.
[3] 'Celui d'Orange qui si a grand renon' (l. 405).
[4] 'Ne quier avoir repos en mon aé' (l. 498).

repose on cushions in a luxurious bed and be fed with dainties from the table. But it is all in vain. Aymeri insists that Guibert shall go and do what he himself did in his youth and, to prove that he is still in his prime, declares that he will not only summon his other sons, but ride with them into battle to conquer a fief for his youngest. So he sends out his messages and his letters and before long the sons and their armies begin to arrive to the joy and pride of their father. In no poem is pride of family so clearly expressed, and the exultation of the elderly parents as they stand at the window of their palace and see troop after troop arriving, each led by one of their sons, is excellently portrayed. So filled with enthusiasm is Aymeri at the sight that he actually begs for the privilege of the first blow at the enemy—a much sought after distinction. He mocks Guillaume unkindly when he returns after a hard fight with only a few horses (Guillaume's love for horses is always an element in his character) for his prey, and he causes great anxiety to his family by his foolhardiness. *Guibert d'Andrenas* has much in common with the other poems of the group to which it belongs, but it is distinguished by its brevity, its colourful language, and its vivid portrayal of the family relationships. The author is familiar with all the epic traditions and characters; the phrases and epithets are those common to all this group of poems— the heathen are 'cette geste grifaigne' who swear by the two gods 'Mahomet et Cahu'; the favourite way to describe a valiant fighter is to say that 'the man he catches is a dead man' ('Cui il consuit morz est et confonduz' or 'cui il ataint tost a son tans feny'), a phrase we find with all sorts of variations in the second half-line in all the poems of the Guillaume cycle and with ever-increasing frequency in the later ones. The number of stereotyped phrases and expressions is in fact such a marked character of the *chansons-de-geste* of this whole cycle, especially those of later date, that it forms one of its most distinguishing features. Even in the more truly epic poems of *Aliscans* and the *Chanson de Guillaume* they are numerous. If a hero deals particularly deadly blows in battle and causes grievous wounds, we are told 'De la menour mourust un amiralz' (the least of them would have killed an emir); a man is in a perilous plight and will certainly perish 'si Dex n'en panse, li rois de Paradis'; one favourite phrase has a familiar ring in English and seems to be peculiar to the poems of the Guillaume cycle, namely, to 'get the worst of it in a battle'—'Or a Guillelme le pis dela bataille' (*Aliscans*). These may be mere tricks of style, but they are typical of the technique of this group, as is the use of the short line at the end of the laisse in so many of the Guillaume poems and, taken in conjunction with the dominating idea of the family—the *geste*, the *lignage*—they give a distinctive character to the whole cycle which is absent from the other more loosely-knit groups. We do not propose to deal further with the poems of this group as they peter-out into further generations and become more romantic and less epic in character, but it would hardly be seemly to close the series without paying a tribute to the father, or rather progenitor of the clan. *Garin de Montglane*, after whom, according to the classification of the 'jongleurs' themselves, the whole *geste* was named, was himself the subject of a little group of poems devoted to his life and adventures. Garin is quite unknown to history, but the arrangers of the cycles needed an ancestor for Guillaume, and at some point, relatively late in the history of the movement we are studying, he became the grandfather of Aymeri and the great-grandfather of Guillaume and his brothers, and the great-great-grandfather of Vivien and Gui and a host of other younger members of the family. It recalls a biblical genealogy: Garin begat Hernaut de Biaulande and Hernaut begat Aymeri and Aymeri begat Guillaume. But Garin had other important sons—he was the father of Girart de Viane and Milon and Renier, who each had their individual history. And Renier was the father of Olivier and Aude, thus forming a link with the Charlemagne cycle. Hence Garin was entitled to some notice by the poets. The most important of the poems of which he is the subject is *Garin de Montglane*, an interminable poem of 13,140 alexandrines typical of the decadent period of our 'genre'. The anonymous poet of the thirteenth century begins in the conventional way by telling us that other 'jongleurs' have celebrated other heroes (whom he enumerates), but all have neglected the first and most important ('Mais tot en ont laissé le grant commencement') of whom he proposes to tell. In reality the poem is a third- or fourth-rate romance abounding in tedious descriptions and absurdities. Charlemagne is alive, and when the hero Garin requests a fief he proposes to play him at chess for the whole of France. Charles loses, but Garin, who is moved to tears by the impotent wrath of the emperor, merely asks for the stronghold of Montglane. The rest of the poem consists of a lengthy description of the winning of this town. There is the love-story typical of these later poems, and other romantic characters are introduced, such as: the enchanter Perdigon, the giant Robastre, a monster with the accompaniment of a cloak that renders its wearer invisible. There is nothing of a true epic character in the whole poem except its length, and its importance is due to the fact that it shows how the later poems which were included in the cycle had degenerated into turgid and tedious romances.

Other poems were added at intervals to fill in the gaps in the genealogies, but it would be idle to enumerate them. There are many signs, besides those of language, of a later date and a change of taste. New characters have appeared; fresh stereotyped phrases, as a rule less bellicose in character, have replaced the old ones. It is Easter time and the birds are singing, flowers are blossoming, and ladies in love are showing a heightened colour. Tents are embroidered with scenes of all descriptions, and chambers are painted; prisons are full of toads and adders ('bas et couleuvres'), and nothing is neglected which will add a touch of colour and enliven the scene. We have moved far from the fierce austerity and the grim seriousness of a *Chanson de Roland* or a *Raoul de Cambrai*. The clear-cut personalities of the older epic poems have been replaced by less well-marked characters. We get confused even amongst the sons of Aymeri; the heathen have lost their original characteristics and the converted pagan often acts as a traitor to his own side; the high-souled Roman matrons whom we have found in Hermenjart and Guibourg have become simpering maidens; the glory of the old genuinely epic poem has departed and we are 'en pleine décadence'. It is time we turned our attention to the third 'geste'; in other words to the cycle of rebellious barons.

CHAPTER IV

THE CYCLE OF REVOLTED BARONS

OR

FEUDAL CYCLE

IN a passage of his *De Nugis Curialium*[1] Walter Map associates the two traitors Isembart and Raoul de Cambrai in disastrous rebellions against Louis the Fat, the son of Charlemagne, thus coupling two of the best known examples of rebellious barons that have come down to us in the Old French epic. These two notable characters have nothing to do with one another in the poems to which Walter Map is probably alluding, but, in conjunction with the even better known Ganelon, they form part of a group whose members are described as being rebels, or worse still, traitors, who have a spiritual ancestry characterized by pride and treacherous behaviour and deriving from Cain, or Judas, or even the devil as the case may be. They were not lacking in courage or renown, and might have been lords of France had they not had pride and treachery in their make-up like the wicked angels who were hurled down from heaven into the infernal abyss.

But besides their spiritual ancestry it was necessary in an age when birth (or pedigree) was considered so important, that the traitors should have a natural ancestry as well as a spiritual, and it was to supply this need that Doon de Mayence was created by the 'jongleurs' as an opposite number to Garin de Montglane, ancestor of the Guillaume-cycle, and to the author of the august royal lineage in the 'geste des rois'. We have seen that Doon was mentioned by name as the progenitor of the traitor family by the author of the poem *Girart de Viane*, but his poetic biography is probably of an even later date than this poem although the important episode of Doon's single combat with Charlemagne bears some marks of an earlier period.

Some apology is therefore needed for beginning our study of this group of poems with a decadent poem of tardy date. But any student, when faced with the above-mentioned passage, might be pardoned for asking: 'Who is this Doon de Mayence, mentioned so expressly as father of the clan?' Who, indeed, but an ingenious invention of

[1] Div. V, Ch. v.

the poet to provide a worthy ancestry for the widely dispersed traitor family, since rebels and traitors and even pagan enemies must have their lineage just as much as the well-born knights and Christians. Otherwise some of the single combats and trials of strength between well-matched adversaries would have been impossible: 'I come of a line of famous knights and will never touch a squire,' declares the pagan Gormont indignantly when attacked by a lately-knighted youth; and King Louis, when he sees so many of his knights dead, remarks regretfully: 'How mistaken I was not to engage this heathen in single combat when the battle began. He is a king and so am I; our joust would have been right and proper.'[1] Hence Doon de Mayence was needed to found the family of rebels, and in the poem which goes by his name he gives them a worthy start as a dangerous opponent to Charlemagne in the combat brought about by their reciprocal insults. In fact, the indecisive battle has to be terminated by the angelic interposition of a bright cloud between the combatants which blinds them, and thus brought about a final reconciliation, reminding us of a similar miraculous intervention in the duel between Roland and Oliver in *Girart de Viane*.

But the history of revolt against the autocratic emperor goes back very much further than this futile and belated attempt to provide an ancestor for the large and disintegrated family of discontented barons. It is possible that the revolt was originally national rather than individual, and this would not be surprising. From allusions in chronicles and poems it seems probable that there was an old tradition, and perhaps a poem, dealing with the so-called *Herupois*, the name given to the inhabitants of the ancient Neustria, the region between the Seine and the Loire in which lay Paris and the Île de France, in opposition to the germanic France or Austrasia, which bounded it on the north and wherein lay Aachen (Aix), the seat of the Frankish emperor. The Herupois, according to the legend, proudly refused to bring their tribute to the Frankish emperor except symbolically at the point of the sword, and Charles, at the advice of Duke Naime, who had property in the disputed neighbourhood, took no action against them. The best account we have of the courageous 'barons Herupes' is incorporated into Jean Bodel's *Chanson des Saisnes* (Saxons), to which we have already alluded. In Bodel's poem the emperor sends his ambassadors to the Herupois to demand the tribute. A council of barons is held in which Salemon de Bretagne—another well-known character whose name is familiar

---

[1] 'Ja est il reis e reis sui jie: / la nostre joste avenist bien.' *Gorm et Isemb.*, 369–70.

from many *chansons-de-geste*—would slay the messengers in barbarous fashion and invade the territory of Charles. But better counsels prevail, and the tribute, cast in iron, is carried at the iron tip of their lances to Aix-la-Chapelle as a symbol of their readiness to fight for their freedom. Charles is much impressed and goes forth barefooted to meet them, and a reconciliation takes place. It is more than likely that both the 'barons herupois' and their leader, Salemon de Bretagne, formed the subject of ancient poems or songs of which we only possess a belated echo.[1] The same may be said of the famous *Ogier le Danois*, who is one of the leaders of the army of Charlemagne in the *Chanson de Roland*[2]—indeed, he is appointed to lead the army corps which is dearest to the heart of the emperor after his own 'baruns de France'. And yet he had been a fierce rebel in his time. But when it is a question of the larger issues, of Christianity against paganism, of right against wrong, the personal element is forgotten and it is a pleasing feature in the *Chanson de Roland*, which is constructed on noble lines, that amongst his trusted knights, even if not amongst the first twelve, are the time-honoured rebels, Girart de Roussillon, Richart de Normandie, Salemon de Bretagne (in the version contained in Ms. V4), and Ogier de Danemarche. It is clear that the 'trouvère' who recited the *Chanson de Roland* could count on these names falling on familiar ears and arousing the flagging interest as the mention of a well-known character never fails to do. Of the four barons just mentioned, Ogier and Girart were probably the best known. Each of them has his roots in history. Ogier (*Otgarius marchio*), as we know from an ancient document,[3] fled to Pavia to the court of Desiderius, King of the Lombards, with the wife and two children of Carloman in 772. The ensuing Siege of Pavia is described by the Monk of St. Gall,[4] who tells us in a dramatic passage how *Otkerus* (*Ogier*), having fled from the emperor, was standing by the side of Desiderius when the vanguard of Charles' army began to appear. To every inquiry of the king as each army corps approaches: 'Surely there is Charles,' Ogier replies: 'Not yet, not yet.' And when at last Charles, clad in iron from top to toe and leading an army in similar garb so that all the fields and open places gleam with iron, appears, a terrified cry went up from the people at the awful iron menace, and Ogier himself fell to the ground half dead with fear. This is hardly enough to account for the reputation that this renegade

---

[1] A reference in *Raoul de Cambrai* to the 'pers de Vermandois' from which the account of the battle is taken seems to point to another possible 'geste' of national rather than individual character.   [2] Cf. l. 3033.
[3] Cf. Pertz: *Mon. Germ. Hist.* II, 195.   [4] Cf. Ch. 17, Bk. II.

knight enjoyed in the epic tradition. There is scarcely a *chanson-de-geste* in which he is not mentioned; his valour, not to say his brutality, became a byword. His legendary history can be pieced together from the various documents, some early and primitive, some of the nature of aitiological legends, which deal with Ogier's life. He owed his epithet of 'le danois' to the fact (or fiction) that he was the son of Gaufroi, King of Denmark. Sent as a hostage to Charlemagne by his father, he is in danger of losing his life when war breaks out afresh. His life is only saved by the fact that Charles is assailed by Corsuble of Italy, and Ogier performs such feats of valour against the enemy that Charles takes him into his favour. This account, which constitutes the 'enfances Ogier', is, however, not the legendary cause of his great war against Charlemagne.

The long-winded poem, *La Chevalerie Ogier de Danemarche*, contains many fine scenes embedded in the savage, bloodthirsty history of Ogier's implacable attitude towards Charlot, the emperor's young son. A quarrel had arisen during a game of chess between Charlot and Ogier's nephew, and Charlot had snatched up the chess-board and hit his antagonist such a blow on the head that he had killed him on the spot. Although the blow was not intended to be fatal, Ogier's anger and grief were fearful to behold. He fairly ran amok:

> Li dus l'entent, vif cuida erragier.
> D'aïr tressue, si saisi un levier,
> De renc a renc se comence afichier.

Nothing, not even the abject apologies and touching regrets of the boy would appease Ogier. He cried for Charlot's blood and persisted in his vendetta so relentlessly that finally an angelic intervention became necessary to save the young man's life. The savagery of Ogier rather revolts us and it was in keeping with this side of his character that later tradition made him responsible for the death of Amis and Amile when the two friends ran into Charlemagne's army returning from a campaign against the Lombards. But Charles did not come far behind him in vindictiveness. When he heard that Ogier, after his capture and imprisonment had escaped death from starvation through a ruse of the wily Turpin,[1] he still refused to make use of his aid against the Saracens. A young squire who rashly exclaimed, 'Oh, if only Ogier were here,' was promptly hung by the emperor's orders. It was only on account of the physical impossibility of hanging three hundred young nobles[2] who surrounded his tent and

---

[1] 'Li arcevesque fu plains de mult grant sens' (l. 9623).
[2] 'Or ara Kalles anqui trop a vengier' (l. 10148).

joining hands, chanted 'We want Ogier', that Charles at last consented to ask Ogier for his help against the common foe. It is a wild story, but related with a certain skill and pathos in a poem which, though not of the first rank, comes near at times in poetic value to the earlier, more genuine epics of the first period. It has a historic value too, for it contains a definite echo of the Lombard war in which Desiderius lost his kingdom. There is an allusion also to the historical basis of Ogier's antagonism to Charles in a few lines[1] in which Ogier recalls his grievances and in which we learn how he fled to King Desier (Desideridus) with the little boys Loeys and Lothier, whom the emperor was intending to kill.

Ogier of Denmark became immensely popular both in France and Italy—many fables were told about his valour. The Pseudo-Turpin chronicle tells us that songs (*cantilenae*) were sung about him on account of the innumerable, wonderful deeds he performed: 'Ogerius rex Daciae cum decem millibus heroum (venit). De hoc canitur in cantilena usque in hodiernum diem, quia innumera fecit mirabilia.' He became thus a national as well as a personal hero.

The same is true to a lesser extent of Girart de Roussillon, another of Charlemagne's trusty knights in the *Chanson de Roland*, and referred to familiarly as 'Gerard li vielz' or 'Gerard le veill (le vieux) de Rossillon'. But, although he is one of the twelve peers over whom Charles laments so sadly, he had been a very bitter enemy in his time. He also has his roots in history. Both he and his wife Berthe are mentioned in documents as early as the year 819. He became 'con : de Paris' in 837, but incurred the displeasure of 'Charles le chauve'. Later on, however, he played an important rôle as Marquis (*Marchio*) of the Duchy of Lyon, and before his death in conjunction with his wife, Berthe, he founded the monasteries of Vezelay and Pothières. But, unfortunately for scholars whose predilection is for the identification of legendary figures with historical prototypes, there are two other rebel barons of the name of Girart amongst the Old French epic heroes, and though their stories differ in detail, they all have one important feature in common, namely their hostility to the reigning monarch. *Girart de Viane* is one of the most notable examples belonging to what we might call the second series of epic poems in France; it cannot be classed precisely with the early group of primitive poems which make up in grandeur for what they lack in picturesque detail, but it contains many genuinely epic scenes. The third Girart, who is not distinguished by being the subject of a whole poem

[1] ll. 4420 ff.

dedicated to himself is 'Girart d'Eufrate' (*de Frete*, or *Fraite*), who figures considerably in the *Chanson d'Aspremont*, first as the sworn enemy, then as the somewhat arrogant supporter of Charles in his battle against the Saracens. Like Girart de Roussillon, he has a wise wife who tries to reconcile him with his lord and does eventually succeed in persuading him to lend Charles his aid against the heathen. But to go back to the first of these three poems, the enmity of Girart de Roussillon against the emperor is much to the latter's discredit, for it is due to Charles insisting on espousing the younger and more beautiful of the two daughters of the emperor of Constantinople, who had been promised to Girart by a solemn agreement. Girart is not unnaturally angry, but the queen promises him her love, gives him a ring, and he goes off with the elder sister Berthe and prepares to make war on Charles (*Martel*). Berthe proves a wise and faithful wife. Had it not been for her Girart would not have survived his many tribulations. The poem[1] has all the usual battle scenes, devastations, sieges, cities taken by treachery and lost again, messengers barely escaping with their lives, and incipient reconciliations rendered fruitless by fresh crimes—but it is redeemed by the delightful scenes in which the outlawed Girart and his wife live by the labour of their hands (he as charcoal-carrier and she as seamstress) for twenty-two years in pitiful surroundings. It is in this part of the poem that a remarkable similarity with the story of Tristan and Iseut strikes the reader. Iseut is, in a sense, doubled; the younger sister, who, though preferring Girart, has been married to the king, remains absolutely faithful to her first love, and when she recognizes him in the ragged, hairy beggar, although in church and engaged in prayer barefooted beside the altar, she cares not that it is Friday but kisses him seven times, and her love returns stronger than ever. But herein lies the beauty of the episode: the queen immediately asks for her sister, and Girart replies enthusiastically that his wife is the best of women and has saved him many times by her sweetness, her good counsel, and her love. And he spoke truly for, during those twenty-two years in the forest, so reminiscent of the forest-life in Béroul's Tristan, she had constantly been his guide, philosopher and friend, and when Girart's case seemed almost hopeless to the hermit[2] on account of his implacable pride and 'démesure', it is Berthe who falls at the hermit's feet in tears (again like Iseut) and succeeds in softening the

---

[1] A critical edition of *Girard de Roussillon* has not yet appeared. Translation by Paul Meyer: *Girart de Roussillon*, ch. de geste traduite pour la première fois, Paris, 1884.

[2] 'No vos sai cosselhar, Dieus vos agut! / Quar aqvest segle e l'autre avetz perdut.'

E

hard heart of her husband. No wonder the poet tells us that she was
wise and courteous and of good stock, for never did preacher speak
better than she:

> El' es savie e corteise et de bone aire,
> Que ne paraule melz nus predicaire.[1]

It is tempting to linger over the delightful scenes in Girart de Roussillon, but they form only a small part of the whole. The earliest
version we possess of the poem contains much of the romantic
element which is absent from the more primitive poems. We have
the hermit and even a magician, and to some extent it is popular in
style. This version, which is probably a *remaniement* of an older
poem, is in a curious intermediary mixed dialect, part French, part
Provençal, and the decasyllabic line has its 'cut' after the sixth syllable
instead of the more usual 4/6 division. But it is pleasant to read, and
must have spread in many a region the fame of the rebel Girart who
ended as a hermit in odour of sanctity, and of 'dame Berthe' who
saved her husband from despair. The two sisters—the queen, who,
though obliged to accept a royal spouse, confesses to Girart, 'eu am
plus tei' (I prefer you), and the wife who tends her husband and
admonishes him that if he accepts the evil better will follow ('quar
si-l mal cuelz en grat mellor conquers'[2])—form a kind of composite
picture of the perfect woman.

Little enough is known of the historic Girart, but that he was a
governor of Provence, that he was in continual strife with an emperor
named Charles (Martel, in *Girart de Roussillon*), that he had a wife
named Berthe, and that he founded monasteries in his old age. From
one chronicle we learn that Berthe defended the town of Vienne
against the emperor during the absence of her husband—and yet in
the poem *Girart de Viane*, to which we must now turn, there is no
mention of Girart's wife. We are in the South of France again in
the poem of the early thirteenth century, the subject of which is the
struggle between Charlemagne and his vassal 'le duc Girart'. The
poem opens with a scene (after the famous description of 'les trois
gestes')[3] rather like the introduction to *Les Narbonnais*. Four young
men (sons of Garin de Montglane) go forth to seek their fortunes,
and two of them—Girard and Renier—betake themselves to the
Court of Charlemagne. They do not meet with the reception they
had hoped for. There are evil-minded men at Charles' Court who
persuade the emperor to send them away. Their manners, in spite of
their good birth, are arrogant and brutal. When Renart de Pevier,

---

[1] ll. 485–6. Extract in Paul Meyer.　　　　[2] ll. 6217–61.　　　　[3] Cf. *supra*.

an unpleasant old man with a paunch like a Lombard,[1] recalls some doubtful action of their father Garin, Renier seizes him by the beard and, tearing out his hairs, makes a bald patch on his chin; on another similar occasion he picks up an old detractor by his beard, leads him running and trotting across the hall against his will and thrusts him into the fire:

> xiiii pas l'a apres lui mené,
> corant trotant trestot estre son gré
> . . . Il vint au feu si la dedanz bouté (ll. 1069-72).

Eventually Renier is provided with a fief and Girart is accompanying the emperor on the hunt when the wife of the recently deceased Duke of Burgundy arrives at the court and throws herself on the mercy of Charles for the provision of a husband[2] to maintain her territory. The emperor immediately replies that he has a nice young man,[3] a son of Garin de Montglane, who will suit her exactly. The duchess accepts gratefully 'car ge suit vostre lige'. But when the susceptible and decidedly unscrupulous emperor looks at the lady more carefully and sees how beautiful she is, he is enamoured with her at once and decides he will keep her for himself, much as Charles insisted on having the more beautiful younger daughter in *Girart de Roussillon*.[4] The duchess demurs and wishes to be given to Girart, to whom she was promised in the first instance, and declares she will never be queen. The emperor points out the folly of refusing such a good offer, but grants her a respite in which to take counsel for 'En conseil querre puet en grant bien trover.'[5] The lady summons Girart to her 'ostel', bids him welcome, and asks him to take her as his wife without delay. Girart is horrified at such boldness—the world must certainly be going mad if ladies are asking men to become their husbands:

> Que or commence le siecle a redoter
> Puis que les dames vont mari demender (ll. 1357-8).

Very sorrowfully the duchess left him—she neither ate nor drank nor slept that night, but went to church and prayed that God would give her Girart. Next morning she sent for him again, but he was so proud that he did not deign to come. The duchess, furious at his refusal, decides that if she could not have the duke she would take the king, and when Charles hears of her decision he announces to his court that he intends to marry her. Rather illogically, Girart now declares that she and her hand had been promised to him, but the duchess replies that Girart had refused her, that she would rather be

[1] l. 803.   [2] l. 1257.   [3] 'J'ai un danzel, molt i a bel enfant' (l. 1265).
[4] Cf. supra.   [5] l. 1323.

dragged by wild horses or drowned or burned than have intimacy with him, and, Girart still vainly protesting, the wedding takes place. But the new queen cannot forget the insult she has suffered, and she determines to humiliate Girart, to whom the emperor, at the advice of his barons, has just granted Viane (Vienne) as a fief to appease him for the loss of Burgundy, and incidentally to get rid of him. Girart accepts the gift and goes to the royal bedchamber to swear his allegiance and kiss the king's foot. In the darkened room the spiteful queen puts out her naked foot for Girart to kiss as she lies beside the king, and Girart unwittingly does so. Had he known he would certainly have killed her straight away, but he did not know, and from this came deadly strife ('mortel encombrier') and great slaughter of gentle knights. She ought to have been killed, remarks the author.[1] So ends the kind of introduction which is, as often, the most original and most interesting part of the poem. The events which follow are for the most part sieges and battles, either general or individual. Most of the space during the long siege of Viane is devoted to the single combat between Roland and Oliver, each of whom has been struck by the other's behaviour and appearance during the siege. Oliver is introduced as the nephew of Girart and the son of Renier and grandson of Garin de Montglane, so that we are in the midst of the Guillaume cycle as Aymeri (destined to become Aymeri de Narbonne), son of Hernaut de Biaulande, is his cousin. Olivier's sister is the fair Aude, who watches the battle from the walls and catches the eye of Roland, Charlemagne's nephew, so that the interweaving of the cycles is complete. Roland succeeds in capturing Aude and riding off with her, but she is rescued by her brother Olivier and the single combat between the lover and the brother proceeds. The romantic element develops in the latter part of the poem. Olivier begs Roland to desist from the battle and he will let him have Aude as a reward, whilst Aude watches the combat from a window and alternately faints and weeps. Dame Guibourg, the wife of Girard, joins with her in their cries and lamentations, but the battle continues with unabated fury. Olivier breaks his sword, but a good Jew provides him with another; Roland pretends to be ill and asks Olivier to let him lie down a little, while Olivier agrees and invites him to lie down on his shield and offers to fan him with his shield so as to refresh him before renewing the combat. The battle is renewed again for 'maltalent' (anger) urges them on, but at long last a cloud descends between them and an angel bids them cease their

[1] l. 1476.

conflict and reserve their strength for fighting against the common foe in Spain where they will receive the martyr's crown for upholding God's law and name against the Saracens. Reconciliation follows, but not before Charles has been captured in the forest and spirited away into Viane where Girart treats him handsomely and salutes him as king in God's name. They issue forth from the town together and Charles informs his anxious knights that he and Girart are now friends and lovers. And so the war is ended.

> Moi et Girart somes ami et dru.
> S'est remese la guerre (ll. 6726–7).

Aude is formally betrothed to Roland on a sweet May morning when the birds are singing and the meadows flowering, and the emperor hopes that an heir will issue from their union who will bring much good to pass. But the author warns us that this will not come to pass as the Saracens and accursed heathen will separate them. And so the poem ends on an ominous note.

We have dwelt at some length on this poem because, although Girart is the nominal hero, the two chief protagonists are in some ways Roland and Charlemagne, just as they are in the *Chanson de Roland*, and this gives us a 'point de depart' for a comparison between poems of varying periods. *Girart de Viane* is 'a poème de jongleur'. The author names himself—Bertrand de Bar-sur-Aube—but practically nothing is known of him though there is reason to think that he was the author of *Aymeri de Narbonne* which would follow our poem in the natural sequence of events. Bertrand tells us that he was 'uns gentis clers' and that he was sitting in a leafy orchard in the merry month of May when a lusty pilgrim returning from St. Jaques came across him and recounted the adventures which he proceeded to put into song, as all the other singers (*chanteör*) had forgotten or did not know this story. This is, of course, merely the traditional form of introduction which became the stereotyped opening for poems during the course of the twelfth century. It is interesting to compare it with the noble approach to his subject employed by the author of the *Roland*:

> Carles li reis, nostre emperere magne,
> Set ans tuz pleins a este en Espagne.

And this in some ways gives the key to the complete difference of impression which the reading of the two poems, separated by perhaps best part of a century, makes on us. The dignity and solemnity of the

early poems has gone. It is not the deep moral issues, the triumph of
good over evil, of the true faith over the false law, which are at stake,
but it is a personal question either of an outraged subject against his
lord or of one incensed vassal against another. Charlemagne, always
in danger of losing his dignity, has now lost it completely. He
filches the beautiful woman from the vassal to whom he had promised
her; he lets Girart kiss his wife's foot instead of his own whilst he
presumably is asleep; his dreams are not of leopards and bears, but of
birds 'qui s'entrebatent', but end by kissing each other, and he stands
up to address his barons, whereas we can only imagine Charlemagne
in the *Chanson de Roland* as sitting in dignified state on his 'falde-stuol
d'or mier'. The archbishop Turpin actually mounts on a chair to
address the knights and, although in their single combat Roland and
Oliver fight fiercely, there is a feeling of comic opera throughout as
when Roland sees Oliver's beautiful sister Aude throw a stone from
the ramparts and declares laughingly that he will never be guilty of
fighting against the fair sex.[1] And yet, in spite of a certain lightness,
the poem has a beauty of its own. The characters are vivid and quick
in their reactions as we may judge from such phrases as 'le sens cuide
changier' (he nearly goes out of his mind), 'a pou n'est forsenez'
(with much the same meaning but perhaps a little stronger) or 'a pou
que n'est desvez', which occur as constantly as they do in other
poems of this epoch; their emotions are suddenly aroused but as
quickly calmed down: when a man is dead and finished with he is
soon forgotten and no amount of grieving will bring him back;[2] the
aristocratic outlook is still prominent, but it is based on nobility of
heart rather than of birth and is unaffected by wealth. 'I care not for
wealth, I am not a merchant' (N'ai soing d'avoir, ne sui pas mar-'
cheänt') exclaims Girart indignantly when the emperor tries to buy
him off with money—'never did my family seek after wealth for
there is not a "borjois" or a merchant amongst them'. Several times
the author puts words into the mouth of his heroes to insist that life
does not consist in the abundance of things a man possesses. Very
finely Renier, Girart's brother, and the father of Olivier and Aude,
expresses the conviction:

> Li cuers n'est pas ne el vair ne el gris.
> Eins est el ventre la ou Deus l'a assis. . . . etc.

Like Guillaume at the end of the *Couronnement de Louis*, Girart
complains bitterly that when a man is poor, he falls into disrepute.

---

[1] 'Devers les dames ne asaudré-ge mie' (l. 4639).
[2] 'Mais en duel fere n'a nul recouvrement' (l. 1257).

Girart de Viane and Girart de Roussillon, whether they be the same man or not, together form a composite picture of the man with a just grievance who dares to raise his standard against a powerful authority even though, by so doing, he is forced to live a life of hardship and misery involving many others besides himself. And yet, so difficult is it to break completely away from the firmly-implanted loyalties of youth, they humble themselves before authority in the end. When Charlemagne has fallen into the hands of Girart towards the end of the long siege and the youthful Aymeri begs his uncle to kill him (a fact remembered by the emperor in the poem of *Aymeri de Narbonne*) Girart replies: 'By no means shall a king of France ever be dishonoured by me', and he swears allegiance to his prisoner, thus effectively bringing the long war to an end. *Girart de Viane* is a worthy example of the poems which combine the epic and the romantic element. The heroes are built on large lines, the battle scenes are vividly portrayed, the interest in the characters and their manifestations never flags. The gallant old Garin de Montglane cannot contain himself when he hears the snort of the battle-horse. The implacability of Girart towards the queen who humiliated him, when he refuses to accept an 'amendise', even though the lady should carry his saddle on her head for the distance of a league, barefooted and in her chemise, reminds us of the similar scenes and the identical 'amendise' refused by Bernier in *Raoul de Cambrai* in which poem the relentless force of the characters is unrelieved by the shimmer of romance which hovers over the poem we have been studying without weakening its basic, epic character. The form is that of the earlier epics, namely, the decasyllabic lines grouped together in 'laisses' of varying length. Rhyme has replaced assonance (except in the short six-syllable line which concludes each 'laisse' on a feminine ending) and the epic technique of hyperbole, litotes ('Et sa moillier que il ne haoit mie'), apostrophe, etc., fit in quite pleasantly with the more sophisticated expressions of 'chevalerie' and 'courtoisie' and noble birth.

A striking deviation from this principle, that a good warrior must have noble blood, and that it is an evil practice to make a knight of a poor man's (vilain) son or even to take his advice[1] is contained in a group of poems which centre round the valiant figure of Garin le Lorrain. One might almost speak of a 'geste des Lorrains' except for the fact that there is only one outstanding poem in the group and

---

[1] 'A Deus! com mal esta a bon guerier
Que de filh de vilha fai cavalier
E fai en senescal o coselher.'
                    Gir de Ross. Ed. Fr. Michel, p. 12.

that it is unwise to multiply the number of 'gestes'. The father of this clan was Hervis, according to the legend the son of a 'bourgeois' of Metz, who had married the daughter of the Duke of Metz, and who fought courageously against the Saracens under Charles Martel, but whose chief claim to notoriety was that he became the father of Garin and Bègue. The bloody feuds between the two great rival families of the Lorrains and the Bordelais form the subject of *Garin le Lorrain*, the central and oldest poem of this group. As one reads the poem one has the impression of reading a graphic chronicle of actual events furnished with a great deal of historical and geographical detail. Much attention is paid to the necessities of life—the commissariat of the army is never neglected, the professional burners (ardeör), couriers (coreör) and foragers (forrier) are always sent out first to collect the prey; suitable lodgings are found for the knights and the actual time of day and state of the weather is described. And yet there is practically nothing historical in the whole poem. True, it opens with the coming of the Vandals ('li Wandre') and the distress of Charles Martel who has to implore the pope's help in making the clergy disburse some of their wealth to furnish his army, a crime for which monkish legend punished him. The Vandals are defeated with the help of Hervi, but Charles is mortally wounded. He dies on the ninth day after the battle, but not before he has rendered back the tithes he had borrowed from the clergy, thus giving the lie to the medieval legend of the emperor's damnation and the metamorphosis of his mortal remains into a stinking serpent that was found in his tomb.

But this introduction with its fragments of history peeping through occupies only a fraction of the space devoted to the completely fabulous tale that follows. Between the two rival families of the Lorrains and the Bordelais the author shows clearly his bias in favour of the former, whom he often speaks of as the 'royalistes'. To the Bordelais belong the traitors—the old fox, Bernart de Naisil ('Renart resemble qu'en la taisniere est mis'), who shoots a surreptitious arrow from a window at his enemy's back, and Fromont, who eventually joins the ranks of the Saracens and actually leads them against the French and whose men treacherously kill the valiant Bègue when they find him alone in the forest. The sympathies of the reader are consistently enlisted on the side of the two brothers, brutal though at times they can be. Their loyalty and courage never fail. Even when the emperor Pepin takes for himself the wife who had been commended to Garin by the dying king Thierri de Moriane, Garin accepts the position humbly, although, like Guillaume d'Orange, he had protected the youthful emperor at the time of his father's death against his potential enemies. They are a noble pair and the universal regret at the death of Bègue, in which even his enemies join, is a testimony to his character:

> Moult est prodons dus Bègues de Belin
> Larges, cortois, sages et bien apris

is the verdict of his host who could not sleep for anxiety when he did not return from his expedition. 'He was noble,' says the monk when asked if he had seen a knight straying in the forest, 'for he deigned to salute me' (Gentilhoms fu, que son salut me fis). The lament of his brother Garin, though conventional in tone, is a beautiful tribute to his character:

> Ha! Sire Bègues, 'Li loherains a dit,
> Frans chevaliers corajeus et hardis!
> Fel et angris contre vos anemis
> Et dols et simples a tres toz vos amis. . . .[1]

a description which recalls the pen picture of Roland riding at the head of his men in the *Chanson de Roland* when the author gives as a reason for his men following him so blindly:

> Vers sarrazins reguardet fierement
> E vers Franceis humeles et dulcement (ll. 1163-4).

Did the author of *Garin le Lorrain* know other poems from which he could draw inspiration? It is hard to say. The only epic hero to whom he refers is Girart de Roussillon, whom he mentions on several occasions as having ravaged the land of the emperor. The rather mysterious personalities Thierri and Estormi de Bourges (known to us from the *Chançun de Willame*) are also mentioned once or twice and always as ignoble characters.[2] Otherwise we are without any indication which would help us to locate Garin amongst the other poems. Nor do we find any references to Garin le Lorrain or other members of his family in other 'chansons de geste'—perhaps on account of its local character. And yet there are a considerable number of manuscripts in which the poem was preserved, and the author gives the impression of having travelled, for he takes us on marvellous journeys across France and round the coast from Bordeaux to Boulogne, which makes its apparent isolation rather hard to account for, especially as it abounds in striking scenes (such as the boar-hunt) and memorable sayings. These are not of a religious character but

---

[1] pp. 262-3. Ed. P. Paris.   [2] *Thiebaus li lerre* = the thief, etc.

reflect the strain of common sense which runs through many of the Old French poems, especially those which narrate the quarrels of feudal barons rather than the inspiration and enthusiasm of the Crusades. The stock phrases which belong to the 'jongleur's' technique are very frequent: *La veïssez*; *Se Diex n'en pense*; *les vaus et les monts*; *por tot l'or que Diex fist*; *le sens cuide derver*; *Qu'il a consuit malement est baillis* (= it is a bad look out for anyone he overtakes) and other stereotyped expressions. But in addition to these there is a sprinkling of more interesting phrases of less common occurrence: *Nature pert* ('nature will out') says Hues del Mans when he hurls a taunt against a man of ignoble lineage; and several times we hear the proverb, familiar to English ears, *Qui son nes coupe il deserte son vis*; very practical is the advice given to a grieving widow: *en grant duel faire onques gaigner ne vis* and the exhortation to liberality which becomes a prince in the words: *Nus avers* (= stingy, mean) *princes ne puet terre tenir*. These are but a few specimens of the language of the poem, but even more interest attaches to the ancient feudal customs which are to be found. The old idea of *compagnonnage* is mentioned on several occasions; the right of *gite* and so many *mangiers par an*; the form of penance which consists in walking barefoot carrying one's enemy's saddle on the head; the dying Bègue's action of taking three leaves between the feet to symbolize the *corpus Deu*—all these are ancient customs of feudal times, some of them reminiscent of similar rites in the poem *Raoul de Cambrai* to which our poem shows a strong resemblance in subject-matter and treatment, for it is a question of family rather than personal feuds. But it is less solemn in tone and lacks perhaps the deep meaning expressed in that poem, and, though the language is colourful, the poetic form is weak. Some of the 'laisses' are immensely long, and the majority have the ending in -i much beloved by poets of the decadent period on account of the frequency with which words, and especially proper names (such as names of saints), ended on that vowel.

This fact is well illustrated by the above-mentioned poem *Raoul de Cambrai*, in which the name of an obscure saint plays an almost preponderant rôle on account of its useful termination. Saint Geri, a little-known bishop in the seventh century, gave his name to a foundation of which the Church subsisted till the sixteenth century and which is frequently mentioned in the poem. Although it is possible to attach an undue amount of importance to the constant occurrence of a convenient name (whether of a saint or church or both), yet it is obvious that this poem has a very strong local interest

—perhaps, indeed, stronger than we find in any other work of the period. The whole action centres round the Cambresis and the Vermandois. There are no exciting journeys across the forests and the wild parts of France where bears and monkeys are to be met, or round the coast, as there are in *Garin le Lorrain*. But there is plenty of excitement concentrated in a more limited area. The historical basis of the story is contained in a few lines of the Annals of Flodoard referring to the year 943, which tell us of the death of Count Herbert of Vermandois and the war that ensued between his sons and Rodolphe de Gouy, who invaded their territory and was killed, much to the grief of King Louis. It will be noted that this historical nucleus of the legend is of much the same dimensions as that contained in the legends of Roland and Guillaume d'Orange. It is difficult to believe that some local legends, written or oral, have not contributed to the twelfth-century poetic and monkish versions we possess of the life and death of Raoul de Cambrai. As in the case of the Guillaume legends, these two versions are closely connected, but the Latin life contained in the Waulsort Chronicle (*Historia Walciodorensis monasterii*) seems to have made use of an older form of the legend, and our present poetic version, which dates probably from the second half of the twelfth century, bears marks of being a 'remaniement' of an older poem. It is impossible even to guess at the date of the earliest form of the legend, but it is noteworthy that the version which has come down to us contains references (as mentioned above) to many ancient feudal customs and the arbitrary action of the king (Louis d'Outremer) in regard to the distribution of fiefs seems to indicate a period before they had become strictly hereditary. There are, moreover, some obscure passages which suggest earlier regional quarrels and hatreds than those immediately accounted for by the poem in its present form. The author speaks of the battle as being 'estraite des pers de Vermandois'.[1] Was there a 'geste des Vermandois' anterior to our poem in which the army included a large contingent of Louis' Frenchmen?[2] We are expressly told in the early part of the poem that Louis would have nothing to do with this quarrel. On several occasions Raoul's mother expresses the greatest contempt for the 'barons d'Arouaise'. They are 'malvais et felon'; they will flee when the battle grows hot; they are good at emptying dishes but not worth a 'fromage en ficelle' in the fight. The poem offers no reason for these strong feelings on the part of Aalais. In a rather obscure passage Bernier seems to have an inexplicable premonition

[1] Ed. S.A.T.F. l. 2457.   [2] See l. 2460.

that Raoul intends some act of treachery towards the sons of Herbert, and we feel that some previous animosity of Raoul against the family may have existed which would have rendered partly unnecessary the undue insistence on Bernier's 'bastardise' as a cause for Raoul's implacable animosity. All these things point to a considerably earlier version than we possess, whether by the 'preus et sages Bertolais' who was present in the thickest of the fight or not we cannot say. In any case the jongleur-poet tells us very charmingly at the beginning of the poem that other 'jogleör' have sung many entertaining songs, but they have left out the best of all (la flor) and this is the 'chançon de joie et de baudor' which he proceeds to relate. We may not quite agree with the description in the title, but it was necessary to excite an interest and create a silence for what was to follow. The only epic heroes he mentions in the course of his poem are Roland and Olivier, and there is a probable allusion to Roland's fight with Fernagu in the description of the armour which with the emperor equips Raoul, and which includes amongst other things the incomparable ('eslite') sword Durendal which was forged by the famous Galans.

Whatever the original poem may have been there is no doubt that the version we possess is a very remarkable epic. The heroes are built on large lines and there is a great underlying truth contained in the poem just as there is the *Chanson de Roland* with some form of which the author was probably familiar. The moral which the hearer was meant to take to heart occurs in one of the opening 'laisses' and is never far from the mind of the narrator: 'Hom desreez a molt grant paine dure' (Uneasy is the life of an unbridled man). *Mesure* is the quality so often insisted on in those lawless times, the lack of which brought death and misery in its train: Roland needed more of it, most of the epic heroes lacked it to a certain degree, but Raoul was the typical *desmesuré*. The villain in the piece is the weak king; the author insists on several occasions that it was the king of Saint-Denis who was in the wrong and that many a noble man is dishonoured by a bad king. Raoul is the tragic hero whose own character and lack of restraint are his undoing. There is another tragic hero in the poem, in most respects a more noble one. Bernier, the bastard, is obsessed by his feelings of loyalty. It is long before Raoul's unspeakable behaviour detaches his loyal friend from him, but Bernier turns at last and it is he who gives the mortal blow to his erstwhile friend. From that moment he is a prey to the most devastating remorse which dogs him all the rest of his days. Everything appeals to us in Bernier: his modesty, his loyalty, his affection for his mother whose death he cannot forgive, and even his pride when he can no longer support the indignities and injuries he has received at the hand of his former benefactor. The characters in this poem are drawn with such consummate skill that in order to do them justice we propose to deal with them in a separate chapter. But it is not only on the psychological side that the author excels. The structure of the poem, working up without undue delay to the final tragedy of Raoul's unhallowed death, the moment of detention when his relentlessly pursued victim hears him utter a blasphemy which makes his downfall certain, the burning of Origny and its church with the hundred nuns, these descriptions are unparalleled in Old French epic poetry. The scene, too, after the final battle, when Raoul the warrior is brought home dead would bear comparison with any of the descriptions in medieval literature. Even Guerri the Red, the mephistophelian uncle of Raoul and his evil genius, is weeping and his heart palpitating with grief as he bears his nephew back on his shield. But the tragic figure in this scene is Raoul's mother, who, in a moment of exasperation at his obstinacy, had cursed him and prayed God that, if he insisted on his wayward course, he might not return alive. She had repented of her words the moment they were uttered. But, alas, the words had gone forth and nothing could recall them though she spent the night in prayer. And now she remembers that she had cursed him ('maudi l'avoit') and her grief is unbounded. It is mixed with other bitterness too; he has been killed by a bastard. 'If only a noble count had killed him, my grief would have been halved,' she cries. And so the 'regrets funèbres' run their course. The young nephew of Raoul—the child Gautier—swears to avenge him; his betrothed laments over him and declares she will never have a husband for the rest of her life (much as the 'fiancée' of St. Alexis lamented over her spouse), and she kept her word.

For a time after his death the land had peace, but alas, it was not for long. The next generation was growing up, and Raoul's nephew Gautier is determined to continue the vendetta against the man who had killed his uncle. There is a fierce single combat between Gautier and Bernier. At length both are carried from the field almost at the point of death. The foolish king has them placed on couches within sight of each other and the invectives continue. Raoul's mother Aalis, at sight of the wounded man who has killed her son, picks up the first thing she can lay her hands on and rushes to kill him, but is held back by the horrified barons at Louis' court. Bernier, who is still tormented by remorse, offers the most abject of penances. He actually

lies stretched in the form of a cross and begs the adherents of Gautier
and the savage old Guerri to kill him unless they will accept his
'amendise'. Only at the intercession of an abbot does the reconciliation take place, and then the weak, wily king shows his true character.
His one wish had been to foster dissension among his powerful
barons, and now he is full of apprehension at the sight of their
accord. By another foolish act he arouses the combined anger of
both parties against himself, and the first, and by far the most important, part of the poem closes on a scene in which the king is threatened
by the combined hostility of the barons he has antagonized by his
weakness and folly: 'Cest coart roi,' says Guerri, 'doit on bien
essillier / Car ceste guere nos fist il commencier.' This is a skilful
ending to the story and shows how antagonistic to the descendants of
Charles the people had become.

From this point the poem changes completely and is clearly the
work of another author. From being virile and powerful it degenerates into a sickly romance in which Guerri's daughter falls in love
with Bernier and, overcoming any possible objections on the part of
her father, marries him. Bernier is captured by Saracens, and the king,
with his habitual malice, wishes to give her as wife to another baron.
She escapes the consummation of this second marriage by the well-
known ruse of a medicinal herb and finally rejoins Bernier. A sudden
impulse causes Guerri and Bernier to set out together on a pilgrimage
to Saint Jaques, but on the way thither Guerri, evil as ever, when
halting at the spot where Raoul had been murdered, treacherously
kills Bernier from behind by a blow from his stirrup as he waters his
horse. One is inevitably reminded here of Hagen's treacherous blow
to Siegfried in the *Nibelungenlied*, and in each case it is loyalty to
another which furnishes the motive, though not the excuse, for the
cowardly stroke. The author tells us that Guerri finally became a
hermit, but we need not linger over this third or fourth-rate continuation of the original poem, merely remarking the rather singular fact
that the second part, though obviously of later date, is in assonances
whereas the first part, in the form in which it has come down to us, is
rhymed. The 'laisses' have the same tendency to length which we
have observed in *Garin le Lorrain* and which contrasts unfavourably
with the shorter, more varied forms of the earlier poems. The
descriptions of individual combats recall those of the *Chanson de
Roland*: *Tant com tint l'anste l'abati mort sanglant* or *plaine sa lance l'abat
mort el sablon*; reminiscent, too, of the *Roland* is the phrase that
'vasclaige' without good sense is worthless. Formulae abound—*qui*

l'i veïst . . .; cui il consuit . . ., etc. Premonitory phrases such as *Mai.
puis en fu Raoul grains et irez* or the author's remark on the curse
uttered by Raoul's mother: *Par cel maldit ot il tel destorbier | Com vo.
orez . . .*, etc., are frequent. But this ancient trick of epic technique
and the many other stereotyped expressions with their skilful variation of detail, only go to prove what an elaborate corpus of accepted
figures of speech and rhetoric must have been in existence by the
time that the earliest extant Old French epic poems appear on the
scene.

In accordance with our plan in this section of working backwards
from the point of view of chronology, another poem, possibly the
earliest of the feudal type which has come down to us, now claims
our attention. *Gormont et Isembart*, of which we unfortunately possess
only a fragment, is in some ways unique. The antiquity of the legend
and of poems (or songs) celebrating it, is attested by a passage in the
chronicle of Hariulf, a monk of Saint-Riquier who completed his
history of the abbey of Saint-Riquier in the year 1088. He briefly
relates the story of the heathen King Guaramond who, aided by the
renegade Esembard (Esembardus), invaded King Louis' territory, was
killed together with thousands of his followers by the French king
but became indirectly the cause of Louis' death as the latter strained
himself in the battle and died shortly after. Hariulf refrains from
going into details because this story—he says—was known 'non solum
historiis, sed etiam patriensium memoria quotidie recolitus et canta-
tur'. What are we to assume from this? Of what nature were the
songs collected and sung by local inhabitants concerning events which
the curious could learn from the traditions of their ancestors ('pris-
corum anctoritate')? Were they like the Germanic lyrico-epic
Ludwigslied which describes the same battle and which is a combination of clerical and popular elements, exhorting people to repent but
full of the delight of battle? It is impossible to answer this question,
but it is noticeable that this poem differs in form from all the known
chansons-de-geste which the language and phraseology allow us to
think of as approximately contemporaneous. *Gormont et Isembart*
reads like a ballad. It is in octosyllabic verse, the lines are assonanced,
and there is a refrain of very ballad-like character at frequent intervals. Were it not for the retarding element introduced by the
insertion of two anecdotes in the body of our fragment we could
almost believe we had an Old French ballad (after the style of the
Old Danish narrative ballads) in front of us. Very ballad-like, too, is

[1] Cf. *Aeneid* X. 503 ff.: *Turno tempus erit*, etc.

the avoidance of circumstantial detail. Gormont, who historically can only have led an invasion of Northmen at this date, has become the traditional enemy, a Saracen, *emperere de Leutiz*,[1] Gormont *d'Afrique*, an *Arab* (or rather *li Arabis*), *cil d'Oriente*, Satan (*Li Satenas*), and on one occasion *Antecri*. He leads an army of Saracens, a mixed multitude of 'gent averse' which includes some *Ireis*! Repetitions and stock phrases abound; nearly all the 'laisses', excepting those in the narrative part of the fragment, begin with some variation of the line: 'Li esturs fut fiers e pesanz' (or 'La bataille fut esbaldie'); the descriptions of the series of single combats, in each of which Gormont lays a noble French knight low (on one occasion the Count of Normandy), are completely stereotyped in character. They are familiar to us from the *Chanson de Roland*; Gormont is so immensely strong that each time he hurls his lance it transpierces his enemy and strikes down a second victim:

> Gormont li lance un dart trenchant
> Par mi le cors li vait bruianz
> Tres lui consuit un Aleman

(on another occasion the second victim is 'un danzel de Lumbardie') and each time the author exclaims:

> Li mielde reis e li plus Frans
> Qui unques fust el munt vivanz,
> Se il creüst Deu le poant ... etc.

even more enthusiastically than the author of the *Roland* when vaunting the courage of a heathen. The earlier part of our fragment consists of a series of individual contests between Gormont and the French knights. After the account of the so far unexplained episode of Hugon's embassy to the heathen King in which the latter was tricked and his lieutenant robbed, which is almost immediately followed by the death of Gormont at the hands of King Louis, the battle becomes more general. The heathen, led and encouraged by the renegade Isembart, alternately flee and return to the fight. On the fourth day after Gormont's death, the heathen having pathetically begged Isembart to stand by them, advance again to the battle and kill many Frenchmen. King Louis comes across the dead body of King Gormont, and after a brief 'regret funèbre' ('Tant mare fustes, gentilz ber / Si creïssiez en Damne Deu', etc.), he acts like a gentleman ('De ceo fist Loöis que prus') and has his enemy carried to his tent covered decently on a shield. Isembart fights furiously; he unhorses

[1] l. 444.

his father in a single combat without recognizing him and makes havoc of the French army. Many times the familiar phrase is applied to him which we have come across so often with a host of variations: *Qui il feri puis ne parla* or *Qui il consuit tut est vencus*, but at last the Saracens, hungry and weary, turn and flee to their barges and ships, and Isembart, attacked from all sides, with three deep wounds in his body, is thrown from his horse and falls at the meeting of three roads ('al quarefor de treis chemins'). He lies there unrecognized and the fragment ends with the devout prayer of the dying man to the Virgin and the God whom he had denied as he lies beneath a tree and, like Roland, confesses his sins with his face towards the east. Isembart is a tragic figure. We can learn from other versions of the story how badly he had been treated by the king—even to the extent of making him turn traitor to his country though he never lost his love and admiration for his native land. Behind the episodes we recognize the background of the weak, faithless king, and the incensed vassal with which we have become familiar.

There are many unexplained and intriguing features about this alluring fragment—the transformation of Gormont into an Arab, the ruse by means of which he was prevented from enjoying his peacock, the connection of the story with Cirencester, the soothsaying of the heathen, the carrying off of the silver 'nef' by the young squire. But all these 'motifs', some well known and others unfamiliar, add colour to the somewhat hackneyed theme of the rebel vassal fighting against his lord, and the noble words of the 'regrets', even though they be somewhat conventional in character, are proof of the skill of the author in manipulating an unaccustomed metrical form. Our chapter concludes, as it begins, with the *démesuré* Raoul and the *reneiié* Isembart coupled together as characteristic traitors by Walter Map.

CHAPTER V

THE *CHANSON DE ROLAND*

THE bulk of this chapter will be devoted to the two great protagonists in the poem we are considering, namely, Charlemagne and Roland, who form in a sense the background and the foreground of the skilfully constructed work. No apology is needed for consideration of a poem which has been the subject of so many learned works, and, incidentally, of a good deal of controversy as regards date, composition and tendency—for the *Chanson de Roland* is one of those rare productions of which it may be said that the more one looks into them the more one finds.

I. CHARLEMAGNE

Like all serious medieval works the *Roland* has a deep meaning ('senefiance'). It symbolizes something. Like the stained glass windows and the frescoes on the church walls, it taught a lesson to the hearers (for it was destined to be recited) which they could not miss if they listened to its enthralling tale. The *Chanson de Roland* might be called the *Pilgrim's Progress* of the Middle Ages. It represents not only the eternal conflict between good and evil, right and wrong,[1] truth and falsehood, but it is also a symbol of the Christian's journey through this vale of tears worked out in the soul of a hero of epic size and grandeur in accordance with the form of expression chosen by the author. How cheerful and self-satisfied Charlemagne is at the opening of the poem:

Li emperere se fait et balz et liez (l. 96).

He has accomplished so much and lost so little for are not his twelve peers, his favourite nephew, his best counsellors, and his beloved archbishop all around him, and his army laden with booty—longing to be home it is true, but otherwise in good trim? There is only one task unaccomplished. He has not taken Saragossa, the seat of the heathen king Marsilic. Only this is needed to enable him to say 'I have fought the good fight, I have finished my course, and now I have qualified to receive the reward promised to the overcomer'. He has come to the most dangerous point in the Christian's career

---

[1] Almost like a refrain recurs the line: 'Paien unt tort et Chrestien unt dreit' (l. 1015), etc.

when humility and dependence on God have given place to self-confidence and self-satisfaction. For now comes the temptation. Satan approaches as an angel of light; just as the emperor is pausing before tackling his last task, a blameless-looking cortège appears. Ten beautiful white mules with reins of gold and saddles of silver, on which are seated ten messengers carrying olive-branches in their hands (but lies in their hearts) can be seen approaching, and soon an alluring offer is made to Charles whereby he may return to France without another battle and take back peace with honour. The emperor makes no immediate reply for he is not 'hasty in his speech and his custom is to speak deliberately ('a leisir'); but he is impressed and reflects that 'Marsilie may even yet be saved'.[1] Moreover, in feudal fashion he must take counsel of his barons. But, whether of his own volition, or whether he is persuaded against his better judgment by his counsellors, Charles yields to temptation and accepts the suggestion made by the heathen king. He sets out for home leaving only a rearguard to cover his retreat, though from his arbitrary and autocratic way of replying to the suggestions of his barons as they offer in turn to take back his reply to Marsilie, it is difficult to avoid the suspicion that at the bottom of his heart he knows he is not acting up to his principles. When the keys of Saragossa are brought to him he has just returned from hearing Mass and Matins, and as he starts on his journey he tells himself that the war is ended.[2] But already the sinister sound of the 'hosts of Midian' might have been heard (if the Christian only had ears to hear them) as they marched in their thousands through the fearsome valleys. 'Dieu, quel dulur, que li Franceis ne-l sevent! AOI.'[3], for the first round of the conflict brings disaster not to Charles in person but to those he loves and cherishes—the twelve peers and the devoted army. Many are the premonitions of disaster which precede the battle and many a tear Charles sheds as things go from bad to worse. But it is of no avail, there is no help in store for them;[4] many an innocent victim falls as the result of Charles' weakness and the ensuing tragedy of which Roland's 'démesure' is but a secondary cause. After the disaster the emperor is overwhelmed with grief and, again on the advice of the barons, decides to avenge the death of Roland and his beloved knights. God has not quite abandoned him, for the sun is stayed in its course until such time as he has completed his vengeance and the whole of Marsilie's army is destroyed, for those who are not

---

[1] l. 156.   [2] l. 705.   [3] l. 716.
[4] 'De ceo qui calt, nen avrunt sucurance' (l. 1405).

slain by the sword are miserably drowned in the river. But the end
is not yet. Charles has another and more personal struggle to endure
and he is well aware of its imminence. He does not doff his armour
as he lies down to rest after the long day's work, but straps on his
helmet and girds on his good sword Joyeuse which has the tip of the
holy lance worked into its golden hilt. The night is fine but, though
he lies down, he cannot sleep, racked with grief as he is by the deaths
of Roland and Oliver and the twelve peers and the Frenchmen he has
left on the bloodstained battlefield. His own exhausted army is
sleeping, and even the horses are too weary to stand as they crop the
grass. There is no self-satisfaction in the mind of Charlemagne now;
he has learnt a bitter lesson, for, as the author remarks at this point,
suffering is a great teacher.[1]

But God has not abandoned His knight although he is crushed by
grief. Saint Gabriel is commissioned to protect the emperor, and all
night he stands beside his head keeping watch over him. At last he
slumbers. His sleep, however, is disturbed by a most ominous dream
presaging a fearful conflict in which his Frenchmen call upon him to
help them and, although filled with grief and pity (like a man in a
nightmare), he cannot go to their help for he is prevented by a lion
in the way. The lion leaps on him and they struggle together, and in
his dream he knows not which of the two, whether he or the lion,
will be the victor. This is followed by another sinister vision of thirty
bears, speaking like humans, who rush from the forest to his palace
at Aix to force him to hand over a bear that he holds in two chains.
A fearful struggle ensues on the green sward; it is all full of fore-
boding and once again the king knows not the outcome, until the
angel reveals it to him.[2]

Thus the way is prepared for the final and decisive round of the
conflict. The conquered Marsilie has sent for help to Baligant, the
Sultan of Cairo,[3] and the Emir has already set forth from Alexandria
with a vast army which is sailing in an imposing fleet across the sea
and up the Ebro.[4] In due course they arrive at Saragossa and before
Charlemagne has finished paying the last honours to his dead knights
the vanguard of this fresh army surges up before him. Soon both
forces are in battle array. The emperor is in a very chastened mood.
He prostrates himself and prays to God most earnestly (*escordeusement*)
that he may receive grace and avenge his nephew. Then he arises

---

[1] 'Mult ad apris ki bien conuist ahan' (l. 2524).
[2] l. 2568.
[3] 'L'amiraill . . . en Babiloine' (l. 2614).
[4] 'Par Sebre amunt tut lur naviries turnent' (l. 2642).

and mounts his swift charger while Naime, his counseller, and Joceranz hold his stirrup for him. He spreads his beard out over his byrnie and all the others do likewise for love of him, and we have a wonderful picture of him, riding with all his warriors as he brings up the rear of his army:

> Mult fierement chevalchet l(i) emperere
> Il est darere od cele gent barbee
> Desur lur bronies lur barbes unt getees
> Altresi blanches cume neif sur gelee (ll. 3316–19).

But they are up against a formidable foe. The Emir, too, has called upon his gods (Tervagant, Mahum, and Apolin), and he has made his followers bow themselves down humbly and pray for victory. The battle is joined, such a battle as there has never been before or since.[1] Evening comes on and it still rages, and the French suffer heavy losses. Then Baligant hears bad news—his son and his brother have been slain. He calls a soothsayer and consults him, but receives no comfort—only the advice to encourage his men to go on and not to put off his fate.[2] Then Ogier the Dane strikes down the heathen's standard bearing the dragon-device, and Baligant begins to have an inkling that he is in the wrong and Charlemagne in the right.[3] Now the crucial moment approaches for Charles and the Emir meet in single combat. Christian has to meet Apollyon and to go through the valley of the shadow of death, for the emperor receives a blow which nearly costs him his life. He is on the point of falling—indeed, he would have done so but that God did not will his death. His protector, Saint Gabriel, approaches him again: 'What art thou doing, great king?'[4] and at the voice of the angel Charles loses all fear of death, his strength and his faith revive, and with his good French sword he gives the heathen his death blow. Apollyon is dead and right has triumphed.[5] Now, one would think, Charlemagne might take his ease and rest on his laurels. But that is never the Christian's lot. His life is a life of toil and sweat and tears—it is an unending battle against adversity. No sooner has Charles returned to his palace at Aix, having slaked his desire for vengeance and brought the heathen queen into the true faith than, in the quiet of the night, when the king is asleep in his vaulted chamber, the angel Gabriel appears again with the divine message that he is to go to the help of oppressed Christians who are crying for his aid in another land. How little he

[1] l. 3394. [2] 'Co qu'estre en deit, ne l'alez demurant' (l. 3519).
[3] l. 3554. [4] 'Reis magnes, que fais tu?' (l. 3611).
[5] 'Mult ben espleitet cui damne Deus aiuet' (l. 3651).

wished to go, for he was a very weary man. 'O God, how toilsome is my life' are the last words we hear him utter as he sheds bitter tears and pulls his hoary beard:

> Deus, dist li reis, si penuse est ma vie!
> Pluret des oilz, sa barbe blanche tiret (ll. 700–2).

and that is the end of the story as far as Turoldus is concerned.

It must not be concluded, however, from what has been said that the *Chanson de Roland* is in any sense an allegory. The author is a born story-teller and the episodes are like a series of vivid pictures woven on a tapestry of which the rather sombre background presents a homogeneous whole. A certain didactic tendency which is to be detected throughout the poems would not repel the medieval hearer at a period when the lessons of the Bible and the Church had to be taught by concrete examples. There are many biblical reminiscences which are almost too obvious to call for remark: Charles surrounded by his twelve peers, of whom one is a traitor, for instance, inevitably recalls Christ and His twelve apostles. Ganelon is indeed a veritable Judas who sells his master for money, since he not only brings about the ruin of his personal enemy, Roland, but he betrays his lord and fails utterly in his duty towards his 'seigneur':

> Malvais servise le jur li rendit Guenes
> Qu'en Sarraguce sa maisnee alat vendre (ll. 1406–7).

'It is *you* he has perjured and wronged,' says Tierri to Charlemagne when he steps forth to fight the 'duel judiciaire' which will vindicate Roland's innocence and prove Ganelon's guilt. The darkness and earthquake which accompany Roland's death are obviously of biblical origin, as are the dreams with their symbolic meanings and the episode of the sun standing still until Charlemagne had completed the defeat of the enemy. What is new and original and due to the genius of the author (whether of our version or an earlier one) is the vividness with which the characters stand out against their edifying background. Even in the embassy scene, which is not conspicuously original, Blancandin is depicted, not merely as the messenger, but as a character and a skilful diplomat who, although he plans most treacherous actions towards the enemy, is an excellent minister of state for his king and a brave knight.[1] Ganelon is a most complicated character who allows personal animosity and private hate to overrule his better feelings and transform him from a respected and beloved leader into a felon and a traitor. He accepts bribes and plays skilfully

---

[1] ll. 24–6.

on the feelings of the enemy even at the risk of his life so as to en-
compass the destruction of the rearguard, in spite of the fact that he
has no feeling of injustice towards his lord, whom he admires and
reveres. There is a deep-seated root of bitterness in Ganelon which
our poem does not fully explain. Roland also had conceived a hatred
against his stepfather[1] and had wronged him in the matter of his
possessions,[2] and this, according to Ganelon's own words, was his
reason for wishing to destroy him. There may have been much more
than this behind it—perhaps some earlier version of the poem
explained Roland's animosity, for this is but one of the episodes
which point to the fact that the poem we possess is not the earliest
version, but the 'remaniement' of a more ancient poem which has
disappeared. Be that as it may, the Ganelon episode throws a great
deal of light on the character of Charlemagne. In his rôle of absolute
sovereign he requires unconditional obedience. The scene in which,
on the advice of Roland supported by the barons, he appoints
Ganelon to be his ambassador to the heathen king—a post involving
danger but requiring a prudent man—is one of the best in the whole
poem. Ganelon rises up in magnificent and righteous indignation at
the impudent suggestion and threatens lifelong enmity to his stepson.
But the young man replies that he is not moved by threats and will
go in his stead if Ganelon wishes it—an offer which it was not within
his power to make. Ganelon accompanies his scornful refusal of the
offer with another alarming threat of what he will do before his great
anger is assuaged. This was too much for Roland and he began to
laugh.[3] Ganelon nearly burst with anger and it is a wonder he did
not go out of his mind. 'I hate you,'[4] he exclaims as he turns to the
emperor and accepts the commission. But he gets no satisfaction
from Charlemagne. When he begs the emperor to care for his young
son Baldwin in the event of his death, the only reply he receives is:
'You are very soft-hearted. Since I command it, go you must.'[5] And
again, when Ganelon still cannot contain his anger against Roland
and the other peers (because they love him so dearly), and actually
hurls a challenge at them, the emperor will stand no more
nonsense: 'Your anger is too great,' he replies, 'now go without
further ado for I command it.'[6] Here we have the autocratic, heavy-
handed side of Charlemagne's character in contrast to the tender side
which appears shortly after, for, strange to say, he too could be very
soft-hearted where his own kith and kin were concerned. He may

[1] l. 3771.   [2] 'Rollanz me forfist en or et en avoir' (l. 3758).   [3] l. 323.
[4] 'Jo ne vus aim nient'—a strong litotes.   [5] ll. 300–1.   [6] ll. 328–9.

even appear weak at times, but tears were no sign of weakness in those days and Charles was always capable of rising to sublime heights when occasion required. There is no real inconsistency in Charles' character. When he sees his nephew lying dead with his face toward the foe, and recognizes the marks made in the stone by Roland's sword, he is grief-stricken and has to be raised up and supported by four of his knights. He utters a heartrending lament for the dead youth both on his own account[1] and that of France,[2] and prays that his own soul may leave his body and go to join those of his lost ones before he arrives at his native land. 'Great is the wrath of Charles,' remarks Duke Naime, the counsellor; Geoffroy of Anjou, his standard-bearer, bids him not to grieve so much but to set about finding the bodies of those who have been slain. Charles rises to the occasion, the more so as he hears that the enemy are approaching. He seizes his beard and, in no weak voice, shouts aloud: 'To horse and to arms, French barons!' He himself is the first to arm, and as he prances proudly ('fait sun eslais') before his assembled troops he calls upon God and the apostle of Rome. There is no sign of weakness in him now as he proceeds to the final battle.

The last episode in the poem is very enlightening as to the character of Charlemagne and shows again the consistency with which it is drawn. Ganelon is to be tried, and Charles has summoned his knights from all quarters for that purpose. He himself is convinced of Ganelon's guilt: he had robbed the emperor of twenty thousand of his Frenchmen, of his nephew and of Oliver, and has betrayed the twelve peers for the sake of filthy lucre.[3] Ganelon pleads skilfully that he had duly challenged Roland and Oliver when they had appointed him to almost certain death, from which he only escaped by his own wit, and that he had avenged himself on them, but that of treason there was none. So convincing is he that the barons begin to waver. Why not let bygones be bygones? they say. Roland is dead and nothing can bring him back now, using a similar argument to one that is common in the feudal cycle, as we have seen—namely, that it is futile to grieve too much for what is past; we gain nothing by sorrowing for the dead. The argument is very plausible when Charlemagne has lost so many valiant knights. 'Let Ganelon live, for he is a noble man and he will serve you loyally henceforth.'[4] But Charles is deeply distressed when he sees that all his knights have failed him. For him right is right and wrong is wrong, and like

---

[1] 'Suz ciel ne quid aveir ami un sul' (l. 2904).
[2] 'Ki tei ad mort France ad mis en exill' (l. 2935) [3] l. 3756. [4] ll. 3809-11.

Michael Angelo's Jeremiah, he sits with bowed head and laments aloud in his grief. But the situation is saved by the knight Tierri, brother of Geoffroy, Duke of Anjou, who steps forth and says courteously to the emperor: 'My lord king, grieve not so much,' claiming the right of ancestry to uphold the cause of justice and prove in single combat with Pinabel that Ganelon is a felon and has betrayed the king's service.[1] So the battle takes place and right triumphs, for Tierri slays his adversary by a mighty blow.[2] The seasoned warriors gather round him and the king takes him in his arms and wipes his face with the fur of his mantle which then, with regal gesture, he throws off and receives another from the hands of those who stand by. On the advice of his counts and dukes the thirty hostages of Pinabel are hung—and rightly so, says the author in justification of this brutal treatment, for a traitor ruins both himself and others.[3] Then all return to their homes satisfied, but above all the rest, the French are eager that Ganelon should die 'par merveillus ahan' and again the moral is impressed upon the hearers that it is not right that a man who betrays another should be allowed to boast of it.[4] Thus a safety-valve has been provided for Charles' great grief and anger,[5] and he is granted the gentle satisfaction of being instrumental in the conversion of Queen Bramimunde to the true faith, before he receives the angelic summons to be up and doing again in the unceasing warfare which constitutes the Christian's life. It is astonishing how, right to the end of the poem, the author has succeeded in developing side by side the symbolic rôle of Charlemagne with its moral import, and the completely human nature of his character, without allowing one to impinge on the other or falsify it in any detail.

2. ROLAND

The only historical or semi-historical reference we have to Roland is to be found, as is well known, in Eginhard's *Vita Karoli*, which, when describing Charlemagne's return from a victorious campaign in Spain, mentions an unfortunate incident that happened on the homeward journey. The Basques (*Wascones*) treacherously attacked the troops composing the rearguard of the French army as they wound their way through the defiles of the Pyrenees, massacred them to the last man, seized their baggage and fled back to the mountains

---

[1] 'Vostre servise l'en doüst bien guarir
Guenes est fels d'ico qu'il le traït' (ll. 3828-9).
[2] l. 3929.
[3] 'Ki hume traist, sei ocit et altroi' (l. 3959).   [4] l. 3974.   [5] l. 3989.

under cover of night. Amongst those who were slain Eginhard mentions by name *Hruodlandus Brittannici limitis praefectus* and one or two others. This title, count of the March of Britainy, does not occur in the *Chanson de Roland*, where the hero is introduced simply as Roland, or *li cuens Roland* (Count Roland). From the very beginning it is made clear that he is the nephew of Charlemagne. We know nothing of his boyhood or upbringing, as one cannot place much reliance on later poems which attempt to make up for this lack of information. The poem of *Aspremont* relates how, as a boy, he escaped from tutelage in order to join Charlemagne's army, and how in the ensuing battle he saved the emperor's life; *Girart de Viane* tells of his single combat with Oliver under the walls of Viane and his wooing of Oliver's sister, 'la belle Aude'. In the *Chanson de Roland* he is the acknowledged 'fiancé' of Aude, and it is possible that some version of the former story existed which would explain the almost exaggerated affection which Charles displays towards his nephew when, for instance, he laments after Roland's death:

> Suz ciel ne quid aveir ami un sul
> Se jo ai parenz, nen i ad nul si pruz (ll. 2903–4).

Such an expression would seem a little hard on his own son whom he offered as a good exchange to Roland's fiancée, were it not that the lament is somewhat stereotyped in character.

In the *Pseudo-Turpin* Roland has a single combat with the heathen Ferragu (Ferracutus),[1] whom he kills after making a valiant attempt to convert him by means of a subtle explanation of the Trinity, the resurrection, and other tenets of the Christian faith. There is no allusion to this fight in the *Chanson de Roland*, although it became very popular in later works and may possibly have been the subject of a poem which has not come down to us. These feats and facts attributed to Roland are probably due to an attempt on the part of the 'jongleurs' to fill out those seven full years which, we as have seen from the first strophe of the *Chanson de Roland*, the French army had spent in Spain. There are references in the poem itself to some of Roland's youthful escapades ('enfances'). We may not, perhaps, attach too much credence to Ganelon's account of his daring and rather childish exploits—how he had presented his uncle with a scarlet apple as a symbol of all the crowned heads he had defeated,[2] and how on another occasion he had washed the fields with water to obliterate the bloody marks of a battle he had fought without his uncle's

---

[1] Cf. supra.   [2] l. 386.

consent.[1] These may be merely the accusations of an aggrieved man anxious to prove that Roland's actions were dictated by pride and folly. Roland's own claims, too, made by the dying warrior as he lamented over his famous sword,[2] are so exaggerated (if those in other versions are added to those of the oldest version we possess, viz., the manuscript of Oxford, the number of kingdoms he had conquered mounts up to fifty-eight) that they must be considered in the nature of a *gab* or vaunt such as the knights of those days indulged in either before or after battle. But there are other allusions in the body of the poem which do throw some light on his youthful character and are entirely consistent with the picture the author has drawn of him in action. Charlemagne himself recounts how Roland had, on a festive occasion, when his knights had been boasting of their feats in fierce pitched battles, vowed that he would never die in a strange land were he not in advance of his men and his peers with his face toward the enemy's land:

> Cunquerrantment si finireit li bers (l. 2867).

Roland's own claims[3] (on a less emotional occasion than that of his lament over his incomparable sword Durendal), to have conquered and taken various strongholds in Spain during the seven years they had sojourned in that country, may, perhaps, be believed, the more so as on the same occasion he recalls a former treacherous act of King Marsilie which has a ring of truth. Roland's methods must have been ruthless, as the author mentions the fact that the 'citet de Galne', which the count had taken and destroyed, lay waste for a hundred years after the event.[4] But other indirect information as regards his character shows us a better and more lovable side. His affection for Oliver was of long standing, as he himself tells us ('This is Roland who has always loved you so much'[5]) in the moving scene in which Oliver, wounded to death and blinded by blood, inadvertently strikes him. Oliver dies calling upon God to bless Charles and sweet France and his companion Roland above all men. Then Roland began very softly to utter his 'regret funèbre':

> Sire cumpaign, tant mar fustes hardiz:
> Ensemble avum estet et anz et dis,
> Ne'm fesis mal, et jo ne-l te forsfis (ll. 2024–7).

Such words as these bear witness to a long and lasting affection between the two men. Nor is it only Oliver in whom he inspires

---

[1] ll. 1775 f. [2] ll. 2316 f. [3] ll. 197 f.
[4] l. 664. [5] ll. 2000–1.

confidence and the desire to have him near when danger is at hand,[1]
but his rather mysterious friend, Gualter del Hum, who occupied a
dangerous post, which he had abandoned after losing all his men, in
his extremity came to Roland for help. The episode, as we have it in
the Oxford manuscript, does not terminate very clearly, but Gualter's
words, when he comes to Roland rather apologetically for having
left his post, are touching and enlightening as to the effect Roland
had on others:

> E gentilz quens, vaillanz hom, u es tu?
> Unkes nen oi poür la u tu fus (ll. 2046-7).

This same effect on others is evident, moreover, in the attitude of his
men and the rest of the army towards him. 'If only we could see
Roland before he died,' exclaim the men of Charlemagne's avenging
army, 'together with him we could give a good account of ourselves.'[2]
Not one of the Frenchmen but weeps for grief and anger and prays to
God to protect Roland until they arrive, and again they repeat their
lament:

> Ensembl' od lui i ferrunt veirement (l. 1840).

But it is of no use, says the author; they have delayed too long and
cannot be in time. There is not an unimportant phrase or incident in
the passages alluding to Roland, and it is obvious why his men
admired and trusted him when we read the description of the con-
fident young warrior as he rides at the head of his troops. The passage
deserves quoting in full:

> As porz d'Espagne en est passet Rollanz
> Sur Veillantif sun bon cheval curant,
> Portet ses armes, mult li sunt avenanz,
> Mais sun espiet vait li bers palmeiant,
> Cuntre le ciel vait la mure turnant,
> Laciet en sum un gunfanun tut blanc,
> Les renges li batent josqu'as mains;
> Cors ad mult gent, le vis cler et riant.
> Sun cumpaignun apres le vait sivant
> Et cil de France le cleiment a guarant.
> Vers Sarrazins regardet fierement
> Et vers Franceis humle(s) et dulcement.
> Si lur ad dit un mot curteisement: . . .[3]

Can we wonder that the Frenchmen acclaimed him as their protector
as he looked fiercely toward the foe and then, turning a humble and
gentle look towards themselves, addressed them in courteous fashion?

---

[1] ll. 2046-7.　　　　　[2] ll. 1805-6.　　　　　[3] str. xci.

Last but not least of the indirect tributes to Roland's attractiveness is the scorn with which his fiancée Aude, on hearing of his death, rejects Charlemagne's offer of his own son ('a very good exchange,' says the simple old emperor) and prefers to follow her lover to the grave.

Every act and every speech of Roland is consistent with the tributes to his character contained in the poem. We have mentioned his impetuosity in the embassy scene and the ruthlessness of which he was guilty in the destruction of an enemy town, which was one of the reasons, perhaps, why the Saracen warriors, one after the other, swore to kill Roland if they came across him in the battle.[1] Ganelon, moreover, had made no secret of the fact that he was Charles' right arm and that he was more responsible for the continuance of the war in Spain than anyone else. Roland was in truth most anxious for the battle. When Oliver remarks that it is likely to begin, Roland replies: 'God grant it may',[2] and then follows the famous declaration of loyalty which is typical of Roland's attitude towards his lord throughout:

> Pur sun seignor deit hom susfrir destreiz
> Et endurer et granz chalz et granz freiz,
> Si-n deit hom perdre et del quir et del peil (ll. 1009–12).

a noble confession of faith which he repeats in almost identical words when things are beginning to look very grim as a vastly superior enemy host approaches, and both Roland and Oliver have begun to realize that Ganelon has been playing the part of the traitor.[3] Roland calls upon his men to acquit themselves well so that they shall never become the subjects of a scurrilous song or a warning sermon. His wish was granted in a curious way, for a thirteenth-century chronicle tells us that there were many people who were impatient for the service to finish so that they might leave the church, as they would rather be told about the prowess of Roland and Oliver than about N.S.J.C.[4] Roland's courage soon became a legend, and there was no danger of his bringing disgrace on his family or causing fair France to fall into disrepute.[5] He has added lustre to the name of his uncle and his country since the beginnings of French literature in the vulgar tongue. The warnings of Oliver as to the size and strength of the pagan army fall on deaf ears: 'So much the better,'[6] replies Roland, and persists in his refusal to sound the horn which would bring

---

[1] 'Se truis Rollant, ne lerrai que ne-l mat' (ll. 893, 902, 914, 923, etc).
[2] 'E Deus la nus otreit' (l. 1008).   [3] l. 1147.
[4] Quoted by Bayot: *Poème moral*, p. 222. Note to line 8132.   [5] ll. 1013–14.
[6] 'Mis talenz en engraigne'—lit. my desire increases thereby (l. 1088).

Charles to their aid. It is at this point that the contrast between the
characters of Roland and Oliver begins to appear. Oliver had
mounted a hillock to 'survey' the enemy forces. They are so numerous
that he cannot count them, and he is much dismayed.[1] For a leader
to act as a scout and try to estimate the strength of the hostile army
(*surveër l'ost*) before the battle was not calculated to inspire confidence
and was sometimes looked upon with disfavour, as we learn from
another poem. In the *Chançun de Willame*, when Tedbalt asks Vivien
to perform this office, Vivien is indignant:

> Viviëns ber, car muntez en cel tertre,
> Si surveez iceste gent adverse,
> Cum bien unt homes e en mer et en terre.
> Dist Viviëns: Nel me devez ja querre.
> . . . Car si m'aprist li miens sire Guillelmes.
> Ja, si Deu plaist, ne surverrai herberge.[2]

Vivien persuades Tedbalt to mount the hillock himself and judge
whether he has enough men to meet the enemy—if not, let him send
to his friends for help. Tedbalt takes Vivien's advice and rides up to
the top of the hill. He sees the sea covered with ships: he looks up
at the sky for the sight of the earth terrifies him, and he almost faints
for fear. He rides down the hill and, coming back to the Frenchmen,
tells them everything, just as Oliver did.[3] But now emerges the
difference in the characters of the two men. Tedbalt is a coward and
his immediate reaction is:

> Franche maisniee, que purrum devenir?
> . . . Alum nus ent pur noz vies guarir.

Oliver is no coward. He may be *sage* (cautious), but he has
merveillus vasselage and he will never avoid battle for fear of death.[4]
He warns the Frenchmen that they will have battle, such a one as
there has never been; he bids them be strong and stand firm so as not
to be vanquished: 'El camp estez, que ne seium vencuz.'[5] But he
speaks differently to Roland. The battle is going to be so unequal
that he beseeches him three times to blow his horn and bring back
Charles and his army. It is evident that Roland has the same feeling
that Vivien had—namely, that it is disgraceful to spy out the attacking
army first and give up the battle before it is begun. In his three
refusals to sound his horn he puts his personal honour first,[6] his family

---

[1] l. 1036.
[2] ll. 162–9. Cf. Xenophon. *On Horsemanship*: Fear . . . . makes a shrewd watchman (or scout).
(Transl.)
[3] Vint as Franceis, si lur ad tut cunté. *Roland*, l. 1039; *Willame*, l. 193.   [4] l. 1096.
[5] l. 1046.   [6] 'Jo fereie que fols / En dulce France en perdreie mun los' (l. 1054).

second,[1] his duty to France third.[2] There is an egotistical note about his refusals, and Oliver again refers to the risk they are running and the fate that awaits the doomed rearguard. But Roland is obdurate and can only see the disgrace of looking at the hosts in the defiles apprehensively:

> Respunt Rollant: Ne dites tel ultrage!
> Mal seit del coer ki el piz se cuardet
> Nus remeindrum en estal en la place
> Par nos i ert et li colps et li caples.

It is clear that Roland puts personal honour before consideration for his men's lives, and it is this to which Oliver refers later when he says: 'Cumpainz, vos le feïstes . . . Franceis sunt morz par vostre legerie.'[3] Roland himself has a twinge of conscience when he sees so many of the faithful barons who had served him long lying dead on the battle-field. As he weeps over them and prays for their souls he says sadly:

> Barons Franceis, pur mei vos vei murir,
> Jo ne vos pois tenser ne guarantir (ll. 1863–4).

The thought spurs him on to fresh efforts, however, in order to avenge them, and he makes the heathen flee before him like a stag before the hounds[4]—one of the very few similes in the poem. Many are the descriptions of his prowess in the battle and the havoc he wrought amongst the heathen. When his lance was broken he drew his good sword Durendal and the Saracens fell in heaps around him.[5] So fierce was the battle that his cuirass and both his arms are covered with blood, as also are the neck and shoulders of his trusty steed. It is just at this point of the story that a certain rift between Roland and Oliver is again apparent. Oliver's lance is broken and he is fighting with the stump. In his hands the fragment of his lance is quite a deadly weapon as he kills three heathen with it, but at last this, too, breaks and splinters completely. At this unlucky moment Roland perceives his friend: 'What are you doing, comrade? What is the use of a stick in such a battle as this? You need iron and steel. Where is your sword Halteclere with its golden hilt and crystal pommel?' 'I could not draw it,' replies Oliver; 'there was no time.'[6] But Roland was urgent and at last Oliver succeeded in drawing his good sword. Not till then was Roland satisfied with his comrade; when he saw the bloodstained sword being brandished and the heathen falling beneath it, he said to himself, 'My friend is fighting furiously now,

---

[1] 'Ja n'en avrunt reproce mi parent' (l. 1076).
[2] 'Que ja pur mei perdet sa valur France' (l. 1090).   [3] ll. 1725–6.
[4] l. 1874.   [5] l. 1341.   [6] ll. 1360–5.

more like himself. It is for blows such as these that the emperor loves
us.'[1] But Oliver gets his own back when the extent of the disaster
becomes clear. The French have suffered grievous losses, and though
they have sustained the first four enemy attacks, the fifth army of the
Saracens is now looming up before them and only sixty Frenchmen
are left to meet the enemy host. Even Roland's courage fails him and
he calls Oliver to him. 'What think you, brother? What had we
better do?' And he cries out in his distress:

> E reis amis, que vos ici nen estes!
> Oliver frere, cument le porrum nus faire,
> Cumfaitement li manderum nuveles? (ll. 1697–9).

He is reduced to asking for help; how can they let Charles know?
But Oliver answers coldly: 'Indeed I know not how. I would rather
die than be disgraced.' The words are practically those used by
Roland on a former occasion.[2] But now the tables are turned.
Twice Roland announces his intention to blow the horn, using the
same words that Oliver had used in the parallel passage earlier in the
poem:

> Si l'orrat Carles ki est as purz passant;
> Jo vos plevis, ja returnerunt Franc.

Oliver replies that he would disgrace his family for all time, that
Roland would not do it when he (Oliver) had suggested it and that
now he would never give his consent. There is almost a touch of
cruelty in the way in which he uses Roland's own words and even
tells him that if he persists in his intention he shall never lie in the
arms of his fair sister Aude. The simple Roland is at a loss to understand Oliver's frame of mind: 'Por quei me portez ire?' he asks, for
to himself it all seemed so natural. Then Oliver's pent-up feelings
burst out:

> Cumpaing, vos le feïstes.
> Kar vasselage par sens nen est folie,
> Mielz valt mesure que ne fait estultie.
> Franceis sunt morz par vostre legerie
> Jamais Karlon de nus n'avrat servise.
> . . . Vostre proece, Rollanz, mar la veïmes.

It was all such a waste, for Charles has need of the help of just such
men as Roland. Here Oliver is expressing an opinion that we meet
with elsewhere in the Middle Ages, namely, that one's first duty is
to be at the service of one's lord, even if it involves at times fleeing
from danger. Guillaume d'Orange was of this opinion as we shall see

---

[1] ll. 1558–60.   [2] l. 1091.

when studying his character in the next chapter. But Oliver's hard thoughts soon give way to his old feelings of admiration for his friend, and he ends up on a note of sorrow rather than anger. 'You are certain to be killed,' he tells Roland, sadly, 'France will be dishonoured. To-day our loyal companionship is at an end and by nightfall the grievous parting will be over:

> Oi nus defalt la leial compaignie,
> Einz le vespre molt ert gref la departie.[1]

It would be lamentable, indeed, if this had been the final parting of the two friends, but the author of the *Chanson de Roland* was much too skilful for this. With consummate skill he brings in the archbishop Turpin at this point. The priest heard the two knights quarrelling, and spurring quickly towards them, began to scold them; with true clerical astuteness he contrived to find a solution of their difficulty and to enable each of them to retreat from his position without losing face. It would be useless to sound the horn now, for it could not help them, but nevertheless it were better to do it so that the king might come and avenge them. Moreover, the Frenchmen would find their bodies and would bury them decently so that they would not be eaten by wolves and pigs and dogs.[2] The solution was worthy of the archbishop, who was such a champion against the heathen, both in word and deed[3] and chose his opponents in the battle so skilfully; for did he not pick out the sorcerer Siglorel, who had once been conducted to hell by Jupiter[4] and the particularly heretical-looking, pitch-black Saracen Abisme[5] amongst the many heathens who fell before his sword?

So the dispute ended; Roland sounded his horn and his manner of doing it was in complete accordance with his character, for weakened doubtless by the long strain of battle, he nevertheless put such energy into the action that the blood flowed from his mouth and his forehead burst from the effort. He spared himself neither risk nor pain, and so loud was the blast that Charles stopped to listen on his journey through the defiles, and Naime the duke heard it, and the Frenchmen caught the sound. Ganelon might try to laugh it off, but the emperor knew full well the meaning:

> Co dist li reis: Jo oi le corn Rollant.
> Unc nel sunast, se ne fust cumbatant (ll. 1768–9).

And Naime remarks:

> Asez oëz que Rollanz se dementet (l. 1795).

[1] ll. 1735–7.   [2] str. cxxxii.   [3] ll. 2243–4.   [4] ll. 1390–3.   [5] str. cxiv.

G

Roland was in distress, indeed, for although he fought on without sparing himself or others,[1] he had damaged himself so badly by the terrific blast on his horn that the pain in his head was almost unbearable, and actually he was a dying man. But the misunderstanding between Oliver and himself is over and together they go forward:

Sire cumpainz, alum i referir (l. 1868).

And now this battle with the fifth and last army of the enemy reaches its peak for the man who knows that no prisoners will be taken puts up a good defence in a losing battle.[2] Roland knows full well that they are doomed; he does not flag but cheers his men on to the end. 'We shall all die to-day, I know. Strike, Frenchmen, for this is my bidding.' 'Cursed be he who lingers,' says Oliver, and at this encouragement the Frenchmen go once more into the fray.

From this point the gentler side of Roland's character comes completely into the foreground, for his actions and words are characterized by humility, gentleness, and courtesy. Oliver is wounded to death and though he fights on bravely for the honour of Charles and of France, in his extremity he calls to Roland and begs him to keep near him as the sad parting is now at hand.[3] Roland has only to look at his friend to see he is a doomed man and he is dismayed—'*or ne sai jo que face*'. He actually faints for grief and Oliver, whose vision is already obscured by loss of blood and approaching death, but who is still wielding his sword almost automatically, not recognizing Roland, strikes him as he comes to his aid and cleaves the helmet on his head. Then Roland, full of grief and pity, addresses him 'dulcement e suef', but, with a faint fear that Oliver might still harbour angry thoughts towards him, he asks pathetically whether the stroke was intentional, as Oliver had not challenged him in any way ('Par nule guise ne m'aviez desfiet'). Oliver recognizes his voice instantly and begs for forgiveness, and on Roland's assurance that all is well the two friends embrace and at this third mention of their parting the author of the poem exclaims:

Par tel amur as les vos desevred ! (l. 2009).

Oliver's dying words were a prayer that God would bless Roland above all other men, and Roland's short lament for him[4] bears an accent of real grief. He loses his senses and is carried hither and thither on his horse Veillantif, but cannot fall as he is firmly fixed in

---

[1] ll. 1865 f.   [2] ll. 1886-7.

[3] 'Sire cumpaign, a mei car vus justez ! A grant dulor ermes hoi deseverez' (ll. 1976-7).

[4] str. cli.

his stirrups. Even in the few short moments of his unconsciousness the disaster has deepened, for all the Frenchmen are dead save the archbishop and Gualter del Hum, who had returned from his outpost having lost all his men. Like Oliver in his extremity Gualter calls upon Roland for help and moral support.[1] This recalls Roland to his senses and the three remaining men keep close together and make a firm stand against the thousands of Saracens. Such terror do they inspire that the heathen dare not approach but begin to hurl darts and spears and shoot arrows from a safe distance. At the first on-slaught Gualter is killed and the archbishop is wounded seriously and his horse killed under him. It was a great calamity when the archbishop fell, but in spite of four spear-wounds through his body, he leapt to his feet and looking at Roland, exclaimed: 'I am not conquered, a good vassal will never give way while he still has life in him.'[2] Once more he gave a good account of himself if the report is to be believed that Charles found four hundred dead and wounded men lying around him.[3] Then Roland, still fighting bravely, paused to sound the horn again to ascertain whether Charles was on his way. The blast, alas, was not like the former one—it had such a quavering sound that Charlemagne recognized at once that his nephew was almost at his last gasp:

> Rollanz mes nies, hui cest jur nus defalt.
> Jo oi al corner que guaires ne vivrat (ll. 2106–7).

So he bade his men ride quickly and sound every horn in the army; the mountains ring with the sound, the valleys echo it, and the heathen hear it with dismay. But it spurs them on to fresh efforts and Roland has much to contend with[4]; but encouraged by the sound of the horn, and side-by-side with the archbishop he plunged once more into the breach. Roland always hated cowards and proud, ill-conditioned men, and now, seeing that the archbishop was on foot and he himself still on horseback, with beautiful courtesy he took his stand beside him:

> Sire, a pied estes et jo sui a cheval,
> Pur vostre amur ici prendrai estal;
> Ensemble avruns et le ben et le mal (ll. 2138–40).

At last the heathen fled, but not until they had killed Roland's horse Veillantif with their darts and arrows and left Turpin a dying man. Roland remained standing alone; all his armour was riddled and torn, but, strange to say, he was not touched in the body.[5] So

---

[1] l. 2046.   [2] ll. 2087–9.   [3] l. 2090.   [4] l. 2123.   [5] l. 2107.

immune did he seem to their shafts that the heathen concluded that
he was invulnerable to mortal man.[1] Roland could not pursue the
retreating enemy for his good steed was dead, but he went to the
archbishop and tended him carefully, binding up his wounds and
placing him softly on the grass. Then gently he addressed him and
asked for his permission to leave him to go and find his dead comrades
and bring them for his blessing. 'Go thither and return,' replied the
dying archbishop. 'This field is yours, thank God, and mine.'[2] So
Roland went and searched up and down for his dead comrades. One
by one he brought them and laid them in order before the archbishop's knees. Turpin is much moved as he gives them his benediction and prays that their souls may be placed among the holy flowers
of paradise. This act of Roland seems like a Christian version of the
reverent act of Walter of Aquitaine in the *Waltharius*,[3] where the
hero places the appropriate heads to the trunks of the twelve knights
whom he has killed in single combat—the knights being, of course,
not Saracens but subjects of a friendly ruler animated by avarice and
anger. When Roland finds the body of Oliver his grief breaks out
afresh,[4] and he does justice to his friend's valour and wisdom in a
short funeral lament as he places his body on a shield beside the
others,[5] after which he falls down in a faint from weakness and grief.

Then follows another scene which is touching in its grandeur.
The archbishop, when he saw Roland faint, was much distressed.
He stretched out his hand and picked up Roland's horn; furnished
with this he tried to reach a running stream to fetch water for him.
But he was so feeble from loss of blood that his heart gave out before
he reached the stream:

> Sun petit pas s'en turnet cancelant,
> Il est si fieble qu'il ne poet en avant,
> N'en ad vertut, trop ad perdut del sang.
> . . . La sue mort li vait mult angoissant (ll. 2227-32).

And now Roland, recovered from his swoon, gets on to his feet
again, though in great pain, and, looking around, perceives the noble
baron, God's chosen archbishop, lying on his back confessing his sins.
His bowels are outside his body, his brains are exuding from his head,
but his beautiful white hands are crossed on his breast.[6] Bitterly
Roland laments him according to the custom of his country and
commends him to the God of heaven as a 'gentleman', a well-born
knight, and a priest who since the days of the apostles was unequalled

---

[1] l. 2153.   [2] ll. 2182-3.   [3] Cf. supra, Ch. I.
[4] '*Idunc agreget le doel et la pitet*' (l. 2206).   [5] str. clxiii.   [6] l. 2250.

'pur lei tenir et pur humes atraire'. For such a soul the gate of paradise would surely be opened.[1]

Now Roland's own death is at hand, but he still has strength left for a characteristic action. With horn and sword he advances a stone's throw and with face turned towards the enemy's land (as he had sworn to die) he mounts a hillock and falls face downwards on to the green sward beneath a beautiful tree. The setting is perfect, for there were four blocks of marble there and he was surrounded by high hills and lofty trees. But there is a moment of danger for his reputation and his peace of mind, for a Saracen has been watching him all this time. Feigning death, the heathen had stained his face and his body with blood and was lying amongst the corpses. He was a fine man, powerful and brave, and now seeing Roland at his last gasp he leapt up and ran towards him; in his mortal rage and pride he thought to possess himself of the sword of Roland. What a trophy Durendal would have been to carry back to Arabia! But Roland was not finished yet. He felt the pull at his sword and came to his senses. 'You are not one of our men,' he exclaimed as he opened his eyes and raising his dearly-loved horn, he smote the heathen a terrific blow on the helmet which killed him outright. 'How dared you touch me, whether by right or wrong. You will be called a fool for your pains—but my horn is split in the middle and all the crystal and the gold-work is destroyed.'[2] Could one imagine a scene, or words more characteristic of Roland? Not much more than a boy in years, but with the strength of a man even though he feels the approach of death, his grief is for his beautiful horn which he has not lost, it is true, but of which the glory has departed. And now his sword—how is he going to prevent that from falling into the hands of the enemy? Above all, no coward must wield it after it has belonged for so long to a very valiant knight—such a knight as will never be known again in France.[3] Now we perceive the 'raison d'être' of those blocks of shining marble which adorned the spot where Roland had laid himself down to die, for, with a mighty effort, he struck the stone with his sword in the hope of rendering it useless. But Durendal resisted all his efforts to break it. Twice did Roland try, but each time, though great pieces of the stone were smashed off,[4] the sword neither broke nor splintered—it merely grated on the rock and rebounded upwards.[5] So the effort had to be abandoned and Roland, after a pathetic lament, feeling that death was creeping down from his head towards his heart, laid himself

---

[1] str. clxvii.   [2] str. clxx.   [3] l. 2311.   [4] l. 2339.   [5] l. 2341.

down once more, this time carefully placing his sword and his horn beneath him. Then remembering his vow he turned his head towards the heathen land:

> Pur co l'at fait que il voelt veirement
> Que Carles diet et trestute sa gent
> Li gentilz quens qu'il fut mort cunquerant (ll. 2361–4).

His last thoughts as he lay thus with his face towards Spain were for 'sweet' France, for his family, for Charlemagne whose kindness to him in his youth (sun seignur ki-l nurrit)[1] he remembers with tears and sighs, and lastly (a significant change of heart!) for himself. After a brief prayer and a final confession of his sins, in simple confidence that his prayer had been heard, he held out his right glove to God. Saint Gabriel received it from his hand and angels carried the soul of the count to paradise.

¶ Roland's character has intentionally been treated at some length as it used to be said that the heroes of the *chansons-de-geste* were types rather than individuals. Although time has modified this opinion, there is still room for insistence on the fact that nothing could be further from the truth. Roland's character, from the first picture of him riding before his men, brandishing his lance with the white pennon, till the last dramatic dying gesture as he holds out his glove to God, is all of one piece and there is nothing in it that does not ring true. His youthful exuberance and quick temper (which rendered him unsuitable for the rôle of ambassador),[2] his lack of moderation ('mesure'), his devotion to his lord and his country, his love for his friends and affection for his men, his gentleness and manly courtesy when misfortune overtakes him, his simple faith in God's mercy and forgiveness—everything combines to depict the character which, with its touch of 'panache', remains absolutely true to itself to the end. No feminine influence comes into his life throughout the poem. It is no kindly aunt like Guibourg, but his uncle Charlemagne who had brought him up from childhood.[3] He had no thought for the fair Aude as, lying at the point of death, he lamented over his horn and his sword and called to mind sweet France, and his kinsmen and his liege-lord. And yet it would be wrong to do him an injustice as she may have been among the many things he remembered which made him weep so bitterly:

> De plusurs choses a remembrer li prist:
> ... Ne poet muer n'en plurt et ne suspirt (ll. 2377 and 2381).

[1] l. 2380.　　　[2] Cf. l. 256.　　　[3] Ki-l nurrit, l. 2080.

The worst reproach that Oliver could bring against him was that he would not listen to reason, that his courage needed to be tempered by good sense and his hardihood by moderation:

> Kar vasselage par sens nen est folie
> Mielz valt mesure que ne fait estultie (ll. 1725–6).

—and, in the end it is Oliver who, knowing his character so well, paid him the highest tribute—'N'ert mais tel hume desqu'a Deu juise'.[1]

Other characters in the *Chanson de Roland* are depicted by a few bold strokes. The heathen range from hideous creatures bristled like pigs,[2] or black as molten pitch[3] to good-looking, fascinating individuals on whom no lady can look without her face breaking out into a smile.[4] Baligant is described with particular care as behoves the Apollyon of Charles' memorable conflict. There is little except their outward appearance to distinguish one from another. They fight well and are no unworthy antagonists for the Christian knights. But the character of the noble heathen has not yet emerged and there is no mercy for them. The only exception is the heathen Queen Bramimunde, who is a good advocate for her wounded husband. When pleading his cause to his friend Baligant who has come from overseas to his aid, she pours forth such a torrent of words that Baligant is obliged to check her with the brief admonition: 'Ne parlez pas tant, ma dame.' The poet's psychological instinct never fails him. There is nothing incongruous or inconsistent in any of his characters. The only apparent exception to this might be found in the character of Charlemagne, but any seeming contradictions in his case are due to the double rôle he has to play. The way in which the two aspects of his character dissolve into one another is but further monument to the author's skill.

The poem begins and ends with Charlemagne. The main theme is never lost sight of, even the retarding elements serve to support it. It never peters out into mere adventure for its own sake as in the romances. In spite of digressions the poem moves on purposefully to the end and, like Montaigne's essay, *Des Coches*, returns to where it started. It contains scarcely a touch of romance to lighten it and yet, even when monotonous, it is saved from dreariness by the flashes of humanity which will keep breaking through.

[1] l. 1733.   [2] l. 3223.   [3] l. 1635.   [4] ll. 958–9.

CHAPTER VI

SOME CHARACTERS IN THE GUILLAUME-CYCLE

I. *GUILLAUME*
II. *GUILLAUME AND GUIBOURG*
III. *GUILLAUME AND HIS NEPHEWS*

THERE is no one work of genius in the cycle of Guillaume d'Orange which has fixed the hero's character for all time as is the case for Roland in the poem bearing his name. And yet, starting from the *Chançun de Willame* and running through *Aliscans*, the *Couronnement de Louis* and the *Charroi de Nimes*, we find definite traits of his character which, taken together, give us a picture of the hero as consistent and true to itself as the one we have been considering in the previous chapter. A study of the four poems just mentioned leaves us with an indelible impression of the warrior—powerful, warlike, irascible, pathetic in his many misfortunes, always ready to help his friends, devoted to his wife and his horse, full of affection for his relations, consistently loyal to his king. He is often discouraged, but still stands like a battered oak tree which has not lost its dignity and—though it is but a shadow of its former self—commands more respect than the other trees which are flourishing all around. It is tempting to think that the description of the defeated Pompey in Lucan's *Pharsalia* (from which this simile is borrowed) returning to his grief-stricken wife and mingling his tears with hers, was hovering in the mind of the author of the *Chançun de Willame* when he described Guillaume's return to the anxious Guibourg after his defeat and losses at l'Archamp. Like Pompey, he is dignified in his retreat, for he is no longer in the first flush of youth when we meet him. Life for him has been one continuous battle against the heathen, of whom it is his prime duty to destroy as many as possible:

> Puis que li hom n'aimme crestienté
> N'a droit en vie, je le di par verté
> Et ki l'ocist, s'a destruit un malfé.[1]
> . . . Tuit estes chien par droiture apelé.
> Car vos n'aves ne foi ne leauté.[2]

[1] *Aliscans*, ll. 1058 f.   [2] Ibid., ll. 1061b–1c.

His work is therefore unceasing and it is no wonder he describes himself as 'celui d'Orange, ki ja repos n'avra'.[1]

Guillaume is the hero of the Midi. The *Chançun de Willame*, the earliest known poem of our group, calls him indiscriminately Willame le Marchis, Willame al curb nes, Fierebrace, Willame le bon franc, dan Willame, but in spite of its northern colouring the author informs us:

> li quens Willame ert a Barzelune
> Si fu repeire d'une bataille lunge
> Qu'il aveit fait a Burdele[2] sur Girunde.[3]

We know, too, that he had already taken Orange in a battle in which 'Tiedbalt l'estormant' had been slain. This proves the existence of a legend, and perhaps a poem, which recounted the story of Guillaume's capture of a town in the South of France and a wife. The constant allusions to King Louis in the poem also go to prove that we have Guillaume here in his double rôle of supporter of Louis, son of Charlemagne, and defender of the south against the Saracens.

But it is not the historical Guillaume who interests us here—it is the Guillaume of the epic poems, Guillaume the father of his clan. It is true that Aymeri is the titular father even in this, the earliest extant poem of the cycle, for both Vivien and Gui, the two nephews of Guillaume, are described in almost identical lines as being sons of Bueve Cornebut, himself a son of Aymeri's daughter,[4] but in each case the next line adds: 'Nefs (nevou) Willame al curbnies (bon cunte) le Marchis'. Aymeri plays no further part in the poem, and his name may have been added as an afterthought for this, as the author tells us, in his introductory lines, is 'la chançun de Willame'. Here as elsewhere the impression is given that Guillaume is the 'chef de famille ou de clan,' surrounded by his nephews, his brothers and his relations, who all enhanced his importance. There were, indeed, no 'orbitatis pretia'[5] in those days. How well the portrait of the baron traced by Ordericus Vitalis fits in with all we know of the epic Guillaume: 'Hic nimirum in saeculo miles fuerat magnae sublimitatis, hostibus terribilis et amicis fidelis. Filios et fratres *multosque nepotes* in armis potentes habuit, hostibusque vicinis seu longe positis valde feroces.'[6] His is the *parage* or *lignage* or *parenté* in which all honour resides, and the members of which, as his wife rather cruelly reminds him, always died on the field of battle.[7] Here we get the idea of 'brothers-

---

[1] *Aliscans*, l. 2190.   [2] = Bordeaux.   [3] l. 935 f.
[4] 'Nez de la fille al bon cunte Aimeri' (ll. 300 and 1440).
[5] Cf. *Tacitus Germania*, Ch. x.   [6] ii, p. 15.   [7] *Chançun de Willame*, l. 1326.

in-arms' (*compagnonnage*), first between the cousins Girart and Vivien who advance side by side with their battle-standards touching—'dous reals compaignuns';[1] and then between Guillaume and Gui where the proximity even of his little nephew seems to give fresh courage to the hard-pressed Guillaume who kept close to him in all his movements and called upon him when in distress.[2] We have seen a similar relationship between Oliver and Roland, and between Roland and Gualtier del Hum in the *Chanson de Roland*, but here it is exclusively between members of the clan. When Guillaume thinks all his nephews have been killed (except 'le petit' Gui whom he had not yet learnt to value), he laments pathetically:

> Qui que en peist, jo sui tuz suls remes;
> Ja mais en terre n'avrai honur mortel.[3]

This relationship, particularly between uncle and nephew, occurs in many of the *chansons-de-geste*. The harmful influence exercised by Guerri the Red over his nephew Raoul de Cambrai will be studied in the next chapter, but it may be noted here that on one occasion the redoubtable Guerri, when discouraged after the loss of his two sons, begs his nephew not to leave him, which Raoul swears not to do. When the latter breaks his oath in the heat of the battle the author of the poem blames his folly sharply:

> Mais d'une chose le taing-je a enfant
> Que vers son oncle fausa de convenant.

The 'companionship' could only be severed by a formal challenge (defi), which, as we have seen, accounts for Roland's remark when Oliver, blinded by blood, had unintentionally struck him: 'Par nule guise ne m'aviez desfiet'.[4] But in a family so united as that of Guillaume d'Orange the breaking of the pact was not very likely to occur.

We are first introduced to Guillaume in the *Chançun de Willame* as to an experienced warrior:

> Sages hom est en bataille champel
> Il la set bien maintenir e guarder (ll. 57–8).

The art of war was no new thing in those days and Guillaume would probably have been described in a Latin poem as 'praelio doctissimus'. He was constantly in request against the heathen,[5] and, so great was

---

[1] l. 471.　　[2] ll. 1574 f.　　[3] ll. 1350–1, Suchier Edition.
[4] *Chanson de Roland*, l. 2002.　　[5] l. 62.

his reputation that even though there were twenty thousand French-men in the army and Guillaume arrived with only five—or four—or three—or even quite alone (*a eschari*), the victory would be ascribed to him and he would have all the credit, however much anyone might object. Indeed, the Frenchmen were being despised by the heathen, who held no one of repute save him.[1] When someone dared to object, Guillaume's nephew Vivien, who had unbounded admira-tion for his uncle, replied with characteristic pride of family that there was no one amongst the Christians or the pagans more courageous in a pitched battle than himself, save Guillaume 'al curb nes le marchis'.[2] They must have been an insufferable family, that Aymeri clan, for they had the superiority both in quantity and quality. Moreover, they were divinely supported at times for our poem tells us later on:

> Co fu grant miracle que nostre sire fist
> Pur un sul home enfuirent uint mil (ll. 1861–2).

Guillaume had, however, undergone two defeats before this divine intervention took place. He had suffered terrible losses in men (in fact two armies) and three of his nephews had been killed. The early part of the poem recounts Vivien's death after a bitter struggle with the army of Desramed, the Saracen king. Guillaume, for whom a messenger had been sent to Barcelona, in spite of the drunken objec-tions of Tedbalt of Bourges and his nephew Esturmi—an unpleasant couple—did not arrive in time to see Vivien alive. Moreover, the pagans, after mutilating his body, had taken it and hidden it so that it should not be found by the Christians. In this account of Vivien's death the *Chançun de Willame* differs from the *Aliscans*. In the latter poem Guillaume arrives to find a spark of life still in his nephew, and a very touching scene ensues in which, with the gentleness of a woman, Guillaume tends his dying nephew and administers the last sacrament to him with a piece of bread he had brought in his pocket. The account in the *Willame* is more tragic, as Vivien's prayer that his uncle should be sent to him[3] is not granted and he dies miserably at the hands of a native of Barbary. When Guillaume receives his dying message he weeps bitterly, the hot tears running down beside his nose.[4] Yet even here we find an example of Guillaume's grim sense of humour which is one of his characteristics. In order to test Guibourg's loyalty (*espermenter . . . sun corage*) he feigns unwillingness to go in search of his nephew on the ground that he is tired and could not bear it, for possibly the enemy might use iron and steel

[1] ll. 78–9.   [2] l. 87.   [3] str. xciv.   [4] l. 101b.

against him !¹ It is a heavy sort of humour, but not inconsistent with his rather insensitive character. In the *Couronnement* he jests at his own expense. When asked whether he feels fit after his battle with the giant Corsolt he replies:

> Oie² . . . la merci Deu del ciel
> Mais que mon nes ai un pou acorcié:
> Bien sai mes nons en sera alongiez.

In the *Charroi de Nimes* he is convulsed with laughter when his nephew Bertrand, who, disguised as a peasant, is leading the convoy, complains that the rough shoes will chafe his feet and that he does not know how to drive the oxen; then he mocks him as he tries with bruised nose and mouth to hoist the wheel of the 'char' out of the mud on to his shoulders. Once again his sense of humour breaks through at the end of the *Chançun* when he tells his famished nephew, Gui, that he will find in the abandoned camp of the Saracens something which could not flee, namely bread and meat and wine.³ His jest at the expense of the Saracen Aerofle in *Aliscans* partakes of the brutal. Aerofle was a worthy foe who stood up valiantly for his faith. But he was riding a magnificent horse which excited Guillaume's envy. The pagan was not to be cajoled by fair words for he could have no dealings with anyone who believed in the virgin birth⁴—always a stumbling-block to the heathen. So Guillaume, still greedily intent on obtaining the horse ('Li quens Guillaumes l'a forment goulousé'), jousted with the pagan and a bitter battle ensued in which finally, with a mighty blow from his sword Joyeuse, he severed Aerofle's leg and thigh completely from his body. Then, in callous fashion, Guillaume mocked him and told him to go and get a crutch made so that wherever he went he would be known as one of Guillaume's victims.⁵ In extenuation of his bad taste on this occasion, it ought, in justice to him, to be added that such vulgar abuse of a fallen foe was an indispensable part of the technique of the single combat from the tenth-century *Waltharius* onwards, nor is it entirely absent from the *Æneid*. But Guillaume went still further on this occasion, for having seized the coveted horse and galloped twice round the meadow on it,⁶ he comes back to where the mutilated Aerofle lies fainting with pain on the ground and gives him the death-blow, thus doing the very thing for which he had angrily blamed his nephew on another occasion.⁷ But Guillaume was a

---

¹ ll. 1014 f. ² Yes. ³ l. 1776. ⁴ l. 1195.
⁵ ll. 1310-12 ⁶ l. 1314. ⁷ *Chançun*, l. 1971.

realist, as was proved on both occasions, and niceties of chivalry did not appeal to him when larger issues were at stake.

It is in this connection that another characteristic principle of Guillaume's actions may be mentioned. He is described in the early part of the *Chançun de Willame* twice over as a skilful general ('sages hom est en bataille champel') and a good tactician[1] in the field. A similar description occurs in *Aliscans* where these two lines have been expanded. The passage may be quoted in full:

> Li quens Guillaume fu molt de grant aïr;
> Molt par fu sages, car bien savoit fuïr
> Et ou besoig trestorner et guenchir.
> C'est grans proece, ce dist, de lui garir;
> Mavais tornois fait maint home morir.
> Puis ke il voit k'il ne puet avancir
> Et ke sa force ne li puet esforcir
> S'il plus demeure, por fol se poet tenir
> Quant por un cop en veut C. requellir.[2]

It will be seen from these lines that the author fully approves the tactics of Guillaume on the principle that:

> He who fights and runs away
> Lives to fight another day.

We have here the old Germanic idea which Tacitus noted in his *Germania*[3]: 'Cedere loco, dummodo rursus instes, consilii quam formidinis arbitrantur.' But it was not only Germanic. Perhaps it was just common sense. Lucan's Pompey, when he surveyed the slaughter of his men from a rising ground decided on flight, because he did not desire, as the wretched often do (sicut mos est miseris), to draw all things in destruction after him and make many others share his ruin.[4] So, too, Guillaume ascended the slope of a hill, and when he considered the menacing size of the pagan army (always a questionable thing to do—had he not warned Vivien against it?) decided, just as Pompey did, that it was the part of true valour to save one's own life and that it was bad tactics to cause a too great slaughter of one's own men. And yet we are up against an interesting streak in Guillaume's character, for in the *Couronnement de Louis* he was strangely unwilling to go to the Pope's help against the Saracens who were attacking in superior numbers. He had just had a bad dream[5] which may have lowered his morale, but he actually wished to send to King Louis for help, which roused his nephew Bertrand to scorn

---

[1] 1. 183. [2] str. xxi. [3] Ch. vi.
[4] Cf. *Pharsalia*, Bk. VII, ll. 649 f. [5] ll. 289–98.

and ire. There are, of course, various reasons for refusal to fight or taking to flight, and the author of the so-called *Poème moral*, a didactic work of the end of the twelfth century, distinguishes carefully between the coward and the prudent man who does not wish to throw away his life:

> S'il amendeir nel peu, mies fist qui en fuit,
> Fous est, ou riens n'aïüe, qui la se fait hardis;
> Revenir encore puet a son seignor, s'il vit;
> Tost li rendrat sa grace, cui il avoit servit.[1]

In any case this was Guillaume's philosophy; it explains much in his character and gives him a certain affinity with the brave yet prudent Oliver. His lament over Vivien for whose idealism he has not much sympathy in spite of his deep affection for him, is almost identical with Oliver's sad reproach to Roland:

> Mar fu vos cors, ke tant par ert vaillans
> Vostre proece et vostre hardement[2]

and he puts his finger on the spot when he says:

> Nies, che t'a mort, c'onqes ne fus fuians
> Ne por paiens un seul pie reculans.[3]

Guillaume's character is not that of the infallible hero who is immune from the lapses and inconsistencies which are never completely absent in the noblest characters, and perhaps occur most often in those marked by strong human affections. He is very tender to his nephews and, in spite of a certain apparent harshness in his treatment of them, they loved him dearly. After losing his three nephews (Girard, Guishart, and Vivien) in the first part of the *Chançun de Willame* he is anxious that the fifteen-year-old Gui should stay at home with his aunt and foster-mother Guibourg. But Gui escapes with the connivance of Guibourg, and having reached the army he mixes with the squires and 'vavassours' mounted on his aunt's saddle-horse with a full-size saddle and shortened stirrups.[4] 'Petiz est Gui e li chevals est granz'. Guillaume, who has taken the oath of his first rank barons, is in the act of addressing his vassals and lesser knights. He was just uttering words of pride and lofty inspiration to the effect that no one except Louis the emperor was in a position to summon such an array of vassals as he: 'and now my proven knights, a pitched battle will never be properly fought unless the "vavassours" and the squires, strong, stout, energetic men like yourselves, carry it through

---

[1] Cf. Ed. A. Bayot, str. 668.
[2] *Aliscans*, ll. 729–30.
[3] Ibid., ll. 740–1.
[4] *Chançun*, str. cxlix.

and hold the field'—when he caught sight of a little figure on a big horse standing amongst them. 'Ki est cil petiz armez', he demanded angrily, adding the scornful remark that there must be a great shortage of men if such as he were needed. But when informed that it was his nephew, his sense of humour and his kindly nature came to the rescue and, shaking his head and weeping softly, he began to blame his wife for letting the boy go.

Guillaume's character is not a complex one. He is marked by intense personal, though perhaps unconscious egotism. Like his reputation which, as we have seen in the *Chançun de Willame*, brooks no rival, so too Guillaume himself will allow no one to compete with him for the first place. He must always be in the front rank. After the fierce battle with Corsolt in the *Couronnement*, his nephew Bertrand suggests in wily fashion that he must be a little tired and might take a rest and give some of the younger ones a chance to show their prowess. But Guillaume would have none of it and tells his nephew that it is useless to oppose his wishes:

> Que (=car) par l'apostre que requierent palmier
> Je ne lairoie por l'or de Montpelier
> Que je ne voise el maistre renc premier
> E i ferrai de l'espee d'acier (ll. 1180 f.).

Nor did Bertrand have any better luck on another occasion in the same poem. Gui d'Allemagne had challenged the emperor Louis to a single combat. The poor weak king had collapsed into tears and Guillaume, according to his wont, had come to the rescue:

> He, povres reis, li cors Deu mal te face!
> Por quei plorez? Qui vos a fait damage? (ll. 2420-1).
> ... Por vostre amor en ai fait vint et quatre:
> Cuidiez vos donc que por ceste vos faille? (ll. 2430-31).

So he proceeded to prepare for the battle, but Bertrand could stand it no longer. He leapt to his feet: 'This is too bad, uncle. You get everything (Tot vos eschiet)—all the battles and all the glory. Your prowess makes ours appear as nothing. I crave this boon, Sire; grant me this combat by your leave'. But Guillaume was adamant. 'No one else accepted the challenge', said he, 'when the king was crazed with fear, and do you think I am going back on my word? Messenger, go and tell Gui to prepare for the battle. Count William will be there to meet him!' He did, however, give his nephew Gui's horse as a sort of consolation prize after the battle.[1]

In spite of the self-assertive, rather truculent side of Guillaume's

[1] ll. 2628-9.

character, the quality that strikes the reader most is his unswerving loyalty to a contemptible sovereign who does not appreciate him, and the constancy of his affection for his own kith and kin—a combination that would have been summed up in Middle High German by the one word *triuwe*. But both his love and his loyalty are human rather than divine. The inspired piety of Charlemagne and Roland does not characterize Guillaume, nor indeed anyone in his cycle. Guillaume's religion was orthodox and not excessive. There is no point in looking to the poems of a later date, such as the *Moniage Guillaume* to give us an idea of it, for when the monks got hold of Guillaume they turned him into a saint, which was certainly not the original character in his poetic history. We have seen that the story of Guillaume and the robbers and other episodes in the above-mentioned poem were identical with those related of *Waltharius de manu fortis* in the Novalese Chronicle. To assess the epic Guillaume's attitude towards religion, it is necessary to go back to the earliest poems of the cycle. The *Chançun de Willame* fixes it once and for all. One episode sums up the faith and the humanity of the man. Guibourg's nephew, Guishart, has been badly wounded and is crying for help. Guillaume approaches him and tells him he will soon be entering paradise. Guishart, who has only rendered lip-service to Christianity, perhaps at the wish of his aunt who is a converted heathen, is not impressed by Guillaume's words. All he wants is a draught of wine or, failing that, even of muddy water, and he would be off to Cordova and never again would he believe in the Christian's God. 'Had I but prayed to Mahomet', he cries in his anguish, 'I would never have had these great wounds in my side'.[1] 'Glut, mar fusses tu nez', exclaims Guillaume, horrified at such blasphemy; 'now you are indeed a dead man. You are so weak you cannot move, but you will never be carried from this field by me'. But the next moment the kindly, large-hearted Guillaume has emerged once more; he stooped and lifted his nephew on to his horse and actually rode back to the palace with the corpse across his saddle-bow so that the body should be brought back to its own kith and kin. Love for his wife and her family had overcome his hatred for the infidel. Guillaume is the most completely human of all the heroes of the Old French epic. His simplicity is touching. In the *Couronnement*, when the worldly-minded Pope came back with a terrifying account of the giant Corsolt, Guillaume replied like a hero of the Old Testament: 'I would fight him if he were five cubits high. If God wishes to

[1] ll. 1201–2.

lower our religion I may be killed and cut to pieces. But if He helps me and sustains me there is no man on earth who can harm me'.[1] The long, efficacious prayer that the author puts into his mouth in the same poem before the battle adds little to our knowledge. It is conventional in character and boastful in its tone. It surprised and alarmed the heathen by its length. Corsolt is so struck by Guillaume's confidence in himself that he inquires his name. Guillaume replies by giving him not only his own name but that of his father, his mother, and his six brothers. Corsolt is greatly impressed and would like to win over such a valiant opponent:

> Car tes lignages est molt de halte gent,
> De tes proeces oï parler sovent (ll. 859–60).

He promises Guillaume great wealth and possessions if he will but renounce his faith and put his trust in Mahomet. Needless to say, Guillaume rejects his offer and cares not for his threats. Tired though he is, he leaps on to his charger without touching either saddle or stirrup, and the battle continues. Each gives the other frightful wounds and the heathen giant remarks ruefully: 'Molt par est fols qui petit ome blasme'.[2] Guillaume receives the blow which slices off the end of his nose,[3] and which was the cause of much of the abuse that Guillaume had to suffer later, for mutilation of this kind was often inflicted on evildoers. But it gave him his famous sobriquet of *Guillaume au cort nez* which was substituted for the original *al curb nes* of the *Chançun de Willame*. A second liturgical prayer, even longer than the first, was placed in the mouth of Guillaume; it contains a reflection on the equality of all men before God at the judgment seat:

> Al jugement ou tuit assemblerons
> La ne valdra pere al fill un boton
> Li prestre n'iert plus avant del clerçon
> Ne l'archevesques de son petit guarçon,
> Li reis del duc ne li cuens del troton,
> Nuls on traître n'i avra guarison (ll. 1007–12).

These lines are rather remarkable put, as they are, in the mouth of a proud knight of impeccable lineage, but the author knew what he was doing when he put them in that of Guillaume, whose pride of birth and arrogance were but the thin bark over a healthy tree-trunk.

In this David-Goliath fight another feature of Guillaume's character is hinted at. He would have preferred to have unseated the heathen who had remained in the saddle although severely wounded, but feared to do so lest he should wound the horse which he coveted.

---

[1] ll. 583–7.   [2] l. 923.   [3] l. 1041.

H

Guillaume's love for horses comes out in most of the poems in which he plays the chief part. In *Aliscans* he treats his Baucent like a faithful companion, sparing him whenever possible and talking to him as if to a human. And the horse replies by neighing, or wrinkling his nose, shaking his head and pawing with his feet for he has the sense of a man.[1] Guillaume never saw a good horse without casting a covetous eye (goulouser) on it. In one of the later poems of the cycle (*Guibert d'Andrenas*) he is mocked by his father Aymeri for bringing back five horses as his booty instead of their captured riders. Roland laments his sword and tries to break it to prevent its falling into enemy hands, but Guillaume's thoughts are all for his horse, and when he reluctantly exchanges the tired Baucent for a fresher horse he has taken from the enemy, he takes off its bridle, its saddle and its *poitrail* to give it a better chance of escape:

> Por çou le fait li marchis au cort nes
> K'il ne soit pris de paiens ne d'Escles (ll. 1371–2).

It has often been noted that Roland had more thought for his sword than for his betrothed, but the same accusation cannot be brought against Guillaume. His thoughts frequently turned to his wife Guibourg when the battle was going badly, and his affection for her is constant except for one brief lapse to which we shall refer in a moment. Indeed, one of the most marked characteristics of the Guillaume cycle is what we might conveniently call, 'le rôle de la femme'. There is still a relic of the matriarchal system in the Aymeri-clan, and this, perhaps, accounts for the fact that the feminine influence is more apparent here than in either of the other cycles. Hermenjart, the wife of Aymeri and mother of his seven sons, belongs to the type of the Roman matron. We do not meet her in the *Chançun de Willame*; Guillaume's mother would be superfluous in a poem in which his wife plays such a considerable part. But Guillaume speaks proudly of her in the *Couronnement* (Et Hermenjart, ma mere o le vis cler) and in the *Charroi de Nimes* (Ms D). When in the latter poem he is insulted and his beard pulled by a heathen who does not recognize him under his disguise he mutters beneath his breath: 'My garment may be torn and my shoes and hosen ill-fitting, yet the lady Hermenjart is my mother and my beard cannot be pulled with impunity'.[2] She is magnificent in *Aliscans*. When Guillaume comes to King Louis at Laon with his pitiful tale of defeat and losses at Aliscans, the feeble king is by no means pleased, for the rough audacity of the

[1] 'Ausi l'entent com s'il fust hom senez' (l. 526).
[2] ll. 1337–40, MS. D. Ed. Łange-Kowal.

count fills him with fear and apprehension. He sits 'dolans et tres-pensés' while the young knights and squires run downstairs and mock the battle-stained warrior who is waiting at the gate. This draws forth the remark from the poet:

> Ensi va d'omme ki chiet en povretés
> Ja n'ert cheris, servis ne honorés (ll. 2416-17).

a reflection which is repeated several times in the poem in slightly different words. Louis gives way more and more to his fear and actually has the entrance to the palace guarded while Guillaume sits outside under an olive tree, and when he tries to arouse their sympathy for Guibourg whom he has left weeping in Orange, the faithless Frenchmen say: 'Let him leave Orange and let the devil take it! He can have Vermandois right up to the port of Wissant'.[1] Then it is that Hermenjart raises her bell-like voice. 'Shame on you, French-men, and on you too, Aymeri, for your cowardice. I have money enough in my treasury and I will pay the mercenaries ('saudoiers') to go and fight':

> Et je meïsmes i serai cevauchant
> L'auberc vestu, lacié l'elme luisant
> L'escu au col et au costé le brant
> La lance el poing, el prumier cief devant.
> Por ce se j'ai le poil cenu et blanc
> S'ai je le cuer hardi et tot joiant
> Si aiderai, se dieu plaist, mon enfant (ll. 2717-23).

She is a worthy mother of the seven famous sons, but the less said about her daughter, the wife of King Louis, the better. Blancheflor had no wish for her brother to become too powerful and tried to dissuade her husband from granting fresh territory to Guillaume. The rage of the latter was so violent at his sister's interference that he abused her scandalously, seized her by her hair and would have killed her had not the knights intervened. His wrath was only appeased by the intercession and humble prayer of his charming niece Aelis who came into the hall where Guillaume, red with anger, was holding a naked sword, Louis was sitting with his head bowed down, and all present were as quiet as if Mass had just been begun:[2]

> A tant es vos la pucele enseignie
> Vestue fu d'un paile d'Aumarie,
> Les iex ot vairs, la face colorie,
> Dou parage est de la geste enforcie
> De la plus fiere ki onques fust en vie (ll. 2906-11).

The real point is in the last two lines—Aelis is a worthy member of

---

[1] ll. 2669-70.   [2] l. 2096.

the great family, the noblest and best which had ever lived. Aymeri
and Hermenjart added their prayers to hers, Guillaume's heart was
moved (*li cuers l'en asouplie*) and peace was restored. Water was
brought and all sat down to a meal, Aymeri beside his wife at the top
table, next to them the emperor with the queen on his left, then the
Marquis Guillaume amongst his brothers. Beside him sat his niece
Aelis who was destined to marry Rainouart, the giant with the club
(*tinel*) who in the second part of *Aliscans* delivered the warrior
Bertrand and six others from the pagan enemy.

Guillaume was susceptible to the charms of his young niece, but
his loyalty to his good wife Guibourg was not impaired. It is true
that for a brief spell in the *Couronnement de Louis*, when far from
home and somewhat elated by his recent victories, he ignored his
obligations to his distant wife and accepted the suggestion of the
'riche roi Gaifier' that he should marry his beautiful daughter. For
the moment Guillaume actually forgot Guibourg[1] and accepted the
king's offer, possibly weakened also in his moral convictions by the
Pope's promise that, if he conquered the giant Corsolt, he would be
at liberty to take as many wives as he wished with impunity. In any
case the marriage was providentially prevented by rumours of wars
from another quarter and Guillaume's reputation was saved. So it is
obvious that Guibourg's fears for the faithfulness of her renowned
husband as expressed in *Aliscans* were not entirely without foundation. When Guillaume set out for France to seek help from the
emperor after his defeat at Aliscans, it was Guibourg who persuaded
him to take this step[2] and bravely declared she would remain at
Orange and hold it against any heathen attack. But her courage gave
out just as her husband was about to set out and, full of grief at his
departure, she begged him not to forget her for he would see many
pretty girls and many noble dames in the land of plenty to which he
was going. Guillaume was greatly touched and tears ran down his
face, and he swore that he would neither change his linen, nor wash
his head, nor drink wine, nor eat fine bread, nor sleep under anything
but his saddle-cloth, nor kiss anyone on the mouth until he was safely
back with her in their palace. And he kept his word faithfully on all
these points. He refused the good fare that was pressed upon him,
and when he met his brother Ernaut and they kissed on recognizing
each other as the custom was, Guillaume slipped his shield in between
so that their mouths did not touch; again, when he found his parents
at the king's court he managed to turn away his mouth when they

[1] l. 1433.   [2] 'Mande secors en France a Saint Denis' (l. 1912).

tried to kiss him.[1] But it is in the *Chançun de Willame* that we have the most engaging portrait of this couple. Guillaume is at Barcelona and is standing with his wife at a window when they see approaching the messenger who has been sent by Vivien to ask for Guillaume's help 'es aluez de l'Archamp'. Once again Guillaume hesitates strangely, or seems to do so, and has to be encouraged by Guibourg to go to his help, so much is he moved by the tidings he hears. The next day he sets off for the field of battle, but disaster overtakes him and he loses his whole army. Meanwhile Guibourg has been busy and has collected another army which she has fed and entertained and waited on at the palace to keep them in good spirits and ready in case of need.[2] When Guillaume returns carrying his ghastly burden (the dead body of Guischart), Guibourg weeps bitterly and Guillaume tries to comfort her.[3] Then Guillaume himself breaks down and tells her that he has lost everything and that now, instead of being a rich baron's wife, she has got a coward, a clown, a cook, a baker for a husband. And the wretched pair weep together.[4] But Guibourg could not bear to see her husband's tears, and when she heard his sighs and groans she forgot some of her own trouble[5] and set herself to encouraging and supporting her husband.

The account of Guillaume's return differs somewhat in the *Chançun* and *Aliscans*, but the characters of Guillaume and Guibourg respectively remain remarkably constant. In the *Chançun* Guibourg herself descends to the gate and admits her husband who is somewhat shocked at his wife having to act as porter. In *Aliscans* she refuses absolutely to recognize her husband, even when he has let down his visor to show his nose, until he has delivered some Christians who are being led away prisoner and cruelly beaten by the Saracens within sight of the very palace at the gate of which he is standing. But it is in the former poem that Guibourg really excels herself and proves her knowledge of the male character. She goes singing upstairs and (with the full permission of her husband), deceives and cajoles the knights she has collected with promises of great rewards into going back to L'Archamp with Guillaume to collect the booty and avenge the dead. She then prepared a Rabelaisian meal for him—a shoulder of boar, a large 'brawn' of pig, a large roasted peacock with plenty of bread and wine—every bit of which he ate without raising his head from the dish,[6] whereupon she shook her head and, smiling in the midst of her grief, remarked 'the man who eats such a meal without

---

[1] ll. 2218 and 2663.   [2] str. cxx.   [3] Plurat Guiburg, confortat la Guillelmes (l. 1304).
[4] l. 1317.   [5] 'Partie ubliet de la sue dolur' (l. 1319).
[6] 'Ne redreçat la chiere ne le vis' (l. 1420).

stopping will never flee in cowardly wise or let down his kith and kin':

> Ja trop vilment ne deit de champ fuir
> Ne sis lignages pur lui estre plus vils (ll. 1433-4).

It is no wonder that Guillaume slept soundly and, on awakening, leapt from his bed like a giant refreshed. So Guibourg in true feminine fashion has gained her end and Guillaume returned to the battlefield.

Guibourg's solicitude for the honour of the famous lineage has become almost more excessive than her husband's for, when the latter was hesitant, she summed up the family tradition in no uncertain words:

> Ço fut custume a tun grand parenté,
> Quant altres terres alerent conquester,
> Tuztens morurent en bataille champel.
> Mielz vueil que muerges en l'Archamp desur mer
> Que tes lignages seit par tei avilez
> N'apres ta mort a tes heirs reprové (ll. 1321-9).

The last that we hear of Guibourg in the *Chançun de Willame* (as distinct from the *Chanson de Rainouart* which follows it in the manuscript) is in entire accordance with the sentiment expressed here. As Guillaume rode off with his newly assembled army, aunt and nephew (Guibourg and the little Gui) watched him depart, and as long as he was in sight commended him to God.[1] But no sooner was he out of sight than Guiot burst into tears because he was not thought old enough to accompany the army and Guillaume had no relative with him ('Ot lui n'en meinet nul sun ami charnel / Fors Deu de gloire ki le mont at salvé'). Guibourg refuses to let him go for fear of incurring her husband's displeasure, but Guiot curtly replies: 'But I can lie, and I will tell him I escaped by force'. He has taken a leaf out of his aunt's book and it is not surprising that when he declares he will bring Guillaume back safe and sound she replies immediately, 'Dunc te lairrai aler'.[2] She lends him her own saddle-horse (*sanbuier*) which she had never lent to a knight before, and Gui rides off quite happily to join the 'escuiers' and lesser knights.

The prominence of the relationship between uncle and nephew in the Old French epic has often been noted and traced back to the early Germanic custom described by Tacitus of considering this relationship as honourable as that between father and son. Indeed, it would seem in the epic tradition to have been more so, for the 'motif'

[1] l. 1513. [2] l. 1542.

of a combat between father and son which occurs in the literature of a number of lands never seems to have been transferred to uncle and nephew. Guillaume's relation to his nephews is most striking. His affection for Vivien knows no bounds and is heartily reciprocated. No doubt there was an element of pride in this mutuality of admiration, for Vivien declares in the opening lines of the *Chançun* that there is no living man who is more courageous in carrying on a pitched battle than himself 'Fors sul Guillelme al curb nies le marchis'.[1] His admiration for his uncle is based first and foremost on his military skill—'Sages hom est en bataille champel'; but he never forgets that it is at Guillaume's palace that he has received 'la grant nurreture'. In the message he sends by his cousin Girart to the uncle whom he knows he can trust ('Guillelm le fedeil')[2] he pathetically reminds him of the battles he has helped him to win. His claims are as fantastic as those of the dying Roland, but they refer to persons he has killed rather than to lands he had conquered. He had slain the heathen Alderufe, beheaded all the twelve sons of the heathen King Borel, fought beside Guillaume under the walls of Orange and actually killed with his own hands 'Dan Tiedbalt l'esturman'. If this claim were true it was no wonder that Guillaume loved him as he had been instrumental in procuring him a wife. But neither the death of Tiedbalt nor that of the sons of Borel is well authenticated, as they are both revived again in *Aliscans*. Such discrepancies were bound to happen but they do not affect the psychology. Vivien is the most appealing of Guillaume's nephews. His men worship him and refuse to leave him even when he absolves them from any obligation to follow him to certain death because he is not their legal 'sire'. His conscience is so sensitive that he is filled with remorse when he believes he has broken the vow made in his youth not to flee a foot's length before the enemy; and, having in a moment of anguish prayed God to save him from death, he recants with touching simplicity:

> Respit de mort, sire, net tei rover
> Car tei meïsme nel volsis pardoner (ll. 825-6).

The only thing he will pray for is that God should send either King Louis or, better still, 'Willame al curb nes' to help him win the battle, and even in this extremity his pride of birth breaks through:

> For sui io mult et hardi sui assez
> De vasselage puis bien estre sun per
> Mais de plus loinz ad sun pris aquité (il. 832-5).

[1] l. 87.　　[2] l. 656.

It is again the great reputation of Guillaume which is insisted on.—
a fame which Vivien cannot emulate as it was won in other lands.
There is little religion in the *Chançun de Willame* and no hint of
pilgrimage routes. Vivien's end is not described in the symbolic
manner of the death of Roland. Like Charlemagne's nephew, he
feels his death approaching ('la sue mort le va mult destreignant')[1] as
he wanders, mortally wounded, about the battlefield. He is so
consumed with thirst that he drinks some brackish water mixed with
blood and brains, but he cannot keep it down. No angel Cherubin
comes to comfort him, and he has no pact with God like Roland.
He dies miserably of his wounds and the pagans hide his body so
that even his corpse may not be found and buried with Christian
rites.

The account of Vivien's end in *Aliscans* differs somewhat, as we
have said, from that described in the *Chançun*. The relationship
between uncle and nephews is just as close and their respective
characters appears in the same light, but the realism of the *Chançun*
has been transmuted into sentimentalism. Vivien has received fifteen
wounds, of the least of which an emir would have died.[2] But he is
found just breathing by Guillaume who, finding it impossible to get
back to Orange, has returned to L'Archamp. He comes across his
nephew lying at the point of death. His breath smells sweeter than
balsam or incense, and his white hands are crossed on his breast.
Guillaume, thinking him to be dead, pronounces three funeral
laments over him, in which he praises his courage, his humility, and
his sweetness of disposition:

> Nies, ainc lions ne fu si cumbatans;
> Vos n'estiez mie estos ne mal querans
> Ne sus vos pers orgueillos ne prisans
> Nonques ne fustes de proece vantans
> Ancois esties dous et humelians
> Et sor paiens hardis et conqerans (ll. 732–7).

Many of the expressions in these laments are familiar to us from the
Chanson de Roland, but the scene that follows is peculiar to *Aliscans*.
As the uncle holds the nephew in his embrace he feels a flutter of life
beneath his hands: 'La vie sent qui el cors li sautele'—and he asks him
tenderly whether he is still alive. 'Yes, uncle', replied the youth, 'but
I am nearly finished for my heart is broken'. Then Guillaume
inquired whether he had received the sacrament on the Sunday
before, and when Vivien replied that he had missed it through arriving

---

[1] Cf. Roland, l. 2232.   [2] 'De la menor morust uns amirans' (l. 727).

too late, but that he is sure God will be merciful to him, Guillaume drew out a piece of bread which he had had in his wallet for a fortnight and bade his nephew eat of it 'en l'enor Deu et sainte trinite', and constituted himself his confessor. 'Sire', said the youth, 'I have a great longing ('molt ai grant faim') for you to put my head in your bosom and give me this bread and then I shall die straightway. But hasten, uncle, for I have not long to live'. Guillaume wept bitterly as he placed Vivien's head on his lap and heard the confession of the sin that was weighing on his conscience, namely, that he had broken a vow made on the day he received his knighthood. He had been forced to turn his back on the enemy and had fled for a short distance which he had not been able to estimate.[1] Guillaume absolved him and he spoke no more except to ask his uncle to salute Guibourg on his behalf (*Mais que Guiborc li rova saluer*). That is all in effect that we know of him (a pure creature of fiction we may suppose) as the poems which were dedicated to him later, such as the *Covenant Vivien*, *Les Enfances Vivien*, etc., merely weave a story round these original data. Vivien does not gain thereby, for the composite picture we have of him in the two earliest poems emerges in its original beauty.

Little more need be said about Guillaume's precocious young nephew Gui whom we meet only in the *Chançun de Willame*. He is the first of a line of youthful prodigies in French literature who harbour great minds and great thoughts in small bodies.[2] He escaped daringly to join Guillaume's army, lied nobly to save his aunt from Guillaume's displeasure, fought valiantly (after a good meal) when Guillaume, dismounted and surrounded, called anxiously for his aid, and acted prudently at the end when he performed an unknightly act to avoid any future evil consequences for his lineage and his country. His indignant answer to any suggestion which he deems unworthy of himself, as, for example, that he might watch the battle from a hill, is simply 'I never heard of such a thing' ('unc mais nen oï tel'), a reply which is repeated on several occasions. So, too, is Guillaume's expression of admiration at any wise remark which issues from his nephew's mouth, 'Cors as d'enfant e raisun as de ber', and it is, perhaps, a sign of his true humility and lack of confidence in himself that he accepts the youthful Gui as his comrade-in-arms who should be at his right hand to support him in the battle:

> Al mien ensemble porte tun gunfanon:
> Si jo ai tei, ne crien malvais engruign (ll. 1673-6).

So far we have barely alluded to another nephew of Guillaume

[1] 'Ne sai com lonc, car ne le puis esmer' (l. 1855).   [2] See supra, Ch. i.

who, though he is not portrayed in such alluring colours as Vivien
and Gui, is designated in nearly all the early sources as Guillaume's
constant companion. Bertrand is one of the warriors mentioned by
name in the *Fragment de la Haye*, once actually with the title of
Palatinus (Bertrand le Palazin). His name is found in an 'acte de
donation' which probably was invented at about the same date as
the *Vita Guillelmis* and which mentions him amongst Guillaume's
relatives: *et nepote meo Bertranno*. But it is from the *chansons-de-geste*
themselves that his function as Guillaume's constant companion and
right-hand man comes to light. In *Aliscans* Guillaume refers to him
as 'de mon lignage la flor'.[1] In the *Couronnement* he rushes to help his
uncle on every possible occasion. He warns him of danger and of
traitors, he accompanies him in exile, he gives him good advice
(namely, not to bother about an ungrateful king any more);[2] he
mounts Guillaume on his own horse and tries to spare him, though
perhaps with a slightly ulterior motive at times. He does not always
approve his uncle's conduct—he cannot understand his hesitation on
certain occasions; in the *Charroi de Nimes* he blames him for quarrelling with the king whom he ought to serve,[3] and he chides him
when he gives way rather weakly to his nostalgia.[4] Guillaume treats
him somewhat cavalierly and mocks him unmercifully at times, but
Bertrand never fails in his loyalty to his uncle, and wherever Guillaume is to be found the proximity of his nephew Bertrand may
almost be taken for granted. Guillaume is greatly distressed when
Bertrand is captured by the Saracens, and he believes him to be dead
—'mors est Bertrans, dont ai an cuer dolor',[5] and, though he is less
spectacular than Vivien or Gui, the portrait of Guillaume would be
quite incomplete without that of his faithful squire and mentor.

Taken all round and pieced together from the various *chansons-de-
geste*, the character of Guillaume d'Orange is indeed extraordinarily
consistent and complete. Judging from the number of poems devoted
to him and his family, he was a popular figure in France, for the
'jongleurs' always had an eye for the main chance when composing
their poems. The old chronicler, Alberic de Trois Fontaines (thirteenth
century), when speaking of another poem (Macaire), tells us of fables
akin to it, for the most part false, which, whether intended to move
people to laughter or tears, were composed for the sake of gain:
'et cetera iste fabule annexa, ex magna parte falsissima quae omnia . . .
lucri gratia ita composita'. How could it be otherwise, for the 'jongleur' had to live and many are the allusions in Old French poetry to

[1] l. 431.   [2] l. 2669.   [3] l. 421.   [4] l. 794.   [5] *Aliscans*, l. 341.

the bad reception of a poor poet who returned home with an empty sack. The surprising fact about the Guillaume poems is that, though so popular in France, they seem to have enjoyed but little favour abroad. There is a dearth of literature devoted to this hero with the vast reputation both in England (though the earliest epic celebrating him must have been composed in this country) and in Germany (where, however, at least one notable poem based on a French original celebrated him). In Italy the heroes of this cycle (the *Nerbonesi*) were known and sung, but nothing like to the extent as those of the royal cycle and certain popular unruly barons. Dante, however, helps to redress the balance by placing both Guillaume and Rainouart in the *Croce di Marte* along with Carlo Magno and Orlandi and other 'gloriosi propugnatore della vera fede' such as Josue and the 'alto Maccabeo'.[1]

[1] Cf. *Paradiso*, Canto xviii.

CHAPTER VII

RAOUL DE CAMBRAI AND SOME OTHER REBELLIOUS BARONS

THE poem *Raoul de Cambrai* has been analysed from various points of view—historical, geographical and cultural. The following pages will be confined entirely to a psychological study of the hero and his immediate family. The poem which has come down to us is, in all probability, not the original version of the legend, and to whose credit should be placed this gem of character delineation must for ever remain a mystery. Whether the author of the original poem was named Bertolai or not matters little as in any case nothing is known of Bertolai except what the author himself tells us in the poem.[1] Whether the character of Raoul was conceived in his brain or was based on a traditional estimate is another insoluble problem, as the only reliable historical reference to Raoul is as brief as that concerning Roland in Eginhard's Chronicle. Relating the events of the year 943, Flodoard writes: 'Heribertus comes obiit, quem sepelierunt apud Sanctum Quintinum filii sui; et audientes Rodulfum, filium Rodulfi de Gaugiaco, quasi ad invadendam terram patris eorum advenisse, agressi eundem interemerunt'.[2] Other attempts at identification of the protagonists in the poem may be left on one side as they add little or nothing to the working out of the plot or the dramatic intensity of the characters. A monastic legend incorporated into an eleventh-century chronicle (*Chronicon Valciodorense*) has obviously used epic traditions relating to Raoul and the other figures in the story, so that we are thrown back on the invention of the poet for what forms the intrinsic value of his work, namely, his skill in portraying character. We can therefore start with an unbiased mind and examine the development and ultimate fate of a young man who, like Hamlet, is cursed with one moral blemish, a root of evil in himself which, watered and fertilized by his environment, brings about his tragic downfall. The skill of the creator, for it is not a question of teamwork here as in the case of Guillaume d'Orange, is seen in the way the action of the tragedy works up to its climax and in the fact that the effect produced on the hearer (or reader) is one of

---

[1] ll. 2442–9.   [2] *Annales Flodoardi*, anno 943.

pity and fear. The moral to be learnt (*Finis tyrannorum semper confusio est*) is a teaching for all time, but the personality in whom it is worked out was a product of his times, when brute force was the order of the day and the softening influences of chivalry had not yet begun to make themselves felt. The manners and customs point to a relatively early date for the poem and the importance attached to the curse of bastardy recalls inevitably the resentment felt by William the Conqueror at the reproach which was attached to his name. The sin of *desmesure* of which Raoul is guilty is not merely the 'stultam superbiam' of which Walter Map accuses him. It is something more subtle. It is excess, lack of moderation, the inability to 'modum servare' praised by Virgil and Lucan. Raoul is a 'desmesuré', an 'hom desreez', a man who cannot walk in step with others, a man with an ill-conditioned mind, almost an 'aliéné', and as such is bound to come to a bad end. Roland had his share of *desmesure* for which Oliver blames him, but Raoul is the embodiment of this dangerous quality which, in those lawless times, was recognized as a menace to society; it has its equivalent in meaning in the Middle High German: *unmâze*.

The portrait of Raoul comes out quite naturally in the course of narrative. He is introduced to us as an infant—his mother's darling—loved and cherished 'amez et gois' (spoilt) by everyone.[1] He grows up a beautiful boy, and at the age of fifteen he is a pattern of good breeding and beloved by all, both his men and his peers.

Unfortunately by this time an evil influence has begun to overshadow his life in the form of a grim, fanatical uncle, an almost Mephistophelian figure who, in his determination to help his widowed sister, instilled into the boy's mind that it was his paramount duty to redeem his father's title and estate with which a weak king had invested someone else. 'Guerri the Red'[2] had already remonstrated with the king and been dismissed with the curt reply: 'The gift is made: I cannot go back on it'.[3] From that moment Guerri never ceased to agitate and keep green in the mind of his nephew and his sister the injury they had suffered. Raoul's mother was by no means loth to listen to his words. She had a strong, proud, imperious character. She told her brother she would rather be burnt alive than accept as husband the man chosen for her by the king, for it would be like a deerhound mating with a common watch-dog. It is true she tried to make Raoul see reason when he was setting out on his mad career, but her fierce love for him and her terrible hatred for his unwilling murderer never diminished. Her proud spirit could not

[1] l. 92.   [2] *Guerri li sors.*   [3] l. 308.

brook the humiliation of knowing that Raoul had been killed by a bastard:

> Diex, dist la dame, cum est mes cuers maris!
> Se l'eüst mort un quens poesteïs,
> De mon duel fust l'une moitiés jus mis (ll. 3596-9).

If character is inherited from the mother as the ancients believed, it is small wonder that Raoul's outwardly attractive nature had the germ of rottenness within.

The years passed and it was time for Raoul to present himself before the king and be accorded the privilege of knighthood. King Louis loved his nephew and singled him out for special honour. He received the helmet which Roland had conquered from a Saracen; a sword forged by Galant[1] which was second only to Durendal, and a steed caparisoned with a carved golden saddle and an embroidered saddle-cloth. Raoul leapt on the horse and showed such skill of horsemanship that the Frenchmen acclaimed him—but the author gives the first ominous hint of the dangerous element in his make-up:

> Bia fo Raoul et de gente faiture,
> S'en lui n'eüst un poi de desmesure
> Mieudres vasal ne tint onques droiture.
> Mais de ce fu molt pesans l'aventure;
> Hom desreez a molt grant paine dure (ll. 494-9).

It was at some stage previous to this in his career that the son of a neighbouring count had conceived one of those boyish admirations for Raoul so familiar to us in fact and fiction. Bernier was the son born out of wedlock to Ybert de Ribemont, who plays an important rôle in the later part of the poem. His infatuation for the handsome Raoul was so great that he left his home and people—against his father's wishes, as we learn later,[2] and attached himself to Raoul's household (*maisniee*, Early English *meinie*). Raoul returned his affection and made him his squire in spite of the fact that his name was tainted with the reproach of bastardy which (as the author well knew) would be of no consequence in a boyish friendship. The two youths grew up together, and it would appear from the poem that Raoul had Bernier knighted and received his fealty ('vostre hom sui liges') at about the same time that he himself had taken his oath to Louis. Raoul was retained at court by the emperor who loved him dearly and even made him his seneschal, and he was thought so well of that many a baron sent his son or nephew to join his household and Raoul loved them and treated them handsomely. The only one to

---

[1] The French equivalent of the Germanic 'Weland the smith'   [2] str. xc.

regret Raoul's increasing popularity was the knight whom the king
had so unjustly invested with his father's fief and whom Raoul hated
from his heart at the advice of his powerful uncle, the 'red Guerri'.[1]

It was just about this time that a most unfortunate incident
occurred. Raoul used to teach the boys who were entrusted to him
the art of fencing, at which he himself was an adept.[2] One Easter as
he came out of church he found the young knights fencing and amusing
themselves. But a moment came when the game took a serious turn
and the jest became earnest. Tempers were frayed, and somehow in
the confusion the two sons of Ernaut de Douai were killed. No one
knew exactly how it happened, but all the barons of the country put
the blame on Raoul and Count Ernaut never forgave him.

Time passed, but ill-will had now begun to smoulder all round.
Raoul, goaded on by his uncle, demanded the restitution of his
rightful possessions and vowed vengeance on the usurper when the
king replied that he could not go back on his word. Finally, however,
harassed on all sides, Louis promised him the next fief which should
fall free at the death of any count in his domain, regardless of the
rightful heirs. Raoul accepted the rash offer and hostages were
exchanged, but the author warns us of what the result of this unjust
action would be:

> Raoux ot droit, tres bien le vos dison:
> Mais l'emperere ot trop le quer felon
> Qi de tel terre fist a son neveu don,
> Dont maint baron widierent puis arçon (ll. 777-80).

Everything was against Raoul, as so often happens when once things
have begun to go wrong. The next fief to fall vacant was the land
of the powerful count Herbert, a man of many friends[3] and the father
of four noble sons. Against everyone's advice and the entreaties of
Bernier, Raoul refused to abandon the gift for any amount of
satisfaction:

> Voir, dist Raoux, ja ne le penserai:
> Li dons m'est fais, por rien nel guerpirai (ll. 942-3).

The investiture was performed: Raoul left Paris and the author adds
that there was no sign of grief at his departure.[4]

The next scene takes place at Cambrai where the lady Aalis was
awaiting her son's return. When she heard with what fief her son
had been invested she received the news with horror. She besought
him not to accept a gift which would bring him into conflict

---

[1] l. 535.   [2] l. 2855.
[3] 'Tant buer fu nez qi a plenté d'amis!' (l. 814).   [4] l. 952.

with the four powerful sons of a man who had always been his
father's friend; who were good knights and much beloved, whereas
he himself could not count on his own supporters.[1] Again and again
she returned to the charge, but it is obvious that it was not so much
the moral injustice to the sons of Herbert which moved her as the
certainty that in the end Raoul was likely to be worsted and would
probably lose his life. She had a clear presentiment ('devinaille') that
Raoul would be slain and his heart torn from his body, and that
Bernier would be the instrument of his death.[2] 'Leave their land',
she pleaded again; 'they will be grateful to you and will help you to
carry on your other war and chase the usurper from your land'. But
Raoul was every whit as determined as his mother and, at last,
infuriated by her reiterated attacks, he exclaimed: 'Shame on the
noble knight who takes counsel of a lady before he goes into battle.
Go to your chamber, madam, take your ease and drink nourishing
potions. A woman's job is to think about food and drink and not
meddle with other matters'.[3] Aalis wept bitterly as she reminded
Raoul of all the sacrifices she had made for him, and at the pitch of
her indignation she uttered the fatal words:

> Et qant por moi ne le viex or laisier
> Cil dame diex qi tout a a jugier
> Ne te ramaint sain ne sauf ne entier ! (ll. 1131–3).

She regretted her words the moment they were spoken and hastened
to church to confess her sin and pray God to bring him back 'safe and
sound and whole', but the curse had gone forth ('a grant tort l'ai
maudit') and it must have seemed like the sealing of his fate when
the first person she met on coming out of church was 'Guerri le sor'.
Once more she tried to bring Raoul to his senses and she is piteous
in her appeal: 'If only you would listen to me, my son, this war
would never be started; though I am old and my hair is white, I have
not yet lost my wits'. But the hardening process which had been
going on in Raoul was only increased by his mother's remonstrances,
and he called to his uncle to set his troops in motion: 'Do not listen
to my mother; she is old and past her prime; my people are waiting
—they are experienced soldiers and will never be beaten in battle'.
And so the wretched war began, and the foragers and burners were
sent out to seize the prey and to burn the farmsteads. But Bernier
held back and was in no hurry to put on his arms.[4]

We have come now to the terrible stage in the life of a man whom

---

[1] Particularly the 'barons d'Arouaise' for whom Aalis shows particular contempt.
[2] 'Ce est li hom dont avras destorbier' (l. 1089.)   [3] ll. 1100–106.   [4] l. 1228.

'nature' and 'nourriture' had combined to spoil, when his lack of control over himself became evident to all. His own knights were afraid to carry out his blasphemous commands when he bade them pitch his tent in the middle of the church, tie up the beasts of burden in the porch, prepare his food in the crypts, chain his hawks to the golden crucifix, and prepare a bed for him in front of the altar so that he might lean against the crucifix. He declared his intention of destroying the place (Origny) and giving the nuns to the squires, because he knew the sons of Herbert loved it.[1] When he found that he had been disobeyed and the tents pitched in the meadows he was furious and demanded to know the reason. Then even his uncle Guerri, his evil genius, reproved him: 'Voir', dist Guerri, 'trop ies desmesurez', and told him that if God was displeased with him, he would soon come to a bad end.[2] So Raoul gave way and the carpets were spread on the green grass.

But the respite was only momentary, for the next morning he gave the order for Origny to be attacked. The inhabitants began to throw up barriers, but the nuns of the convent poured forth, each with her psalter in her hand, with Marsent, Bernier's mother, at their head, to plead with Raoul, and very pitifully they pleaded:

> Sire Raoul, valroit i rien proiere
> Qe .j. petit vos traisisiés ariere?
> Nos somes nonnes, par les sainz de Baviere;
> Ja ne tenrons ne lance, ne baniere,
> Ne ja par nos n'en iert .j. mis en biere (ll. 1323–8).

Raoul answered insultingly, but Marsent again begged him humbly to spare them, promising to perform the most menial duties for his army. Then Raoul did one of those sudden drops into kindliness and humility which were characteristic of him and promised out of respect for her to grant her request and leave them in peace. Bernier went to see his mother and explained to her his dilemma; how that he was Raoul's liege-man and had received so much from him that he could not fail him until such time as all would commend his action.[3] Marsent answered nobly: 'You are quite right, my son. Serve your lord and God will support you'.

Then followed another of those unfortunate incidents which dogged Raoul's career. In spite of the truce, three of his men went out on a marauding expedition, and as they returned heavily laden with spoils they were pursued and attacked by ten men from Origni and two of them were killed. The third escaped and came and told

---

[1] 'Por ce le fas li fil H. l'ont chier' (l. 1243).   [2] l. 1276.   [3] l. 1385.

I

a lying story to Raoul of the savage attitude of the inhabitants. Raoul
was beside himself with anger ('le sens cuida changier') and ordered
an immediate attack on the town and the fortress. He swore by God
and His strength that if all the inhabitants were not 'afolé et pendu',
he would not think he was worth a straw.[1] 'Baron, touchiez le feu!'
he cried in his mad fury—and they did so, for they all hoped to gain
something out of the confusion that would follow. The houses
caught fire, the ceilings fell in, and it was pitiful to see the children
burnt. The nuns fled to the church but it did not help them, for the
fire spread rapidly. The cellars flowed with wine, the flitches burned,
the larders collapsed, and the fat made the fire burn all the fiercer.
The flames rose to the highest clock-tower and it was a blazing
furnace inside the church. All the nuns perished in the flames and
the burning flesh could be smelt amidst the ashes. Even the stoutest
knights wept for pity, and when Bernier saw to what a pitch things
had come he nearly went out of his mind with grief and anger. The
fire was too hot to approach within a lance-throw, but he found his
mother lying dead beside a slab of marble with her psalter still
burning on her chest. This was the decisive moment for which he
had waited:

> E! R. fel, dex te doinst encombrier!
> Le tien homage avant porter ne quier.
> Se or ne puis ceste honte vengier,
> Je ne me pris le montant d'un denier (ll. 1513-16).

And what was Raoul doing while these dreadful things were
happening? He was the real author of the trouble ('fait ot le destorbier'), but there was no sign of repentance for the broken truce or
the burning and grilling ('ardoir et graaillier') of the nuns. He returned
to his tent after the slaughter looking handsomer than ever and the
barons unrobed him. He called his seneschal, and demanded food—
roasted peacock and devilled swan, and venison in abundance so that
even the lowest should have his fill. 'Nominedame!' exclaimed the
seneschal, 'what can you be thinking of? ... It is Lent when we all
ought to fast. To-day is Holy Friday when sinners adore the cross,
and we miserable men have burnt the nuns and desecrated the church.
God will never forgive us unless His pity overcomes our cruelty'.
Raoul listened and declared that his squires had been affronted, but he
admitted that he had forgotten all about Lent and asked for the
chessmen. These were not denied him and he sat down ill-humour-
edly in the meadow. But just as he was on the point of checkmating

[1] l. 1452.

his adversary he leapt to his feet, threw off his cloak for the heat, and called for wine.

The next phase in this 'rake's progress' was a grievous one, for he lost his best friend. Amongst the young men who hastened to bring him wine was Bernier the son of Ybert, who had just seen his mother burnt to death. As he handed the goblet on bended knee Raoul remained for quite a space of time so engrossed in his gloomy thoughts that he did not look up, and Bernier was so exasperated that he swore he would spill it on the ground if Raoul did not take it. A momentary regret for his incivility caused him to apologize, but in the next breath he began to denounce the sons of Herbert and swear that he would drive them out of the land. This brought Bernier to his feet and he put forward his case.[1] His first admission is striking in its fairness and veracity. 'Raoul, my lord, you often act so nobly and yet at times you are most blameworthy'. He then proceeded to defend his father and his uncles (the sons of Herbert) and to accuse Raoul bitterly of being the cause of his mother's death. She was dead now and there was no remedy for that, but it was no wonder that he was angry and wished to help his uncles and avenge his shame. Raoul replied with abuse and even accused Bernier of being in his camp to betray him by learning his secrets from his barons, and actually of having designs on his life.[2] Bernier replied with dignity to the foul accusations against himself, his father and his mother (whose character he defends), and to Raoul's constant taunts about his bastardy he is driven at last to say that he would engage any well-armed knight in a 'trial by combat' to prove that no man is a bastard unless he has denied God,[3] and that even Raoul himself, outrageous though he was, would not take up arms against him on that score. Upon this Raoul, who had been listening with his head bowed in his hands, was so incensed that he picked up a large fragment of a spear which the hunters had left lying on the ground and struck Bernier with such force that he broke open his head and sent the blood streaming down his fine ermine cloak. Bernier seized Raoul in his anger and would have killed him, but the knights ran up and separated them. Then Bernier bade his squire fetch his arms, his hauberk, his sword and his helmet, for he would not remain a moment longer.[4] Thus the two friends parted and became the bitterest of enemies in spite of the fact that Raoul, with one of the sudden changes of mood

---

[1] 'Hui mais orez la desfense Bernier . . .' (l. 1637).
[2] ll. 1568-9.   [3] l. 1709.
[4] 'De ceste cort partirai, san congié' (l. 1727).

which characterized him, was horrified at what he had done and turned to his barons in dismay to ask for their advice as to how he might appease Bernier. One and all they blamed Raoul and justified Bernier's action. They counselled an offer of apology if Bernier could be induced to accept it. In all humility Raoul was guided by their decision and offered to make a public apology. But he had gone too far and Bernier replied bitterly: 'Who could be satisfied with such a reconciliation? You burned my mother who loved me so dearly and then you broke my head. I swear by God I will never be reconciled to you until this red blood, which you have caused to flow down, goes back to my head of its own accord. Only then will my lust for vengeance be satisfied'.[1] At this the unpredictable Raoul humbled himself still further. He knelt before Bernier, clothed only in his tunic and, in memory of their old friendship, he answered him in fair words[2]: 'Alack, Bernier, you spurn my apology; then I offer you generous amends, not because I fear a conflict but because I wish to be your friend'. With this in view ('Por ce le fas' twice over), he offered to walk a distance of fourteen leagues accompanied by a hundred knights each carrying his own saddle, and he himself would carry Bernier's saddle on his head. He would go on foot leading his war horse and would proclaim to every common soldier or waiting-maid that he passed: 'This is Bernier's saddle'.[3] It was a handsome offer from such a proud man, and his knights exclaimed at it saying, 'Qi ce refuse vos amis ne vieut estre'. And Raoul went even further in his access of humility for he actually made a personal appeal to his old friend:

> Berneçon, frere, molt ies de grant vaillance;
> Pren ceste accorde, si lai la malvoillance (ll. 1781-4).

But Bernier was too deeply wounded and refused the offer of amends unconditionally until such time as his blood should flow upwards towards his head.

War was now inevitable between the two great families. Bernier passed over to the other camp accompanied by a few faithful followers and the four sons of Herbert gathered their forces together and pitched their camp beneath the walls of St. Quentin.[4] Even at the eleventh hour a counsel of prudence decided the sons of Herbert to send a messenger to see whether a reconciliation with Raoul were possible 'for he is the king's nephew' argued one of the brothers, 'and if he were to be killed we should bring disaster on ourselves. Let us

---

[1] ll. 1746-52. [2] 'Par grant amor li a dit raison bele' (l. 1758).
[3] l. 1777. [4] l. 2080.

send a messenger and ask him to withdraw a little from our lands.
Let us act prudently for "Hons sans mesure ne vaut un alier".' So two
successive messengers (the second of whom was Bernier at his own
request) were sent. Raoul, in spite of Guerri's advice, or in his
contrariety perhaps because of it, refused any attempt at a 'rapproche-
ment' and dismissed the first messenger summarily, telling him to go
quickly lest he should spy on his way of life.[1] When the second
messenger, Bernier, however, made on behalf of his uncles a generous
offer to accept Raoul's 'amendise' and pardon all that had gone before,
Raoul with another sudden drop into humility replied: 'Friend, this
is an act of true friendship. By Him who suffered on the cross, your
proposal shall be considered in good faith'. Once again he consulted
his uncle, even beseeching him to agree:

> Fai le, biaus oncles, por amor Dieu te prie.
> Acordon nos, si soions bon ami.

But the fates were against him, for Guerri, annoyed by the fact that
his advice had not been taken the first time and that Raoul had
accused him of cowardice, turned the tables on his nephew, telling
him that he dared not go into battle and had better flee to Cambrai
whilst the war was carried on without him. Bernier perceived that
this constituted a final answer. He gave a formal challenge by the
old feudal custom of plucking three hairs from his ermine cloak
through the meshes of his hauberk and throwing them at Raoul with
the words, 'Vassal, je vos desfi!'

War was now declared and was pursued on either side with the
utmost ferocity, which made the cowards tremble, the valiant men
rejoice, and the men of goodwill weep for pity. Many a valiant knight
had to be content with three blades of grass for the last sacrament as
he committed his soul to God, for there was no other priest in the
battlefield. Bertolai, who was present in the thickest of the fight,[2]
made a song about it. The noise was so great that you could not have
heard God thundering.[3] There were the customary single combats
described in the conventional way. Guerri fought ferociously ('cui il
ataint, n'a de mire mestier') and overthrew more than fourteen
knights, but his own two sons were slain, to his intense grief. So
shaken in his morale was he that he besought Raoul not to leave
him alone in the battle and he would pledge his faith to support his
nephew against ten men attacking him and remount him if he was

---

[1] 'Mon convine esgarder' (l. 2159).
[2] 'De la bataille vi tot le greignor fais' (l. 2447).
[3] l. 2480.

unhorsed. Raoul entered willingly into the agreement but, as he fought his way through the mass of enemies, he broke his covenant with his uncle and left him in the lurch. For this foolish, irresponsible ('legier') action he paid afterwards with his life. The battle proceeded with great slaughter on either side. It had rained and soon the ground was thick with slush and blood so that the horses grew weary and even the swiftest were slowed down and stumbled. Then Ernaut found himself face to face with the lord of Cambrai. The incident of his nephews' death still rankled in his mind, and as soon as he was within earshot he hurled the reproach at Raoul of having killed them. Raoul replied that he would kill more of them and Ernaut himself if he got the chance. A bitter single combat ensued in which each knight delivered frightful blows, after one of which Raoul, who was almost stunned and rather sobered, stated that he had no wish to exculpate himself, but he himself had not killed the two boys. In the next round it was Ernaut who was worsted, for he received a blow which shattered his helmet, travelled down his left side and severed his left hand from his arm—a disastrous blow for he could no longer hold his shield. There was nothing left for Ernaut to do but to turn and flee and only a fool would blame him.[1]

It is difficult to do justice to the next scene of the grim tragedy to which everything has been working up and gathering momentum. In his headlong flight Ernaut lost all sense of pride and turned again and again to beg for mercy, offering to give up everything and become Raoul's 'man' if he would but spare his life. But his prayers only brought forth fresh bursts of anger from Raoul who had now lost all sense of decency. Various knights whom Ernaut spied in the distance as he fled before his pursuer were called upon to help him in his distress, but each in turn fell a victim to Raoul's mad fury, including even the gigantic Jean de Ponthieu whom he had always feared and even now would not have dared to attack had he not called to mind his father Taillefer, who had been such a valiant warrior. Coarse jokes escape him as, when having deprived one knight of his leg, he shouts: 'Now Ernaut has lost an arm and you a leg; one of you can be my watchman and the other my doorkeeper'. Such taunts were not unusual but they add to the brutality of the scene. At last Ernaut was at his last gasp and he called upon the Saviour of Souls: 'Holy Mary, queen of heaven, my death cannot be averted now for there is none of the milk of human kindness[2] in this

[1] l. 2871.
[2] Lit. no dew—*point de rousee*.

devil'. And as Raoul shouted after him that his doom was sealed he saw that there was indeed no ray of hope:

> N'en puis mais, sire, tex est ma destinee,
> N'i vaut defense une poume paree.

But, though Ernaut did not know it, the climax was approaching and relief was at hand. Raoul, flushed with success, declared: 'You speak truth for your end has come. This sword is about to sever your head from your body':

> Terre ne erbe ne te puet atenir,
> Ne Diex me hom ne t'en puet garantir
> Ne tout li saint qi Dieu doivent servir (ll. 3017–20).

At last Raoul's self-confidence had over-reached itself. There had been a spark of the fear of God in him before; though it was barely visible it had flickered up on occasions as we have seen. But now it had gone out, a subtle change had taken place in him. He had denied God's power and these words were his undoing. Ernaut breathed a sigh of relief and immediately plucked up heart. 'By God, Raoul, now you are indeed a renegade and a proud, wicked, and presumptuous man. Now I care no more for you than for a mad dog, for nature could have helped me had God so willed it'. He turned again in flight, but this time he drew his sword, and then the unforeseen happened, for there was Bernier galloping towards him armed at all points. Ernaut forgot his hand in his joy and cried out to him for help. When Bernier saw what had happened to Ernaut he was deeply moved and a shudder of fear went through him right down to his toe-nail.[1] He saw Raoul approaching rapidly but before he struck him he appealed to him once more. He offered to accept Raoul's 'amende', call off the battle and hand over his land if Raoul would but have pity and be reconciled and leave off pursuing a man as good as dead. But Raoul's spark of pity was extinct. He took no notice of Bernier's prayer but rushed at him savagely. The fateful battle which ensued swayed to and fro, but *God* and *Right* (Diex et Drois) were on the side of Bernier and he gave Raoul a blow which, crashing through his jewelled helmet, cut right through his head. The knight, wounded to death, fell from his horse, for no man could have remained upright after such a blow. The sons of Herbert rejoiced and were glad, but it would not be long before their joy would be turned into sorrow. Thus ends the third act in the tragedy, and in the fourth and fifth the curse merely works itself out till both sides, grown weary of the

[1] l. 3045.

struggle, made an uneasy peace, only brought about by the idea of waging war against their common enemy, the faithless king.

Raoul's death had not been so instantaneous but that he had made a dying effort to raise his sword and strike another blow at his enemy. But the sword sank from his lifeless hands and fell its full length on the ground. With his dying breath he addressed God, the Judge of all, and begged the Virgin for her aid. But there was no word of repentance in his prayer—only vexation that his strength had gone and regret that he had ever been invested with the land. Bernier wept beneath his helmet, but Ernaut was still longing to avenge the loss of his hand, and in spite of Bernier's reminder that one should never touch a dead man, he struck Raoul again on the head and, as if this were not enough, he plunged his sword into the body. Then the knight's soul finally left his body. 'May God receive it', adds the poet, 'if one ought to pray for it'.[1]

The battle dragged miserably on until Guerri the red, having lost many of his men, decided to ask for a truce until he had buried his nephew. This was granted by the sons of Herbert, and Guerri, searching amongst the corpses, forgot to look for those of his sons so intent was he on finding his nephew. He found him lying beside the giant John whom Raoul had killed. John was the tallest knight in France, but when their bodies were opened it was found that his heart was no larger than that of a child, whereas Raoul's was much bigger than that of an ox capable of drawing a plough. When Guerri saw this he was so moved with indignation that he called off the truce and the battle began again.

But this last episode throws a flood of light not only on the sentiments of the poet towards his hero, but on the character of the man whose downfall he has so skilfully depicted. Raoul was 'greathearted'; he was a 'magnanimous hero' in the literal sense of the word. The author has summed up the situation in well-chosen words:

> Biax fu Raoul et de gente faiture;
> S'en lui n'eüst i. poi de desmesure,
> Mieudres vasals ne tint onques droiture (ll. 494–6).

Had that germ of evil in his character been sterilized or killed at an early age he would have been a splendid man—he would have been a perfect knight and feudal lord. As it was, not only did his 'ego' develop unhinderedly, but the germ was actually watered and fertilized by a misguided mother and an unscrupulous uncle until it

[1] 'Dame Diex l'ait, se on l'en doit proier' (l. 3157).

absorbed his whole being. But in the purifying of death his real nature appeared. The much gentler and more sensitive character of Bernier acts as a foil to his tempestuous friend. Bernier is equally brave, and conscientious to a fault. Like Raoul he seems to have inherited the characteristics of his mother whose courage and candour command our respect. He had imbibed from her his sense of loyalty, for, when doubtful as to whether his lord Raoul had forfeited his allegiance and he should go over to the enemy's camp, she replied quietly: 'Ser ton signor, Dieu en gaaigneras'.[1] The contrast between the two mothers is as interesting as that between the two sons, one marked throughout by pride and anger, the other by gentleness and humility.

After the death of Raoul the poem becomes less convincing. The laments of Raoul's mother and fiancée are more or less conventional in character. The mantle of Raoul falls on his nephew Gautier, who, in his turn goaded on by the sinister Guerri the Red, continues the war and is filled with implacable hatred against Bernier for killing his uncle. Bernier's remorse knows no bounds and the author allows him to demean himself almost to excess in trying to heal the breach between the two families. Louis comes out in his true colours and it is only in making common cause against him that the rival factions at last agree to become peaceful neighbours and join forces against the king. There is little in the poem to soften the impression of fierce passions playing themselves out in individuals; the religious element is almost entirely lacking, and the moral of the poem, which is ethical rather than religious, is summed up in the one pregnant line: 'Hom desreez a molt grant painne dure'.[2]

We have only considered the poem as far as line 5,555, as the second part is by common consent assigned to a different author. It is different in both form and contents as it is written, strangely enough, in assonances, although of later date. Its contents are those of the average decadent epic. There are descriptions of battle-scenes and deeds of heroism, but they are interspersed with love-scenes, abductions and marital ruses such as abound in the 'romans d'aventure'. Bernier, after his reconciliation with his former enemies, marries Guerri's daughter, but the good faith of the wily old warrior can never be counted on, and finally, mindful of the death of his nephew, he kills Bernier from behind with a treacherous blow of his stirrup as he is watering his horse at a stream. The action is reminiscent of Hagen's cowardly method of killing Siegfried in the *Nibelungenlied*.

[1] l. 1387.   [2] l. 498. 'Hard is the lot of an unbridled man.'

In each case the deed is explained but not excused by a conflict of loyalties in the mind of the murderer.

Raoul's name and character were well known in the twelfth and thirteenth centuries both to poets and chroniclers. In Walter Map he is introduced, as we have seen, as one of the disturbers of the reign of Charlemagne's son, Louis, in connection with Gurmundis, who fought against him with Ysembardus. An attempt was made by the compilers of the *Geste des Lorrains* to bring him into the lineage and complications of their cycle. But Raoul stands by himself, and deserves to be judged solely by the one poem from which his character emerges as a complete whole; it is not to be regretted that, as far as we know, no garrulous prose-version was ever woven around the original subject and Raoul never became the hero of distorted stories in other lands.

If *Raoul de Cambrai* can be taken as a product of the period in which unruly barons, taking advantage of a weak king, fought amongst themselves to the great detriment of the countryside, there is no lack of rivals to him in this sphere. Reference has just been made to what is sometimes called the *Geste des Lorrains*, though this is rather an ambitious title for the two or three poems composing this group—although it must be admitted that in their entirety they assume the imposing proportions of 56,000 lines. Not all the component parts of the cycle have as yet been published, but the two volumes published by Paulin Paris under the title of the *Roman de Garin le Loherain* undoubtedly give us the most important part of the series. We are not likely to find great interest in the long sequel devoted to the two sons of Garin and the history of Hervi de Metz, the father of the clan, pales before that of his two sons Garin and Bègue.

The subject of the poem, or rather the group of poems, relating to the family (*geste*) of the Lorrains has much in common with *Raoul de Cambrai*, but the treatment in the two cases is quite different. The background is similar; a weak king (Pepin here, corresponding to Louis in *Raoul de Cambrai*) whom no one respects; turbulent barons engaged in constant clashes with each other and a prey to boredom when not engaged in strife: 'This is a good scrap', says Bègue on one occasion—'this is the kind of game I prefer to all others' ('Sor totes choses itex gieux m'abelit'). 'What a devil you are', ejaculated King Pepin, who was not cast in such heroic mould; loyalties, hatreds, women whose chief function is to mourn for slain husbands when they are not being treated as pawns in the distribution of lands; a very meagre religious ingredient chiefly perceptible in a few acts of ritual, but a large slice of common sense expressed in wise saws and proverbs; and pervading all the poem a feudal dispensation which, both as regards tenure of land and juridical customs, seems to belong to much the same period as that depicted in *Raoul de Cambrai*. But there is no one character (like that of Raoul) which grows and develops before our eyes and whose gradual decline and fall we follow with apprehension and sorrow. Instead of this there is a galaxy of valiant knights, members of two great rival families at constant war with one another. The family (or *geste*) of the Lorrainers is depicted throughout as mainly loyal to the king. Its two chief representatives, Garin and Bègue, sons of Hervi de Metz, are types of the best products of medieval knighthood, marked throughout by courage, loyalty, gentleness to women, and a strict sense of honour. A streak of brutality there is naturally in their composition. The fact that Bègue cuts out the heart of a fallen foe and throws it in the face of an infuriating enemy telling him to salt and roast it, must not be taken too seriously, as it is but indicative of the ferocity of those times. Bègue and his brother Garin are 'gentlemen'; those with whom they come into contact recognize it. The monk who was questioned by Bègue's late host as to whether a knight had passed that way replied simply 'Gentilhom fu', and the host himself hearing that his guest was missing, said sadly:

> Moult est prodons dus Begues de Belin,
> Larges, cortois, sages et bien apris.[1]

The laments for him strike the same note. Though somewhat conventional in character they convey a true estimate:

> Frans chevaliers, corajeus et hardis,
> Fel et angris contre vos anemis,
> Et dols et simples a tres toz vos amis.[2]

And again:

> Tant mare fustes frans chevaliers gentis!
> Dous et loiaus, simples et bien apris.[3]

To complete these testimonies to his character the poet tells us that the legend which was inscribed on his tomb was:

> Ce fu li mieuldres qui sor destrier seist.

These panegyrics are all tributes to the character of Bègue—but they

---

[1] Ed. Paulin Paris, Vol. II, p. 251.
[2] Lament of Garin for his brother.   [3] Lament of Bègue's wife.

can equally well be applied to Garin as the two brothers merge into a kind of composite picture of a gallant soldier of the epoch.

The interesting point, however, of all these descriptions is that they do not apply to knights of blue blood, nephews of emperors or sons of great barons. Instead of the monotonous insistence on aristocratic birth and noble pedigree, the emphasis in this group of poems has shifted to a good heart (fin cuer) and a tradition of loyalty—'Cuer ne puet mentir', we are told several times and Bègue when, telling his wife that friendship is of more worth than 'le vair et le gris' or any other possessions, adds the following noble sentiment:

Li cuers d'un homme vaut tout l'or d'un païs.[1]

In actual fact Garin and Bègue are the sons of Hervi de Metz, a rich bourgeois, a 'vilain', a man of the people. It is true that Hervi's father, Thierri, had married a duke's daughter, but it is the paternal lineage that counts. This pedigree is never forgotten or glossed over in the poem. Another Hervi, surnamed 'le vilain', is a godson of Hervi de Metz. His advice, contrary to aristocratic prejudice, is taken before a battle; on one occasion Bègue, echoed by the whole army, exclaims: 'Li vilains a bien dit'. The 'vilain's' son, Rigaut, cousin of Garin and Bègue, is completely peasant-minded. When he is knighted he refuses the ritual of the bath which he deems quite unnecessary, although another passage tells us that he had come into contact with no water except what dropped from the sky for six months. When invested with the knight's mantle he seizes a knife from a bystander and cuts off its train saying he will be able to run and jump better without it. The king and the onlookers are a little shocked at his behaviour, but not for long, and he distinguishes himself so much in the jousts that he fills his friends with admiration and his enemies with fear. Garin and Bègue have another disreputable relation in Menuel Galopin, a cousin, frequenter of taverns, who has no longing for rich neighbours but just wants to be left in peace and enjoy life in his own way. When he is summoned to take a message for his cousin—besieged in his town Belin, he goes somewhat unwillingly. Bègue offers to make him a knight if he will quit his evil ways, but he merely laughs and replies that he prefers the taverns and the wenches. He gives much the same answer to Garin's wife when he arrives at Orléans and she wants to entertain him at her house, telling him she has three hundred barrels of wine. 'It is the company I like as well as the wine' ('La compangnie aime moult lez

---

[1] Ed. Paulin Paris, Vol. II, p. 218.

le vin'), he replies, at which Helois laughed heartily. It will be seen from this that no need was felt to be ashamed of humble relations, and there is no hint on the part of the author at any incongruity between knighthood and humble life—a refreshing contrast to sentiments expressed in some of the *chansons-de-geste* and the bulk of the *romans courtois*.

The upbringing of the two young men, however, had been according to knightly traditions of the period. They had lived for seven and a half years with their uncle, the Bishop of Chalons, and it is specially mentioned that Garin was 'de lettres appris' and could read both Latin and his mother tongue. They grew up handsome youths and King Pepin knighted them after a festival at Paris at the same time that the two sons of Hardré, one of the king's counsellors, received the accolade. The king was especially attached to Bègue and gave him a rich gift—'tote Gascoigne li dona a tenir'—a mark of special favour which annoyed Hardré. However, the four young men became companions-in-arms and fought in the king's battles.

About this time messengers came from Thierri, King of Moriane, that he was hard beset by four Saracen kings who had attacked his territory. The king, weak as usual in this group of poems, bowed his head and called to his vassals for advice. Then Hardré came out in his true colours. He reminded the king that his land was still poor and exhausted from his wars with Girart de Roussillon: 'Take my advice, king, winter will pass, April will come, grass will grow and our horses will have enough to eat'—prudent advice perhaps, but not heroic. When Garin heard it from the dismayed messenger he called to his young companions: 'Let *us* go and help Thierri; we are young and we shall win glory'. All agreed and they went to the palace where Garin was spokesman: 'You ought to have consulted your barons, king—not the old bearded men ('les chenus, les barbés') who want to sit at home at ease and sup their cup of wine at night ('Et au couchier le vin et le claret').' Hardré rebukes them angrily, but the young men gain their point and the emperor summoned his army.

The next episode is a crucial one as it relates the beginning of the great animosity between the two families. Garin sends out a scouting party to estimate the enemy's strength. They mount a rock the better to 'surveer l'ost', and again we see the evil effect this may have on an unheroic mind. The heathen enemy lies spread out for seven and a half leagues. Even Bègue, who was one of the party, was silent for a moment before he turned to his neighbour and said: 'What think you, Bernart?' Bernart de Nasil, of whom much more will be heard presently, said:

> Ralons nos en en cest nostre païs.
> Folie fut grand quant nous vinmes ici
> Contre chascun de nus sunt il bien mil.

Bègue's reaction was exactly the opposite. His answer is almost like a 'gab'. 'I wish every heathen in the world were there. You would see them all miserably perish, for I myself would kill a thousand'. Then Fromont, Hardré's son, asked his uncle Bernart what he thought, and the ominous reply was 'J'ai veü Sarrasins', and he and others of his party all counsel a retreat while the going was good. But Bègue was angry and insisted upon engaging the enemy. Whereupon Fromont refused to go in spite of Garin's reminder that they were brothers-in-arms:

> Mes compains estes et plevis et jurés.
> Vos sairement, vos fiance acquitez
> Et el nom Dieu avec moi en venez. (Vol. I, p. 102)

And on Fromonts' repeated refusal he says sadly: 'Ce poise moi,' but he adds that Fromont must accept the dilemma into which he puts him ('un giu vos part') that, if the heathen are defeated, he shall have no share in the spoil. Fromont accepts the proposition and abstains from the fight. Further trouble arises when, after the heathen are defeated, Fromont claims not only his share of the booty, but the daughter and land of King Thierri (who had died of his wounds in the battle) which the dying king had offered to Garin. The first 'chanson' ends with the summing-up of the poet:

> Iluec comence li grans borroflemens
> Dont furent mort chevalier ne sais quant.
> . . . Chansons commence de grant efforcement
> Onc ne fu mieudre, en cest siecle vivant.

By this time the protagonists have clearly emerged: Hardré, his son Fromont and his nephew Bernart de Naisil on the one side; Garin and Bègue with other members of the family on the other. It is obvious from the beginning that the Bordelais (i.e. Hardré and his followers) are 'the villains of the piece', full of guile, spite, perjury, and hatred. In the incessant wars between the two families which fill the rest of the poem they are practically always the incentors to the fight, and they will even descend to treachery to get rid of a hated enemy. Bernart de Naisil is about the worst of this undisciplined crowd. When trying to do an evil turn to his most hated enemy

Bègue, and prevent help from being sent to him, he insults the queen and says the king ought never to have married such a 'folle garce'. He was suitably punished for this insolence, for the queen summoned everyone in the town, even the butchers, to avenge her, and Hardré got four teeth knocked and was nearly killed by Garin, who came to the rescue. On another occasion he wanted to lay hands on the king, an unpardonable act, but was prevented by Fromont, who did not forget that he was the king's man ('Je suis ses homs'). But his meanest piece of treachery was when he shot an arrow at the departing Bègue's back from a window just as an agreement had been reached and Bègue was completely unsuspecting. He is constantly described as 'Bernarz li lerres' (Bernart the thief), or 'li lerres de Naisil', and is compared to a fox in his lair when he has barricaded himself in his castle. But the poet gives him his due as an accomplished soldier, one who knew how to yield, or flee, or fight as occasion required—'Car bien en fu norris tout son aé'.

Another unpleasant person is Isoré li Gris, Fromont's nephew, who, like Hardré and Bernart, had 'le cuer felon'. But he was not such an out-and-out villain as Bernart, though his enemies considered him as having an evil nature. 'Nature pert', says a former friend when Isoré, forgetting their earlier relationship, attacked him and laid waste his land—'nature will out, and you betray your birth by your deeds. If I ever had you in a high court, I would summon you for treason'. It is only just to add that Isoré admitted that he was in the wrong and drew off with his followers. He was eventually killed by Bègue, who fights him in a 'duel judiciaire' for falsely accusing Garin of a treasonable intention against the king, which had its origin in Isoré's own brain.

It was Fromont who, as has been mentioned, was the occasion (though not the real cause) of the outbreak of hostilities between the two great rival families although Garin and Fromont had been 'compaignons d'armes' for many years before the severence of their friendship when Fromont defaulted from the battle. 'Amé vous ai de fin cuer leaument', says Garin when trying to prevent the rupture. But after the death of his father Hardré, in an unfortunate tussle between the two parties, Fromont developed into the implacable enemy of the two brothers. His character deteriorated and eventually he became an enemy to his country, for a later chapter tells us that he went over to the Saracens and denied Jesus Christ. And yet he was not altogether bad; he was not treacherous like the foxy Bernart, but he shared with the other members of his family that trait of unforgivingness and jealousy which was the ruin of them all. In fact, the 'desmesure' which caused the downfall of Raoul and brought so much confusion in its train, is one of the characteristics of the unruly barons. The loyal ones are not entirely immune, but it is the ruin of the evil, ill-conditioned ones. They are their own worst enemies, and how often they have to be reminded that, in trying to spite their enemies they are damaging themselves—'Qui son nes coupe, il deserte son vis' is sometimes a warning of the poet, sometimes a caution put into the mouth of a friend who—unavailingly for the most part—tries to restrain them. Christian ideals play but a small part in the ethics of the knights on both sides; even in their grief, or expressions of sympathy, both good and bad alike are governed by practical considerations. 'Do not grieve so much', said the old Duke Hervi to the queen after the death of her husband:

> En grant duel faire onques gaigner ne vis;
> Duel sor dolor, ne joie sor joir,
> Home ne fame ne le doit maintenir.

This is a sentiment we often find expressed in the poems dealing with the turbulent barons who so frequently found themselves obliged to console the sorrowing relations of those killed in their service with the note of resignation contained in the phrase: 'Li vif aus vis, li mort aus morz'. There are some fine scenes in the poem *Garin le Lorrain* and much worldly wisdom. The only historical element is to be found in the first 'chanson' which describes the incursions into France of the Vandals under Charles Martel. This part has been neglected in the foregoing analysis which has been confined entirely to the characters of the conflicting warriors. It is, however, in the early part of the poem that we are introduced to Hervi de Metz, the father of two famous sons. He plays somewhat the rôle of Guillaume d'Orange in the support he gives to Charles Martel in his battles against the Saracens and the wise advice he gives to the pope on the subject of the 'dîmes' without which those battles could not have taken place. Still more does he remind us of Guillaume when, after the death of Charles Martel, he assists at the coronation of the 'damoisel Pepin', and swears to support him against all his enemies:

> De mainte gent i ot grant contredit
> Qui ne le volent otroier ne sofrir.
> Hervis l'entent, a poi n'enrage vis
> Et jure Dieu et le cor Saint Denis
> Qui fera mal au damoisel Pepin
> N'a la reine, au gent cor seignori,
> Jamais nul jor ne sera ses amis.

But alas, the king fails him miserably (at the advice of his evil counsellor, Hardré) and Hervi forswears his allegiance to the king and
fights his battles alone. He is killed pursuing the Saracens and his
two sons in their turn presented themselves before the king, who
received them kindly and took them into his service. But the telling
of all this is not in the dramatic style of the *Couronnement* where every
actor (especially Guillaume) stands out in stark relief; moreover, the
interminable 'laisses' on the vowel 'i' give great monotony to the
chronicle of events. It is not till we come to the death of Bègue that
we have a really fine piece of story-telling of a rather unusual character. An uneasy peace had followed the continual fighting, and for
seven and a half years Bègue had remained in his own land. Weary
of inactivity, he decided to go and visit his brother Garin and to
hunt, on his way, a famous boar of which he had been told. But the
forest in which this boar had been located was in Fromont's territory
and it was a most foolhardy enterprise. But adventures are to the
adventurous ('Par aventure vient li biens el païs') and nothing would
turn Bègue from his purpose. The inevitable happened. Bègue, in
his eager pursuit of the animal which had been roused and, contrary
to the habit of boars, had left the wood and taken to the open, got
separated from his companions. The boar was a monstrous one with
formidable habits, and an independent character. When surrounded
by dogs, it raised its eyebrows, rolled its eyes, screwed up its nose,
and proceeded to kill the dogs one by one—then it rushed at Bègue,
but was killed by a skilful spear-stroke. Night came on and Bègue
found himself alone. He lay down to rest beneath a willow tree and
sounded his horn to recall his men. But unfortunately he was heard
by a gamekeeper who, seeing him well equipped, with a valuable
steed beside him, after obtaining Fromont's permission, gathered a
few other 'gloutons' (amongst whom were Estormi de Bourges and
Thiebaud—known to us from the *Chançun de Willame*) and returned
to the resting man. Bègue appealed to their sense of honour, but in
vain. He even told them who he was, but urged on by Thiebaud,
they attacked him, and after killing several of them he was himself
smitten down by an arrow in 'la maistre veine del cuer'. Truly, as the
poet remarks: 'par glouton est mains maus arivés'. Bègue uttered a
brief prayer for his wife and children, then taking three blades of
grass between his feet in lieu of the 'corpus Deu' (the Eucharist), he
quietly expired. When all this became known and the murdered
man was brought in looking magnificent in death, and surrounded
by his dogs howling for grief, the knights and barons were astounded

K

at his beauty and convinced of his nobility: 'Gentis hons fu, moult l'aimoient si chien', they say, and when Fromont, now elderly, came to see what was happening, he recognized the count and was horri-fied. He ordered the highest honours to be paid to the dead man, and himself spent that night at the head of the bier. Many laments followed from all who knew him, but nothing could bring him back to life, and Garin undertook the painful task of conveying the corpse back to Belin and trying to console the widow, though quite 'boul-versé' by grief himself. Thus perished a very noble knight—'li mieuldres qui sor destrier seist', and it was true of him what the poet had said at the beginning of the poem about Garin: 'En son vivant maintes peines sofri'. But there is no hint of 'démesure' in the character of the two knights.

In spite of the similarity of background and allusions to ancient feudal customs very reminiscent of those we find in *Raoul de Cambrai*, there is no definite evidence of any knowledge either poet may have had of the other author's work. There is an allusion to Roland and his single combat with a heathen, presumably the Ferracutus of Turpin's Chronicle. There is, as has been remarked, an easily recog-nizable likeness between the rôle of Hervi de Metz in connection with the young king and that of Guillaume d'Orange in several of the poems of that cycle. Rather more surprising is the introduction of the two base characters, Estormi de Bourges and Thiebaut (li glous del Plaisseis), his brother, known to us from the *Chançun de Willame* where they play an equally ignoble rôle. But for the conception of the characters in the two rival families, the consistency with which they are painted, we must give the author of the poem full credit. The characters do not develop before our eyes, as in the case of Raoul de Cambrai; they are in that sense types. But the wealth of detail concerning them, and the realistic touches, give us an impression of figures drawn from the life, just as the author's constant insistence on the importance of a good commissariat for the army makes us feel that he is working on experience and not solely on imagination, a feeling which is absent from other accounts of turbulent barons of a more stereotyped character. The fact, moreover, that Garin and Bègue were descended from bourgeois stock shifts the emphasis from impeccable pedigree to the necessity of a good, loyal heart. Dis-loyalty to old friends and companions-in-arms is lamentable, but disloyalty to the king was unthinkable. This is what distinguishes the loyal faction from the Fromont-Hardré clan, whose disloyalty brought them into the group of traitors who became notorious in Old French literature.

So far we have dealt with baronial feuds, but there is another group of turbulent barons whose quarrel is with the king rather than with one another. Of these we have an excellent example in any of the three Girards—Girart de Roussillon, Girart de Fraite, and Girart de Viane.[1] We may take Girart de Viane as being the most suitable example of these rebellious subjects, for in the poems dealing with them it is with a type rather than a character that we have to do—a type characteristic of an epoch before a strong king had begun to curb the power of his more powerful and often unruly barons. Girart de Viane was of noble birth and the bond of lineage links up this cycle with that of Guillaume d'Orange, for he is a descendant of Aymeri de Narbonne. But the great difference between Guillaume and these lusty barons is that the former was loyal to his sovereign lord, whereas the latter were more often in open revolt against him. They devastate his land, rebel against his decrees, humiliate and insult him, but end up as his loyal subjects and supporters when they have had their fill of an unsettled life of insubjection. We have seen how Ogier of Denmark and Girart de Roussillon present a similar right-about-turn and appear as pillars of strength in Charlemagne's army.[2] Girart de Viane started as a humble official in the royal household, but he soon got tired of supervising the cooking, and both he and his brother Renier demanded recognition of their services and their birth. Certain barons were in favour of buying them off with money, but this soon brings out their chief characteristic—a colossal pride in their ancestry and knightly calling: 'I care not for money, I am not a merchant' says Renier:

> Einz mes lignage n'ala avoir querant
> N'en i a nul borjois ne mercheänt
> Ne ja ne l'ier en trestot mon vivant (ll. 700-3).

It is not that poverty matters, for 'honour peepeth in the meanest habits'; many a poor man is brave and strong, a fine knight and a noble gentleman.[3] But it is their pride of birth and their arrogance which makes them such a thorn in the side of a weak king. Girart is so rude to the king and so cavalier in his treatment of the duchess of Burgundy that the king is glad to get rid of him by presenting him with the town of Viane (Vienne). Like the other barons of his group he is violent, brutal even—but always strictly within the framework

---

[1] Cf. supra, Ch. IV.   [2] Cf. supra, Ch. IV.
[3] 'Vassaus de cors et frans om et gentis' (l. 611)

of feudal custom. He is quick to anger, but as quick to be appeased when the offender turns out to be one of his own kith and kin. At one moment he orders his nephew to be hung, at the next he embraces him because he recognizes a family trait ('Bien traiez a ma geste'), thus linking up Girart who fought against the emperor all his life with the noble clan of Garin de Montglane.

There is another rebellious baron without whom our chapter would be incomplete. Isembart was probably the chief character of a poem that has only come down to us in very fragmentary form. From other sources it can be gathered that he had very real grievances against King Louis of France; had been obliged to leave the country, and had joined the forces of the heathen King Gormund[1] and, having been given a position of command in the army, took part in an expedition against the land of his birth. He had given up the Christian faith, hence the epithets of *reneié* and *margari* (same meaning) which are attached to his name in the poem. He was greatly attached to King Gormund and trusted by his men. But he had never lost his admiration for his fellow-countrymen, and had warned King Gormund before starting and on the voyage that they were a tough nation ('gent adurée') who would never give up their land, and he cannot resist an affectionate reference to them—'la gentil gent e l'onurée'. He even has a good word for the emperor: 'A, Looïs, bons emperere / cum as France bien aquitee', when he sees his own master dead. He was loyal to the heathen army, however, as long as they trusted him, and fought on relentlessly for four days, taking heavy toll of the French:

> Qui il consuit, ne s'en ala;
> Qui il feri, puis ne parla,
> Se Damnes Deus nel suscita (ll. 580-2).

At one juncture he was engaged in single combat with a Frenchman, Miles li Gaillarz, and would have killed him had not an elderly knight came to his rescue. The rescuer was none other than Isembart's father, who gave his son such a blow that he pierced his shield. 'Maistre Isembarz' replied by an even more powerful blow which unhorsed Bernart but did not wound him. Thereupon he leapt on his father's horse and rode off without a word. The poet adds that it was a sin and a shame that he should have unhorsed his own father, only that he did not recognize him. Had he known him, he would not have touched him for there would have been other matters to

---

[1] NOTE. *Gormund* is the form preserved in the manuscript but the form *Gormont*, employed by the editor, will be used when the poem is cited.

occupy them.[1] Then the heathen, weary, hungry and discouraged, turned and fled, and escaped in their boats. Isembart was left, still fighting, until he was pierced in three places and hurled from his horse. The pursuit went on and the fallen knight was not even recognized. As he lay dying where three roads met he remembered the God of his youth, and he uttered a prayer that would be his salvation.[2] He did not pray for himself alone, but for those who had killed him, ending with a humble appeal to the Virgin:

> Sainte Marie, genitrix,
> Mere Deu, dame, 'Isembarz dist,
> Depreiez en vostre bel filz,
> Qu'il ait merci de cest chaitif.

The fragment ends as he drags himself with difficulty beneath a leafy olive tree, turns his face towards the east and confesses his sins. It is the pathetic story of a grievously-wronged man, obsessed by a desire for vengeance which leads him to act against his better judgment and die in the attempt rather than submit to an injustice. This is, in fact, the moral lesson to be learnt from all the poems of this group— revenge may be sweet, but the injury caused by relentless vengeance returns with boomerang effect on the head of the man who nurses a real or imaginary grievance. One feels that Isembart was a noble-hearted man but tainted by that same sin of 'desmesure' which was so fatal to good and bad alike. Had his heart been opened it would perhaps have been found to be as large as that of Raoul de Cambrai. In any case his end was just as miserable.

[1] l. 577.   [2] l.633.

CHAPTER VIII

THE HEATHEN IN THE OLD FRENCH EPIC

OUT of the confused and tangled strains of legend, history, tradition, and propaganda which compose the fabric of epic production in medieval France it seems almost impossible at first to obtain any idea of these formidable rivals to Western civilization which even approximates to the truth. And yet a careful scrutiny of the poems enables us to pick out, not only certain particular characteristics, but also those general tendencies in the swing of public opinion which nearly always become sensible in contemporary literature, sometimes increasingly so when that literature ceases to be of the first rank. We will start our study with the *Chanson de Roland*, not only because of its outstanding merit, but because being one of the earliest—if not the earliest—of the known epic poems it is the least spoiled by the stereotyped and artificial features which mark the later poems and produce a fixed type rather than a recognizable character.

The *Chanson de Roland* gives us a perfectly rational idea of the heterogeneous mass of the heathen as they struck a poet probably not far removed in date from the launching of the First Crusade in 1096. There is no hint of a knowledge of this crusade (unless it be a passing allusion to the finding of the holy lance), no mention of the Holy Sepulchre, of Jerusalem (except a legendary one), of Antioch, or of any of the heroes, spiritual or warlike, of the First Crusade. The scene is laid in Spain and all the action unfolds itself in the land which had been the hunting-ground for expeditions against the Muslims during the eleventh century. But Turoldus has introduced the religious, crusading spirit which was a marked characteristic of the extreme end of that century, and the invaders of Spain are invested with a moral glamour to which they were perhaps not entitled. It is a great tribute to the author's skill and—perhaps first-hand—knowledge of the pagans he describes, that he differentiates clearly between the somewhat decadent type of Saracen to be found in Spain in the eleventh century, when the gentler arts had partially replaced the pursuit of arms, and the more virile types that accompanied the Sultan of Cairo on his expedition from North Africa in answer to their request for aid. It is noticeable moreover that some of the tenets generally attributed more specifically to the Muslim faith (such as the promise of the immediate joys and delights amongst the flowers of paradise to those killed in a holy war) have passed into the Christian teaching and become an incentive to courage and contempt for death. There is, in fact, a marked parallelism in the descriptions of the two rival camps of this crusading epic and it is not always obvious which has served as a model for the other. Charlemagne is surrounded by his twelve peers; Marsilie is introduced in the same way. Each potentate is seated on a throne ('faldestuel', mod. Fr. fauteuil), the emperor's being of pure gold, the heathen king's of ivory. Their knights are seated around them in oriental style on silken mats ('paile', 'paile d'Alexandre'). Of the two kings, Charlemagne gives the stronger impression of an eastern monarch by his autocratic attitude towards his knights when they rise to speak unbidden.[1] Each has his 'wise man' beside him—Duke Naime, the counsellor, is never far from the emperor's side; Marsilie is flanked by Blancandrin.[2] Each takes counsel of his barons according to the feudal custom, and the preparations for the battle proceed on similar lines. But subtle differences soon begin to make themselves felt. The heathen king's one object is to get Charlemagne out of Spain which he considers is his property. He listens to the advice of his counsellor who does not hesitate (1) to make a promise with every intention of breaking it; (2) to offer a large bribe from the fabulous wealth of the East (bears, lions, dogs, 700 camels, 1000 moulted falcons, 400 mules loaded with gold and silver, 50 waggons loaded—presumably with similar treasure); (3) to show a complete disregard for the lives of the hostages who would have to be sacrificed even though they included his own son. This was characteristic pagan advice—it is true it did not shock Ganelon, but Ganelon was a traitor who considered that any means would justify his end. On the other hand a certain amount of sympathy must be felt for the heathen king. For seven years Charles had been devastating Spain, pulling down her strongholds and razing her cities to the ground. Marsilie asks the messenger, quite pitifully: 'When ever will he be tired of waging war?'[3] Marsilie was not cast in a very heroic mould; he was, in fact, anxious about the future and not feeling at all sure of the capacity of his own army:

> Jo nen ai ost qui bataille li dunne
> Ne n'ai tel gent ki la sue derumpet (ll. 18–19).

He could put 400,000 knights into the field if necessary and yet he

---

[1] 'Alez sedeir, quant nuls ne vos sumunt' (l. 251). Cf. ll. 259, 272.
[2] 'Blancandins fut des plus savies paiens' (l. 24).
[3] 'Quant ert il mais recreanz d'osteier?' (l. 528).

preferred to act with guile and deploy his huge army in sections against the 20,000 Franks who formed the rearguard of Charlemagne's army. Undoubtedly the Saracens who composed Marsilie's army were a very mixed crowd. The epithets of Moor or Saracen was used as a generic term in the chronicles of that epoch to cover the infidels of Spain, the Berbers, and other mixed races of the Levant: 'c'est un vocable ethnographique de significance imprécise au Moyen Age puisqu'il a servi a désigner aussi bien les Berberes de Maghreb et les Sarrasins d'Espagne que les Arabes mêlés aux autres éléments des races du Levant'.[1] This is an excellent description of the 'Saracens d'Espagne' in the *chanson*, who include Berbers[2]; a duke from the land of Dathan and Abiran[3]; long-haired men of immense strength from a devil's land where no dew falls and nothing grows; an African clad entirely in beaten gold,[4] and other strange folk ranging from 'black as molten pitch' to 'white as the flowers in May'.[5] Apart from individuals, they are not outstandingly good fighters. They have lost the unbounded enthusiasm of the earlier Muslims who were inspired by the threefold incentive of thirst for martyrdom, visions of paradise, and belief in pre-destination, all of which seem to have passed over to the Christians. History tells us that Cordova had become a city of wealth and luxury by the tenth century, and the result of this had been a relaxing of the sinews of war: 'The sword of the Saracens became less formidable when their youth was drawn away from the camp to the College; when the armies of the faithful presumed to read and reflect'.[6] 'Paiens s'en fuient' is a phrase which occurs rather often in this poem; they may profess that they will not quit the field for fear of death, but in the next line we are told:

> Dist l'un a l'altre: E car nos en fuiums!
> A icest mot tels cent milie s'en vunt (ll. 1910–11).

A hundred thousand seems a large army to take to flight, but no quarter was given in those days between Christian and heathen and no prisoners taken.[7] When Marsilie had lost his right hand in the encounter with Roland, and was informed that his son (on his way to his rescue) had lost his life, he immediately took to flight and, on reaching Saragossa, gave himself up to despair. Bramimunde, his wife, and more than 20,000 Muslims wept and wailed and beat their

---

[1] Cf. Boissonade: *De nouveau sur la Chanson de Roland.*
[2] 'Rois Corsalis . . . Barbarins est et mult de males arz' (l. 885); 'Barbarins est d'un estrange païs' (l. 1236).   [3] l. 1215.   [4] ll. 1550–2.
[5] 'Peiz ki est demise' (l. 1635); 'blancs cum flur en estet' (l. 3162).
[6] Gibbon: *Decline and Fall*, VII, p. 151.
[7] Cf. ll. 1886–7.

breasts. They cursed Charles and 'France dulce', and then proceeded to abuse their own gods—Apollin, whom they hung by the hands to a pillar and then trampled underfoot, Tervagant whose carbuncle-stone they took from him, Mahomet whom they thrust into a ditch for pigs and dogs to devour.[1] It will be noted that the one god of the followers of Mahomet has been replaced by a trinity of gods. It is not very clear whether one of them was *primus inter pares*, though, on the whole, more godlike qualities were attributed to Mahomet, who is called upon during the battle as their protector ('garant')[2] and actually worshipped:

> Mahomet levent en la plus halte tur;
> N'i a paien ne-l priet et ne l'aort (ll. 853–4).

We are told at the outset of King Marsilie:

> Li reis Marsilie la (Saragosse) tent qui Deu non aimet:
> Mahumet sert et Apollin reclaimet (ll. 9–10).

This signifies a great change either in the Muslim conception of the deity, or perhaps merely in the Christian conception of the Muslim creed. The Koran was a testimony to the unity of God and the Saracens always professed to be greatly shocked at the Christian polytheism. When Mahomet died in 682 and fanaticism was suggesting a ray of hope for the mourners in the assertion that he was not dead but in a holy trance, Abubeker, his faithful friend and father-in-law, appeased the tumult: 'Is it Mahomet', said he to the crowd, 'or the God of Mahomet you worship? The God of Mahomet liveth for ever, but the apostle was mortal like ourselves'. The so-called *Anonymous* who, as an eye-witness, wrote an account of the First Crusade, quotes on several occasions the oath: 'iuro vobis per Maehomet et per omnia Deorum nomina', which he places in the mouth of a heathen.[3] Tradition gave the number of mystic names of God as seventy-two,[4] but this could hardly have been the source of the three (or four) heathen gods and the idols and images so often referred to in the *chansons-de-geste*. A comparison of the earlier poems is instructive and may throw some light on the relative dates. The author of *Chançun de Willame* does not mention Apollin or Tervagant, the two rivals of Mahomet in the *Chanson de Roland*. Moreover, he puts Mahomet in his proper place: 'Deus est on ciel, et Mahomet en terre', describing their respective functions.[5] In *Gormont et Isembart*

---

[1] Cf. ll. 2579–91.   [2] l. 868.
[3] Cf. *Gesta Francorum et AliorumHieroso lymitanorum*, Ch. xxi, xxxix.
[4] Cf. Gaster (M.): *Studies and Texts in Folk-lore*, I, 268, 391 f., 406 f., 438, 444 f.; II, 1075. London, 1925–8.   [5] l. 2115.

there is no mention of Tervagant, but the heathen king swears by Apollin on one isolated occasion. As Gormont is referred to by the biblical terms of *l'antecrist* and *le Satenas*, it is tempting here to connect the heathen deity Apollin with the Apollyon of the Apocalypse[1], whose name meant 'destruction' rather than with Apollo, the sun-god of the Greeks, as has generally been done.[2] In the early and perhaps the oldest part of *Garin le Lorrain*, the *Wandres* (Vandals) and the Saracens in general (described indiscriminately as *paiens, sarrazins, esclavons, esclers* and *hongrois*) are referred to by the collective name of 'la gent Mahom', or 'la mesniee[3] Apollin'; Hervi de Metz informs the heathen King Godin with whom he is engaged in single combat that God is greater than Apollin,[4] again tempting us to think of Apollyon rather than Apollo as the adversary. There is no reference to Tervagant in the poem. So far back as our sources in the vulgar tongue go, we may therefore reasonably assume that the tradition of the three gods in the *Chanson de Roland* popularized the idea of the picturesque heathen trinity—'Apollin le felun' with his sceptre and crown, Tervagant with his flashing carbuncle, and Mahomet their protector, each with his standard and his statue (*ymage*)—which was followed by so many later poems, sometimes with the addition of a fourth, or even a fifth deity.

The traits of the heathen, as portrayed by Turoldus, are as vivid as those of their gods. Some of them are fantastic, others true to type, just as we find in the early chronicles. Whether repulsive or of lady-killing appearance,[5] they are magnificent in their battle array, armed with triple Saracen hauberks, good Saragossan helmets, swords of famous steel, good shields and lances of Valentian metal. They own beautiful Arab steeds ('destriers Arabiz') which were often objects of envy to the Christians. There are sorcerers ('encanteür') and sooth-sayers amongst them (as one would expect in an Arab army), one of whom had paid a visit to hell under the guidance of Jupiter and his black art.[6] Baligant himself consults a soothsayer when in doubt as to the issue of the battle. Of the braver, or nobler ones, the author gen-erally makes the pious remark that 'he would have been a valiant knight had he been a Christian'.[7] Some of them are genuine, orthodox believers, like the Count Turgis of Turteluse who puts Mahomet in

---

[1] Ch. ix; v-7.
[2] Cf. Boissonade, loc. cit., p. 247.
[3] =household, Old English *meinie*.
[4] 'Car mieus vaut Diex que ne fait Apollin.' Ed. P. Paris, Vol. I, p. 31.
[5] l. 957. [6] l. 1391. [7] l. 899, etc.

his proper place, at the same time assuring the king that victory will be on his side:

> Plus valt Mahum que seint Pierre de Rume,
> Se lui servez, l'onur del camp est nostre (ll. 922–3).

But Mahomet failed them only too often and their souls were carried off to hell by devils[1] or, as the *Anonymous* would say: 'reddiderunt infelices animas Diabolo et Sathanae ministris'.[2]

It will be obvious from the above that Turoldus held the conventional views as regards the heathen and was influenced by the clerical assumptions of his time. This is especially true of the first half (roughly) of the *Chanson de Roland*, which is concerned mainly with the clash of personalities (Ganelon, Roland, and Oliver). After the death of Roland[3] a more interesting, because more truthful, description of the heathen is to be found. Letters had been sent from Marsilie to his liege-lord, the Sultan of Cairo,[4] an ancient survival of Virgil and Homer (!), to come to his aid. A warning accompanied the letter that if the emir did not come and attack the Frankish warriors[5] Marsilie would desert his gods and the images to whom he prayed, accept holy Christianity and make peace with Charlemagne. But the 'amiral' did not need pressing, and having assembled a huge army in the north of Africa, he set sail from Alexandria and soon arrived in Spain, where the brilliantly-lighted ships illuminated the countryside as they sailed up the Ebro to Saragossa. As Baligant's envoys passed through the streets of the town towards the palace they heard a great noise; the citizens and the remnants of Marsilie's army were weeping and wailing with all the appropriate signs of grief, and blaming their gods, who had been so useless to them. When, in friendly wise, they gave the heathen salutation in the name of Mahomet, Tervagant, and Apollin, Bramimunde replied indignantly that their gods had gone into retirement and had completely abandoned them at Roncevaux and what was to become of her—a poor miserable, deserted woman with a useless husband? 'Hold your peace, lady',[6] replied the messenger as he began to unfold his master's plan of campaign.

Henceforth it is the Arabis (Arabites of the *Anonymous*, etc.) with whom we have to do: 'Paien d'Arabe des nefs se sunt eissut'.[7] The Arabis were the picked fighting men, the 'aristocracie militaire musulmane', the 'élite de la chevalerie',[8] mounted on swift Arab

---

[1] 'L'arme de lui en portet Sathanas' (l. 1268).   [2] Op. cit., Ch. xviii.
[3] l. 2396.   [4] 'En Babiloine Baligant ad mandet' (l. 2614).
[5] 'Ki si sunt fiers, n'unt cure de lur vies' (l. 2604).
[6] 'ne parlez mie itant' (l. 2926).   [7] l. 2810.   [8] Cf. Boissonade, loc. cit., p. 194.

horses and mules, a very formidable foe. Charlemagne, as he 'performs his prance' (*fait sun eslais*) in front of his army, realizes his danger and calls upon God and the apostle of Rome for their help. After describing the formation of the French army the poet passes to that of the Saracen army, which is organized on parallel lines. Baligant, too, made his 'eslais' before the army, in the course of which he leapt a ditch fifty feet wide. He has the build of a true cavalryman:

> La forcheüre ad asez grant li ber,
> Graisle ad les flancs et larges les costez,
> Gros a le piz, belement est mollez,
> Lees les espalles . . .
> . . . De vasselage est suvent espruvet.
> Deus, quel baron, s'eüst chrestientet (ll. 3155–65).

Baligant was a learned man ('de sa lei mult par est savies hom') as well as a valiant knight. Like a good Muslim he exhorted his men to abase themselves before the battle, and their helmets fell forward as they all bowed their heads to the ground.[1] Then the emir formed his army-corps (*escheles*) just as the emperor had done. They were composed of mixed troops, some of which can be identified geographically and some are of fabulous origin. Three of the best ones he kept back for his own use against Charles and the Franks, and foremost amongst these were the Turks. Clearly Turoldus had the same opinion of Turkish valour as the *Anonymous* who tells us that: 'nullus homo naturaliter debet esse miles nisi Franci et illi' (Turci), and goes on to say that if only they believed in the Trinity no one could find better knights 'potentiores vel forciores vel bellorum ingeniosissimos' than they.[2] The author tells us, moreover, that they made fearful noises ('stridere et garrire') as they rushed into battle, and precipitated the Franks by thousands into heaven to receive the crown of martyrdom. But to return to our poem, Baligant, in his certainty of victory, stood aside from the battle and reserved himself for the single combat with Charlemagne, on which he was determined.[3] He promised his men many fair wives and much treasure if they vanquished the Frenchmen and the Arabs replied with an encouraging shout. They fought magnificently[4] and both sides suffered heavy losses. The battle became almost unbearable—'mult fort a suffrir'—since the French and the Arabis were well matched. The poet's words 'Mult bien i fierent Franceis et Arrabit' remind us again of the 'Franci et illi' of the *Anonymous*. The emir called on his three gods, promising them

---

[1] l. 3274.   [2] Bk. III, Ch. ix.   [3] ll. 3326–8.
[4] 'Ki puis veïst li chevaler d'Arabe' (l. 3473).

statues of pure gold, but even as he was praying a knight arrived to tell him that his son Malprimis and his brother Canabeus had both been slain in single combat with noble Frenchmen, one of whom was the emperor himself. This was small consolation to the emir, who bowed his head and thought he would die of grief. The parental feeling often seems to have been stronger amongst the Arabs than the Franks, who had retained the old Germanic tradition of nepotism. So great was Baligant's grief on this occasion that he began to lose confidence in himself and his cause. He called his wise soothsayer Jangleu and asked him for a forecast of the result of the battle:

> Que vus en semblet d'Arrabiz et de France,
> Avrum nus la victoire del champ (ll. 3511-12).

The soothsayer replied: 'You are a dead man, Baligant; your gods will never save you. Charles is a fierce enemy and his men are valiant. . . . Nevertheless, call up your best troops for the attack and *delay not the appointed end*'.[1] The idea of his predestined end did not alarm Baligant, as it was an accepted belief among the Muslims. He put his white beard outside his armour, gave a clarion call on his horn and rallied his noisy troops,[2] who forthwith slew seven thousand of their opponents. But the French knights rallied too, and Baligant's standard-bearer was killed and the standard fell to the ground—an incident which was always recognized as a signal of defeat by the Arabs. Straightway a glimmer of light told the emir that he was in the wrong and Charlemagne in the right.[3] Moreover, terrified at the disappearance of their standard, the heathen were beginning to flee. Charlemagne shouted his well-known battle-cry *Munjoie*, and the emir replied by his own of *Preciuse*, and each recognized the other by the loud, clear tones of his voice. Now the climax is at hand, for the decisive battle for the cause of religion cannot be decided without the death of one of the antagonists,[4] or, indeed, at any rate without one or the other confessing his error.[5] Each makes his appeal to the other —that of Baligant has a certain pathos: 'Charles, reflect and make up your mind to repent towards me. You have killed my son and most unjustly ('a mult grant tort') challenged my land. Become my man ('deven mes hom') and swear fealty to me; be my lawful vassal from here to the East'. Charlemagne's reply is uncompromising: 'I will have no love or peace towards a heathen. Embrace Christianity and

---

[1] ll. 3513-19.
[2] 'Cil d'Ociant i braient et henissent
Arguille si cume chien i glatissent' (ll. 3525-6).
[3] ll. 3553-4.   [4] l. 3578.   [5] 'Jusque li uns sun tort i reconuisset' (l. 3688).

the Law of God; then I will love you and you will become the servant of the Omnipotent'. Charlemagne never forgot his mission; but his words were of no avail and the combat was renewed. The emir struck the emperor a fearful blow which sliced off a large piece of his flesh and made him totter, but divine intervention saved him, restoring his strength and courage. His next blow was a fatal one for Baligant and the battle ended with the flight of the heathen 'for God willed it so'.[1] As they approached Saragossa in their headlong flight they came within the view of Queen Bramimunde, who was watching from her high tower, surrounded by the clerks and canons of her faith. But, the author reminds us, they are not true priests and they have not tonsured heads. Bramimunde called out in despair: 'Mahomet, help us! Dear lord, our men are vanquished and the emir has perished shamefully'. The news was too much for the stricken Marsilie. He turned his face to the wall, weeping bitterly; then he bowed his head and died of grief still in his sinful state. Living devils received his soul.[2] The rest of the campaign was soon accomplished. The emperor took possession of Saragossa, caused the town, the synagogues and the mosques (*mahomeries*, cf. the *machomaria* of the *Anonymous*) to be searched for statues and idols which his men straightway shattered with iron mallets and axes so that no witness to their falsehood should remain. The baptistries were filled with water in which 100,000 heathen were baptized (on pain of death in the case of refusal) and the emperor set out for France with the captured queen whom he was determined to convert by peaceful means. Thus the cause of right has triumphed and the author remarks piously: 'Mult bien espleitet qui Damnedeu aiuet'.[3] This is the moral which detaches itself from the second part (as we may call it) of the *Chanson de Roland*. The first part (up to the death of Roland) is a study of characters, and the most heinous crime is the treachery of one of Charlemagne's own knights. But in the second part the protagonists are the royal representatives of the rival faiths. Charlemagne may emerge victorious in the end, but he has a worthy antagonist in Baligant and the moral scales are not unevenly weighted. The Christians and the heathen, too, are well-matched: 'Mult bien i fierent Franceis et Arrabit'. The victory of Charles was due to the 'seinte voiz de l'angle', for right must triumph in a 'combat judiciaire'. There was no desire for vengeance left in the emperor once the question was settled, and the poem ends (after the trial of Ganelon) on the consoling note of Bramimunde's conversion, sponsored by

---

[1] l. 3625.　　[2] 'L'anme de lui as vifs diables dunet' (l. 3647).　　[3] l. 3657.

many dames of high degree. But there is a hint in the last *laisse* that Charlemagne will have to be off again on his toilsome quests—for hitherto the action has been confined entirely to Spain.

It is not without a certain poetic irony that a woman becomes a connecting link between the rival forces of the (two) conflicting religious ideals. Charlemagne allowed himself to be touched by the beauty of the Saracen queen who, until her husband's death, was the faithful, and as far as we know, the only wife of the Moslem king. Had she, perhaps, been a little attracted by the handsome Christian knight Ganelon, when he came with treacherous suggestions to the Saracen court? At all events, she had presented him with two very valuable pieces of jewellery to take back with him—both of solid gold, set with amethysts and jacynths, and worth all the wealth of Rome.[1] The dazzling riches of the East must have had great attractions for the soldiers of less sumptuous climes, but it would be surprising if the beautiful oriental woman did not possess even greater charms for the knights of the West. That this was so is illustrated very forcibly in the history of the epic Guillaume d'Orange, for already in the earliest poem of his cycle he is wedded to the erstwhile heathen princess Guibourg. Under her pre-baptismal name of Orable, she had been the wife of the rather mysterious pagan 'Thiebaut l'esturmant',[2] who had been defeated under the walls of Orange (desuz Orange) and robbed of his wife. In the *Chançun* Vivien claims to have slain 'dan Tiedbalt', but the fact that we find him still alive in *Aliscans* proves that he already existed as the useful legendary character of an ill-treated husband, whose chief crime was to be a pagan with a beautiful wife. Guibourg, whether from conviction or other causes, had deserted her faith and received the Christian religion, of which she had become a staunch supporter:

> Nen out tel femme en la crestienté
> Pur sun seignur servir e honorer,
> Por eshalcier sainte crestienté
> Ne pur la lei maintenir e guarder (ll. 1489–92).

It is true that in the *Chançun de Willame* the heathen do not carry much conviction of first-hand knowledge as they do in the *Chanson de Roland*. The only Saracen whose name is mentioned is the King Desramé who, perhaps, represents a vague recollection in the jongleur's mind of one of the famous Arabic rulers who bore the name of Abderrahman. Otherwise the 'Saracens', as they are called in the *Chançun*, present a kind of jumble of Moors, Northmen, and even

---

[1] ll. 637–9.   [2] Cf. *Chançun de Willame*, l. 678, etc.

Saxons, and the fantastic geographical details do not help us in identifying them. The interest of the poem lies in the characters themselves, and their relation to epic traditions, and from this point of view Guibourg is important as representing the bridge between Christian and heathen and the human relationships between the two opposing forces which form such a delightful contrast to the indiscriminate slaughter and destruction which prevailed around. The two Frenchmen who play such an unworthy part in the first section of the poem are more cowardly and ready to flee at the first sign of danger than any of the *pute geste*—'les Sarazin de Saraguce terre'. When Esturmi, who has seen the heathen disembarking with their Arab horses on to the sandy shore, is asked by 'Tiedbalt de Beürges', 'Qu'en loez, Esturmis?' he receives the immediate reply: 'Alum nus ent pur nos vies guarir!'[1] and Tiedbalt actually tells his friend to destroy the battle-standard which might betray them in their flight. This Esturmi does, placing the lance with its white ensign across his saddle-bow, breaking it in halves with his two hands and trampling it in the mud. It is doubtful whether any of the heathen would have performed such a dastardly and ominous act. The final battle, in which Guillaume is at last victorious, concludes with the death of Desramé. He has been badly wounded and is left lying covered with blood and sand on the battlefield. Now he sees Guillaume approaching, accompanied by his nephew Gui. With a last heroic gesture he leaps unaided on to the back of his charger ('de plaine terre salt sus en l'alferrant') and advances, painfully, to the encounter. But he soon succumbs again and is given the *coup-de-grâce* by Gui as he lies on the ground. The Saracen's last thoughts are for his faithful steed.

Vaguer and vaguer become the references to the heathen when we come to the barbled story of Guillaume's battles in *Aliscans*. Desramé is still their lord and the forces are composed of contingents from 'Inde Superior' and Palerne, and of those grouped under the title of 'li estraneor'. They are at times 'la gent Tervagant', elsewhere '*la gent Apollin*'; elsewhere they are *Turs*, *Persans*, and *Esclavons*. One group, qualified as 'vachiers', are of the '*maisni. Gorhant*'; they are horned both back and front. In another passage reminiscent of the *Chanson de Roland* (the battle of Roncevaux is mentioned), they become the 'Sarracens d'Espagne'. Guillaume's attitude towards them is interesting. When he is reproached by Tiebaut's son for having stolen his father's wife, he replies: 'You speak folly. If a man does not love Christianity, if he hates God and scorns charity, he has no right to live. Anyone who kills him has destroyed a devil'.[1] Another passage in the same poem describes the single combat of Guillaume with Aerofle, the brother of Desramé. The episode clearly corresponds to the one in the *Chançun* in which the heathen king Desramé lost his life. In each case it is the final battle before Guillaume succeeds in returning to Orange. But in *Aliscans* the description is much elaborated. Aerofle is 'li plus fiers Turs, dont onques fust parlé' and, although what we might call the character of the good heathen has not yet evolved, yet Aerofle appeals in a nobler and more sympathetic light than Guillaume himself. In fact Guillaume's rôle is an ignoble one. At first sight he covets the heathen's horse and determines to secure it. He tries at first to obtain it hypocritically by making friends with Aerofle.[2] But the heathen refuses to be well-disposed towards anyone who believes in the Trinity and in the Virgin birth; moreover, he very naturally reproaches Guillaume for having robbed his brother (Desramé) of his town (Orange) and his friend (Tiebaut) of his wife (Orable). Only if these are given back will he be reconciled to the Frenchman.[3] 'You ask too much', replied Guillaume, and the battle began.

The two warriors fought hard, as they were well matched—the Turk and the Frenchman.[4] They found time, however, in the brief intervals of fighting, for one of the discussions of the relative value of their two faiths which became so popular in later chronicles and *chansons*. Aerofle is eloquent and more orthodox than some of the heathen we have seen. He begins by assuring Guillaume that Christianity will benefit no one; its baptisms, its masses and sacraments, its marriages and its orisons are nothing but a fraud, indeed the whole belief is based on a deception. God is in heaven and does not trouble Himself with the earth. 'It is Mahomet who, at His command, gives the wind and the rain, the fruits of the trees, the wine and the wheat. It is Mahomet whom we ought to believe and try to propitiate'. This interesting exposition, which had a widespread popularity, did not convince Guillaume, who merely replied: 'Glous, de tot chou vos desment'.[5] The battle was then renewed and continued savagely until, by divine aid, Guillaume severed the leg and thigh of the infidel—just as he had done to the heathen King Desramé in the parallel passage in the *Chançun*. Aerofle had been a worthy antagonist, but Guillaume mocked him unmercifully as he lay wounded on the ground. He seized the coveted horse, taking no

---

[1] ll. 1058–61.   [2] ll. 1185 f.   [3] l. 1200.
[4] Cf. the *Franci et Turci* of the *Anonymous*.   [5] l. 1228.

notice of the heathen's piteous appeal for his beloved steed,[1] of which he enumerates the virtues. Finally, as the heathen faints for pain, he shamefully seizes his sword and cuts off his head with it. It must be admitted that in the whole episode the balance of nobility and refinement of feeling is on the side of the Turk. The authors of these early crusading epics were by no means blind to the failings of their compatriots, any more than the chronicler who tells us of the action of the Christians in digging up the Turkish dead after their warriors had bravely returned to the battlefield to bury them, and robbing them of all their possessions.[2]

And yet something subtle is happening in the background. We have seen how Guibourg formed a kind of bridge over the chasm which separated the adherents of the Crescent and the Cross. But an even stronger link, because not due to mere natural physical attractions, is described in the continuations of both the poems describing Guillaume's exploits and misfortunes at Alischans. The exhausted hero has been persuaded by his wife to go and seek help against the ever-increasing pressure of the Saracens at the court of King Louis. The king has at last been induced to put an army at Guillaume's disposal and a hundred thousand men are about to set out. Just on the eve of their departure Guillaume chanced to spy a tall youth coming from the kitchen into the palace. He was well grown and handsome, but his face was blackened and disfigured by the smoke of the fire, at which the cook had kept him working all night. The young squires had been making fun of his appearance, and at last he lost his temper and became violent; whereupon fifty of them rushed at him, meaning to kill him. Guillaume's father, Aymeri, who was also at the court, arrived just in time to save him from their hands, and Guillaume, who had noticed the young man's unusual strength, turned to King Louis and said: 'Sire, who is this young man whom I saw fighting with your squires? . . . By St. Denis, he is a formidable foe'. Then King Louis told how he had bought him from some merchants; how he believed him to be an infidel (*escler*), but the boy could not remember anything of his childhood; how he had sent him to work in his kitchen because he feared and disliked him on account of his strength; and how, in spite of his many requests, he had refused to have him baptized and had kept him there in the kitchen for seven years, until he had become completely 'asoté'. When the king declared that he quite expected the young man would brain him one

[1] 'Por l'amor Dieu, mon cheval me rendes' (l. 1323).
[2] *Anonymous*: Bk. IV, Ch. xviii.

day, Guillaume burst into his loud laugh and said: 'Give him to me, Sire; he shall return home with me and I will see that he has plenty to eat'. The king agreed willingly and Rainouart (for he was so called) left the kitchen and was allowed to join Guillaume's army, to his immense joy. His gratitude to Guillaume for having saved him from servitude and menial jobs was unbounded.[1]

Rainouart was a heathen, a son of Desramé and therefore brother to Guibourg, but although she, with feminine instinct, soon had a suspicion as to his origin, Rainouart himself was in ignorance of the fact. He is by no means a mere comic character as has sometimes been assumed. He was devoted to Guillaume and he fought unwaveringly for him even against his own father, who was in the Saracen army. He knew what he was doing on this occasion (unlike Isembart in the poem *Gormont et Isembart*), for he recognized his father: 'You are my father, I know, for I am Rainouart, your son. But I am Guillaume's man ('Hom sui Guillaume') and I love him from my heart. If you harm him I will do the same to you'. He admits no loyalty whatever to his own kith and kin—only to his friend and protector. Then an unfortunate thing happened. The main battle was over, thanks to the valour of Rainouart, and at long last Guillaume was returning home victorious. Owing to a kind action in saving a poor man's field from the Saracens who were pillaging it, Rainouart was delayed, and when he arrived at Orange the gates were already shut and he was too late for the magnificent feast that Guibourg had prepared for the warriors. Rainouart was very angry, but, even more, he was hurt at Guillaume's forgetfulness, and the author of *Aliscans* admits that Guillaume was greatly to blame:

> Li quens Guillames fist forment a blasmer
> Que Rainouart a mis en oublier (ll. 7507-8).

His bitterness was increased by the thought that the omission was due to pride on the part of Guillaume, who did not deign to sit at table with him[2] in spite of the fact that he had fought so hard against his own folk and had, in fact, won the battle for the Christians and rescued Guillaume's own relations from captivity. But it was not pride, it was sheer thoughtlessness on the part of the Christian knight. He made a humble apology to Rainouart when he realized how seriously his feelings had been hurt. It was not till Guibourg intervened, however, that Rainouart's anger was appeased and he dissolved into tears and forgave Guillaume for her sake.

The episode ends on a note of reconciliation. We next find

---

[1] ll. 3316 ff.   [2] l. 7515.

Rainouart seated by the side of Guillaume, the Saracen and Christian cheek by jowl, and therein lies the importance of the episode. Rainouart tells his story to the assembled 'baronage' and pays Guillaume the tribute he deserves for his large-heartedness:

> A grant travail i ai lonc tems esté;
> Plus de .vii. ans, je cuit, i sont passé,
> Tant que Guillaumes i vint, s'i m'a rové;
> Ansamble o lui m'en a ci amené.
> Soe merci, molt me tint en chierté,
> Et je l'ain plus qu'home de mere né (ll. 47–53).

It is a reconciliation based on human affections in which knightly conventions can be flouted, race can be ignored, and differences of creed overlooked or accommodated. Religious revivals and chivalrous ideals had not yet begun to soften manners at the date to which these earlier poems belong. It was pure humanity which made Guillaume, out of love and pity for a fellow mortal, take up the uncouth slave who was turning spits in the kitchen. On Rainouart's side it was love and gratitude to Guillaume which made him sacrifice all his natural relationships. In this way, without realizing it, he had helped to build the bridge between the forces of paganism and Christianity and prepared the ground for the conception of the 'good heathen' which we find in so many of the later poems and which coincides with certain tolerant elements which made their appearance in actual fact when the first fine careless rapture of the early crusades had begun to wane.

It is fairly obvious from the above that the story of Rainouart, although it formed a kind of sequel to the Vivien and Guillaume episodes in *Chançun de Willame* and was incorporated into the poem of *Aliscans*, belongs by its character to a somewhat later period than that which produced such poems as the *Chançun* itself, the *Chanson de Roland* or *Gormont et Isembart*. The uncompromising attitude of the Christians towards the heathen in the mass, the generally unsympathetic treatment they receive at the hands of the authors, and the complete lack of chivalry evinced by the Christian knights towards their infidel foes, justify us in considering the earliest versions of epic poems which have come down to us as roughly contemporary with the earliest chronicles of the crusades—e.g. the above-mentioned eyewitness-author of the First Crusade known under the name of the '*Anonymous*'. The heathen are consistently bad, although in a few isolated cases it may be admitted that *if* they had been Christians they would have been valiant barons. Generally speaking, they have been created only to be destroyed. It was even permissible, against all the rules of knighthood, to kill a wounded man as he lay defenceless on the ground, to prevent the possibility of his having any heirs.[1] And yet the delightful inconsistency between Guillaume's humanity and his religious principles comes out even in the *Chançun*, where his actions belie his words. He picks up the wounded Guishart and carries him back to Orange in spite of the fact that he had at first refused to do so because his nephew had denied his Christianity. In general, however, the earlier poems do not betray a sympathetic attitude towards the heathen although the chronicles confirm the fact that the Christians were guilty of just as flagrant acts of barbarism as the pagans themselves—indeed, sometimes of even more savage ones.

By the middle of the twelfth century, however, a different attitude towards the heathen can be traced both in the chronicles and the poems. We may take the chronicle of the *Pseudo Turpin* as a sort of signpost, as its arms point both backwards and forwards. Just as the author is certainly indebted to epic legends for some of his material and probably for other elements in his work, of which the origin is not quite so clearly indicated, so certain of the later epic poems are based on the *Chronicle*, the borrowings being sometimes unacknowledged, at other times not only acknowledged but even exaggerated. The author of this so-called *Historia* is most impartial. Obviously in a clerical work of this sort with all its edifying moral deductions, the ultimate victory must always lie with the Christians; the Saracens and 'perfidious Jews' (who are now introduced into the picture) must succumb to the victorious army of God's elect. The general impression left on the reader, and clearly intended by the author, however, is that the pagan is a very gallant foe, capable of noble actions, ready to be convinced of a greater law than his own if his reason and his principles allow it. The first of the two great single combats which occupy the bulk of the work, bring this out very clearly. A certain pagan African king, by name Agolandus, had acquired the whole of Spain for himself, having invaded it with a large army and killed, or turned out of the towns, all the Christians who had been left to garrison it by Charlemagne. On hearing of this the emperor returned to Spain with large armies. After various vicissitudes, in which the Frankish army was mainly victorious, Agolant retired to Pampeluna and informed Charlemagne that he would await him there. Knowing that he was up against a formidable enemy, the emperor returned to Gaul where with great energy ('cum summa

---

[1] Cf. *Chançun*, ll. 1972–4.

cura') he summoned all his vassals from far and near and even released the prisoners and presented them with perpetual freedom on condition they served in his army for the expulsion of the treacherous enemy from Spain. With his vast army, under many famous leaders (viri famosi heroes), all propagators of the Christian faith in the world, he proceeded to besiege Agolant in Pampeluna, to which city he had retreated. Agolant, however, preferred to fight in the open —moreover, he greatly desired to see Charles.[1] This wish was gratified by a temporary truce during which Agolant, with sixty of his generals advanced in procession to meet the emperor, who came forth into a wide, open field for the interview. As soon as the heathen arrived at the appointed place ('tribunal Caroli'), Charlemagne vented his displeasure and declared that he would demand a large indemnity for all the damage that had been done to Christian life and property in Spain. Agolant was very much impressed and delighted by the fact that Charles knew his Arabic speech ('loquelam suam arabicam') which he had learnt as a boy at Toledo, where he had spent a considerable time. Then followed the usual discussion in which each upheld the superiority of his own religion. 'Valde indignum est', said Agolant, 'ut gens nostra tuae genti subjaceat, cum *lex nostra magis quam vestra valeat*; nos habemus Mahumeth, qui Dei nuncius fuit nobis a Deo missus, cujus praecepta tenemus; imo Deos omnipotentes habemus, qui jussu omnipotentis Mahumeth nobis futura manifestant,[2] quos colimus, per quos vivimus et regnamus'. Charlemagne replies that the pagans hold 'vana praecepta vani hominis'. After stating the Christian belief in the Trinity he asserts that the Christians' souls go straight to Paradise and eternal life after death, whereas the pagans proceed to Orcus, adding rather illogically: 'Unde liquido patet, quod *magis valeat lex nostra quam vestra*'. Agolant suggests that equal numbers should be pitted against each other from either side and that the result of the battles should decide the question. It is rather like a toss-up—heads I win, tails you lose, were it not that such large issues were at stake. In the event the Christians were victorious and Agolant, affirming that the Christian faith had proved its superiority, promised Charles that he and his army would come to the Christian camp for baptism the next day. This satisfactory solution, however, was not to come about. When Agolant came over next day to be baptized, he saw the emperor dining in the midst of a distinguished group of soldiers, canons, bishops, and abbots, all

---

[1] Ch. xi, 'desiderabat enim Carolum videre'.
[2] The function of Tervagant in *Le Jeu de S. Nicholas*.

reclining round the laden tables in their distinctive garbs. But his attention was caught by a group of thirteen miserably-clad beggars in a corner who were consuming a meagre meal—('parvo cibo et potu utentes') whilst the others were feasting. On inquiring who they were he was told 'Haec est gens Dei, nuntii Domini nostri Jesu Christi ... quos unumquemque diem ex more pascimus'. Agolant was profoundly shocked at the lack of liberality towards God's messengers displayed in this custom. He had no further use for a religion which sanctioned such inequality of treatment. He returned to his own people, bade them refuse baptism, and be ready to fight the next day.

The author takes this opportunity of delivering a homily on the uselessness of faith without works. It is obvious that his sympathy is with the heathen king, whose conscience, in spite of his false religion, was far more tender than Charlemagne's. It is true that in the ensuing battle Agolant is killed and the Christians wallow up to their knees in the blood of the heathen, but this was the foregone result of a battle in which the excellence of the 'lex christiana' was at stake.

A somewhat similar course of events is narrated in the second important single combat which occurs in this chronicle of fabulous events. A young giant (de genere Goliad) named Ferracutus, possessed of forty men's strength, seeks the pleasure of a *singulare certamen* with one of Charlemagne's knights. The unwary victims come out against him one after another. Ogerius Dacus (= Ogier the Dane) is carried off like an unresisting sheep, Constantinus rex Romanus and Oellus, count of Nantas,[1] are carried off likewise, one tucked under each arm. Finally Roland came out at Charles' request, but he, too, was ignominiously picked up and placed upon the heathen's steed to join the other knights in prison. But Roland, recovering his strength and putting his trust in God, managed to seize Ferracutus by the chin and threw him backwards on his horse. Both knights fell to the ground, but straightway leapt to their feet and mounted again. Soon, however, their horses were killed, their swords thrown aside, and they fought on foot with fists and stones. At last, Ferracutus, who, it must be remembered, had already fought several combats, asked for a truce. This was granted by Roland, and they arranged to resume the battle next day, without horses or lances, whereupon each repaired to his base. On the following day they returned to the fight, Ferracutus armed with a sword and Roland with a long twisted staff (club). They fought till noon with their

---

[1] Whose innumerable miracles, the author tells us, were recounted in a *cantilena*—cf. Ch. xi.

respective weapons and the large round stones which lay in numbers about the field. Neither was yet seriously wounded, but this time Roland asked for a truce and Ferracutus, being very sleepy, lay down for a nap. Roland, seeing this, came up and slipped a stone under his head that he might sleep the better. This delightful act of courtesy from a Christian to a heathen is indicative of much. As yet it is only courtesy from man to man, the spontaneous recognition of nobility in a well-matched foe in spite of his being a 'heathen dog', but it is difficult to imagine such a contingency either in the *Chanson de Roland* or the *Chançun de Willame*. In the grim battles of the earlier poems only abuse was heaped on the head of a dead or living foe. Having slept sufficiently, Ferracutus sat up, and we have the most engaging spectacle of the two young knights sitting side by side discussing the eternal verities in a completely amicable manner. Many are the arguments and illustrations used by Roland in his exegesis of the Christian faith.[1] Some of his arguments are far-fetched and the heathen exclaims: 'Rolande, cur tot verba inania profers?' But Roland is not discouraged and even illustrates the mystery of the Resurrection by the homely legend of the lion which wakes its still-born cubs to life after three days by his breath. Ferracutus is not convinced, however, in spite of the long and ingenious series of arguments. We are back again at the idea of the toss-up. 'I will fight you again now', says Ferracutus, 'on the agreement ('tali . . . pacto') that your religion is the right one if I lose, but the false one if you are vanquished; that the people of the losing side will be shamed, but there shall be praise and honour to the winning side for ever'. 'Done' ('*Fiat*'), replied Roland, and the battle was renewed, with the inevitable result that Ferracutus, who called in vain on Mahomet for help, was killed (by a thrust through the navel, the secret of this vulnerable spot having been revealed by the simple heathen as they sat side by side before the battle), though it was only by divine help (Deo juvante) that Roland overpowered his adversary. It is notice-able that the chronicler says nothing about the heathen's soul being carried off to hell.

Charlemagne's character, through this so-called *Chronicle*, is so reprehensible on several occasions (as has been mentioned in a previous chapter, cf. page 28) that it throws into relief the admirable side of the pagan's behaviour when the rival protagonists are brought into conflict. The African King, Agolant, became a popular character in the fiction of the twelfth century when he was adopted by the

[1] Cf. supra, Ch. III, p. 26.

authors of the *chansons-de-geste*. The battle between Roland and Ferracutus (Ferragu, or Fernagu, in the later poems) excited so much enthusiasm in the audience when it was recited, that foolish people would exclaim: 'If only I were a knight like that, I would soon be a champion in the tourney'.[1] Many are the references in the romances, the rhymed chronicles,[2] and even in the troubadour poetry of the second half of the century to Agolant, Aumont his son, and *Ferragu le duc*. The epic poem in which Agolant—and even to a greater extent his son Aumont (or Eaumont)—plays a large part, is the *Chanson d'Aspremont*, which has already been cited in a different connection in a previous chapter: Agolant, a typical heathen king, sends an arrogant message to Charlemagne that Africa already belongs to him and that he has now crossed the sea into Calabria and proposes to crown his son Aumont, King of Rome. A heathen knight, Balant by name, delivers the message faithfully and admits that the chief object in his master's mind is to do despite to the Christian faith.[3] Charlemagne prepares accordingly, sending out a summons to all his noble knights to join in his crusade,[4] and, as in the *Pseudo-Turpin*, he offers freedom to all prisoners who will go and fight to avenge the cause of Jesus Christ. Meanwhile Aumont, who is in charge of 100,000 Turks, ravages the land. His armies carry the four pagan gods (the three well-known ones and Jupiter) on scaffolds in front of them, having done obeisance to them before starting out. The battle sways to and fro, most of the success being on the side of the Christians. Aumont and his men are pushed back until at last, after a three days' battle Aumont, who is parched with thirst, stops beside a spring of water, dismounts, lays aside his shield, sword and spear, and stoops down to drink. He is surprised in the act by Charlemagne himself—'Es vos Karlon qui descent del rocier'. Aumont is dismayed, but the emperor reassures him with the chivalrous words:

'Paien' (dist Karles) 'ne te caut d'esmaier.
Ja, par mon cief, n'en avrai reprovier
Que om sopris ait par moi encombrier' (ll. 5796–9).

He then bids him recover his arms and remount his steed, and challenges him to fight for the spring which is in his territory. So a great single combat between the two powerful warriors, one lord of the East and the other lord of the West, takes place. Aumont soon

[1] Cf. *Poème Moral*, ll. 3151–2.
[2] Cf. Philippe Mousket: *Chronique rimée*, ll. 5732–6055, obviously based on the *Pseudo-Turpin*.
[3] 'Chrestienté violt a grant tort despire' (l. 130).
[4] 'Venes od moi en cest pelerinage' (l. 867).

perceives the magic virtue of the precious stone in Charles' helmet
which even his own marvellous sword Durendal cannot shatter. So
having recourse to his physical strength, he seizes the emperor with
both hands and a wrestling match ensues:

> Karlon aert ('seizes') li paiens malostru
> Et l'emperere raert lui a vertu (ll. 5987–8).

Charles, who is the older man of the two, begins to flag, and
Aumont at last gets possession of the helmet. Then indeed the
emperor's fate would have been sealed but that God did not intend
his warrior to be vanquished and in the nick of time young Roland
('Rollandin'), his nephew, appeared on the scene and joined in the
fight on his uncle's side. Roland, a mere youth, fought so well that
Aumont, who had been brought to his knees, realizes that he has the
makings of a valiant knight and, regardless of more important issues,
prays Mahomet that his sword Durendal may fall into the hands of
the victor should he be killed:

> Que trop seroit granz dels et fors irors
> Se cete espee portoit om pereços (ll. 6043–4).

Aumont is broadminded enough to wish for a worthy possessor of
his valued sword, even though it should thus pass into the hands
of his enemies. This is in striking contrast to the fanatical action of
Roland in the *Chanson de Roland*. The dying warrior exerted himself
to the utmost to break his sword (the same Durendal) so that it
should not fall into the hands of a pagan enemy.

Aumont inevitably succumbs in the unequal contest, but the
author himself assures us that Charlemagne would never have
returned to France and worn a crown again if it had not been for his
God and his nephew Roland. He is honest enough to admit this
when he returns to his anxious knights and Naime remarks:

> Se cis rois fust leves et baptisié
> Plus hardis om de mere ne nasquié (ll. 6120–1).

After this tribute to his courage Aumont was carried beneath an
olive tree and buried. Again there is no mention of the heathen's
soul being fetched by a devil, although he died unconverted. His
fate recalls that of Roland as, like his predecessor, he had refused
to sound his horn and summon his father to his aid because he had
made a vow to Mahomet that he would never sound it on account
of the Frenchmen. The influence of the older poem is obvious, but
the change of attitude in respect of the heathen is striking. It is even

more so if we examine another of the characters who plays an important rôle in the younger *chanson*.

The case of Aumont is that of a gallant enemy who is capable of sublime action in his last moments, but never wavers in his devotion to a mistaken cause and therefore falls a victim to his loyalty. In Balant, however, a different type appears. Here is another heathen who commands our respect. But he has something in addition to the gallantry and disinterested love of horse or sword which we have seen in Aerofle and Aumont. Balant has a mind which is capable of perceiving the truth. He is, in fact, 'une âme bien née', an 'ager bene praeparatus' which is ready for the good seed to be sown in it. When converted he will never give up his new faith merely to save his skin, but is capable of whole-hearted loyalty to his new master. The case is not that of Rainouart who had been brought up in a Christian court since earliest childhood, nor yet of the two ladies Bramimunde and Guibourg, each of whom may have been impelled by the strong attraction of a noble warrior to abandon their own faith.

Balant was sent as a messenger to Charlemagne from King Agolant to deliver his challenge. It had been foretold by a heathen soothsayer (a favourite heathen type in the *chansons-de-geste*) that of the three known lands Europe, Asia, and Africa, two would bow down to the third. Agolant, therefore, who already possesses Africa, fired by a desire to become a second Alexander,[1] sends an aggressive message to the emperor that he will conquer Apulia and Sicily during the summer and be crowned King of Rome in the following winter. Balant delivers his message courageously, ending up with a dreadful threat:

> Se vostre tieste ne tendes sus son brant
> Et de sa loi n'estes reconissant
> Jo ne donroie de vo vie un besant (ll. 323-5).

Charlemagne was so angry at these words that he made as if to strike him, but Duke Naime ran forward and prevented such an improper act. A messenger must be properly treated in such a noble court, and the duke proceeded to act as the perfect host, even offering Balant the pick of his horses to replace his own tired mount. At the banquet (for it was a feast day) Balant was overcome (like the Queen of Sheba) at the opulence of everybody and everything he saw, at the number of kings and noble barons, at the knives with which they cut their food, and at the way they conversed together.[2] He began to

---

[1] Cf. l. 418   [2] 'Come cascuns parole a son voisin' (l. 421).

feel that Agolant had undertaken a task beyond his strength and—a much more important matter—his faith in his own gods began to weaken. So worthless did they appear to him that he transferred his faith to the true God (Dameldeu), realizing that he was doomed unless he was loyal to his new faith.[1] On his way back to the pagan king he longed for the French court where he had received so much kindness and would willingly have had himself baptized at once; but he had not yet accomplished his mission and it would have been a disloyal act ('vilonie'). Agolant's first question was: 'Did you see Charles?' 'By Mahomet, I did', replied Balant, and then gave such a description of the emperor and his court (which was as superior to all others as gold to baser metals)[2] that evil-minded barons accused him of having been bribed,[3] and for a time Balant was in disgrace. Meanwhile Charles prepared for his campaign and summoned all his vassals. He then decided to send someone to spy out and estimate the enemy's strength. After much discussion Duke Naime set out for Aspremont where he arrived after many adventures, only to be in danger of losing his life at the hands of infuriated Saracens.[4] He was saved by Balant who swore that the man they had captured was not Duke Naime but someone of no importance—a mere 'serjans u canberier' to whom the king should pay no attention whatever. The ruse succeeded and Naime was allowed to depart, but before he set out Balant confided to him his desire to be baptized and raised at the font ('baptisié et levé'). Naime received this good news joyfully; it gave him greater pleasure than a message from the heathen queen that she would like him to become her lover and that she would be willing for his sake to abandon Agolant and give herself up to him. Naime replied that, although he had no wife, she would find plenty of Frenchmen better-looking than himself, and he had no time for dalliance whilst serving his king. This episode, viz. a heathen princess falling in love with a young Christian knight and quite shamelessly sacrificing husband or father to obtain her end, became an almost stereotyped feature of the decadent *chansons-de-geste*. Naime, however, showed no surprise at the offer and accepted a magic ring before he departed, leaving a weeping Dido behind. Balant pressed some of his treasures on the duke, but they were refused. However, a beautiful snow-white Arab horse was accepted on behalf of Charlemagne with the promise that as soon as the war was over the donor would embrace the Christian religion. During the battle Balant fought faithfully on

---

[1] ll. 438–40.   [2] 'Com est ors cuis sor kevre et sor metal' (l. 572).
[3] l. 624.   [4] l. 2410.

behalf of his lord though he prayed earnestly that he might not die before receiving baptism, and when things began to go badly for the heathen, he could not resist the temptation of recalling his own words of warning:

> Ja mais la mer, ce cuit, ne passeron;
> Loins est Aufrique, ja̓ mais ne le verron (ll. 4627–8).

His own son Gorhaut was killed by Ogier le Danois in the course of the battle. Balant was so infuriated at this that, regardless of the danger to body and soul, he spurred straight for Charlemagne and struck him with his lance of eastern steel, only to be hurled off his horse by a return blow from the emperor. Angrily he leapt again into the saddle, but found himself surrounded by a threatening group of French knights amongst whom he recognized Duke Naime. He only escaped death at the hands of Ogier by recalling himself to the memory of the duke, who said reproachfully: 'You said then that you believed in God. Are you going to obey His law?' Balant replied emphatically: 'Oïl voir, Sire, des or mais en avant'.[1]

The next we hear of Balant is on the solemn occasion of his baptism after the death of Aumont, when the first great battle is over. With the permission of the Pope he was brought forward by Ogier and Naime. Four archbishops and the rest of the clergy, with the help of the Pope, prepared and blessed the font. Balant was stripped to his trousers and plunged three times into the water. The emperor raised him up, and so much oil ('cresme') was used for the occasion that it could not have been bought for 100 marks.[2] His name was changed to Guitequin but his part in the play is now finished.

The case of Balant is fairly typical of a number of good pagans who from their first appearance on the scene are marked out in some way as potential converts. They are essentially of noble birth, they are valiant soldiers and, although they remain loyal to their rightful lord until they are free from their obligations, something tells them from the beginning that the Christian faith is superior to their own. It is hardly likely, as the author of *Aspremont* would have us believe, that it was the splendour of Charlemagne's court that dazzled them, for they must have been accustomed to great magnificence and wealth at the courts of the emirs and sultans of Africa, or more particularly of Spain. Sometimes, doubtless, there were reasons of a prudential nature when the fate of prisoners taken by either of the opposing armies is remembered. The heathen Clargis in the poem *Les Narbonnais* was taken prisoner but offered to conduct a messenger

---

[1] l. 5747.   [2] l. 7059.

whom Aymeri wished to send to the French Court through the lines of the pagan army. He had a great longing to see his wife and children again and, although he refused to change his faith at the moment, he hinted that if the French army was finally victorious he might do so at a later date. He was evidently marked out for conversion, for he was saved by God in a battle later in the poem and obviously reserved for the edifying scene at the end, where he declares that he has long desired to be a Christian[1] and begs to be baptized. His companion in baptism was his cousin Forré, a much more interesting character. Forré was the brother of one king and the son of another. He was taken prisoner early in the battle when a tent full of treasures was captured by the French army:

> Et un danzel qui mout estoit cortois,
> Forrez ot non, mont fu sages des lois,
> Chanberlans fu a l'amirant persois
> E nepo.qant si fu ses peres rois (ll. 2983 f.).

He was very alarmed when he saw the Frenchman enter the tent, for he was not a fighter. He was a man of science, in fact, a doctor: 'Je sui bons mires; ja mellor ne verrois.'[2] The skill of the Arab doctors was well known at that time, and Aymeri immediately tells him to have no fear for he shall accompany him to his palace. He commends Forré to his barons and tells them to take good care of him. The name Forré is hardly ever mentioned in the poem without the epithet of 'le bon mire'—'the good doctor'—indeed, we might almost say 'the beloved physician' for Aymeri was devoted to him. His skill was soon in request, for Aymeri himself was badly wounded in battle shortly after. The prisoner was sent for immediately and was promised great rewards if he could heal his captor. Forré, who was used to a fatalistic creed, was seized with surprise and pity when he saw the grief-stricken countess weeping and fainting again and again. He set to work at once, turning the count over and over (*envers et adent*), gently washing his wounds with wine, plastering them with a good ointment, then binding them skilfully. He treated the state of lockjaw by inserting a knife between his teeth,[3] then mixed an aromatic spiced drink of priceless value from a plant which had its origin in Paradise. It had such magic power that no man, however badly wounded, but became 'as sound as a fish when the liquid passed down his throat'.[4] Forré then bade them kill a peacock, and Aymeri was able to sit up and take nourishment, after which he had a good

[1] l. 7884. [2] l. 3990. [3] l. 4315. [4] l. 4324.

long sleep. It is small wonder that, when he awoke, without a trace of pain or weakness, he was full of gratitude to 'le bon mire':

> O voit Forré, antre ses braz le prant:
> Ja le besast s'eüst bastissement (ll. 4329–30).

But the time was not quite ripe yet. Forré had another cure to perform. Aymeri's youngest son Guibert was captured by the Saracens and nailed to a cross. He was delivered by his brother Aïmer, but had horrible wounds from his maltreatment. He would certainly have died but for Forré, who was immediately sent for by Hermenjart when she saw her son: 'Demander fet le bon mire Forré'.[1] But this time Forré made a condition. He will only heal Guibert if he and his cousin Clargis are set at liberty. Aymeri in turn replied that he would only release the two prisoners if Guibert was restored to health. Guibert was completely recovered by the end of a month:

> Et li bons mire a de Guibert pansé,
> Dedans un mois l'a i si respassé
> Que bien pot porter armes (ll. 5304–6).

Soon after this, Forré and Clargis were both baptized. Count Guillaume stood sponsor to 'le bon mire', who had healed both his father and brother, and there was great joy in the court over the repentant sinners.

The case of Forré is a more interesting one than those of the majority of converted pagans, as it expresses a historic reality. It is reported that in Spain during the tenth century the life of the Catholic princes was entrusted to Saracen skill, and that in the year 956, Sancho the Fat, King of Leon, was cured by the physicians of Cordova. The school of Salerno, which was so famous in the twelfth century and so constantly mentioned in literature of the period, helped to introduce the Arabic sciences into Italy. But Spain was the centre of learning, and when Borel, Count of Barcelona, came to Aurillac to pray ('orandi gratia') and was asked 'an in artibus perfecti in Hispaniis habeantur', he replied very promptly in the affirmative.[2] This was when Gerbertus, the future Pope Sylvester II, was a young man (end of tenth century), but we may assume that the reputation of the Saracens in Spain was not yet dimmed at the time of the earliest Old French epic poems, in which the scene shifts continually from Spain to Italy and back again.

The legend of another 'good heathen' which enjoyed great popularity both in France and other lands takes us back again to Spain.

---

[1] l. 5274.   [2] *Richer Historia*, III, xliii.

In the two thirteenth-century poems *La Destruction de Rome* and its sequel *Fierabras*, we hear of the attack on Rome by Laban d'Espagne and his son Fierabras d'Alexandre, and, in the second poem, of the counter-attack of Charlemagne and the eventual defeat of the Saracen king and his army. King Laban had heard that some of his subjects had been ill-treated by the inhabitants of Rome—a city which belonged to him by ancient right. He immediately set out with a vast army and crossed the sea to proceed to the help of his subjects. A fierce battle was fought on the outskirts of the city, and soon we have the first hint of future salvation in the soul of the king's young son, Fierabras. The 'apostoille de Rome' was fighting vigorously with the ensign of St. Peter fixed to his lance, when he was unhorsed and thrown to the ground by Fierabras. On removing his helmet and head-piece in order to cut off his head—under the delusion that his antagonist was a king or an emir—Fierabras found to his surprise that his head was tonsured. Disgusted at what he found, he told him to go back to his psalter and his bell-ringing as it was more suitable for a priest than bearing shield and lance in battle. 'Off with you, mount, and may Mahomet curse you' he told him as he gave him back his horse. The Pope was overjoyed as Fierabras conducted him from the field, and the author remarks:

<blockquote>Grant curteisie en fist, si le lesse aler (l. 666).</blockquote>

This courtesy on the part of Fierabras and his intolerance of a treacherous action a few lines later on, prepare us for the rôle he is to play in the following poem—*Fierabras*—in which Charlemagne, bringing his twelve peers and a large army, comes to the help of the inhabitants of Rome with the fixed intention of rescuing the holy relics which Laban had seized when the city was captured.

Fierabras, with the arrogance of youth, was the first to defy the Christian army, and he challenged any six of Charlemagne's knights to come out and fight him. He was particularly anxious to meet Roland, or Oliver, Ogier the Dane, or Gui of Burgundy in single combat. Roland, who had been grievously offended by some foolish words of Charlemagne, refused to go out against him; whereupon Charlemagne, in a fit of anger, struck him on the nose with his gauntlet, making the blood flow down freely. Roland retired in dudgeon to his tent, and Oliver, obliged to take up Fierabras' challenge, does so under a feigned name. A more or less conventional battle ensued. Fierabras takes great pains to protect his horse from blows directed against it by Oliver, whose own horse had already been killed. So both knights were now fighting on foot, and Fierabras was so astonished by the French knight's strength that he adjured him by his God and his baptism to reveal his true name. Oliver confessed his identity and the battle continued, whilst Charles watched from his tent and prayed earnestly for his knight. He is reassured by an angel and, in fact, the battle soon turned in Oliver's favour, for Fierabras was seriously wounded in the flank. Realizing his helpless condition, Fierabras surrendered, promising that, if he might be brought before the emperor, he would embrace Christianity and hand over the relics which his father had seized. Oliver yielded to his entreaty and, as it was impossible to fight his way back carrying the heathen on his horse, he deposited him at his own request under an olive tree, well aside from the beaten track lest he should be killed and die unbaptized, in which case his soul would be damned. Here Charlemagne found him and was only prevented from giving him his 'coup-de-grâce' by Fierabras's repeated promise to accept baptism and return the relics. So doctors were summoned, Fierabras's bowels were replaced in his body, a potion of herbs was administered and within fifteen days he was well enough to be baptized. He received the name of Florien, but as long as he lived, the author tells us, he was always called Fierabras.

Such is the history of Fierabras. It is more edifying than that of his sister Floripas, who, in order to secure the French knight with whom she has fallen in love, brutally kills the jailor who was in charge of the captive knights, throws her nurse out of the window into the sea when she tries to frustrate her wicked designs, urges the knight she has freed to go and kill her father, Laban, whilst at his dinner, and is yet shameless enough to encourage him to be baptized and save his soul when he is captured at the end of the poem. Floripas is merely one of a line of repulsive females who became rather popular in the decadent period of the *chansons-de-geste*. In a sense they derive from Guibourg, the converted wife of Guillaume d'Orange, but time and tolerance had softened this lady's traits and mitigated her action. Her roots go back as far as the earliest traditions, and we do not know the details of her previous union with Tiebaut or the actual cause of her desertion of family and faith. Guibourg may or may not have been an enchantress of doubtful character before her marriage to Guillaume, but at all events her behaviour after her conversion was exemplary. It is to be hoped that the same transformation took place in the case of the horrible Floripas and Sebiles[1] of the later poems and

---

[1] Cf. *Chanson-des-Saisnes*—supra, Ch. XI, p. 237.

their foolish simpering sisters who fell in love with French knights in the poems of the decadent period.[1] There is as little trace of courtesy towards women in the earlier poems as there is of chivalry between Christian and heathen. Both these features developed in the course of the twelfth century, and the result was to change completely the nature of the poems and to turn the rough-hewn, masculine epic of the earlier period into courtly romance.

[1] Cf. *Guibert d'Andrenas*, etc.

CHAPTER IX

THE TRAITOR AND HIS PUNISHMENT

WHEN Guillaume was describing the Day of Judgment in the *Couronnement de Louis* and emphasizing the fact that all would be equal there and no one could help anyone else, he finished with the statement: 'Nuls om traïtres n'i aura guarison'. In the course of his long prayer he had just mentioned Judas who had betrayed his Lord and had received the punishment due to him. Judas was, of course, the stock example of a traitor and, although in French secular literature Ganelon took his place, it is impossible to think of Ganelon among the twelve peers of Charlemagne without being reminded of Judas among the twelve apostles. Here, then, was a spiritual genealogy and, until the craze for physical lineage and family associations invaded the Old French epic, this was quite enough to stamp the traitor as a lost soul for ever: *Guenes li fel* was a successful rival of *Judas le felon*. It would be superfluous to dwell further on the case of Ganelon, which has been discussed in a previous chapter, except in so far as it throws light on the conception of what constituted treason at the period when his name became synonymous with the term. The author of the *Chanson de Roland* was in no doubt as to the nature of Ganelon's crime, and it is not till the very end of the poem that a clever argument nearly saved Ganelon from the judgment he deserved. But the result of the 'combat judiciaire' proved that Thierri was right when he declared that:

> Guenes est fels d'iço qu'il le traït,
> Vers vos s'en est parjurez e malmis.[1]

Ganelon had broken his oath, his *fidem inviolabilem* ('s'est parjurez') and had harmed his lord ('Vers vos s'en est . . . malmis') besides having injured[2] his peer Roland whilst he was in the emperor's service. Thierri was therefore just in giving his judgment:

> Porço le juzjo (juge) a pendre et a murir
> Si cume fel ki felonie fist.

Ganelon was a double-dyed traitor, although it was generally his treachery towards his brother-in-arms Roland that is insisted on in later poems. He had betrayed Roland to the heathen King Marsilie,

---

[1] *Chanson de Roland*, ll. 3829–30.   [2] forsfesist, l. 3827.

thus causing his death and thereby bringing loss to the emperor. For this reason he was judged 'a modo de traïtor'.[1]

Fulbert de Chartres, in a letter to William, Duke of Aquitaine, expounding the relations of a vassal to his lord in the year 1020, describes the obligations of the man who had sworn fidelity to his lord—obligations which he always ought to have in mind. Amongst these are two which bear specially on the cases of treachery which come before us in the Old French epic poems: (1) '*ne sit domino in damnum de corpore suo*', and (2) '*ne id bonum quod dominus suus leviter facere poterat, faciat ei difficile, ne id quod possibile erat, reddat ei impossibile*'. Either of these infractions of his obligations to his seigneur would have condemned Ganelon and any of his so-called 'parenté'. In the famous passage of *Girart de Viane* quoted above[2] the second or traitor 'geste' is attributed to Doon, 'cil de Maience' who became the ancestor of a formidable lineage amongst which was to be found Ganelon 'qui . . . fist la grant felonie' and many 'chevaliers barons' of great renown, who would have been lords of France had it not been for the pride and treachery which caused their downfall, just as it had that of the wicked angels who were cast out of heaven. It will be noted from this that the so-called traitors were not thought of as contemptible villains, cowards, or men of low degree. Like Ganelon, about whom the author of *Roland* is not sparing in his praise, who was a handsome knight with a devoted following, these relations of his ('li parent Ganelon', as the author calls them), were men of courage and authority and would have ruled France had they not been full of pride and envy. This description might easily lead to some confusion and did so in some of the later poems and chronicles. It might be applied to the rebellious barons who fought against the emperor and caused both king and country untold harm. But these unruly subjects had in almost every case suffered grievous injustice at the hands of their sovereign. Isembart, Raoul de Cambrai, Girart de Roussillon, and Girart de Viane had legitimate grounds for renouncing their allegiance and turning against their former lord. They were rebels who defied their lord, but not technically traitors because the sovereign had a duty towards his subjects and the obligations of *auxilium* and *consilium* between lord and vassal were reciprocal. When Charlemagne is handing over the crown to his son in the *Couronnement de Louis*, he tells him not to be offended by a poor man's claim: '*Ainceis le deit aidier et consilier*', and among the instructions given occurs the warning never to commit a treasonable act towards anyone

---

[1] Cf. Macaire, l. 23.   [2] Cf. Ch. II.

('Ne traïson vers nului ne ferez'), for in so doing he would become *malefidus* or *foi-menti*. We find the same idea expressed in *Ogier le Danois*, where the emperor is told frankly that he himself has committed an act of treachery:

> Traï l'aves par vo grant coardie,
> Come traïtres li as ta foi mentie (ll. 5441–2).

But it is natural that the more frequent occurrence of treason should be that committed by a vassal against his 'seigneur'.

Apart from the case of Ganelon, perhaps the best examples of treachery are to be found in the *Couronnement*, where we have the rather stock example of an ambitious man who hopes to take advantage of a weak, youthful king, to seize the power for himself. The scene is well known: the emperor, by the mouth of the archbishop, had announced his intention of handing over the crown to his son; his loyal subjects rejoiced that they were not to have an outsider (*estrange rei*) thrust upon them. But the feeble youth hung back and Charlemagne was so angry that he abused him coarsely, declared that he should be tonsured and put into the church to ring the bells, and receive a pittance so as not to have to beg. Here was the opportunity for the traitor to put himself forward. Up sprang Arneis d'Orliens who was sitting by the king's side and made the hypocritical suggestion that, as it would be the death of the boy even if anyone were to knight him, he himself should govern the kingdom for three years, at the end of which time he would hand it over to Louis if he had proved himself capable of inheriting it. Charlemagne agreed to this; all the relations of Arneis were rejoiced and thanked the king with their flattering tongues, and the traitor would have become king at once had not Guillaume, the loyal subject and the arch-enemy of all traitors, appeared on the scene. He had heard the news from his faithful squire Bertrand and, girding on his sword, he rushed to the church. The whole scene is so characteristic of Guillaume in action that it is worth recalling. He strode into the church, broke through the crowd of knights, and finding Arneis already prepared for his new rôle, was just about to sever his head from his body when he remembered that it was a mortal sin to shed blood in a church, so he thrust his sword back in its sheath. Nothing daunted, however, rolling up his sleeves, he pushed his way forward, seized the traitor by the hair with his left hand ('le poing senestre li a meslé el chief') and with his right hand dealt him such a blow on the neck that he killed him outright. Then, according to the custom of those days he added

words to his deeds: 'He! Gloz!' dist il, 'Deus te doinst encombrier!'
'What did you mean by betraying your rightful lord whom you
ought to have loved and cherished?' Later on in the same poem
Louis is in trouble again from members of the traitor stock.[1] This
time it is Duke Richart, the father of Acelin, who has plotted against
the young king. The affair is urgent as he is just about to have his son
crowned in the church. A porter, loyal to the real king's cause, gives
due warning to Guillaume of what is about to happen, and he once
again arrives on the scene in the nick of time. It is noticeable that the
porter, who has been serving in a subordinate capacity under the
traitor, acts strictly within the feudal framework in presenting his
glove and making a formal challenge (*defi*) to his former master
before acting on Guillaume's behalf, thus guarding against any
accusation of treachery on his own part. He is then free to give
Guillaume all possible help against the traitors.[2] Guillaume acts
promptly. In view of the numbers of those supporting the traitor
(amongst whom, sad to say, are priests and canons, bishops and
abbots) he disposes his forces carefully before he goes and kneels down
in church to pray for the safety of Louis. A monk who recognized
him came and touched him on the shoulder and informed him that
all those 'qi por aveir ont le mal plait basti'—in other words, the
traitors—are assembled in the Church of St. Martin, and promised
that he himself would be responsible for the sin incurred if Guillaume
would go and kill them all in church—'car il sont tuit traïtor et failli'.[3]
Guillaume laughed heartily and replied: 'Blessings on the head of
such a monk as you', but he retained his scruples as to murder in the
cathedral and, having rescued Louis, instead of killing his opponents
by the sword he had them all driven out of the church by sticks and
blows, and when they had all been chased or dragged out by force
he commended them to eighty devils:

> Qui traïson vuelt faire a seignorage
> Il est bien dreiz que il i ait damage (ll. 1774–6).

The case was rather a difficult one as most of the pretender's supporters in this uprising were churchmen. 'Give me your advice', said
Guillaume to his knights: 'Just because a man is tonsured and reads
the lessons in church, ought he to be allowed to commit treason for
the sake of gain?'[4] 'By no means, Sire' replied his knights; 'he ought
to be hung like a common thief'. On this counsel Guillaume felt free

---

[1] 'Le lignage Alori' (l. 1499).   [2] l. 1614.
[3] l. 1699.   [4] ll. 1749–50.

to act, and having killed or taken prisoner all the traitors' adherents he turns to Acelin himself:

> Traître lerre, li cors Deu te confonde !
> Por quei faiseies ton dreit seignor tel honte?
> Richarz tes pere ne porta onc corone (ll. 1913–16).

'How shall we kill him?' he asks his nephew. Bertrand replies by drawing his sword to cut off the man's head, but Guillaume stops him. 'God forbid that he should die by the sword of a valiant knight', said he, and, not deigning to touch the traitor with any of his weapons, he snatched a stake from a nearby palisade and struck him with it so violently that Acelin fell dead at his feet.

> Einsi deit on traïtor justicier,
> Qui son seignor vuelt traïr et boisier.

Guillaume had one more affray with a traitor before his strenuous years described in the *Couronnement de Louis* were over. Acelin's father, Richard, after making 'une feinte paix' with Guillaume, ambushed him on a journey through his land and threatened his life by superior numbers. Once again, however, Guillaume was victorious and had the traitor at his mercy. He would not grant him a soldier's death, but had the wounded man bound, put on a horse and taken to Orleans where he handed him over to the king. Richard languished for a while in a dungeon and then died miserably. Such was the end of traitors whether they be of noble blood or no. Charlemagne, old aristocrat that he was, warned his son against making a 'vilan', or the son of a magistrate or a functionary (*veier*), his counsellor for they would betray him for gain.[1] But dukes and counts were no more immune from committing treachery (Richard was Duke of Normandy) than men of lower rank. When Richard was setting a trap to catch Guillaume, his knights warn him that the citizens of the town would not allow it, and they add: 'Traïson n'est pas bone a comencier'. Guillaume himself was scrupulous if his loyalty to his lord was at stake. When he was obliged to leave Rome hastily in response to King Louis' urgent appeal for help, he abandoned his affianced bride without a murmur; when, however, the broadminded Pope suggested that he should leave Rome to be governed in his absence by Galafre, the emir who had embraced Christianity after his defeat, Guillaume was indignant, for such a transfer of responsibility was not within his right and would have been contrary to his duty as a vassal. It would have been

---

[1] l. 208.

detracting from the royal authority. 'You speak folly', he said; 'I have never yet been guilty of treason, nor do I mean to be now.'

It is clear from the above examples taken from the *Couronnement* that the function of a traitor was to betray (traïr) or to injure (boisier) his lord. There is no reference to Ganelon in the poem although the disaster of Roncevaux and the fate of the twelve peers is recalled. There is an allusion in a rather doubtful line[1] to the 'lignage Alori' which, from the context, is evidently a family of traitors; but the families or *gestes* were not yet constituted to anything like the same extent as we find in the poems of later date, the only one of importance to be mentioned being the 'lignage Aimeri', famous for its numerical strength as well as its loyalty and courage. Guillelmes sees such a large company of nephews and other relations coming to his assistance at one point that the author remarks:

> Tant buer fu nez qui plenté a d'amis (l. 1486).

This gave him a strong position against the wiles of any traitor and strengthened him in his loyalty.

It is in the poem *Garin le Lorrain* that we are introduced to a group of traitors whose names became almost synonymous with treachery in the Old French epic and whose actions give us a very clear idea of what constituted felony, or treason, in the state of society which the poem reflects. It has been noted in a previous chapter that this poem belongs to a group of 'chansons' which, although not very archaic in form, present a feudal state of society as yet unaffected either by religious revival or chivalrous ideals, and are consequently a valuable source of information about early customs and modes of thought. Although the subject is the feud between two rival clans or families, yet the relationships and obligations between vassals and their lord form just as important a part of the narrative as those between rival landowners. The two families may almost be taken as representing good and evil respectively for the Lorrainers are consistently loyal, brave, and generous (an occasional act of brutality was in keeping with the manners of the times)—whereas the Bordelais were almost as consistently treacherous and self-seeking, though not lacking in physical courage. They are nearly all closely related—Hardré, of whom we hear first, was the father of Fromont and Bernart de Naisil, the most contemptible of the group, was his uncle. As usual, it is rather difficult to distinguish between all the cousins and their respective uncles. In the early part of the poem which is occupied

[1] l. 1499.

with the inroads of the Vandals during the reign of Charlemagne, the king is supported, and his battles against 'la gent Mahon' are fought by the powerful baron Hervi de Metz, who inspires such fear into the heathen by his enormous strength and courage, that on their return to their headquarters they take back the report that the devil has fought against them and conquered them. But Charles Martel died, and Hervi, having summoned the princes, had his son Pepin crowned at St. Denis.

Many of the barons, so the poem tells us, were against the coronation, and Hervi, to strengthen the hands of the young king, commended him to the care of Hardré until such time as he himself should return from looking after his own affairs. Hardré accepted the charge and Hervi departed after giving practical advice to Charles' widow not to grieve unduly:

> En grant duel faire onques gaigner ne vis;
> Duel sor dolor, ne joie sor joir,
> Home ne fame ne le doit maintenir.

Shortly after this Hervi took to himself a wife who bore him his two famous sons Garin and Bègue, and seven daughters who were responsible for the nephews who play such a part subsequently in the poem. But Hervi was not allowed to remain long in a state of conjugal bliss, for the Hongrois invaded Gaul, devastated the countryside, and laid siege to Metz. Hervi was obliged to send to King Pepin for help. The king was at Laon (called Mont-Loon in the poem) with Hardré and Amauri, and now the true character of Hardré displays itself, for, as the author says:

> 'N'ot plus felon, jusqu'a l'esve del Rin,
> Cil les destruie qui confondit Caïn !'[1]

The scene which follows is reminiscent of a similar one in the *Couronnement de Louis*. The weak king consulted his counsellors Hardré, Heudon, and Amauri (of whom the author again remarks: 'N'ot si felons en soisante païs'); Count Hardré advised him to take no action in the matter as his land was still lying waste from his war with Girart de Roussillon and Hervi was powerful and had many friends. Thus Hardré, in pretending to serve his king, proved a false friend to the man who had raised him to the position he held and was branded as a felon. Nevertheless, when Hervi's two handsome sons Garin and Bègue came to court and were well received by the king, he was glad for his own two sons Fromont and Guillaume to

[1] Ed. Paulin Paris, Vol. I, p. 52.

be associated with them and become their youthful companions. The king had an affection for them all, but his special friend was the little Bègue who became his page. Eventually the king gave Bègue a rich gift:

Tote Gascoigne li dona a tenir.

Many were envious of him but most of all Hardré, who was both grieved and angry, and the jealousy in his heart increased, thus paving the way for the acts of teachery that were to follow. For history repeated itself. King Pepin was appealed to for help against another Saracen invasion and once again dejectedly turned to his counsellors for advice. After a short consultation, Hardré, the most evil man in Pepin's kingdom, spoke for them all. He reminded Pepin how his father, Charles Martel, had fought many battles against Girard de Roussillon; had made many widows and orphans, and had impoverished his kingdom. 'Winter will pass', said he, 'April will come again, and our good horses will have grass to feed upon. Then we will go to the help of the besieged if they can hold out till then'. Garin was indignant at such villainy and wickedness ('villenie et grant pechié') and he and Bègue with their two young companions went to court and obtained leave from the king to go to the help of King Thierry without the assistance of the old ones ('les barbés / Qui le sejor aiment et repouser'). Hardré was angry, but even his own son Fromont blamed him and permission was given, to their great joy, and many young men were knighted in advance. One more attempt was made by Hardré to stop the expedition. King Pepin, who accompanied it himself, was taken seriously ill, and Hardré had already given orders for all to return to their own homes when Garin took matters into his own hands. He forced his way to the king's bedchamber, diagnosed Pepin's complaint as an ulcer, and declared he would be well by the morrow. Thus Hardré's order was annulled and the expedition set out again. Hardré's motive throughout was self-aggrandisement and not solicitude for the king, who would have suffered loss in his person and his domain, had he not actively resisted the enemy from without. Hence his action fell within the category of perfidy, for he was not acting in accordance with his oath of fidelity and was rightly included in after times amongst the stock list of traitors and enrolled in the family of Ganelon.[1]

In the poem we are studying the question of heredity is paramount. During the very expedition which Hardré had tried to suppress, the tendency to unfaithfulness and disloyalty becomes apparent in his

[1] Cf. *Ph. Mousket Chronique*, ll. 8457 f.

own son. Garin and Bègue were in command of the royalist army; Fromont and the other young men had assured them of their support: 'Commandez-nos, ferons ce que vourez'. Soon, however, a difference of opinion arose. At Garin's suggestion a party was sent out to reconnoitre the enemy position and assess their strength. The party consisted of Fromont, his uncle Bernart de Naisil, Bègue, and one or two others. Bernart's immediate advice was: 'Ralons-nous-en en cest nostre païs / Folie fut quant nous vinmes ici', so familiar to us as the reaction of the less noble knights when they saw, before the battle, the strength of the enemy. Fromont agreed with his uncle, but Bègue answered indignantly: 'Or avez-vous mal dit', and insisted that they should ride straightway against the foe, whereupon Fromont replied that he preferred to listen to his uncle and he refused to accompany the army. This amounted to breaking his oath and Garin warns him:

> 'Vous dites mal', ce dit li dux Garins:
> 'Mes compains estes et jurés et plevis
> Et li rois a et commandé et dit
> Que vos fassiez del tout a mon plaisir.'

Fromont refused to change his mind and withdrew from the field, though he was warned by Garin that, if the enemy were beaten, he would receive none of the spoil, and Garin kept his word although Fromont came back after the battle was over under the pretence that he had come in the hope of putting the Saracens to flight. The episode is interesting as an example of the serious relationship between brothers-in-arms. Fromont had 'faussé son serment' to Garin just as much as if he had been disloyal to the king.

This was the beginning of the breach between the two rival families, and after this original display of disloyalty, as may be imagined, Fromont goes from bad to worse. King Thierry, in aid of whom the expedition under Garin had originally started out, was unfortunately mortally wounded in the battle. On his deathbed he called Garin to him and bequeathed to him his land and his daughter in return for his protection. Garin accepted the offer on condition that the emperor gave his permission ('se le me loue l'empereres Pepins') according to the feudal custom, and he was formally affianced to her. On the return of the army to Mont-Loon, Garin reported the victory to the king and mentioned the bequest made to him by the dying Thierry. 'I grant it gladly', replied Pepin; 'no honour is too great for you who have served me so well as all my people will witness'. This was overheard by Fromont who was standing by, and he nearly burst with anger. 'I forbid this, King', he shouted in his fury ('moult felenessement'); 'you promised me the next fief that fell vacant and I claim this one for it suits me well'. With unusual courage the king replied boldly: 'You have no claim at all; when a father makes a gift to his child (in this case the daughter), the child cannot lose it even by a decree of court. If another fief falls vacant, you shall have it'. Then Garin answered Fromont without anger: 'You were my companion-in-arms and I loved you dearly. You and your relatives deserted me in the battle, but in spite of that, had you told me before that you would like for yourself the maiden and the land, I would have given up my right. But now I see that pride and "felonie" have caused your action and I would not give you a jot or tittle of my possessions'. Bitter accusations followed on both sides in which the word traitor was bandied about, and at last Garin, after taunting Fromont with his lineage, for an ancestor of his had murdered his 'signor-lige', gave a formal challenge to Fromont and his kith and kin in respect of the town of Soissons which had been wrongfully snatched from his own cousin Beranger. Garin ended with an accusation and a threat:

'Se vous i truis et au deseur en vieng.
Je vous trairai a m'espee le chief;
Ensi doit-on traïtor chastoier
Qu'a tort honnist son signor droiturier'.[1]

Guillaume d'Orange would have considered that even this treatment was too good for a traitor, but the words made Fromont furious and he rushed at Garin. Garin felled him at a blow and a general mêlée followed. At this point Hardré appears on the scene again. The king was young and helpless—no one took the slightest notice of him. But Hardré, hearing the noise and, presumably, guessing the reason for it, seized a sword 'un brant d'acier' (although the other knights would be unarmed as the affair took place in the king's palace. Hence the author's remark: 'Li glous le prent'), rushed with his followers into the hall and decapitated fourteen of Garin's men. Garin, pinned into a corner, snatched up one of the fire-irons with which to defend himself, but was in imminent danger of losing his life as Hardré pressed in on him sword in hand, thirsting for his blood. Garin would certainly have been killed, but God also had an obligation towards a loyal subject and He did not permit it:

Mais Dieu ne plot, ne la soie pitié;
Ja n'iert honis eui Diex veut bien aidier.

[1] Ed. Paulin Paris, Vol. I, p. 130.

The rescue was effected by one of Garin's nephews, Hernaut d'Orliens, a noble and vigorous man (no 'vilain bergier'), who appeared at this opportune moment with 7,000 knights well armed and mounted. The tables were soon turned as, when Hernaut heard what was happening, he immediately shouted to his men in a spirit of true family loyalty: 'Or avant, chevalier!... Cis est mes oncles, je ne le dois laissier'. In a moment the palace was besieged, the doors broken open, Hardré's men routed, and Hardré himself stretched dead on the floor. Most of the dead bodies were just thrown out of the palace, but traitor Hardré's corpse was hurled into a ditch.

Thus ended a double-dyed traitor who had consistently given the king bad advice ('domino in damnum de corpore suo') and had tried his utmost to harm the king's loyal barons ('qui vous ont moult servi de cuer entier'). But there was more behind it than this, for the poem alludes to an act of treachery in the past when Hardré had betrayed Pepin's father during the war that he waged against Girart de Roussillon. His whole lineage was tainted ('Ainc ses linages au votre n'obeit') and his name became a byword. His son Fromont carried on the tradition for his next intrigue, when he saw that it was hopeless to try and carry off the princess who had been allotted to Garin, was to marry without the king's permission a wife who would secure his position among the barons—the sister of Baudouin de Flandres, who had recently lost her husband. When the suggestion was first made to Fromont he welcomed it at once, but added that on no account was Pepin to hear of it for he would never consent to the marriage.[1] So the marriage was contracted secretly and hastily consummated lest the news should reach the ears of the king. No wonder, after this act of disloyalty, that the son born from this union (Fromondin) caused much damage later to the cause of Garin's family. Fromont himself went from bad to worse, for we learn later in the poem that he deserted the king's cause altogether, denied Jesus Christ, and joined the army of the Saracens. This, however, is anticipating, for Fromont's intrigues are not yet ended.

The next traitor to appear upon the scene from amongst this veritable nest of traitors is Bernart de Naisil. Although he did not attain to the same sinister reputation in the Old French epic traditions, he is one of the vilest characters of this disloyal family. It will be remembered that he was one of the little group who, when the extent of the enemy army was discovered, valued their personal safety more than the peace and prosperity of the country. Now the

[1] Ed. Paulin Paris, Vol. II, p. 151.

opportunity had arrived for him to indulge his restless thieving instincts. On the death of his father, Hardré, Fromont had besieged Garin's nephew, Hues de Cambrai, in St. Quentin as an act of reprisal. Garin appealed to the king for help in resisting the treacherous action on the ground that by marrying without the king's consent, and now by besieging Cambrai and laying waste the land, Fromont and his new relations were trying to rob the king of all his possessions ('*trestoute honor tollir*'). This constituted an act of treason, and Garin insisted that the king should not merely denounce Fromont but summon his whole army to frustrate his designs ('*ensi doit rois son roiaume tenir*').

The king followed this advice and sent out his messengers (even the cooks and the wine-bottlers were pressed into the service), and a large army was assembled at Laon. Fromont, on his side, sent an urgent message for help to his uncle, Bernart de Naisil, who was delighted at an opportunity for displaying his valour and improving his somewhat shady reputation, for had he not counselled retreat on a former occasion and forfeited the fruits of victory! Without delay, for a good warrior must not be caught napping ('*Qui bien guerroie, ne l'estuet pas dormir*'), he crossed into Garin's own territory and began to lay the country waste. Having seized everything of value he could lay hands upon, he distributed the booty and led his jubilant army by forced marches into the land of Auberi de Bourgogne (another of Garin's nephews), and laid siege to Dijon. Meanwhile the king had summoned Bègue to join his forces. Bègue was at his fortress of Belin, living unsuspiciously amongst his enemies, for news of Hardré's death had not reached him. Having learnt the truth, he slipped out of the palace away from his former friends, summoned his own adherents and started to join the king's army. On the way thither an urgent messenger arrived from Auberi, who, as we have seen, was besieged by Bernard ('Li lerres de Neisil') in Dijon. This put Bègue in a dilemma—was he to proceed on his way and join the king's army, or was he to be deflected from his course and go to his nephew's assistance? In true feudal fashion he put the case to his counsellors who could be depended upon to give him '*conseil . . . bon et leal et fin*', for his followers were like himself. It is obvious that this was quite a difficult question to have to decide, and it gives us a good example of how the obligation of '*consilium*' functioned amongst loyal knights. 'Listen to me', said Duke Bègue, 'warfare is in progress in France and Pepin has sent for me, but Auberi of Bourgogne is in great straits; I know not how to decide between

these two rival claims. What is your decision, my loyal friends?'
No one spoke for a moment, then Hervi (surnamed '*li vilain*') arose
and answered respectfully but characteristically: 'My advice is, so it
please you, that you do not go to France to help King Pepin, for he
and Garin both have many supporters; but that you go speedily to
the help of Auberi for he has but few friends. When the fighting is
over in his country, then you can go to France and join the great
King Pepin.' All were unanimous in endorsing this advice and the
army set off. There were many ups and downs in the war after this,
sometimes one side winning a temporary advantage, sometimes the
other. At last King Pepin, who was weary of the desolation which
was being brought upon the country, sent a stern message to Fromont
to come and make amends ('droit faire') for the disloyalty and aggres-
sion of which he had been guilty:

> 'Fromons', dist il (the messenger), 'Pepins m'envoie ci
> Et si te mande que ta foi as menti;
> Sans son congié que tu as fame prins,
> Par ton orguel as son baron assis.'

If Fromont refuses he will be treated as a 'foimenti' and an outlaw
with not a corner of land where he can rest. But Fromont still defied
the king and the war continued—'Dont mainte dame en remaint
sans mari'. Finally, however, Bernart de Naisil was taken prisoner
and an uneasy peace was made by which Bernart's stronghold of
Naisil was restored to him in exchange for the possessions he had
taken from Auberi ('*les pertes Auberi*').

The most glaring example of a traitor's rôle was still to come,
however. The Princess Blanchefleur had been promised and affianced
to Garin. By a disgraceful ruse on the part of Fromont and an
unscrupulous archbishop, the banns were stopped on the grounds of
'parenté' and the easily-swayed king was persuaded to take her to
wife himself. At this point Bernart de Naisil stands out in all his
meanness and cunning. Garin, with a disinterested display of courtesy
and loyalty, admitted the distant relationship and refused to quarrel
with Bernart on the subject. But Fromont and his friends continued
to conspire in an effort to win the well-endowed princess for one of
their party. The archbishop saw the conspirators with heads together
and pointed it out to the king: 'If you do not make haste, emperor,
you will lose Blanchefleur after all'. So the king wedded her quickly
and she was crowned at Paris. Thus Bernart was defeated in this last
attempt to score a point off Garin, but he determined to try once
more to detract him in the eyes of the king. He was filled with envy

when he saw Garin serving the king with wine at the wedding feast, and in his mad jealousy he tried to snatch the cup from his hands. Garin treated him humorously at first: 'Do you want to drink, Sir Bernart?' said he; 'I can give you some better wine than this'. But Bernart was not in joking mood and pulled hard at the cup. Garin could not stand this and gave him such a blow with the cup that he cut off his hair and his eyebrow. Then the mêlée began. They fought with everything they could lay hands on. Bègue, who was superintending the feast, called up the cooks and the kitchen-boys who gave a good account of themselves with pestles and mortars, ladles and spits. Fromont's followers were driven from the palace, and in the hasty exit Fromont's son was killed by a blow on the head from 'uns povres gars qu'ot les mustiax rostis'. Fromont himself and Bernart and others of their party were caught and imprisoned by the king. Things had now become so desperate for Bernart and his party that an even viler plot was hatched. The idea came, as might be expected, from Bernart. 'We will soon get out of this prison', said he to Fromont. 'I will tell the king that Garin intends to murder him on account of the queen from whom he has been parted. I will swear that he promised Blanchefleur to you for your brother Guillaume and received a bribe of sixty marks of pure gold. If he denies it, either "Isoré le gris" or myself will undertake the proof against him and by this means we will escape and get back to our own lands'. This bold suggestion was carried out. Bernart obtained an audience with the king and accused Garin of having threatened his life because of Blanchefleur, and alleged this as his reason for his attack on Garin. The king was horrified to hear such a thing about Garin whom, as he said, he loved more than anyone else in his kingdom. Garin was immediately sent for and confronted with Bernart, who repeated his accusation before several others. 'You lie', declared Garin; 'if any man dared accuse me of having said such a thing, I would make him take back his words before the sun was up'. Then Bernart called upon Isoré to make his statement and Isoré made a formal challenge and offered his pledge ('*gage*') which was supported by his family and his friends. Garin did the same, but the weak, ungrateful king refused to recognize his hostages, to which Garin replied: 'If my kith and kin fail me now I shall never go forth to fight the Saracens again'. A messenger went and told Bègue what had happened to his brother. Without even stopping to put on his cloak Bègue hastened to the palace and asked angrily why his brother had been treated in this way. 'So help me, God', he cried, 'I hold nothing from Garin, nor any portion of my dear father Hervi's inheritance, so no court can prevent me from standing guarantee for my brother'. All agreed that he could take up the pledge and fight on behalf of Garin, so the pledges were exchanged and all made ready for the trial by combat. An interesting description follows of the preparations and formalities in connection with the duel which was about to take place, for it was a case of perjury and treason—both equally serious in the eyes of God. Bègue was full of confidence for he knew his cause was just and therefore his opponent was doomed for: 'Hons desloiaus ne puet longes garir'. Bernart was not unnaturally seized with sudden fear for his champion and suggested to the emperor that a day should be fixed when both sides could come together and a reconciliation take place. Bègue would have none of it and replied indignantly:

> 'Il ont de murte ci apellé Garin;
> De traïson ne doit on plait tenir'.

So the preparations for the combat continued. Isoré swore on the holy relics that Garin was guilty of treason towards the king, and Bègue took up the gauntlet (or, as the Old French puts it: 'took him up') on the score of perjury. The battle took place amidst tremendous excitement. It lasted for hours and each in turn gave and took tremendous blows. At last Isoré began to falter, and when his nephew Guillaume shouted to him to cut off his opponent's head, he replied: 'You don't know what you are talking about—you are not beneath my shield. Rather go and beg King Pepin to take pity on us both'. Bègue had been unhorsed and had broken his sword, but he remembered the spare sword that the knights always carried attached to their saddle-bows, and drew it from the prostrate horse. He himself was badly wounded in head and chest, but he managed to deal Isoré another blow on his helmet which clove through everything and struck him dead to the earth. He was so incensed against the man who had just clamoured for his head that he tore the heart from the body and threw it in Guillaume's face. 'Take this', he shouted—'your cousin's heart, and have it salted and roasted'. It was brutal, but he had received great provocation and they were wild times.

Thus ended the man who had perjured himself and thereby become a traitor in accusing a loyal vassal of treachery. In the royal city the rejoicing was great; the queen was overcome with joy and the bells were rung, and Bègue took measures to get healed of his wounds. Bernart retired in dudgeon to his fortress of Naisil like a fox to his

N

den ('*Renart resemble qu'en la taisniere est mis*'). We need not follow
Bernart in his later activities. He was a menace to the countryside—
he is a *lerres* (thief), a *briseur de chemins, le viex traître, parjuré, foi-menti*;
he never kept an oath, and the last we hear of him is when he shot an
arrow at Bègue's back as he left the castle after a reconciliation had
taken place between the rival forces. And yet, like Ganelon and other
traitors, he was a worthy opponent-in-arms and certainly no coward.
On one occasion the author of the poem tells us:

> Bernars fu preus, de grant nobilité;
> Bien le sachiez, s'il eüst loiauté,
> N'eüst meillor en trestout le regné.

In most of the cases we have examined the traitors were not
altogether bad, but a mixture in which the bad predominated and
the good was buried under layers of pride, jealousy, spite, and
unscrupulousness which kept it effectually smothered. Nevertheless,
they had natural affections like other men, and were generally willing
to risk anything for the good or advancement of their own kith and
kin. The rather mysterious Isoré le Gris definitely had his good
moments (like Raoul de Cambrai), where he confessed himself in
the wrong and refused to fight against a former benefactor. But he,
too, was drawn into the evil faction and died trying to defend a
perjured man.

The traitors discussed in the foregoing section belonged to the class
of turbulent barons who were not necessarily in rebellion against
their sovereign, but transgressed against the moral code of their epoch
by their behaviour one to another. Like Ganelon, they were traitors
because they sought to injure loyal subjects of the king and in so
doing injured the king himself. They were of equally noble birth
as their opponents and sometimes there was an element of ill-fortune
which accounted for the fact that they so often found themselves on
the side of opposition to the king's interests. A far more ignoble type
was what one might designate a 'traître de profession'—the kind of
traitor who had a grievance against no one in particular, who always
tried to catch the ear of his lord and was ready to perform any
dastardly deed for the sake of gain. It was traitors such as these who
offered to assassinate Bueve d'Aigremont in the poem *Renaud de
Montauban*, with whom the emperor had just made peace, and it is
characteristic of the degenerate character of Charlemagne in the later
poems that he agrees to the proposal: 'Kill him', he says, 'and I will
pay you well'. In accounts of sieges there is often a traitor ready to

obtain the keys of the city for the enemy—such as the rôle of 'Hervi de Lousanne' in the same poem who plots to hand over to the emperor the stronghold in which the four sons of Aymon have fortified themselves. He is described in the poem as 'li cuivers renoiés / Qui en liu de Judas fu laiens herbergiés'.[1] The sons of Aymon were rebels against the emperor, but never would they have been capable of a mean action and their behaviour throughout is in striking contrast to that of Charlemagne.

All these traitors had generally had a common ancestor in Judas or Ganelon. In the somewhat isolated poem *Aiol* (which will be discussed in a later chapter) the relations of Ganelon were numerous, and Hardré was joined with him in being responsible for a large and degenerate clan:

> Plus furent de .L. d'un parenté,
> Des neveus Guenelon et de Hardré,
> Et des parens Makaire le desfaé.[2]

The mention of Makaire in the last line of this passage brings us to another traitor who made his mark on Old French literature, not so much on his own account, but on that of his opponent in the 'trial by combat'; this was no member of a rival family, or loyal subject of the king, but a faithful hound. The poem which introduces us to this particularly vile type of traitor has been published under the name of *Macaire* (by Guessard), although in the version which has come down to us the traitor bears the name of Macario, for the poem is in a barbarous form of Italian similar to that in which a number of Old French epic poems has been preserved to posterity. In all probability a French version of the story in the customary decasyllabic metre formed the basis of our poem. The author was well acquainted with the Old French epic heroes of the different cycles. He mentions Roland and Oliver and their betrayal and death. He tells us how Charlemagne toiled and suffered all his life to maintain Christianity, never listening to foolish counsel (conseio d'infan), but fighting the heathen and inspiring them with dread all his life, till after more than two hundred years Guillaume and Bertrand appeared on the scene to carry on the struggle. But the story he relates has nothing to do with these valiant heroes and their kith and kin. It is Ganelon and his family—'ceux de Mayence (qui de Magan)'—who interest him and constitute the background for the arch-traitor of the poem and his wicked deeds. It is obvious from the allusion to Mayence that the

---

[1] *Renaud de Montauban*, Ed. Michelant, p. 70, ll. 13–14.
[2] *Aiol*, Ed. Soc. d. a.t. ll. 4438 f.

author is familiar also with the cyclic framework into which all the heroes of the earlier poems are pressed, probably at the end of the twelfth century or beginning of the thirteenth. Doon de Mayence, as we have seen, was an ancestor invented by the 'jongleurs' to introduce a certain unity into the family of traitors and bring it into correspondence with the existing 'gestes' of the emperor and Aymeri de Narbonne. Thus Ganelon, the hoary traitor, became one of the notorious gang who never ceased to cause trouble—who waged war incessantly on Renaut de Montauban and betrayed Roland and Oliver:

> Senpre avoit guere cun Rainaldo da Mote Alban,
> Et si trai Oliver e Rolan,
> E li doçe pere e ses compagna gran.[1]

Now it was the emperor's wife who became the object of hatred to one of these wicked men—'Li mal Macario, li fel el seduant', who hoped by seducing his wife to harm the emperor himself. When Blanchefleur (as the author of this poem calls the lady who was better known to posterity as 'la reine Sibille') indignantly refused the advances of Macario, she was compromised in the eyes of her husband by the ruse of introducing a dwarf into her bed, to be found there in the morning when the emperor came back from attending matins. The weak king, always listening to the counsel of the flattering Macario and ignoring that of Duke Naime, was persuaded into allowing the sentence of death to be passed on her, and she was about to be burnt alive when the priest, who was struck by the obvious truthfulness of her confession, pleaded for her and the sentence of death was commuted to one of banishment. She was accompanied into banishment by a young knight and his faithful dog. Macario, infuriated by the turn things had taken, pursued the fugitives and killed the knight, but the queen and the hound managed to escape into the forest. Now the loyalty of the animal stands out in contrast to the disloyalty of the treacherous man. The dog kept watch over his master's corpse, till, forced by hunger, he made his way back to Paris where the knights were assembled at their daily repast. Rushing into the hall, he leapt on to the table; perceiving Macario, he sprang upon him, gave him a savage bite, then seized as much bread as he wanted and made off before he could be stopped. This happened several days running until the knights and the emperor began to suspect some foul play. The dog was followed into the forest—the dead knight's body was discovered (the queen had fled) and it was

---

[1] *Macaire*, Ed. Guessard, p. 18.

clear to everyone that the dog's action pointed to the murderer. Charlemagne had Macario brought before him and asked him if he had killed the knight Albaris (Aubri). Macario denied it and offered to prove his innocence by battle, feeling himself safe on account of the number of his relations which made the knights hesitate to take up the challenge—such an advantage was it in those days to belong to a numerous family. 'Take counsel of your knights', was the advice of the wise Duke Naime, and the king did so, encouraging them to have no fear of any man. But still they hesitated for fear of reprisals (Tant dotent la soa segnorie). Then Naime spoke again. He admitted that 'ceux de Mayence' were powerful and honoured and that there was no more numerous clan in the kingdom—'let the one who challenged Macario take him on in this fight', said he. 'Let Macario be provided with a big stick and let him and the dog be brought into the ring and fight it out. . . . If the dog is vanquished, the man can go free, but if Macario gets the worst of it let him be judged 'como traitres et malvasio renoié'. The emperor took his counsellor's advice and the duel was fought amid tremendous enthusiasm. The whole of Paris turned out to watch. One of Macario's relations was at such a pitch of excitement that he broke through the lists and narrowly escaped being hung by the angry crowd on the spot. He fled precipitately, but he did not escape, for he was caught by a peddling cobbler, and handed back to the emperor who had set a price of a thousand pounds on his head. The emperor commanded that he should be first strangled and then burnt—so serious an offence was it to interfere with a 'combat judiciaire'.

The battle between the man and the dog was terrible. The dog bit, the man struck furious blows with his stick. Both were wounded and bleeding, but the struggle lasted till the second day. Macario called in vain upon his relations to help him, but the emperor allowed no one to move from his place. At last the dog leapt at the throat of his opponent and threw him to the ground where he held him in his grip. This was the end of the battle and Macario asked for a priest to hear his confession. The poor man (if we may pity him) could hardly speak, for the dog would not lose his hold on his throat. The priest, who was admitted into the ring to hear his confession, was the same 'abé' who had heard that of the queen, so that he would know whether Macario was speaking the truth. But the crime had been so heinous and the miracle of such a man being vanquished by a dog was so great that the priest insisted on a public confession. Charlemagne and Naime and all the public, good and bad, must be summoned and the sin publicly confessed before the dog could be expected to release his strangle-hold on the man's throat. So, as best he could, Macario confessed the whole story and swore in God's name that he was telling the truth. Then Charlemagne turned to Duke Naime and said: 'What shall we do with such a felon who betrayed my wife by his guile and killed Aubri whom I loved so much?' Naime replied: 'He must be taken and first drawn (*trainé*) through Paris by a strong, swift horse and then burnt. And if any of his relations object, we will do the same to them'. The dog had not yet loosed his grip and could not be moved; but the emperor begged him in an ingratiating voice to let his victim go for love of him. And the dog granted his request as if he had the intelligence of a human. Then Macario was taken, 'drawn' by horses up and down the streets of Paris with all the population, small and great, running after him and abusing him, and then burnt in a large fire which was prepared for him in the open space where the battle had been fought. He was buried by his kith and kin of Mayence who shared in his disgrace, and there the author leaves him with the comment that he received the recompense of his deeds ('Segondo l'ovre n'oït en son loer').

The rest of the poem deals with the terrible war occasioned by the treatment of Blanchefleur between Charlemagne and the emperor of Constantinople, the queen's father. The most interesting and loyal character in this part of the story is that of Varocher, the peasant who had taken pity on the queen in her exile and remained faithful to her throughout, even though in so doing he had to desert his own wife and children. He was knighted and duly rewarded in the end, after fighting a duel with 'Ogier le danois' and many other exploits. The tragedy was that the queen's avengers were fighting against her erstwhile friends. The author of the poem dwells on this sad eventuality which was entirely due to the treachery of Macario and his clan ('qui de Magance') in whom the emperor had placed his confidence and who brought him shame and dishonour. The first of this dangerous family, he insists again, was Gaines (Ganelon) who betrayed the twelve companions in Spain and caused twenty thousand of their followers to be killed. Through Macario an even more regrettable strife had arisen between Christians, which it was not in the power of any man to quell.

The story of Macario and his duel with the dog enjoyed the most extraordinary popularity of perhaps any of the medieval French romances. It struck the popular imagination, not by reason of the villainy of the traitor, but on account of the fidelity and sagacity of the dog. Alberic de Trois Fontaines introduces it into his Latin Chronicle in the thirteenth century (his narrative being based on a slightly different version than that of our poem *Macaire*); the *Menagier de Paris* cites the dog as an example of fidelity to wives in his well-known work written for the instruction of his young wife. Olivier de la Marche (fifteenth century) relates the story in his *Livre des duels*, and about this time it began to be represented in prints and paintings—one of which on the mantelpiece of a hall in the castle of Montargis gave the dog his famous name of the 'Chien de Montargis'. Jules Scaliger thought the dog deserved something even better—that it ought to be executed in bronze! Cretin (at the beginning of the sixteenth century) spoke of the combat between man and dog as being 'de merveilleuse grace'. The story seemed unable to die. It was translated into Spanish prose; an imitation appeared in England under the name of *Sir Triamour* in which the villain Macaire has changed his name to Marrock. In 1814 the French author Guilbert de Pixérécourt wrote a 'melodrame historique' entitled *Le Chien de Montargis* which was staged at the Théatre de la Gaieté and had tremendous success. This was translated into German and put on the stage by the Grand Duke of Saxe Weimar, to the great annoyance of Goethe, who was director of the theatre at that time, as he thought it derogatory to the dignity of a theatre for a dog to appear on the stage.[1]

It is difficult to give any precise dating for the poem we have just been examining. If, as seems probable, it is an Italianized version of an Old French poem, it would probably be not far wrong to consider the original as an example of what might be called the second series of *chansons-de-geste*. It has not the grim seriousness of the earlier poems; the author is acquainted with the older poems, but he also knows versions of Renaut de Montauban and other poems in which the traitor-clan connected with Doon de Mayence play a rôle. He constantly mentions the numerous relations and the powerful following of Macaire as making any resistance against the traitor extremely dangerous. Most of these characters of the 'geste' of Doon de Mayence are to be found again in another poem which also, though not one of the really archaic poems, has not entirely fallen a victim to the romanticizing element which invaded the epic roughly in the second half of the twelfth century, when the genuine epic poems were

[1] All these and many other details of the history of the story of the traitor Macaire and his assailant have been brought together in the interesting preface to his edition of *Macaire* by Guessard, published in 1866.

fighting a losing battle with the elements of romance. The author of *Aiol*, the *chanson-de-geste*, which is one of the few that has broken away from the customary rhythm of the decasyllabic line by placing the pause after the sixth syllable instead of the fourth, has placed the traitor Macaire almost as much in the foreground of his work as the hero Aiol himself. Macaire has not the distinction in this poem of being the only medieval knight known to us who fights a duel with a dog; nor does the author show any sign of having heard such a story about him. In *Aiol* the traitor dies the normal death of the felon. He was attached to the tails of four strong horses, just as Ganelon was, and torn to pieces. He is, moreover, not spoken of as being of Mayence, but is almost always called Macaire de Losane. He is a traitor of the vilest sort—he has the king's ear ('li mavais losengiers') and is always whispering bad advice into it or drawing the king into a corner ('a un recoi') to influence him against some loyal knight—generally Aiol, whose father he had ruined previously in order to obtain his possessions. He has hosts of relations, nephews of Ganelon, of Hardré and himself. His friends bear well-known traitor names such as Bernard, Alori, and Sanse. Aiol treats him with great courtesy, and on one occasion, when his horse has been ridiculed by Macaire, proposes a race between their respective steeds. The race takes place and Macaire's horse is beaten, but its rider refuses to pay the wager which had been agreed upon and is cast into prison. There is nothing too mean for him and in the second part of the poem, which is of later date and more romanesque than the first, he throws Aiol's two sons into the river in his last futile attempt to damage his arch-enemy.

It will be seen from the examples in this chapter that the traitors from Ganelon onwards are all actuated by the same motives: love of gain, jealousy, meanness, and an unscrupulousness which makes them willing to break their oath of allegiance if necessary. They are traitors because they harm their liege-lord either directly, or indirectly through those who serve him, and this is felony. They are types rather than characters, as their characteristics do not change much, and the mere names—Ganelon, Hardré, Fromont, Bernard, Macaire became so familiar that when they were used in the later epic poems to denote a traitor of any description the audience would know at once what to expect. It is interesting to note that the author of the so-called *Pòeme moral*, to which allusion has been made before, gives the name of Hardré to the perjured counsel who is called in by the unjust, avaricious judge to bear false witness against a man of means whom he wishes to ruin.[1] It was for the later poems to sweep all the traitors into one big family or *geste* and later still the family became a faction. We shall see in the chapter dealing with the fate of the Old French epic in Italy how the descendants of Doon de Mayence became the clan of the Maganzi which was constitutionally opposed to the followers of the lords of Clermont (patronymic of Roland's family), much as the family of the Orsini was opposed to that of the Colonni.

[1] *Pòeme moral*, str. 347–8.

CHAPTER X

SOME ISOLATED *CHANSONS-DE-GESTE*

I. *GORMONT ET ISEMBART*

IN spite of the ingenious attempts of the *jongleurs* of the thirteenth century to make all the poems fit into certain categories by unscrupulously forcing the heroes into one or other of the acknowledged *lignages* or *gestes*, there are some which resist all efforts at classification. An independent 'chanson' of this description is the poem, or rather fragment of a poem, generally known under the title of *Gormont et Isembart*. It is true that Walter Map[1] coupled the hero Isembart with Raoul de Cambrai and hinted at a relationship with Ganelon, but Isembart does not really belong either to the ranks of the rebellious barons or the traitors, although he partakes of the features of both, nor is he in any way related to Ganelon. It is true that he transferred his loyalty from one lord to another (which was pardonable under certain circumstances) and abjured the Christian faith (which was unpardonable); but the first of these acts produced a proof of a new loyalty to which he remained true, and the second was atoned for by his repentance and death. The transference of loyalty, as will have been seen from the previous chapter, was fairly common among the pagans who, for reasons either of prudence or a nobler sentiment, became renegades to their religion and embraced the Christian faith. The opposite process is rare. We know from history that it was not an uncommon occurrence in the early days of Islam, but in a period dominated by the Church it was less likely to happen and still less likely to be celebrated in chronicle or in song. It might occur to an author of the thirteenth century to invent a counterpart to the popular *motif* of a heathen princess attracted to a Christian knight by imagining the similar fascination exercised by a noble heathen on a Christian princess. The so-called *Menestral de Reims* relates in his chronicle (or better-named *récits*) how the wife of King Louis of France—the Elinor of evil repute—fell in love with the chivalrous Sultan Saladin from accounts she had heard of his valour. She arranged an elopement, but was caught with one foot in the boat which was to take her to her lover, brought back, and repudiated by her husband. Shortly

---

[1] As we have seen, Ch. IV, p. 48.

after she became the wife of Henry II of England. Such an event, however, was not likely to become a commonplace of epic poetry, as it reflected little credit on the heroic French character. The same would be true in the case of a French knight who for any reason abandoned his country and his faith to become the ally of a heathen invader. A traitor like Fromont in *Garin le Lorrain* might be expected to deny Jesus Christ and join the Saracen forces, or, like Ganelon, to side with the enemy in order to satisfy his own desire for personal vengeance; but these were evil-minded villains whose characters were consistent with their treachery. In the poem we are considering the case is different. The hero is a 'reneiez', a 'renegat', a *margariz* (much the same meaning), and yet in spite of this he is a sympathetic figure, a prey to a clash of loyalties, who inspires us with interest and pity rather than with scorn.

Our fragment, for unfortunately only a fragment of some 660 lines remains to us of the poem, plunges us into the middle of a furious battle between the French and the Saracens which, by an anachronism common to epic traditions, reproduces a real victory of Louis III of France at Saucourt over the Northmen in the year 881. This victory had already been celebrated in an old High German poem (the so-called *Ludwigslied*) of monkish origin which has nothing to do with our poem, but is of interest on account of the contrast it presents between the elongated, alliterative style of the Germanic poem with its solemn religious bias and the ballad-like, almost sprightly character of its French counterpart. What the poems have in common is the heroic character and inherited fighting qualities attributed to the Frankish king. The *rithmus teutonicus* calls the heathen (*heidine man*) who sailed across the sea[1] by their proper name—'Northmen'—and insists on their complete rout by the victorious king in praise of whose valour the author is almost lyrical. But, panegyric though it is, the poem proves that the battle had left its impress on men's minds and was, from an early date, celebrated in song. Moreover, the character of the king in French poems seems to have preserved something of its nobility, whereas the customary character of a comprehensive King Louis, in the *chansons-de-geste*, is mostly despicable.

The French poet, at a much longer distance from the event, has obviously drawn largely on his imagination. But we do not know what the original poem (for there is evidence of previous versions) owed to chronicles and poems in which his story had been celebrated. The earliest version of the story of Gormont and Isembart that we

[1] *Ober seo lidan*, l. 11.

possess (apart from the description of the battle) is due to a monk of Saint-Riquier, a name which is prominent in the poem and helps to localize the legend. Hariulf, who wrote his *Chronicle* in 1088 and revised it in 1104, tells us that the story was repeated daily by local folk ('non solum historiis, sed etiam patriensium memoria quotidie recolitur et canitur'), and if anyone wants to know all about it, he adds, he must learn it from the tales of his grandfathers. If such a statement is true it would not be surprising if a combination of faulty memories and a certain love of improvisation had rendered it uncertain in people's minds whether Gormont was the 'Godrun' celebrated in Asser's *Life of King Alfred*, or the 'Wurm' defeated by Charles the Fat in 882, or whether the several heroes, owing to a certain similarity of name, had combined to produce a single figure out of elements borrowed from all three. Be that as it may, King Gormont in our poem is: *Celui d'Oriente*, the *Sathanas*, the *Arabi*, the *emperere de Leutiz* and the *Antecrist*—a sufficient number of names to suggest that the author did not treat the heathen king and his identity very seriously. The gist of the poem, as we can reconstruct it chiefly from a longish account in Mousket's *Rhymed Chronicle*,[1] and a German translation of the fourteenth century entitled *Lohier und Mallart*, is very briefly as follows: A heathen king (Gormont) has invaded France with a vast, mixed army of 'Saracens' (here as in the *Willame* a thin disguise for Northmen); fighting under his standard is a French knight named Isembart who, having been grievously wronged by the Emperor Louis, had fled the kingdom and joined forces with the formidable pagan king in hopes of avenging his wrong. After feats of valour on both sides, Gormont is killed by King Louis who, however, strains himself fatally in the affray; the heathen flee back to their ships, and Isembart, left alone and mortally wounded, turns to God and prays for forgiveness. But, embedded in the narrative, are allusions and episodes for which no source has yet been discovered. There is the valiant young standard-bearer of King Louis (*le fiz Charlun* in spite of history) who, on hearing Gormont blaspheming against the God of the Christians,[2] rides like a whirlwind to attack this antichrist, against the will of the emperor who pleads with him not to desert him, saying pitifully:

> Se tu esteies ore occis,
> dunc n'ai jeo mais suz ciel ami.

This sounds much more like the stock Louis, Charlemagne's feeble

---

[1] Thirteenth century, cf. supra.
[2] 'Quant Damne Deu out si laidir' (ll. 198, 206).

son, in the *chansons-de-geste*, but he retrieves his character later in the poem by courage and chivalrous behaviour. Hugue answers the emperor proudly that he must accomplish his destiny:

> Pruz (fut) mun pere e mun ancestre,
> e jeo fui mut de bone geste
> e, par meimes, dei pruz estre (ll. 218–20).

And so he rode to his doom, for Gormont smote him a terrible wound in his left side which hurled him from his horse. But even then, when Gormont told him that he would have no use now for either a doctor or a priest, the valiant youth replied: 'You lie! You have only cut off a little piece of my garment ('peliçon'). You have not finished with me yet'. He leapt to his feet and, taking the battle-standard in both hands, would have killed King Gormont had not help arrived. Yet still he made another tour of the field and came back again to Gormont, but this time Gormont drove his lance into the young man's body and he fell again to earth. At this dramatic moment Isembart the renegade ('le reneié') recognized the horse that Hugue had been riding as the one that had been stolen from him on a previous occasion. The stealing of the baron's horse by Hugue when he had gone to Gormont's camps as a messenger, and a mysterious allusion to a trick of Hugue's in serving the king with a peacock but making it impossible for him to eat it or open his mouth except to talk nonsense, are among the unexplained episodes in the narrative part of the poem. The same is true of the theft from the heathen's tent of a gold cup by Hugue's nephew, who now tried in vain to avenge his uncle. King Gormont, however, in spite of his pride of birth refused to demean himself by fighting with a squire, as was to be expected in this aristocratically-minded society, whether heathen or Christian:

> Fui de sur mei, garz paltenier!
> Jeo sui de lin a chevalier,
> de riches e de preisiez;
> n'i tocherai oi esquier (ll. 356–9).

This was quite in keeping with the character of Gormont for, in spite of the many bad names he is called, he was a valiant knight and a noble character:

> Li meudre rei e le plus franc
> qui unques fust el munde vivant
> Se il creüst Deu le poant (ll. 29–31).

King Louis had a high regard for him and, when he saw so many of his men lying dead on the battlefield, was filled with regret that he had not engaged in single combat with him at the beginning of the battle, thus sparing many a noble knight. There would have been nothing derogatory in such a duel: 'Ja est il rei et rei sui jeo'. In all probability Louis would have had the worst of it, for Gormont was immensely strong. He had already given the death-blow to some of the first knights of France, and on two occasions the dart, or javelin, killed not only the knight at whom it was aimed but, passing through his antagonist's body, killed the man who was standing behind him—on one occasion a 'danzel de Lumbardie', on the other 'un Aleman'. King Louis' army was composed of mixed forces as well as Gormont's, in which men of Ireland (Ireis) fought side by side with Africans. The 'joust' between the two kings took place. Gormont hurled his fatal three javelins (darz), but God in His pity preserved the emperor's life so that the weapons did not enter his flesh.[1] Then King Louis gave up the idea of a regulation 'combat singulier' (or *jouste*) to decide the matter according to the rules, and struck Gormont a blow over the head with his lance that split him in halves to the middle. But the blow cost him such an effort that he almost fell, and saved himself by grasping the horse's neck. As he raised himself with difficulty in his heavy armour he bent his stirrup-straps three fingers' length, and strained himself so badly that he lived for only thirty days after his victory. This result of the battle is described in Hariulf's Chronicle which tells of the ravages and destruction wrought by the heathen invaders and the vast numbers of those who were slain by King Louis and his Frenchmen. Hariulf tells us also that it was Isembart (Esembardus), a Frank of noble origin, who had incited Gormont to invade the frontiers of France, thus becoming a traitor to his own country. This is emphasized in the poem for, when things are going badly and Gormont with his standard is laid low, the heathen themselves accuse Isembart of having betrayed them and brought them to France, under false pretences. They may have had some reasons for doubting whether Isembart would stand by them in their danger, for in his lament for Gormont, Isembart had openly declared: 'A! Loöis, bon emperere / cum as oi France bien aquitee!' The author is unsparing in his praise of Louis for he tells us that he was a good knight, a valiant fighter and a true counsellor to his fellow-Christians. Then he adds:

> Ceo dit la geste, e il est veir,
> puis n'ot en France nul dreit eir (ll. 418–19).

thus ending the relation of Louis' exploits with a scrap of historic

[1] ll. 386–7.

fact culled from a chronicle and illustrating again the intermingling of fact and fiction. For, although the Emperor Louis and the heathen King Gormont represent rather blurred portraits of historical figures, about whose identity the author himself was not very clear, Isembart seems to have even less claim to an historical origin. His rôle was probably an imaginary one introduced to add interest to a somewhat vague story formed of a patchwork of indistinct reminiscences of rival kings centering round a town in England of the name of Cirencester and the neighbourhood of Saint-Riquier in France. Hariulf mentions Isembart very briefly; we do not know what the stories and songs referred to by Hariulf related about him. But it was probably left to the French poet to create the rather pathetic figure who is the chief point of interest in the poem we are studying. For Isembart is torn in two. He is not convinced that his cause is right, like a Roland or a Vivien. He has committed a heinous sin in betraying his king and his faith. Even a heathen had warned him that he was bringing down a judgment on his own head, and he himself had warned Gormont of the grave danger of fighting against a race as noble as that of the Franks. And yet, having embraced the cause of his nation's enemies, he is true as steel to his new lord and the somewhat unsavoury crowd with whom he fights and whose leader he is. When the heathen saw their king lying dead they turned and fled towards the coast uttering loud cries.[1] Isembart, now designated as *le Margari*, hearing the noise, spurred his horse towards the spot where the standard was lying, and at the sight of Gormont's dead body he swooned three times. He realized that there was small chance of a successful issue to the battle now that his adopted lord was dead, and that his own fate was sealed. The prophecy of a heathen soothsayer came into his mind:

> 'Allas!' dist il, 'veir dist le sort,
> Si jeo veneie en icest ost.
> Que jeo i serreie u pris u mort.
> Or sai jeo bien que veir dist trop' (ll. 426–9).

Nothing daunted, however, he rallied the fleeing heathen, telling them that flight was useless in a foreign land and exhorting them to avenge their generous master who had bestowed lands and strongholds and rich gifts ('le ver, le gris e le ermin') upon them. But the heathen would not listen[2] and the familiar 'paien s'enfuient' resounds again and again in our ears. Their cowardice inspires Isembart to fresh efforts and he fights on furiously, killing a cousin of King Louis

[1] l. 422.   [2] l. 448.

and two more of the noblest-born Frenchmen. In a second lament over the dead body of Gormont, more eloquent than the first, Isembart refers to the fact that he had warned the king about the fighting qualities of the French several times, both at Cirencester, which he describes as 'voz cuntrees', and on the galley coming over to France. This curious reference to Cirencester, which does not occur in Hariulf, but is mentioned in Asser's *Life of King Alfred*, has done much to confuse the issues in any attempt to identify the Gormont-Godrum personage. But the noble words of the 'regret funèbre' throw light on the character of the hero Isembart. After a tribute to King Louis and an admission that Gormont has paid dearly for his attempt at invasion, he declares that he will not fail the subjects of his adopted liege-lord as long as he has a sword at his side:

> Ja ne faudrai a sa meisnée
> pur tant cum puisse ceindre espée (ll. 487–8).

This time the heathen rally and return to the attack, and you might have seen many a lance splintered and many Saracens laid low on the grassy plain. We are reminded of Vivien and his men (in the *Chançun de Willame*) when the heathen, in their distress, call upon their leader: 'Pur le tuen Due, sire Isembart / gentil, ne nus faillir tu ja! / Nu ferai jeo, dist Isembart, / tant cum li miens cors durera'.[1] Then the fight was renewed for the fourth day in succession after the death of Gormont. The two armies pass with a kind of rhythmical parallel motion through each other's ranks, killing and wounding as they go. Louis performed the chivalrous action in the midst of the battle of having Gormont's body carried to his tent and placing the bodies of Hugue and his squire (Geudon) covered with a cloak beside him. Isembart met his aged father ('le viel Bernard') in the midst of the fighting and, not recognizing him, he struck at him fiercely and unhorsed him, but fortunately did not wound him. It would have been a sin and a crime to unhorse his father if he had recognized him, remarks the author—adding rather naïvely: 'If he had known it, he would never have touched him, for they would have had other things to talk about!'[2] So the fierce battle went on and Isembart wrought much havoc amongst 'our Frenchmen'.[3] But the heathen turned at last in despair against their leader and even cast in his teeth that he was a renegade and a 'fel Margari' and that he had got them into France under false pretences only to betray them. This must have been a bitter moment for Isembart, but he fought on even after his

---

[1] ll. 509–12.   [2] ll. 576–7.   [3] l. 577.

heathen had fled to their boats with the haste of a stag pursued by the hunters. It was a forlorn hope, however; soon he was struck through the body in three places and hurled from his horse to the ground where he lay unrecognized. As he lay, hidden by a thicket at the cross-roads, he remembered 'Damne Deu', and was moved to utter words which would be his salvation, for he called upon the blessed Virgin for her intercession and he implored mercy from the God of the Christians who died on the cross on a Friday and rose on the third day. Then spying a leafy olive tree nearby, he crawled painfully to it, seated himself on the fresh grass and turned his face towards the east. Our fragment ends with him lying on the ground confessing his sins like Roland. A better ending could hardly have been devised.

It is difficult to assign any definite date to the fragment of *Gormont et Isembart* as, indeed, is the case with all the older poems. The language, vocabulary, and assonances are distinctly archaic in character. But antique words and phrases do not prove that the work is antique which uses them. As W. P. Ker has said in connection with ballad-poetry in general: 'All that is proved is the tenacity and perseverance of the old poetical diction'.[1] The terminology is stereotyped—we have the 'escu frait et malmis', the 'hauberc rompu et desafré', the splintered lances and shattered helmets; the blows which leave no doubt as to their effectiveness. Many are the changes rung on the description of a powerful knight's blows which has been noted as of frequent occurrence in poems of the Guillaume cycle. The octosyllabic line has shortened the phrase but the sense is the same:

> Qui il consuit, nel laist en sele:
> vestue l'a de mort novele (ll. 45–6).
> Ki il consuit, ne s'en ala;
> Ki il feri, puis ne parla (ll. 580–81).
> Qui il consuit, tut est vencu (l. 616).

The heathen in the mass are conventional and flee at regular intervals. There is much that is reminiscent of both the *Chanson de Roland* and the *Chançun de Willame*, but there is no reference in our fragment to any other poem or any other hero of legend. There is, however, a striking difference of atmosphere in our poem from that in the Crusading epics. The fighting is just as grim, the individual heroes are just as valiant, but there is a conciliatory spirit running through which is completely absent from the *Roland* or the *Chançun*,

---

[1] Proceedings of the British Academy. Vol. IV: *On the History of the Ballads*, 1100–1500.

though there is a trace of it in the *Rainouart* poem which is a continuation of the latter. The representatives of the rival forces
are generous to their antagonists; Isembart praises first his original
liege-lord, then his adopted one almost in the same breath.
Though he has been absolutely loyal to the pagan forces fighting
under him, he prays for his compatriots who have brought
about his downfall. His prayer has none of the self-assurance
which breaks through that of Roland as he hands his glove to God.
It has more the character of the penitent thief's prayer in the Mary
legend, or the moving words of Theophile in the miracle play:

> 'Sainte Marie, genitrix
> Mere Deu, dame', Isembart dist,
> 'depreez en vostre beau fiz.
> Qu'il eit merci de cest chaitif!'

Gormont, although he has burnt the church of Saint Ricqier and
devastated the country of his opponents, is a good lord to his own
men, the giver of 'le ver, le gris e le ermin', of 'l'or e l'argent e les
soudees / e les pelices engulees', more like a bounteous sovereign of
romance than of epic. In the episode of father and son fighting—a
very old one in literature—the unnaturalness of the situation is
softened by the fact that Isembart and his father did not recognize
one another. In this episode Isembart is called 'Maistre Isembart'—
somehow we cannot imagine Roland being called 'Maistre Roland'
any more than we can imagine Vivien speaking 'o la voiz clere' or
a young Lombard being called 'un danzel de Lumbardie'. Not
unconnected, perhaps, with the difference in tone is the difference in
style of the poem. The fragment suffices to give an idea of the
ballad-like character of the whole, especially in those parts where
descriptions of fighting are concerned. It has all the characteristics of
ballad poetry: the sort of refrain which follows each of Gormont's
victories over a French knight; the repetitive line which introduces
each fresh phase of the battle in slightly different words (*Fier fut l'estur
e esbaudi*, etc.), omitted from the narrative part but picked up again
when the battle is resumed; the details of time—three days, four days,
etc.; the exact descriptions of the combatants involved. It has the
tragic motive common to the epic and the ballad and a unity of
action which is equally characteristic of both types of poetry. It
keeps to the point with its definite tragic problem, in this case a
conflict of affections and loyalties. The relation of ballads to epic
poetry has often been discussed and it is hard to decide from the
present state of the fragment whether we have to do with a narrative

ballad derived from an older epic poem or an original ballad with narrative digressive interpolations. The poem has not the grace of a true ballad, but it has the lively conceptions and the lyrical spirit. Most of the ballads, in spite of their style, celebrate a tragic mistake, a fight to the finish or a good defence. It has been said that *Chevy Chase* is the counterpart of the *Battle of Malden* and the hero of *Percy Reed* more like a Northern hero than a knight of romance. But Percy Reed might equally well be compared with a French paladin—indeed, his death at the hand of traitors when he is discovered asleep and alone after a hunt is strikingly like that of Bègue in the poem *Garin le Lorrain*—and *Chevy Chase* might with equal justice be considered a counterpart to *Gormont et Isembart*. We have already described the joust between the two kings in the latter poem—both well matched in strength and pride of birth. The words of Douglas as he defies 'the Percy out of Northumberland' in the ballad are almost like an echo of the same theme:

> To kille alle these guiltless men
> Alas it were great pitye!
> But Percy, *thou art a lord of land,*
> *I an earl in my countrye*—
> Let all our men on a party stand
> And do battle of thee and me.[1]

In both cases the end of the encounter was tragic, but the words of Percy as he laments over the corpse of his valiant foe are again strangely reminiscent of our poem:

> He took the dead man by the hand
> And said: 'Woe is me for thee!
> To have sav'd thy life I'd have parted with
> My lands for yeares three,
> For a better man of heart nor of hand
> Was not in the north countrye'.[2]

II. *LA CHANSON D'AIOL*

Amongst the isolated *chansons-de-geste* there is one, not perhaps of the first water, yet by no means devoid of merits, which deserves a place of honour on account of its originality. The *Chanson d'Aiol* has been badly tampered with. It has been furnished with an introduction and a continuation obviously of later date than the original (or at any

---

[1] str. xviii.   [2] str. xxxvii–viii.

rate older) form of the poem. The additions are composed in quite a
different style and are very inferior in quality. The original poem (if
we may so call it) is, like the majority of the epic poems, in the
decasyllabic metre, with 'laisses' of varying length bound together
by assonances which have not yet been replaced by rhymes. But
one has only to pronounce a line or two of the poem to notice a
difference of rhythm caused by the fact that, in the vast majority of
lines, the pause is after the sixth, instead of the customary fourth
syllable:

> Cui il consuit a cop / ne puet durer,
> Ja mar mandera mire / pour lui saner (ll. 4047–8).

In this example the difference is easily seen as it is one of the stock
phrases of the jongleurs' 'répertoire' and constantly occurs, as we have
seen, with the more normal division of words:

> Cui il consuit / n'a talent de chanter.

This seemingly slight change must have given quite a different lilt
to the poem when it was recited and it necessitated a difference in
phrasing, as in the above example. The six/four cut is by no means
unknown in Old French literature. It occurs in the Franco-provençal
poem, *Girart de Roussillon*, and in some of the early Old French
'romances' or so-called 'Chansons de toile' and in the burlesque poem
Audigier mentioned below.[1] None the less, it shows a certain indepen-
dence on the part of the poet for which he must be given credit. For
the rest, the style, the diction and the vocabulary of *Aiol* justify us in
placing the poem amongst those which are intermediate in date
between the oldest and more primitive Old French epic and the
decadent poems which mark the end of the epic output in France
and caused it to die a natural death.

Aiol is, as we have said, an isolated poem and celebrated an isolated
hero. Attempts were made by irresponsible writers of the thirteenth
century (e.g. Alberic de Trois-Fontaines) to make Aiol dangle at the
end of the already swollen lineage of Garin de Montglane. But the
attempt was as foolish as it was futile and Aiol remains a solitary
figure. The plot of the poem is briefly as follows: Aiol is the son of
a certain Count Elie who has been maligned and wrongfully dis-
possessed of his lands by the machinations of the traitor Macaire. We
are back in the reign of 'Louis le fiz Charlon', whose ear was always
open to the lies of the flatterer. Elie is poor and sick and lives miserably with wife, child, and horse in a sort of annexe to a hermit's cell.

[1] p. 207.

We may note here the spate of hermits which invaded the Old French epic and romantic literature when the individual saint began to replace the collective church and the individual knight, fighting for his own glory, formed the centre of the picture instead of the army of Christian warriors in conflict with the heathen. With the approbation of his father, but strongly against the wishes of his mother, the boy Aiol ('Aiol li enfes'—the child) set out to seek the emperor's court and retrieve his father's fortune. He is given much good advice both by his father and the hermit before he sets forth clad in miserable clothing and mounted on an emaciated horse. His father's last words to him as he rides off are an appeal not to forget his lone, lorn mother if God should prosper him in worldly things.[1] As he departs, his mother, Avisse, faints three times for grief, but Aiol brooks no delay in setting forth on his quest.[2] After brief adventures with robbers and Saracens he arrives at Poitiers where he is mocked by everyone for his sorry appearance. But he is taken in and supplied surreptitiously with a clean shirt by a well-to-do burgher who would have done more for him had his wife not objected to such liberality. Aiol departed the next day, not forgetting 'le service Dieu' as his father had instructed him.

After further adventures Aiol arrived at Orleans where he found a hostel at the house of the Countess Ysabiaus, who is actually his aunt but does not recognize her nephew in the unsophisticated but courageous 'enfant Aiol'. The countess's daughter fell violently in love with him at first sight. She tended him and looked after his horse. She helped him to undress and put him to bed with many soothing touches. She begged for the privilege of being his 'drue', but Aiol firmly resisted temptation. Unwillingly she left him, but could not sleep for thinking of him, whereas Aiol slept soundly till morning. He was determined not to love this one nor another,[3] until he had performed the task he had set himself. On his arrival at Orleans he was mocked again for his appearance but never failed to answer courteously. Even the king who saw him from the window of his palace was in doubt of him at first but changed his mind when Aiol fought valiantly for him and took his enemy prisoner. Louis, then, became so grateful to him that he loaded him with benefits, much to the annoyance of the traitor Macaire who was constantly drawing the king into a corner,[4] and whispering spiteful words into his ear. Aiol did not forget his father and mother in his prosperity,

---

[1] ll. 532–3. [2] l. 549. [3] l. 2216–7.
[4] 'A une part le trait a un recoi' (l. 3046).

but sent back a portion of the gifts he had received with an account of his doings since he left home. He remained courteous to the end, even to his enemy Macaire, and the epic story ends with a marvellous horse-race between Marchegai, Aiol's singular-looking steed, and the well-groomed horse of Macaire. In spite of a handicap unwillingly accepted by Macaire, Marchegai won an easy victory and gained a large prize for his mastery. Aiol remained unrecognized to the end, and to every question put to him as to his identity he would only reply 'On m'apele, biaus sire, l'enfant Aiol'. The continuation of the poem, which is in alexandrines, degenerates into a second or third-rate romance relating the subsequent fantastic adventures of Aiol with digressions of the usual kind.

It is impossible to read the first part of the *Chanson d'Aiol* without being struck by the similarity between the plot in this poem and that of the Arthurian romance *Perceval*, Chretien de Troye's latest and unfinished work. In the *Roman de Perceval*, or *Perceval le Galois* as it is usually called in the manuscripts, we have the same 'motif' of a young boy who has been brought up in a wilderness (*gaste foreste*) owing to his father's misfortunes, and who leaves a sorrowing mother to go and seek his fortunes at the king's court. He, too, sets out dressed in most unsuitable clothes. The advice given to Aiol by his father and the hermit has its counterpart in the wise counsels given to Perceval by his mother and the 'prodome' whom he meets shortly after he sets out. In each case the advice boils down to very much the same thing—viz. the avoidance of bad company and the frequenting of wise men:—'Ne pren a mavais home acointement' (*Aiol*, 330); 'Avuec les prodomes alez' (*Perceval*, l. 564).

In each case also some instruction in arms is given to the simple youth who has been brought up in the backwoods—to Aiol by his father Elie who had been a valiant knight before his misfortunes, to Perceval by the same 'prodome' who gave some demonstrations of the fighting art which were beyond the powers of Elie as he lay on his bed of sickness. Both Aiol and Perceval are furnished with an efficacious prayer containing the mystic names of God—in the case of Aiol the prayer was committed to him by the hermit in the form of a 'brief',[1] whereas Perceval had it whispered into his ear[2] and repeated until he knew it by heart. There are other details which the two poems have in common, such as the fight with a lion in which the lion's two front paws pierce his assailant's shield. But by far the most interesting comparison for the light it throws on the different

---

[1] l. 463.　　　　[2] l. 6482.

attitude towards women in the two different types of poem, is to be
found in the episode, common to both, of the advances made to the
hero by a young woman. We have mentioned the episode in *Aiol*
where the maiden could hardly be persuaded to leave Aiol's bedchamber. The poor girl covered him up carefully,[1] then looking at
him longingly, she asks him for a kiss[2] and pleads with him to be her
'ami'; but Aiol, who was ignorant in matters of love ('Le deduit de
puchele n'ot pas apris / Car il avoit esté el bois noris'),[3] begged her
to go back to her room and go to bed with her maidens, for it was
high time. He knew he would forget his mission if he listened to
her, for the author adds sententiously:

> Car amistet de feme fait tout muer
> Le corage de l'home et trestorner (ll. 2221–2).

This is the unromantic attitude of a man towards a woman characteristic of the *chansons-de-geste* of the best period. We have noticed
how Roland was too preoccupied with other things to give a thought
to 'la bele Aude' in the *Chanson de Roland*, and how Bernier turned
down the proffered love of a young girl in *Raoul de Cambrai* because
he had no time for such things. In the parallel episode to the scene
we have just described, however, in the *Roman de Perceval*, the contrast is most striking and most instructive. In the romance, Perceval
arrived at a beleaguered castle in which a young girl was threatened
by a hostile army and an unwelcome lover. Perceval was received
with joy and put in the best guest-chamber. He had already retired
to bed when the maiden, who had observed his courteous method of
conversation as she sat beside him after his arrival, came to his room
weeping and poured out her grief. Perceval was revelling in the *eise*
and *delit* of a comfortable bed and not missing the further pleasure of
feminine society in the least, for he, too, had no knowledge of the
'deduit de pucele'.[4] He had fallen asleep without a care ('il n'estoit
de rien an espans'),[5] whilst the young girl was spending a sleepless
night. It was when she could bear it no longer that she went to
Perceval's room 'come hardie et corageuse'. She met with no stern
refusal. It was the man who drew her into his bed and asked for a
kiss and drew the coverlet over her, and 'don't think he didn't enjoy
it' adds the author.[6]

The absence of this chivalrous attitude towards women in the
Chanson d'Aiol justifies us in thinking that, if there were any borrowing by the author of one poem from another, it must have been on

---

[1] *Aiol*, l. 2157. [2] l. 2173. [3] ll. 2161–2.
[4] *Perceval*, l. 1938. [5] l. 1944. [6] l. 2063.

the part of the author of *Perceval*. It is true that in the text of *Aiol* there is a mysterious reference to 'the horses of King Arthur'. But it is tempting to suppose that the writer of the manuscript or the copyist misheard or mistook the word *Bucefalu* and substituted for it the words *le roi Artu*, as the next line clearly refers to the propensity of Alexander's horse for human flesh: 'Ne puet consentir home que tout ne tut'—a propensity illustrated in many manuscript illuminations of the Alexander cycle in the Middle Ages.

There is a unity about the character of Aiol which is striking. He never allows himself to be deflected from his course. It is true that the first part of the poem ends with his triumph in the horse-race and not with a tragic defeat, as befits the epic hero, but he has many humiliations and 'déboires' to put up with first. Like Guillaume d'Orange (in *Aliscans*) he learns from bitter experience that 'poverte si fait home molt angoisous'.[1] When warned by a pilgrim that at court he will feel rather out of place on account of his ragged clothes, his twisted lance, and his loose stirrups, he replies sorrowfully, in the same words as another hero of epic (Girard de Viane):

> Ja n'est mie li cuers / n'el vair n'el gris,
> N'es riches garnimens / , n'es dras de pris,
> Mais est el ventre a l'home / u Diex l'asist (ll. 1581 f.).

an interesting example of the common stock of phrases and tags (some good and some bad) of which the 'jongleurs' of that period availed themselves. Aiol's pride of birth fits in perfectly, too, with the epic scheme. He is 'de fiere geste'[2] and scorns to take anything from the treasure of those he has conquered for:

> Ne sui pas marchëans / qu'aie borsée,
> Ains m'en vois reconquerre / l'onor mon pere (l. 766-7).

This is the only serious reference to his lineage (*geste*) for, as remarked above, Aiol is an isolated hero. This is not the case, however, with the other protagonist of our poem, viz. the traitor Macaire, the character which by itself alone connects the *Chanson d'Aiol* with the epic tradition.

Macaire, familiar to us already from the poem of that name (or rather *Machario* to give it its correct form), is a member of a large clan. There were more than fifty of them in the immediate neighbourhood of the court—nephews of Ganelon, Hardré, and Macaire.[3] They were all traitors and mercenaries and flatterers (*fels traitres, soudoiiers, malvais losengiers,* etc.). But Macaire de Losange (we do

---

[1] *Aiol*, l. 2031.   [2] l. 2124.   [3] Cf. l. 4439.

not hear of *Maience* here) is the head of all this great lineage and he had the ear of the king. It was he who had caused Elie to be disinherited by his jealous slanders, and he was just as jealous of Elie's son Aiol as soon as he began to be honoured by the king. His character is altogether despicable, but he does not end as Machario does in the Franco-Italian poem, fighting a duel with a dog. We leave him in prison after the horse-race in which the 'combat judiciaire' is decided between two animals and not between an animal and a man. His mischief-making career is continued in the second part of the poem, at the end of which he suffered the due reward of his deeds by suffering the same death as Ganelon in the *Chanson de Roland*.

The other real personality in the *Chanson d'Aiol* is the hero's horse, Marchegai, a worthy member of the group of famous horses who figure in the Old French epic. Marchegai has the sense of a man and responds to every action of his master. He shows his goodwill by a responsive leap (fourteen feet) like Guillaume's faithful Baucent in *Aliscans*. He was 'maigre et confondu' in appearance but his strength and endurance were amazing. He had a good 'flair' for a villain. If he saw a worthless fellow about to obstruct his master he had but to raise his right foot and give him a tap on the chest and the man's corpse lay on the ground beneath his feet. When a drunkard from the tavern tried to seize his bridle and make off with it, Marchegai laid back his ears, galloped after the man, seized him by the nape of the neck and gave him such a shaking that the 'glouton' fell back half dead. We note the barbarity of the time, for Aiol finished what Marchegai had begun. He turned the horse round so that it trampled on the body and broke three of the man's ribs; then stooped down and recovered his bridle—whereupon the author remarks:

> Onques si fais chevaus ne fu trovés;
> J'oï le mestre dire qu'il fu faés (ll. 1439-40).

Aiol's affection for his strange-looking horse was more steadfast than that of Guillaume for Baucent. Guillaume was quite ready to abandon his own horse if he saw a chance of a better one, for he was a great connoisseur of horse-flesh. But Aiol was rewarded for his constancy, for in the race between his own steed and that of Macaire, in spite of a considerable handicap, Marchegai won by a large margin, whereas Macaire's horse was so winded that it could neither run nor move and the knights and bourgeois gathered round and beat the poor creature with sticks and poles, calling it a 'recreant roncin' and threatening to cut off its tail.

There are other characters in the *Chanson d'Aiol* which only play a minor part but are nevertheless worthy of attention for the light they throw on habits and manners prevalent at the time our poem was composed. The 'borgeois' in the cities through which Aiol passes do not make a pleasant impression. They mock Aiol and his horse mercilessly when they first perceive him, and although some feel shame when he answers them courteously, yet the dejected appearance of both seems to have been treated as quite a legitimate source of amusement. The drunkards ('lechëor') from the taverns are anxious to get hold of his horse and harness, his armour and his clothes to pawn them for food and drink in a way reminiscent of the thieves in the *St. Nicolas* of Jean Bodel:

> Li vostre haubers sera au pain portes,
> De vostre elme arons vin a grant plenté. . . . (ll. 1031 f.).

On one occasion even the knights and their ladies, as well as the rich bourgeois, from their upper windows poke fun at him as he rides through the town with his helmet all on one side because of its broken straps, his twisted lance, and his ancient shield.[1] But Marchegai held his head up proudly as he trotted through the streets of Orleans, and Aiol showed something of his nobility in his face, for the Countess Isabiaus and her daughter Lusiane were at once struck by his appearance and offered him shelter. So, too, did a certain rich citizen who detected in Aiol a likeness to his father Elie whom he had once served.

But on the whole one is left with a rather sordid picture of life in the city and the rich, vulgar butcher's wife, Hersent, who had come penniless to the town five years before with her husband, but had amassed great wealth (in fact they possessed two-thirds of the city), by fair means or foul, presents an aspect of town life in the second half of the twelfth century which is confirmed by other works of roughly the same period. But Hersent was easily put to rout by a few sharp-pointed words from our hero and hissed through the town by a crowd of citizens crying:

> Troves aves vo maistre, dame Hersent,
> Onques mais ne veïmes home vivant,
> Qui vos osast respondre ne tant ne quant (ll. 2719–21).

and the roar of laughter in the market which greeted Hersent's husband when he regretted that he had not his butcher's knife handy

[1] ll. 1949 f.

to avenge his wife's honour was so loud that it would have been impossible to hear God thundering:

> Dont lieve la risee el marchie grant,
> Que n'i oïssies mie nes Dieu tonant (ll. 2732–3).

When Aiol came back with flying colours from defeating the king's enemies, Hersent feared reprisals for having mocked him before and sent a considerable peace-offering in the form of fourteen barrels of 'Vin d'Aucoire' (Auxerre) and the same number of hams (*bacons*)—again reminding us of descriptions of life in Arras in the comedies of Adam de la Halle and Jean Bodel in which the 'vin d'Auxerre' flows freely. Aiol acts up to his noble, generous character throughout. The good fare was distributed amongst knights and citizens who had become penurious owing to their misfortunes; he did not even forget the porter who had at first prevented his joining in the battle by refusing to let him out of the gate. The king made an announcement that for the coming year everything Aiol wished for or ordered should be charged to the exchequer, at which the citizens and merchants greatly rejoiced as they knew much gain would accrue to them by such a transaction. The only person who was displeased was, very naturally, the traitor Macaire, who also remains true to type throughout the poem. There is thus a unity about the poem in that everything tends towards the same end which is the object lesson contained in the line twice repeated:

> Chil cui Dex vieut aidier n'est ja honi(s) (l. 2229).

or

> Cil cui Diex vuet aidier, il est troves (l. 800).

The author of *Aiol* was evidently familiar with the literature of his period. The diction, the phrases (e.g. *cil qu'il consuit*, etc.; *n'oïssiez Deu tonant*; *si veïssiez*, etc.), the ideas are those which occur frequently in the *chansons*, which we may look upon as belonging to a sort of middle period—even if the attitude towards women and a certain brutality characteristic of the poems of an earlier date give an archaic flavour to the poem. References to other poems hardly occur, except the allusion to Audigier and his mother (not his wife), Rainberge, the hero and heroine of a burlesque, or satire, of the *chansons-de-geste* and their exaggerated ideas of knighthood. The family of traitors, including Ganelon and Hardré as well as Macaire, was evidently familiar to the poet, and one may assume from this that the poems in which those characters occur were not unknown to him. A curious passage in alexandrines[1] has been introduced, in which the deterioration of morals in France is castigated and a possible reference occurs to an event which took place in 1200—viz. the marriage at a very early age of two children of princely families. But the whole passage could be left out without causing any detriment to the poem; in fact, the reverse, as it bears the stamp of composition of inferior quality. The theme of the poem in the version we possess remains, as stated above, perfectly simple—the man who remains loyal to his obligations and performs his duty single-mindedly will be helped of God and never overwhelmed by untoward circumstances. This theme is worked out in the first part of the poem without undue digressions, unnecessary descriptions or fantastic adventures. The trials endured by Aiol are not brought upon him by his unfilial behaviour as they are in the case of Chretien's Perceval, but they serve as a discipline in the development of an unformed character, although the *Aiols li enfes* of the epic poem is not such an uncouth boy as the hero of romance.

III. *LE PÈLERINAGE DE CHARLEMAGNE*

The poem, generally known under this name, or—more correctly— that of *Voyage de Charlemagne à Jerusalem et à Constantinople*, has given rise to almost as much discussion as the *Chanson de Roland*, as regards its date and its place in the history of the Old French epic. As with so many of the medieval poems, it is impossible to determine with any degree of certainty the exact period of its composition even to a decade. Language is deceptive; historical allusions are few; all we can do is to note certain features of the poem and try to locate it in the Charlemagne legend, taking our cue from the character of its contents and its personages. This is not to say that language is no guide at all. There are certain features in the *Pèlerinage* which definitely point to the early Middle Ages. Rhyme has not yet replaced 'assonance' and the poet distinguishes carefully between certain sounds (e.g. *en* and *an*, *ié* and *é*) which afterwards tended to become confused. The state of the language has much in common with that of our earliest epic poems, though the poet has chosen the twelve-syllable line (alexandrine), which marks it off from the rest of the *chansons-de-geste* as these are almost uniformly composed in the decasyllabic metre. We note an absence of the constant 'chevilles' which disfigure the later poems and the poet displays considerable

[1] ll. 1624–1884.

skill in bringing vivacity and even pathos into his rather ponderous long lines. A striking example of this occurs in the conversation between the emperor and his wife at the outset of the poem.

The *chanson* falls into two distinct parts somewhat unskilfully spliced together. The first part is the description of Charlemagne's pilgrimage to Jerusalem in search of relics. It is a peaceful pilgrimage recalling those of the eleventh century before the events which gave rise to the First Crusade. The second part, which has no such pious motive, is the account of Charlemagne's visit to Constantinople to vindicate his title to be the 'sansper' emperor on earth. It is only towards the end of the poem that we realize that obtaining the relics, with their extraordinary 'virtue', was a necessary preliminary in view of the accomplishment of Charlemagne's object, thus giving to the poem a certain unity which would otherwise have been lacking. The idea of Charlemagne's visit to the East was a not unnatural consequence of his relations with oriental potentates, which received a considerable share of attention from his admiring chroniclers. Both Eginhard and the Monk of St. Gall recall with obvious pleasure the friendship of the Frankish emperor with the sultan Haroun el Rashid. Then the legend arose that Charles himself had been to the East and, whatever the first form of this legend may have been, it was soon expanded and exploited by the monks in an unworthy attempt to guarantee the authenticity of their relics by asserting that they had been brought back from the East by Charlemagne and presented to their particular church. Such an attempt would explain very satisfactorily the first part of the French poem (apart from the introductory scene between the emperor and his wife). Charlemagne was credited with having constructed a route to Constantinople—the 'viam quam ... Carolus Magnus, mirificus rex Franciae aptari fecit usque Constantinopolim',[1] and his name, coupled with that of his son Louis, was used by Pope Urban II in his speech at the Council of Clermont in 1095 to incite the knights and warriors of France to take up the cross and gird on the sword against the Saracens: 'Moveat vos et incitet animos vestros ad virilitatem gesta praedecessorum, probitas et magnitudo Caroli Magni regis et Ludovici filii ejus, altiorumque regum vestrorum, qui regna Turcorum distruxerunt et in eis fines sanctae Ecclesiae dilataverunt.'[2] The author of the Old French epic poems would probably have endorsed these words about Charlemagne but suppressed them about his son Louis.

[1] Anonymous, Ch. iii, cf. supra.
[2] Cf. Roberti monachi S. Remizii: *Historia hierosolymitana*, Ch. i.

The question here presents itself: When did the 'mirificus rex Franciae', the king distinguished by 'probitas et magnitudo', begin to become an object of ridicule and satire? In the *Chanson de Roland*, in spite of occasional lapses, he is an august personage, he can give absolution, he has direct intercourse with angelic beings, and miracles are performed for him; he rides magnificently at the head of his army of bearded warriors. In the poem we are about to examine, on the other hand, although he still rules over a mighty kingdom, he is conceited and vindictive, capable of sudden petulant anger and even of undignified fear. A brief analysis of the poem will give the best idea of the spirit which pervades it.

Charlemagne was at the Church of Saint Denis one day, surrounded by his vassals and accompanied by his wife who, like himself, was wearing a magnificent crown. As he looked at his wife a wave of pride surged over him and, drawing her a little to one side, he said: 'Lady, have you ever seen a king on earth whose sword and crown became him so well?' His wife, never renowned for her wisdom, replied: 'Emperor, you esteem yourself too highly; I know a king who wears his crown amongst his knights more nobly than you do'. She soon regretted her thoughtless words, for Charles was furious on account of those standing round who might have overheard them. 'Where is this king? Tell me at once so that we can wear our crowns together. Then your friends on one side and my knights on the other can decide the question. If my Frenchmen agree with you I will abide by their decision; but if your word proves false, you will pay dearly for it, for I will strike off your head with my sword'. The poor queen bitterly regretted her idle words. In vain she declared that the other king might be richer but was not so valiant; in vain she offered to undergo a trial by ordeal and be thrown from the highest tower in Paris to prove that she had spoken with no evil intent. She was forced to blurt out the truth—viz. that she had in mind the King 'Hugo le Fort', emperor of Greece, Constantinople, and Persia, and the finest knight from there to Antioch. 'By my head', said Charles, 'I will go and find out'. The shaft had gone home very badly: 'You ought not to have thought such a thing about me. You have made me very angry':

> 'Par ma feit', dist li reis, 'molt m'avez irascut.
> . . . Nel deüssez penser, dame, de ma vertut.
> Ja n'en prendrai mais fin tres que l'avrai veüt' (ll. 51, 56–7).

Then the outraged emperor commanded the knights in his immediate entourage—Roland, Oliver, Guillaume d'Orange, Turpin, Naime,

Ogier, Bernard, and Bertrand, and others from the two well-known *gestes*—to prepare for a journey. He only informed them of the real reason for his departure incidentally, but stated that he had been bidden thrice in a dream to go to Jerusalem to worship the Cross and the Holy Sepulchre, and warned them that they would probably be away for seven years. So the expedition was prepared—not as a fighting force but as a peaceful pilgrimage, the knights being equipped with staves and scarves instead of swords and shields. The necessities of life, however, were not overlooked as the emperor ordered them to load 700 camels with gold and silver and they piled high their mules and pack-horses with vessels, clothes, armchairs (*faldestoels*), and silken tents. Thus they started, leaving a weeping queen behind them. But the emperor had not learnt his lesson; for no sooner were they away from the town than he called Bertrand (a wise choice) aside and asked him if he had ever seen such a noble army of pilgrims —eighty thousand in the front rank!—'Ki ço duit et governet bien deit estre poant!'[1] Bertrand was more discreet than the queen, and made no reply. So the emperor and his great company went on their way across Bavaria and Hungary and Greece (the description of the journey is obscure in our text, especially the line containing the reference to *la grant ewe del flum* and *croizpartie*),[2] till they arrived at Jerusalem and turned in at the church in which Christ had celebrated Mass with His twelve apostles. The twelve original seats were still there, and a thirteenth, barricaded and sealed, which was that of God Himself. Nothing daunted, Charlemagne went and sat in it, a thing which no one had ever done before. He was full of joy and pride and his appearance was so awe-inspiring ('tant out fier le visage') that a Jew, on coming into the church, nearly collapsed with fear, like the poor bishop of whom the Monk of St. Gall tells us in his chronicle (chapter xxv), and hastening straight to the patriarch, begged to be baptized at once. The patriarch, on hearing of the arrival of such an imposing leader, went forth to meet him and there was a scene of mutually respectful greeting. Charles was invested with the full name of 'Charlemaine' for having sat with impunity in the seat of God. Many sacred relics were handed over at his request, to be deposited at Saint Denis. These included such important ones as a nail which had pierced Christ's feet, the crown of thorns, the chalice, dish and knife which Christ had blessed and used, and many others. So strong was their efficacy,[3] that a paralysed man was healed straight

[1] l. 97.   [2] ll. 103–4.
[3] 'Les reliques sont forz deus i fait grant vertuz' (l. 292).

away. The emperor, full of joy, had them sealed in a golden casket and handed them over to Archbishop Turpin's care. For four months Charlemagne and his knights remained in Jerusalem, living in lavish style and not at all as became pilgrims. The Church of *Ste Marie la Latine* was constructed—so named because merchants of all nationalities and tongues brought their wares to it, and God, who insists on just weights and measures, was depicted symbolically on the roof.[1] With this good work the sojourn of the Frankish emperor in Jerusalem came to an end, and after a promise that in return for the relics he would summon an army for an expedition against the Saracens in Spain—a promise which the author tells us he faithfully kept when Roland and the twelve peers met their end[2]—the emperor departed, giving the subtle reason that he must go and look after his kingdom.[3] When night came, however, and the Frenchmen had retired to their lodgings (*ostels*), Charlemagne sent the word around that they were to be ready at break of day to set out in search of the king who had been praised by his wife at his expense. The knights were delighted when they heard that further adventures lay ahead of them, and the next morning they mounted and set off for Constantinople.

The second part of the poem is in a less serious vein and the lack of any vestige of historical truth is obvious. It is not in the nature of a crusading epic, for Charles wins a perfectly bloodless victory over his rival—a fact on which he congratulates himself:

> Molt fu liez et joios Charlemaignes le ber
> Ki tel rei ad cunquis sans bataille champel (ll. 858-9).

Nor is it a monkish legend, in spite of the part played by the relics and the intervention of the angel. It is in the nature of a burlesque although it might well serve as a warning against drunkenness and its consequences. It follows on quite naturally from the first part. Charlemagne and his company (who seem by now to have dwindled in number), having got under weigh, arrive at Jericho with palms in their hands and shouting the pilgrim's cry: *Ultre*(e), *Deus aie*![4] They were met by the patriarch but did not linger. After an exchange of greetings they proceeded on their way, crossing rivers and healing the blind and the maimed by the strength of their relics. At last they espied the spires and domes of Constantinople glittering in the sunlight. As they advanced they perceived knights and ladies, all beautifully clad, disporting themselves in the orchards. Charles rode up mounted on a sturdy mule and inquired pleasantly of a knight: 'Amis,

---

[1] l. 213.   [2] 'Quant la fu morz Rollanz, li xii per od sei' (l. 432).
[3] l. 217.   [4] l. 243.

u est li reis? mult l'ai alet querant'.[1] 'Ride straight forward and you will find him', replied the knight, and sure enough there was King Hugo, seated on a golden plough drawn by two mules, holding the reins in gloved hands and intent on ploughing a very straight furrow so as not to waste his time. The advantage in this poem is not always on the side of the most Christian king. The two potentates greeted each other in friendly wise, Charles introducing himself as Charlemagne, the uncle of Roland[2]—a proof of Roland's great reputation. King Hugo descended from his golden plough which he left lying in the field, assuring Charles that there were no thieves in his country. The French party was then conducted to the palace where another 7,000 richly-clad knights were seated playing 'as esches et as tables' as in the *Chanson de Roland.* The palace was wonderfully adorned with paintings and columns; it had the magic quality of turning round like a wheel when the wind blew in from the sea, rather like the 'chastel faé' of Tintagel, which was said to disappear at regular intervals. When Charlemagne saw all the wonders of the palace he forgot his pride in his own household and remembered his wife's words:

> La sue manantise ne priset mie un guant;
> De sa mullier li memb(e)ret que manecé out tant (ll. 363-4).

Whilst he was in the act of looking and marvelling and congratulating the king, the wind rose, and round the palace began to turn like the arms of a windmill.[3] It was a terrible storm with raging wind, snow and hail. The crystal windows, however, kept out the raging elements so effectively that it was as peaceful inside the palace as a sunny day in May. But the palace continued to turn so fast that Charles could not stand upright, and the Frenchmen covered their faces for fear as they lay flat on the ground, some on their faces and some on their backs ('adenz et sovin'). It was quite a new experience for the emperor and he did not like it at all. 'Will this go on for ever'?)[4] he asked the king. 'Have patience', replied Hugo, and sure enough the storm abated as evening approached. Then came the banquet with the king's wife and fair-haired, fair-skinned daughter who inspired Oliver with love at first sight. The guests were plied with wine and food (venison, crane, wild duck and devilled peacock), entertained by 'jongleurs', and finally put to bed with softest of pillows, sheets of silk, and beautiful bedspreads of fairy make. More wine was sent in to them by the wily king as each of the knights

---

[1] l. 279. [2] 'Jo ai(a) nun Carlemaine, Rolland si est mis nes (mon neveu)'.
[3] l. 372. [4] 'Ne serat jamais el?' (= *otherwise*).

chose the bed he would sleep on. Then comes the famous scene of the 'gabs', the *vanteries* or 'boasts'. All the knights were feeling merry after the *claret* which had been flowing in profusion. It was the emperor himself who proposed that each of them in turn should *gab*, i.e. declare what impossible, or, at any rate, unbelievable, task he would perform on the morrow. But King Hugo, before retiring to bed with his wife, had placed a spy in the bedchamber concealed in a hollow pillar, with instructions to report the Frenchmen's intentions to him. We need not describe all the different *gabs*—but it is note-worthy that Roland's boast was in connection with his famous horn, whereas the *gab* of Oliver was not at all in keeping with the character of that wise and courteous knight as we find it in the *Chanson de Roland*. The *gab* of Turpin, too, combining the skill of circus rider and clown, seems rather like a parody of the ability of the famous prelate. The rest were mere boasts of strength and prowess. The spy listened and marked each boast, and his comments to himself showed how he distinguished between harmless braggings and threats shameful to his lord. When the king heard the substance of the boasts he was naturally very angry and swore that all the Frenchmen should be forced to accomplish them next day on pain of death in the event of failure. On the following morning, Charlemagne, after his customary devotions, proceeded to meet the king, unsuspectingly carrying an olive branch in his hand. He was met with black looks: 'Charles, porquei gabastes de moi et escarnistes?' The emperor is forced to confess humbly that both he and his knights were all drunk the night before. He in his turn reproached King Hugo for his breach of hospitality in having him spied on during the night, for, said he, 'It is the custom for Frenchmen, when they go to bed, to boast and say things in jest, some of which are wise and some foolish'.[1] But Hugo was deeply offended and swore they should perform their boasts or die. So Charles had recourse to penitence and prayer, and an angel appeared to him who rebuked him sharply for folly but told him not to dismay. He then arose and crossed himself and encouraged his knights to come boldly to the palace.

The first *gab* of which the king demanded the accomplishment, believing in its impossibility, was that of Oliver, because it involved his daughter's honour. It was only partially accomplished, it is true, but the maiden had been so charmed by her seducer that she lied to her father the next morning and King Hugo was told to his dismay that the *gab* had been accomplished. Next came the *gab* of Guillaume

[1] ll. 650–7.

d'Orange and his feat of lifting a huge stone, throwing it over the palace and catching it the other side before it fell, was performed also with divine help. But the feat which reduced King Hugo to submission was that of Bernart, which brought the waters up out of their channels and the sea out of its bed and threatened to submerge the whole palace. Hugo was obliged to retreat from one storey to another, ever higher, until at last he sued for mercy as his life began to be in danger. Charlemagne was quickly moved to pity, for one should always be 'easy to be intreated' before humility.[1] He prayed that the floods should cease, and God performed this miracle 'por amor Charlemaigne'. Hugo, seeing that God was on the emperor's side, swore to become his man, to hold his kingdom from him and to grant him all his treasure. A grand procession was formed, both kings wearing their crowns. Charlemagne was taller than Hugo by one foot, four inches, so the Frenchmen recognized that their king was the most powerful potentate on earth and Charlemagne's wager was won. Soon the return journey to France was started. Oliver resisted the pathetic appeal of the king's daughter to accompany him: 'Car m'en portez en France, si m'en irai od vos';[2] his first duty was towards the emperor and his love must give way before that. Joyfully they set out for France, and Charles, after distributing the precious relics he had brought back with him, graciously forgave his wife for love of the sepulchre at which he had worshipped. So this curious poem ends, having brought Charlemagne back to the place of departure, viz. the *mostier saint Denis*. As we have said, the language of the *Pèlerinage*, with its Anglo-Norman colouring, compares favourably with that of the *Chanson de Roland* of the Oxford manuscript. And yet there is much in the poem which indicates a later date and gives it an air of romance. The author evidently knew the *Chanson de Roland* for he refers to the emperor as Roland's uncle, bases the boast (*gab*) of Roland on the renown of his famous horn, and actually refers on one occasion to the disaster of Roncevaux in which the peers were all slain.[3] He knew the clan of Guillaume d'Orange, several members of which he mentions among the knights of Charlemagne, showing thus a mingling of the clans such as we find in several early works.[4] He was evidently familiar with the character and known propensities of the various knights, for it is the truculent and rather greedy Guillaume d'Orange of the *Charroi* and the *Couronnement* who whispers to his nephew Bertrand, 'What a pity

[1] l. 789.   [2] l. 855.   [3] l. 232.
[4] E.g. the *Fragment de la Haye*, cf. supra, Ch. II.

you and I have not got this in France to turn into money', when he sees King Hugo's golden plough lying about unguarded on the grass. There is obviously a touch of parody in the story of the *gabs*, but it is not coarse parody such as we find in the poem *Audigier*, except, perhaps, in the case of Oliver (*le sage, le pieux, le corteis* of the *Chanson de Roland*). But even this is redeemed by the charming description of the young girl who was so frightened when Oliver entered her bedchamber and yet behaved so courteously[1] and begged him piteously not to dishonour her. She is very different from the brazen hussies who threw themselves at the head of the heroes in the early epic poems. But once she had given way she lied nobly to protect her newly-acquired lover from the effects of having proved himself unable to accomplish his vow. She is a heroine of a *roman courtois* rather than of a *chanson-de-geste*.

But it is when we come to the descriptions that we seem to be right in the middle of the twelfth century. Accounts of the East were now flowing back into France with the returning knights—particularly, perhaps, after the Second Crusade. We are in the age of *mirabilia*; 'le merveilleux' has invaded epic production. Here is the hall built 'par compas', the columns of many-coloured marble, the automatic figures which bow and smile to each other and seem to be alive:

> Li uns esgardet l'altre, ensement (cum) en riant,
> Que ço vus fust viaire que tut fussent vivant (ll. 360–1).

This is the sort of description we find in *Le Roman de Thèbes*, or even in *Flore et Blancheflor*, where wonderful feats were performed by the images on the bogus tomb of Blanchflor. The *Chronicle* of Robert de Clari, in which he describes the fall of Constantinople in 1204, describes many such *automata*, some of which were on a grand scale, for a whole contest was played by images of men and animals 'getees de cuivre', which played 'par encantement'—rather like, a football match played in an automatic machine by inserting a penny in the slot, but on a much larger scale and wonderfully made so as to look as though they were alive. The dazzle of the East runs through the poem. The carbuncle gives a brilliant light in the hall, the chairs and tables are of gold, the beds run about on silver castors and are marvels of workmanship like the 'lit merveilleux' in Chrétien's *Roman de Perceval*; the pillows are of velvet and the sheets of silken material, the counterpanes had been embroidered by a fairy.[2] The description

---

[1] 'Porquant si fut corteise' (l. 710).   [2] l. 431.

of the Church at Jerusalem fits into the oriental pattern. Its decoration was an exposition of the orthodox creed and the iconography which dominated Byzantine art. Starting from the animal creation of birds and fishes, it passed to the cycle of the great Christian festivals (. . . 'les curs de la lune et les festes anuels'),[1] thence to the armies of holy martyrs and virgins (. . . 'de martyrs et de virgines), and from that to the 'granz majestez' which could only be represented symbolically.[2] The relics need not detain us, although they were the very special ones of the holy nails, the crown of thorns and the arm of St. Symeon, and many others. These had been made familiar by the monkish legends as early as the tenth century and were claimed as the property of many rival churches. Robert the Monk of St. Remi (quoted above) had claimed for Constantinople many holy relics which had been salvaged from the pagan inroads in Asia and Africa[3] and had found a 'receptacle' in the capital of the East.

But it was left for Robert de Clari, a hundred years later, to become really lyrical about Constantinople and its wonders. His description of the emperor returning to the city after a successful campaign merits our attention for the analogy it bears to the description in our poem of King Hugo riding on his golden plough. The Emperor of Constantinople was on a four-wheeled chariot of gold ('un curre d'or'), in the midst of which was a platform on which a throne (caiiere) was placed. Round the throne (or seat) were four columns which bore an awning to keep off the sun ('un habitacle qui aombroit le caiiere'), which had the appearance of being entirely of gold. Here sat the emperor, fully crowned (tous coronés), and was drawn in state from the gate of the city called the *Porte d'Or* to his palace. The comparison between this procession and that of King Hugo in the *Pèlerinage* can be made by quoting the lines of the poem:

> Trovat le rei Hugon a sa charrue arant;
> Les conjogles en sont a or fin reluisant.
> . . . Une chaiere sus tienent d'or soz pendant.
> La sist li emperere sor un cossin vaillant,
> . . . A ses piez un eschame neielet d'argent blanc.
> Son chapel en son chief; molt par sont bel li guant;
> Quatre estaches d'or mier entor lui en estant;
> Desus i a jetet un bon palie grizain.

There are a few more picturesque details in the poem, such as the gloves and the foot-stool—but the main features are the same except

---

[1] l. 126.
[2] Cf. Norman Baynes: *The Byzantine Empire*, Ch. xi.
[3] *Historia hierosolymita*, Ch. iv.

for the important fact that Hugo's chariot was a plough and he was earnestly engaged on drawing a straight furrow. One could hardly imagine a gentler parody of the enthusiastic accounts brought back by crusading knights of the dazzling East, and once more a chronicle has provided the material for a poet to embroider.

IV. *AMIS ET AMILES*

Some apology is needed for including among the heroic poems generally ranged under the title of *chansons-de-geste* a legend of an entirely different character. *Amis et Amiles* does not strictly belong to any of the cycles; its heroes are not kings, or princes, or even unruly barons. Battles do not form its staple content, for there is but one in the whole story and that between only two individuals. No great issues, such as the triumph of Christianity or the struggle for supremacy between a king and his barons are at stake. It is the strength of an idea that gives the legend its epic value and its unity, for it is the theme of indissoluble friendship which governs it from beginning to end. It is, indeed, the exaltation of a fidelity so great that it exceeds simple friendship.

At once certain examples spring to one's mind that would be familiar to medieval poets whose two great sources of inspiration were the Bible and the Latin poets. David and Jonathan swore a solemn oath ('God do so to me and more also') to stand by each other under all circumstances, and we are told that 'the soul of Jonathan was knit to the soul of David'[1]; Nisus and Euryalus were bound by such a close tie that Nisus says to his friend: 'Te vero . . . jam pectore toto accipio, et comitem casus complector in omnes . . .; tibi maxima rerum verborumque fides.'[2] Their love was completely mutual[3] and one was willing to cheat in the games in order to give the other the victory,[4] a not unworthy precedent for the 'tricked ordeal' which forms the pivot of our legend. Other elements would, of course, be present in a medieval version, but the fundamental theme remains the same.

The story is briefly as follows: Two young men (Amicus and Amelius in the earliest known version) were born on the same day although in different localities, and in the Christian versions, christened by the same prelate. They were so alike, both in character

[1] 1 Sam. xxiii. 1.   [2] *Æneid*, IX, 276 f.
[3] His unus amor erat—ibid., l. 182.   [4] *Æneid*, V, 331 f.

and appearance, that they were indistinguishable even to their closest friends. At a suitable age they sought the king's court, where they won high favour with all except one jealous individual who had hitherto been in the king's confidence. One of them (Amicus in most versions) got married in due time and founded a home of his own. Amelius remained at court and proved only too attractive to the king's daughter who could not disguise her love for him. Watched and betrayed by the jealous favourite, the lovers were in danger of losing their lives, but before summary justice was executed, a duel (*duellum—combat judiciaire*) was arranged between the treacherous spy and the lover. Amelius, knowing that he was guilty and could not expect to triumph over his enemy if he perjured himself, went in haste to consult his friend. Amicus immediately suggested an exchange of rôles and garments which would enable him to fight the battle for his friend without swearing to a lie. The combat took place and the traitor-spy was killed. Amicus married the king's daughter without the fraud being discovered and then returned home. Meanwhile, his friend Amelius had replaced him and lived with his wife, but had placed a sword between them in bed out of loyalty to his friend. The exchange of personalities was again effected and each took possession of his rightful spouse. Shortly afterwards, Amicus was smitten with leprosy. Turned out brutally by an unfeeling wife, he set forth to ask help of his friend, who received him gladly. They learned that leprosy could only be cured by children's blood, and Amelius sorrowfully, but willingly, killed the two sons who had been born to him in the interval and used their blood to restore his friend to health. By a miracle, however, the children were resuscitated and found by their parents sitting up in bed, playing happily. Thus each of the friends in turn proved himself to be 'a friend in need', and having been faithful to each other in their lifetime, they were buried together, so that even in death they were not divided.

Such is the outline of the story which is common to all versions of the legend and had a wide popularity in the countries of Western Europe. The earliest known version is contained in a poem in Latin hexameters written by a monk of the Abbey of Fleury, Radulphus Tortarius, who flourished roughly in the second half of the eleventh century. The poem occurs amongst a group of letters (*Epistolae ad diversos*) which were probably written not later than the last decade of that century.[1] The particular epistle which concerns us here (No. 11) is in praise of friendships, beginning with the story of Damon and

---

[1] Cf. De Certain: *Archives des Missions Scientifiques*. V. Ire. Série, 118 f.

Pythias, then relating in more detail the story of Nisus and Euryalus, etc., and finishing up with that of Amicus and Amelius, which is told with greater elaboration than any of the others. It is a strange story, says the author, but is known in Gaul and Saxony, and though learned men despise it, there may be some truth mixed with the fable. Did Tortarius invent the story, combining certain well-known popular themes into one united, well-motivated whole? It is impossible under present conditions to say. Nor is it, perhaps, profitable to discuss, for there were many versions of the Jonathan and David relationship. In any case the epistle has by no means a popular character. It is full of reminiscences of Virgil, Ovid, and other Latin writers who were studied in the schools at that time. Sometimes the verbal correspondence is so great as to prove actual borrowings from the Latin texts. The description of the sudden love awakened by Amelius in the breast of the king's daughter is obviously inspired by that of Dido's love-sickness in Virgil and the duel, in which one of the fighters as he leaps forward (*emicat* in both texts) slips on the blood of a slain animal and falls ignominiously, to the joy of those watching, is clearly based on the classical text. The references and similes are entirely non-Christian: 'savage Cupid' shoots the dart which wounds the prince's daughter; the traitor (Adradus) is told to wash out his crimes in the waters of Phlegethon beneath the eyes of the Stygian judge after he has sought the waters of dark Erebus. The similes of the lioness robbed of her whelps and the bristly wild boars fighting savagely whilst the herd looks on have a very Virgilian ring. It is necessary to insist on the pagan character of Radulphus' poem because it has been cited as a proof of the feudal and Christian origin of the legend; it has also been stated that the two heroes bore the character of saints favoured by signs of divine predestination in the earliest known texts.[1] This is not true of the Latin poem which bears no traces of being a hagiographical legend.

The second part of the story is in some ways more medieval in character than the first part. The cure of leprosy by children's blood was a well-known fable in the Middle Ages. It is most familiar to us in the romance *Der arme Heinrich* by the German poet, Hartmann von Aue. It is hard to say where it originated. Perhaps the simple statement in the Bible that Naaman's flesh became 'as that of a little child'[2] started some train of thought or superstitious conjecture. Tortarius admits that he is relating strange things (*mira*) when he

---

[1] Cf. Bédier: *Les Legendes Epiques*, Vol. II, pp. 186–7.   [2] 2 Kings v. 4.

tells of the cure, but adds that he had heard them many times with his own ears from many sources. It is clear from the poem that the author was familiar with some of the Old French epic legends already existing, for the name of the courtier (*aulicus*), the traitor of the Latin poem, is *A(r)dericus* (Old French *Hardré*), who is an accepted traitor in the epic tradition. Moreover, in a rather unlikely episode, he has exploited some version of the Roland legend, for the anxious princess who, be it noted, was the first to fall in love, on seeing her lover hard-pressed after losing his sword, managed to get her father's sword which she fetches from his bedchamber delivered to him. This sword is the identical one which 'magnus Karolus' had presented to his nephew Roland and wherewith the latter had killed many thousands of heathen (*millia multa . . . pagani populi*)—a proof, if it were needed, that some version of the *Chanson de Roland* was current in the second half of the eleventh century. The name of the king, Gaiferus (Old French Gaifier), too, has a familiar ring.

The combat judiciaire ('duellum') is described at length by Radulphus. It accounts for eighty out of the 204 lines. It is inaugurated in the approved fashion; hostages are given and the priests bring out the 'sacra pignora' on which the combatants swear. There is chivalry between the knights—Amicus will not take advantage of an unarmed enemy when Adradus falls; but rules of combat were not as strict as they became later, for no messenger would have been allowed to enter the lists and bring a fresh sword to one of the combatants when these duels became more formal, as we find them in the later *chansons-de-geste*.

Very different in every respect from the Latin poem of Radulphus is another Latin version of the legend which enjoyed a wide circulation in the twelfth century. The *Vita Amici et Amelii carissimorum* is to be found in many manuscripts—often accompanied by the *Chronicle* of the so-called Faux-Turpin. The *Vita* is a monkish version of the story, and it is interesting to see the treatment the story received when it was utilized as an instrument of propaganda. All the possible Christian elements have been elaborated. The young men are predestined by angelic announcements, regenerated by baptism, exhorted to carry on the *miliciam Christi'* and observe the rites of Holy Church. It is the young man in the *Vita*—Amelius—who casts amorous eyes on the king's (Carolus magnus—in the '*Life*') daughter, but we are warned not to think this a strange case (*casus extraneus*), for there was not a more holy king than David nor a wiser

than Solomon. When he calls upon Amicus for help the latter has
not the slightest scruple about taking his friend's place in the judicial
combat. From the recess of his wise breast ('ab archano sapientis
pectoris') he replies: 'Let us change garments and horses; you set out
for my house without delay and I, *with God's help*, will do battle
with the treacherous count for you'. Just before the battle begins,
however, he has a prick of conscience: 'Heu michi, qui mortem huius
comitis tam fraudulenter cupio!' He knows that if he kills him he
will be guilty before the supreme judge ('supernum judicem') and
that if he is overcome it will be recounted to his eternal shame. So
he suggests to his opponent that they should abandon the mortal
conflict, in which case the count might be assured of his friendship
and service. Ardericus—convinced that he is fighting for the truth—
refused indignantly and the battle took place after the customary
oaths. It is described in exactly two lines. The 'delator impiissimus'
is killed and Amicus cuts off his head. Shortly afterwards Amicus was
smitten with leprosy. There is no hint of this being a punishment for
his sins. On the contrary, it is a mark of divine favour: '*Quo scriptum
est: Omnem filium quem Deus recipit, corripit, flagellat, et castigat*'. The
account of Amicus' wanderings and his eventual cure is long drawn
out and adorned with angelic visitations, prayers and pious ejaculations in the well-known style of monkish *Lives*. On the very day of
the miraculous cure the wicked wife of Amicus was snatched away
by the devil and, falling over a precipice, expired.

The *Vita* proceeds to relate how, after a number of years, the Pope
Hadrian sent to Charles for help against the Lombard King Desiderius.
Charles collected a vast army composed of 'gentes Francorum,
Anglorum, Theutonicorum, etc'. who flowed into Italy like rivers
flowing into the sea ('sicut omnia in mare flumina videntur fluere').
The Lombards and their king fled. This is not surprising, as for every
priest in the army of Desiderius, Karolus had a bishop; for every
monk an abbot, for every knight a prince, for every foot-soldier a
duke or count. Further, where Desiderius could send one soldier to
the battle, Charlemagne could send thirty. The description is a
variant of the scene in the Monk of St. Gall where the emperor, clad
in iron armour, and all his iron-clad followers struck terror into the
heart of the Lombard king. A battle was fought at a place called
Mortaria in which many were slain on both sides—amongst them
Amelius with his comrade Amicus. Two churches were built on the
spot to commemorate the victory, and the emperor had Amicus
buried in one and his son-in-law Amelius in the other. The next

morning, however, the sarcophagus containing the body of Amelius was found peacefully resting beside that of his friend. Thus in death they were not divided. Such is the hagiographic legend into which the simple story, as related by Radulphus Tortarius, had developed. It is interesting to compare with this the poetic version (with which we are chiefly concerned here) represented by the Old French epic poem *Amis et Amiles*, which occupies in many ways a middle position between the two Latin versions and illustrates in an illuminating manner the difference between the treatment of a subject by the monks and the 'jongleurs'. We have seen that the poem of Radulphus is completely non-religious, whereas the *Vita* is permeated with sickly clerical sentiment and biblical tradition. The *Chanson*, on the other hand, is neither the one nor the other. The prayers are conventional in character and similar to most prayers in the poems of the twelfth century; the admonitions are common sense; the onslaught of leprosy is a retribution for the sin of bigamy and not a proof of the love of God. It was not an instrument of propaganda; it was left to the pious *Vita* to invent the story of the two coffins coming together in the same church. It uses but does not abuse the touching story of friendship, linking it up with the idea of 'compagnonnage' which we have noted in so many of the heroic poems. There is no need to assume its Germanic origin in particular. The basic idea is Hebrew (David and Jonathan), classical (Nisus and Euryalus, etc.), Byzantine (Cosmo and Damien), Germanic (Gunthar and Siegfried). It contains elements of all these stories because the idea is a universal one. It is a theme of all time. Accurate dating is impossible. The form is that of the majority of epic poems of the twelfth century—viz. the decasyllabic lines united by assonances which show tendency to become rhymes. Each 'laisse' is terminated by a *vers orphelin* of six syllables—also a common feature of the *chansons*, particularly those of the Guillaume cycle. It has the conventional opening lines of the period:

> Or entendez, seignor gentil baron,
> Que deus de gloire vos face vrai pardon. . . .

which contrast so unfavourably with the simple majestic début of the *Chanson de Roland* ('Carles li reis, nostre emperere magne', etc.), or even that of the less evocative *Aliscans* ('A icel ior que la dolor fut granz', etc.); but are not so trivial as those of the later more romantic poems which sing of spring and birds and flowers ('Ce fu a Pasques la feste seignorie', etc.). There is, indeed, much in the poem that

recalls the earliest epic traditions. Charlemagne has replaced the Duke
Gaifier of the Radulphus version. He has kept up his habit of going
regularly to Mass and Matins before he betakes himself to his garden
(vergier). He is 'joianz et liez' when he sees his knights distinguishing
themselves in battle; he instantly detects the voice of a traitor:
'Hardré, dist il, cuer avez de felon.'[1] We are back in the *Chanson de
Roland* when we read:

> La veïssiez un estor commencier,
> Tant escu fraindre, tante lance brisier.

The description of the fight between Hardré and Amicus is drawn out
to the extension of its limit. Hardré loses first an ear and then an eye
before he loses his head. As much gory description is introduced as
the subject will allow. But the theme which welds the rather lengthy
poem into one united whole is, of course, that of the indissoluble
friendship of the two heroes. The idea of 'compaignie' runs through
the poem—initiated by a plighted troth, cemented by a natural
compatibility of character and the remarkable similarity of appearance which makes the two friends interchangeable. At the very
beginning of the poem they swear to this remarkable form of friendship:

> Il s'entrafient *compaignie* nouvelle (l. 200).

They are continually drawn to each other like two lovers[2] and the
poem sometimes develops into a kind of quest. They will not accept
the same form of loyalty towards any other man. When Amiles feels
he has let his friend down by neglecting his advice he is filled with
remorse, and on finding himself on the spot where they plighted their
troth he exclaims:

> Ci fumes nez; et juré et plevi
> La *compaignie* entre moi et Ami.
> Il l'a gardé con chevalier de pris
> Et je com fel et com deu annemis (ll. 912 f.).

Loyalty to this friend takes precedence of loyalty to the wife. When
Belissant, the emperor's daughter, marries Amis, who is substituting
for Amiles, she has to swear that she will never cause strife between
the two friends. When Amis is thought to be dying of leprosy and
is too weak even to be carried to church, Amiles is heartbroken at
the thought of the coming separation: 'La compaignie se va molt
departent', he cries, reminding us inevitably of the poet's words at

---

[1] l. 252.   [2] Cf. Tristan and Iseut.

the parting of Roland and Oliver (for they, too, had plighted their troth to each other):

> Oi nus defalt la leial cumpaignie,
> Einz le vespre mult ert gref la departie.[1]

Even one of the little boys, though terrified at the sight of his father coming in with drawn sword, as soon as he heard that his own death will mean the life of his father's friend, exclaims:

> Or nos copez les chies isnellement,
> . . . Quant vos compainz aura garissement (ll. 3005-6).

It is human traits such as these that we owe to the 'jongleur', and it is to the characters themselves, rather than to the episodes that the poem owes those distinguishing features which enable us to place it in the pattern of the Old French epic. The two heroes are, of course, models of faithfulness, for this is the essence of the story. But they are attractive in other ways, for they are both equally beautiful and brave:

> Il s'entresemblent de venir et d'aler
> Et de la bouche et dou vis et dou nes,
> Dou chevauchier et des armes porter
> Que nus plus biax ne puet on deviser.
> Dex les fist par miracle (ll. 38-43).

Their courage is seen in action when they fight against the emperor's enemies; their charming lack of suspicion is seen in the way they defend Hardré's reputation after the battle and accept the offer of his daughter in marriage—an offer which he first made to Amiles but which, fortunately for himself, Amiles passed on to Amis, saying: 'Mes compains l'ait qui plus est conquereres'. Thus Amiles was spared from being united to the horrible woman who comes from a family of traitors and never ceases to torment her husband and try to sow trouble between him and his friend. There is no hint in the Latin versions that the cruel wife was related to the impious traitor. The fact was probably invented by the 'jongleur' in order to bring his poem into the orbit of other *chansons-de-geste* by attaching at least one character in his poem to a well-known 'lignage'. By so doing he would account for her atrocious behaviour, for she is endowed with many more evil traits in the *chanson* than in either of the Latin versions. The treatment of both the feminine characters and the complete lack of gallantry towards women on the part of the men gives an archaic flavour to the whole poem. Amis accepts without a murmur

---

[1] *Chanson de Roland*, ll. 1735-6.

the daughter of Hardré who is thrust upon him, and Amiles is
shamelessly wooed by the king's daughter Belissant, who catches him
by guile. When she forces herself into his bed it is only because he
thinks she is a maidservant that he consents to be her lover. When
he learns the truth by her own confession ('Par bel engieng voz ai
prins et maté'), he is angry at first, though he lets no word of regret
fall from his lips when he confesses his imprudence to his friend.
Amis, too, has no spark of chivalry towards his wife, for when he
tells Amiles (with whom he is about to exchange places) how to treat
Lubias if she is difficult, he says:

> S'elle voz dist orgoil ne faussetez
> Hauciez la paume et el chief l'an ferez (ll. 1068–9).

Amiles does so with excellent results and, like Hermenjart when
treated in the same way by Aimeri, Lubias appears to consider it
a perfectly natural proceeding. This absence of chivalry towards
women definitely helps us to place our poem and rank it among the
epics rather than the romances. Both the feminine characters are
entirely consistent with this, for even the emperor's daughter is, as
we have seen, capable of deceit and guile. She feels a prick of conscience during the battle between Amis and Hardré, for she knows
that the latter was not lying in his accusation. She mutters beneath
her breath[1]: 'God knows that what Hardré has sworn and pledged
is true and that he has not lied with a single word'. But she feels free
nevertheless to pray that God will protect her lover and lay the traitor
low.[2] The poet seems to treat the ruse as a matter of course, just as
Béroul treats the narration of Iseut's trickery when she swore her oath
after crossing the stream on the back of her lover disguised as a leper.
Belissant emerges in the end, however, as a loyal wife who respected
her husband's wishes and was willing to place herself in his affections
below his friend. It is Lubias, the wife of Amis, who is the really
bad woman—the '*saevissima conjux*' of Tortarius' poem. She is evil
from beginning to end, but the spitefulness of her character comes out
most luridly when her husband has been smitten with leprosy. She
insults him and reproaches him; she abuses the bishop who will not
at first release her from him; she banishes the sick man to a miserable
hut ('*habitacle*') and tries to starve him; she illtreats her own son and
locks him up when he wants to take food to his father. Finally she
goes in procession to church accompanied by two knights preceded
by a 'jongleur' singing songs of love and friendship! As they pass the

---

[1] 'entre ses dens, que nus ne l'entendit' (l. 1435).
[2] ll. 1436–40.

hut the leper (Amis) comes out and begs for a crumb from her table, but Lubias merely tells him she is sick of him and hopes he will be dead before a month is over:

> Ja deu ne place qui tout a a jugier,
> Que vous soiez passez un mois entier,
> Trop en sui annuiie (ll. 2352-5).

In the *Vita* Lubias comes to a violent end as she richly deserves. But in the *Chanson* her fate is not so grim. Amis, who has a beautiful, unselfish character all through the poem, at first refuses her advances when he returns home handsome and cured of his leprosy. He orders her to be bound and shut up in the same hut that he had inhabited with a little piece of bread.[1] But his kind heart melted and he soon had her fetched back and reinstated in her territory.

This insistence in the *Chanson* on the bad character of Lubias is entirely in keeping with epic tradition. She came of bad stock—of a '*put lin*' out of which no good could come. The traitor family was a large one as we have seen, and Hardré was one of its outstanding members. His name, like that of Macaire, is well known in the *chansons-de-geste* as a worthy descendant of Ganelon, or Doon de Mayence, as the case may be. His evil character creates a foil for the gentle character of Amis and Amiles. Soon after the first meeting of the two friends, at which they embraced so rapturously that they nearly passed out,[2] we are introduced to Hardré:

> Huimais orrez de Hardré le felon
> Qui porchasa la mortel traïson (ll. 2289-90).

The very words remind us of Ganelon, and he is never spoken of without such epithets as *fel, losengiers, traitres, lerre, parjurs, de put lin,* etc. He sits beside the king and whispers malicious things into his ear. He has a large following for his clan is numerous—'couzin ou frere, tuit furent d'un paraige'. After the first round in the battle, in which he has lost an ear and an eye, he sends for his *filluel* and, in the conversation which follows, his devilish character comes out for he gives his adopted son much the same advice as the devil gave to Theophile in the 'miracle' of Rutebuef:

> Je te chastie, bians filleus Aulori,
> Que n'aiez cure de dammeldeu servir,
> Ne de voir dire, se ne cuides mentir,
> Se vois preudomme, panse de l'escharnir,

---

[1] '*un quarteret de pain et ne mie trop grant*' (l. 3447).
[2] 'Tant fort se baisent et estraignent soëf
A poi ne sont estraint et define' (ll. 180-1).

> De ta parole, se tu puez, le honnis,
> Ardez les villes, les bors, et les maisnils,
> Metez par terre autex et crucefiz
> Par ce serez honorez et servis (ll. 1625–33).

It is obvious that Hardré has sold his soul to the devil. The next day, when the battle is about to begin, Amiles prays to God (a very conventional prayer it is true) that he may kill this 'glouton' and see his dear compagnion once more. Hardré, on the other hand, blasphemes God and puts his faith in the devil:

> Ier fiz bataille el non dou criator,
> Hui le ferai el non a cel seignor
> Qui envers deu nen ot onques amor.
> Ahi diables! con ancui seras prouz (ll. 1660–4).

From this moment his fate is sealed, like that of Raoul de Cambrai when he blasphemed God and His saints.

We have lingered over *Amis et Amiles* partly on account of its wide popularity in the Middle Ages, partly because it is a good example of the way in which a popular story could be pressed into the epic mould, so that not only its form but its character also could be worked into the accepted pattern. The 'jongleur' has attached it loosely to the Charlemagne cycle by transforming the Duke Gaiferus (of Radulphus Tortarius) into the Emperor Charlemagne. But its link with epic tradition is rendered much closer by the introduction and development of the character of the traitor, an element which, it is important to note, is also prominent in the earliest version we possess. It is interesting also to see how the hagiographic version (as represented by the *Vita*) and the poetic versions (as represented by our *chanson*) developed on independent lines, each incorporating into the story those features which were characteristic of its *genre*. It would take us too far here to go into the relations between the Old French epic, the English version, *Amis and Amiloun*, the Anglo-Norman *Amis e Amilun*, and others. Suffice it to say that in general the poetic versions, in spite of many differences in detail, have the majority of episodes in common. As an example of this we might mention that in all the poems we have reviewed the lady is the first to make advances (in each case in a rather overbearing manner) and the punishment of the wicked Lubias is to be immured in a small building and fed on bread and water. In the *Vita*, on the contrary, it is the man who first casts amorous glances on the woman, and the savage Lubias (or Obias) is hurled by the devil to her death. The English and Anglo-Norman versions are not brought into the Charlemagne cycle nor is the traitor given his well-known name. He is simply alluded to as the 'steward' and the 'senescal' in the two poems respectively. Another peculiarity of these two poems is that the parts of *Amicus and Amelius* are completely reversed. It is obvious that the legend was a popular one in the twelfth century and that there were divergent versions, the later ones being more romantic in character. The Old French prose version (*Li amitiez de Ami et Amile*) and the 'Miracle de Nostre-Dame', both dating from the fourteenth century, are based on the *Vita*, the former being an almost literal translation of the Latin text. The moral of the legend was used as an 'exemplum' by preachers in the fourteenth century.

Thus the story wound its way through the Middle Ages, becoming more and more fantastic with passing time. The development reaches its peak, perhaps, in the *Roman de Miles et Amis* by Antoine Verard, in the fifteenth century. In this version, which is stuffed with adventures on the one hand and trite maxims of bourgeois philosophy on the other, the most attractive figure is a faithful and intelligent monkey whose appearance halfway through the poem introduces us to the primitive legend of the two loyal friends! From this and other similar works it passed into the editions of the *Bibliothèque bleue* which gave it its final form.

Q

CHAPTER XI

THE OLD FRENCH EPIC OUTSIDE FRANCE

I. *IN ENGLAND*

IT is no exaggeration to say that all the literary movements which flourished in Western Europe during the Middle Ages sprang from the soil of France. Their origins are mysterious and elusive: we cannot do much more than study the soil from which they sprang and note the fact that the great movements of the crusades and the religious revival in the eleventh and twelfth centuries served both to fertilize that soil and spread the seeds over a wide area. Some of the plants produced had a richer growth in France than in the lands to which they were transplanted; others found a more congenial soil outside the country of their origin, though the transplanted shoots never broke completely away from the parent plant. Some might consider that the lyric production of the twelfth and thirteenth centuries—possibly, too, the wealth of romance—which appeared in Germany and elsewhere, belonged to the second of these two categories, but to the first, without a doubt, belongs the epic production in the stricter sense of the word, i.e. in the sense in which it applies to the 'genre' we have been considering. This is partly due to the nature of epic poetry, but partly, too, to the fact that the heroes were national in character and consequently of much greater importance in their own country than elsewhere. True, Charlemagne had an international reputation, and he did, in fact, enjoy a wide popularity and fame until he was eclipsed by a more fabulous royal hero in the shape of King Arthur. Guillaume d'Orange, on the other hand, was little known outside his own country. We do not hear of him in England, and it was, perhaps, unfortunate that the poem which celebrated him and his exploits in Germany was composed in a language and style extremely difficult to understand. But the fact remains that he could not have become a very popular hero outside his own country, and the French poets themselves did not help matters by giving the title of 'matière de France' to all those poems dealing with their home-grown heroes, even though their activities were often directed against a common enemy.

In England one might, however, have expected a better fate,

considering the close ties which existed between the two countries after the Norman Conquest. English poetry had, moreover, an epic tradition behind it which might have made it more ready to embrace its foreign relation. Unfortunately, however, there is a scarcity of English productions for a long period before and after the year 1100, just about the time when epic poetry was at its height in France. The absence of anything corresponding to the earlier Old French epic poems is the more noticeable because the earliest known manuscripts of both the *Chanson de Roland* and the *Chanson de Guillaume* were probably written in England by Anglo-Norman scribes. Yet the former gave rise, as far as we know, to no immediate adaptation or imitation and the latter apparently had no result at all.

There has come down to us, however, a fragment of a *Song of Roland* in Middle-English alliterative verse to which, perhaps, not quite full justice has been done. If due consideration is given to the fact that some 200 years (or possibly more) had elapsed since the story of Roncevaux received its first poetic form, some credit must be given to the author for passing on to us even the faintest echo of the original. The fragment consists of 1,049 lines and begins at the point of the story where Ganelon returns from the heathen court to Charlemagne's camp, bringing rich gifts and a false promise couched in fair and flattering words: 'he told many tailis and all was lies'. He informed the emperor that there was no need of further fighting, for the sultan would come within fifteen days and receive the Christian faith. He is sanctimonious in his words:

> Ther is no prow to pryk þer men pece sought!
> If that mercy and myght mellithe togedur
> he shall have the mor grace ever aftur (ll. 32–5).

Amongst the gifts he brought were many fair ladies, and good wine, with the subtle intent of lowering the morale of the French army. It had the desired effect. The author describes vividly how:

> It (= the wine) swymyd in þer hedis and mad hem to nap;
> they wist not what þey did, so þer wit failid.
> when they wer in bed and thought to a-restid,
> they went to the women þat were so hend (ll. 70–3).

This detail is known to us from the *Chronicle of Turpin*, who preaches a little sermon on the rights and wrongs of the fact that both those who sinned with the women and those who did not met their death indiscriminately on the battlefield. The English poet does not stop for this, but proceeds to tell of Charlemagne's ominous dreams and the interpretation given to them by his wise men. It is obvious, as we proceed in the English version, that the model was an early one. The characters are completely in accord with those of the best epic period. Roland is beloved of his peers:

> With Sir Roulond to rid they were bold;
> For he in word and work greved us neuer,
> nor sparied schewing of sheldis for non þat lyuyd ever.
> For dred of dethe, he hid never his hed (ll. 209–12).

The affection and loyalty is, as in the *Chanson*, mutual:

> 'Now wise us crist!' quod Roulond, 'one word;
> We be *fellos* and *frendis*, God be our gid' (ll. 303–4).

The insistence on *fellichip* and Roland's grief when it must come to an end give his character that human touch with which we are familiar:

> Not for his own sake he soghed often,
> but for his *fellichip* þat he most louyden (ll. 600–1).

Constantly he cheers his comrades, not only with the thought that they will sup that night with the saints in heaven where Christ feeds the souls of the blest, but with the heartening words of a true leader of men:

> let our hertis be hie, and togedir rynn,
> that no hethyn hound of our men wyn.
> but he by it with blod, his brest with-in (ll. 375–7).

His indignation when Oliver suggests that he should blow his horn, is expressed in brief words:

> 'Abid,' quod Roulond, 'and suche wordis blyn!
> Olyver, art thou aferd of this sight?' (ll. 534–5).

But his words to his men, as always, express his character best. All the princes begged him to blow his bugle for help—not for dread of death but out of love to their lord.[1] Their joining in the request made Roland really angry, and he answered in stern words:

> Ye knyghtis, for shame shon ye never,
> have ye broken eny bone, or eny harm tid?
> May ye schew in your sheild eny strokeis wid?
> Is not your compony hole as they come?
> Flee fast þat is afferd, þat he wer at home! (ll. 560–4).

When they understood that their lord was determined to fight to the bitter end, they took comfort and cried: 'Cursed be he that flies and yields any foot of the field this day'. So the next morning the battle was renewed and the author gives us the usual description of the

[1] ll. 551–2.

many single combats between heathen and Christian. Both Oliver and Roland performed prodigies of valour. Of Oliver, we are told that never were so many slain by one man,[1] and then we find the phrase: 'Whom he raught in the rout, his lif last',[2] so familiar in its Old French form: 'Cui il consuit', etc.

The names of the twelve peers do not tally exactly with any extant version of the *Chanson*. Some of them we recognize, others not. 'Richard þat russelen fonge' is obviously 'Girard de Roussillon'. Turpin is mentioned, both among the list of knights at the beginning and later for his deed of valour in killing the richly dight African[3] who had just struck down Amys of Almayn (= Fr. Anseis). 'Ly þer', said Turpin as he cursed him and rode away bidding the fiend fetch him off to hell.[4] The names of the heathen, too, are much disfigured. Grandoine, son of Capuel the King of Cappadocia, appears as Cadwel; he and his horse are cloven through the middle by a tremendous stroke from Roland in all the known versions, but the Middle-English description is, perhaps, the most vivid:

> He (Roland) rent hym unredly enyn to the sadill:
> on either sid of the horse down he did wadill (ll. 990–1).

Valdabrun (of the continental version), who took Jerusalem 'par trahison', has become 'Dalabern of Valern' who took Jerusalem 'with a gyn'.[5] Ganelon, the traitor, has remained his evil self, but the author knew all about the 'pute geste' for he mentions Herdres (= Hardré) and Mark(is) (= Macaire?) and others of his numerous kin ('his kyn many').[6] Some of the episodes differ from those with which we are familiar. Sir Gauter (= Gautier del Hum) is sent out to reconnoitre the enemy and returns alone before the main battle begins, having lost all his army in an ambush. He comes back broken-hearted at his defeat and convinced that Ganelon has betrayed them:

> I wold foulis had ete me, so I were at my end.
> Gwynylon hathe us gilid, I may say now;
> that ever he was born, a tratur to prove (ll. 365–7).

The fragment ends, moreover, on an unexpected note. Roland, seeing that defeat is inevitable, realizes that they must seek help from Charles. He does not propose to sound his horn, however, but to send a messenger:

> I red we send a man to feche our lord;
> say we be sore hurt and socour we wold.

[1] l. 792. [2] l. 796. [3] '= Malquiant le filz al rei Malcud' in the *Chanson*, Ms. O.
[4] l. 975. [5] l. 955. [6] l. 403.

One wonders how he actually met his death in the English version, for in the known accounts it is caused by his effort in sounding the horn and not at the hand of his foes.

There are, of course, differences in style between the English poem and the earlier poems. Romance has crept in and we are told that as the day dawned and the sun rose:

> dew disked adown and dymmyd the floures,
> And foulis rose and song full Amorous (ll. 580-1).

The 'Gates of Spain' are described as being full of craggy rocks and ancient hills and so narrow that three men could not go in at once.[1] The 'strange weather' that occurred in France as the armies fought is described with a pastoral touch:

> Foulis fled for fere, it was gret wonder;
> bowes of trees þen brestyn asonder:
> best ran to bankis and cried full sore,
> they durst not abid in the mor.
> . . . the wekid wedur lastid full long
> from the morning to the evynsong (ll. 851-7).

Finally a blood-red cloud arose in the west and shone down on the men who died in the battle. They died with resignation after having been blessed by Turpin and assured of God's love. Every man took off his helmet and, looking upwards, lifted his hands and thanked Christ who had defended them up to that point. Then Roland prayed 'Criste kep us cristyn that ben here / to serve your soper with seintis dere'. The supper promised to those slain on the battlefield may appear more gross than the flowers of paradise which appear in earlier poems; the descriptions may be more trivial and the general tone less solemn and sublime: but the action is rapid, the characters are consistent (as far as can be judged by the fragment) and the poem has its moral content for we have such an occasional remark as:

> It is good to be wise in ded and in thought (l. 310).

or

> He must take heed that with evil dealeth (l. 249).

Less profound, perhaps, but as applicable to human affairs as the Old French 'mult ad aprins qui bien conuist ahan'.[2]

It was natural that the story of Roncevaux with its intense patriotism and its glorification of the part played by Charlemagne and his knights against the threat from the East should make a greater appeal

---

[1] l. 127.   [2] *Chanson de Roland*, l. 2524.

to the continental nations than to the inhabitants of an island less exposed to the common enemy of Christendom. Moreover, the victory of Charles Martel in 732 had checked the rapidly advancing tide of invasion and Oxford had been saved from the fate imagined by Gibbon of having the Koran taught in its schools and the revelation of Mahomet proclaimed in its pulpits.[1] But there was one subject that had a perennial appeal whatever the nationality of the hero or the cause at stake. This was the unequal combat between a gigantic heathen and a much smaller but more nimble opponent—in fact, between David and Goliath, a permissible simile because the smaller man is always supported by divine strength and the giant is always defeated in the end. There are many descriptions of such combats in the *chansons-de-geste*, epic encounters between royal combatants— Charles and Baligant, Louis and Gormont, Guillaume and Corsolt; nor was the popularity confined to the *chansons-de-geste*, for we have Tristan and Morholt in the Tristan legend and many another such episode in the romances. But there are two outstanding matches of strength to the popularity of which abundant tribute is paid in allusions of more or less contemporary authors. These are the single combats between the two great friends Roland and Oliver and the two heathen giants Fernagu (*Ferracutus*) and Fierabras respectively. The first of them, *Roland v. Fernagu*, was widely known from its inclusion in the *Pseudo-Turpin Chronicle*.[2] It was translated into English and is contained in the famous Auchinlech manuscript together with *Sir Otuel*[3]—a version of the Old French poem *Otinel*. Little would be gained by going into these two translations in detail, although the second—Sir Otuel—gains a certain importance from the fact that the story forms a section of the *Karlamagnus-Saga* (of which more later) in which Otuel appears under the same name as in the English version. It has been suggested that the story was transmitted to the Icelandic author through the medium of the English version, which would be an interesting light on the literary relations between the two countries in the twelfth century.

The story, however, which seems to have had the widest circulation in England is that of the fight between Oliver and Fierabras and the circumstances under which the combat took place. The two main English versions are *Sir Fyrumbras*, a poem in somewhat free verse with partial alliteration, and a metrical version known as *The*

---

[1] D. and F., Ch. vi.
[2] See Ch. IV, p. 25, where an account of the classic fight is given.
[3] Ellis: *Metrical Romances*, ii.

Romaunce of the Sowdone of Babylone and of Ferumbras his Sone who conquerede Rome. Of these two adaptations of French models the latter is the more comprehensive, though much less diffuse work, as it includes the two distinct narratives: (1) the destruction of Rome by Laban (or Balan) of Spain and the capture of the holy relics, (2) the battle between Oliver and Fierabras d'Alexandre and the recovery of the relics. *Sir Fyrumbras* begins at what we might call the second half of the story. Rome has already been conquered by the Saracens, the relics have been seized by Fierabras. We are plunged 'in medias res' with a reference to the emperor's ill-timed remark that in the recent fighting the veterans had made a better show in the battle than the young knights. This gave great offence to Roland, who had fought bravely, and who not unreasonably accused Charles of wanting to praise himself: 'Thou madest that auaunt, soth to saye, / for to praise the selve'.[1] So indignant was he that when the heathen champion Syre Fyrumbras of Alexandre approached and defied the Christian army, he refused to undertake the battle against him when requested to do so by the emperor. Consequently Oliver, although wounded, had to undertake the combat. All this is in complete accord with the French and Provençal poems on the subject, although the actual version on which it is based is difficult to determine. The duel is long drawn out. Oliver fights at first under a feigned name (Garin in the English poem), but at last, when pressed by the heathen, who soon discovers that he is fighting with a seasoned warrior, he admits: 'Olyver ys my name rizt, a doꝑꝑeper am of France'. It is interesting to note how the original meaning of the 'douzepers' had been lost in English where a single knight as here is often called a 'dozeper'. The rest of the poem, which recounts the struggle between the two armies, follows its French models closely, but it is long drawn out in the English poem, especially in the later part where the metre changes for some unaccountable reason, and to each rhyming couplet is added a short line which generally contributes little to the sense but much to the length of the work. The characters are similar to those in the French versions. Sir Fyrumbras' conversion is very rapid after he has received the deciding blow from Oliver's sword, as in the English version the sermon pronounced on the battlefield by the ardent Christian proselytizer is completely absent. The Emperor Charlemagne is just as autocratic and, indeed, unreasonable as he often is in the later epic stories. But he was truly concerned for the

---

[1] l. 158.

fate of his barons captured by the Saracens and his depression is quite infectious when we read:

> Than set he him down in drury mode
> and dropede for hure sake (l. 1103).

The daughter of the Emir (Balan), like so many heathen maidens in the decadent epic poems, had set her heart on marrying a French knight. When the barons, including most of the 'doþþepers', were taken prisoner by Balan's army and shut up in a dungeon, Floripas shrinks from nothing in her effort to see them. She kills the warder who obstructs her passage with a blow from a stout stick, but much worse is her treatment of her nurse (maitresse) who also tries to restrain her. She threw her out of the window into the sea and left her to drown. This episode occurs in all the different versions but the English author treats it with evident relish. He describes at length how she pretended to lean out of the window to look at something and got her nurse to do the same as though she would speak privately to her. Then she signed to an attendant to approach from behind. As she and the nurse leaned further and further out with heads close together, the attendant seized the nurse's legs and heaved the poor woman right out of the window:

> By the legges lifte he þe schrewe þan and scef hur out ech del,
> þan ful down þat olde trate into þe salte see.

Floripas was then free to visit the French knights and bring them food and balm for their wounds. She comforted them with all her might and main and bade them be 'glad and blythe'. Towards her own father, on the other hand, she was completely without filial feeling. . Towards the end of the poem, after the final defeat of the heathen and the capture of their king, Charlemagne is anxious that Balan should be baptized. He had a huge vat filled with clean water and summoned the bishop for the ceremony. In view of the emir's rank three of the most valiant knights, Roland, Oliver, and Ogier, were allocated to him to prepare him for his baptism. They had to take off his clothes by force for he turned and twisted so much ('tornde and wende fast'), but in the end they got them off whether he would or no. Then, surprisingly, in the English version, Charles preached to him and enumerated the articles of Christian faith, beginning with how Christ was born of the Virgin 'Wyþoute wem and wyþoute hore / As sunne goþ þorz þe glas' and ending with the promise of heavenly bliss if he will but 'do the deed'. Balan, however, was adamant as in the basic versions. He sweated with anger and spat in the font in despite of God Almighty. His son Fyrumbras pleaded with his father in vain, a contrast to his sister Floripas ('þat burde bryzt') who besought the emperor to slay him at once. Balan had almost yielded and was about to step into the water when the bishop informed him that a public recantation of his faith was necessary. This was too much and the heathen struck the bishop with his fist, knocking out three teeth. Fyrumbras pleaded once more on his knees, but Floripas insisted that it was waste of time. Her brother remonstrated with her: 'Sustre ne ys he þy fader; Tak of hym pytee', but at last it was apparent that all appeals would avail nothing and Charles asked for a volunteer to slay the 'heþene hounde'. Ogier came forward and without more ado Balan lost his head. Much of this was in the French original but the English poet relates the episode with gusto and with many a telling phrase, especially where the 'burde bryzt' is concerned. He betrays no repugnance to the callousness of Floripas, who is described elsewhere in the conventional terms of the French beauty; he knows other epic poems and refers to the stock traitors as well-known characters. His work may not be original but it is not without merit and must have contributed greatly to the renown of Sir Fyrumbras in England.

The Romance of the Sowdone of Babylone and of Ferumbras his Sone is another version of the same story and includes the introductory destruction of Rome. It is a more attractive poem both on account of its greater compactness and its less laboured metrical form. Originality can no longer be claimed, for it is a translation[1], in some cases almost verbal, of a French version of the legend which was published in 1938 by L. M. Brandin (see *Romania* LXIV). The two parts of the poem are clearly distinguished—the first part which relates the destruction of Rome by the Soudan of Babylong, *alias* Laban d'Espagne, ends with a temporary discomfiture of the heathen and the emperor's provocative remark that his seasoned warriors have won the battle and the 'yonge of age' should follow in their footsteps. He is even more irresponsible than in the previous poem for he adds:

> These hethen houndes we shall a-tame
> By God in magisté
> Let us make myrth in Goddis name
> And to souper now go we (ll. 935–9).

The second part, which is more strictly the legend of Fierabras, opens with a prayer of the heathen to 'red Mars Omnipotent' to give them

---

[1] See Hausknecht, Ed. E.E.T.S., Preface, p. xxxiii.

victory over the 'crystys doggis'. We do not find this in the French versions, and it may well be an addition on the part of the translator, as is a similar invocation occurring in other English poems. It is not an isolated addition, for a short moral has been added to the prologue, ending with the words:

> For the offences to God idone
> Many vengeaunces have befalle;

moreover Charles' words to his young knights receive their justification:

> For worthynesse wole not be hadde
> But it be ofte soughte,
> Nor knighthode wole not ben hadde
> Till it be dere boghte.

In fact, the translation, though often literal, is not slavish. It partakes more of the nature of a romance than the French by reason not only of its short four-lined stanzas but also of its references to spring[1]; its descriptions of unknown people; its references to chivalrous love and the necessity of acting like a gentleman,[2] and its obvious enjoyment of feminine guile—for Floripas, in order to get her nurse to come to the window tells her to come and see the porpoises! Floripas, moreover, refers to a local custom when desirous of celebrating her betrothal to Sir Gye (Duke of Burgoyne), she produced from her father's treasure a golden goblet 'ful of noble myghty wyne' and said:

> 'my love and my lorde.
> My herte, my body, my goode is thyn',
> And kissed him with that worde,
> And 'Sir' she said, 'drinke to me,
> As the Gyse is of my londe;
> And I shalle drinke agayn to the,
> As to my worthy hosbonde'.
> Thay clipped and kissed both in fere
> And made grete Joye and game,
> And so did alle that were there (ll. 1928–37).

There is a very English ring about this. Perhaps we may say the same about the behaviour of the emperor who did not stand for a symbol of justice in England as he did in France. He was always anxious to be merry. He did not preach a sermon to Laban when he ordered 'a grete fat' to be prepared for his baptism, and he very readily came to the conclusion (after the soudan had 'spitted in the water cler' and struck the archbishop) that there was no hope now for

---

[1] 'To the semely seson of the yere' (ll. 963 f.).   [2] l. 1273

his conversion. His attitude, moreover, was somewhat callous towards a gallant opponent:

> 'Duke Neymes' quod Charles tho,
> 'Loke þat execution be don,
> Smyte of his hedde! God gyfe him woo!
> And goo we to mete anoone (ll. 3183–6).

There is no hint in the French original that Charles was as fond of his food as he appears to be on several occasions in the English rendering.

The descriptions of the 'heathen houndes' and their mysterious rites are very colourful in the *Sowdone*. The army consists of three thousand Saracens, some blue, some yellow, some pitch black. They drink 'wilde beestes blood' to make them more ferocious ('to egre here mode') before they go into battle. When Laban and Sir Ferumbras had captured Rome and conveyed the holy relics to Spain they celebrated the victory by an offering to their gods. They burned frankincense 'that smoked up so strong', they drank blood, ate milk and honey and serpents fried in oil, and shouted: *Antrarian, antrarian*, a loud cry 'that signyfied Joye generalle'.[1] These are spontaneous elaborations in a translation which is at times, as we have said, almost verbal. In the description of the curious game of live coal, for instance, almost every word corresponds. This was a practical joke played by Lucafer of Baldas on Duke Neymes, which burnt his beard badly and led to savage reprisals. The French version mentioned above describes the game as follows:

> Cil (Lucafer) a pris un agoile, si le fist a filer,
> Le chief de la file fist a un perche lier.
> Puis a pris un carbon, sur l'agule fist poser . . .
> Par tiel air sofre le carbon les cinteles fist voler
> Si qe la barbe duc Neimes en fist tut bruler.[2]

This is rendered in English by:

> He teyde a tredde on a pole
> With a nedel thereon ifest,
> And ther uppon a quike cole.
> . . . Duke Neymes had a long berd
> King Lucafer blewe even to hym.
> That game hade he neuer before lered
> He brent the her of Neyme's berd to the skyne.[3]

It is not surprising that Duke Neymes was furious and smote Lucafer such a blow in the face 'that both his eyen bresten oute' ('Ke les us de sun chief en fist hors voler'), threw him into the fire and held him

---

[1] ll. 689–70.   [2] *Fierabras*, 89, 3–4; 98–9.   [3] *Sowdone*, ll. 1999–2006.

down with a 'fyre-forke'[1] until he was roasted to coal. The details of this episode are not the same in all the versions, either French or English, but those in the *Sowdone* clearly reproduce those in the French version on which it is based.

The translator has not, however, always been so fortunate in his rendering of the original. In one passage he has mistaken *mastes*[2] for *maistres* and has placed these on the main top armed with maces to threaten the Christians. The curious line which occurs twice: 'Le vent ont bone: dient cil notonier' has clearly not been understood as it becomes: 'The wynde hem served, it was ful goode' in one passage and 'The wynde hem blewe ful fayre and goode' in the other. The names, too, presented a difficulty. The well-known ones are faithfully reproduced, but 'Foukes li vaillant' has become 'Folk Baliante'; 'Bernard li prud conte' appears as 'Bernarde of Spruwse', Briez of Nantes as 'Bryer of Mountez', and 'Neiron li barbe' as 'Miron of Brabane', etc.

Enough has been said to indicate the relation between the French and English versions. The *Sowdone* has a slightly more moral tone than the original in spite of Charlemagne's lapses into levity, but the author does not take so much upon himself as Caxton in his translation of a prose romance entitled: *The Lyf of the Noble and Crysten Prynce Charles the Grete*. Here both Charlemagne and Roland are severely castigated for their display of temper after the battle for Rome—Charlemagne for his lack of restraint in hitting Roland; and Roland for his lack of respect towards his uncle. But this interesting version is far too removed from the Old French epic to detain us here. Its interest for us lies in the fact that it was the first romance to be printed—a proof of the popularity the Charlemagne stories still enjoyed in England in the fifteenth century. There is no doubt that of these romances the one relating Fierabras' duel with Oliver, his conversion to Christianity, his loyalty to his new lord, and his valour in the cause of his new faith, had a first place in the affection of the fiction-loving public both in English-speaking and French-speaking lands. There are numerous references to the hero in Middle-English works and in Barbour's *Bruce*, the king is described as relating to his followers the whole story of 'worthy Ferumbrace' who was overcome of the right doughty Olywer and of the discomfiture of Laban (Lawyne) and the recovery of the holy relics.[3]

---

[1] Cf. 'Fr. un forche sur son col le voit fichier'.
[2] l. 154.
[3] Cf. Ed. Skeat, 3, 435 ff.

II. *IN GERMANY*

The poems and groups of traditions which compose the Old French epic cannot be said to have made any considerable contribution to Middle High German literature. Charlemagne never became a popular figure in the German-speaking lands. Although the twelfth-century *Kaiserchronik* speaks of songs devoted to Charlemagne ('Karl hat ouch andere liet'), there was no spate of heroic literature devoted to his memory. This may seem surprising at first—but Germany had its own epic tradition and, during the twelfth century, evolved its own epic legends which had no connection whatever with Charlemagne. The only two French poems which, as far as we know, gave rise to poetic versions of any importance in Germany were the *Chanson de Roland* and *Aliscans*. We cannot cavil at their taste.

The *Ruolandes-liet* has been preserved in several manuscripts so that it must have enjoyed a certain amount of popularity (among the 'spielmann' fraternity). In one of these manuscripts the poem is provided with an epilogue in which a certain Pfaffe Kuonrat names himself as the author and tells us that a 'Duke Henry' had commissioned him to undertake the work at the desire of his wife; but that he had been obliged to translate the French original first into Latin before he converted it into German. If this epilogue can be relied upon, the date of the translation can be approximately fixed before the middle of the twelfth century—possibly as early as the year 1131. This would make it a valuable contribution to any reconstruction of the original text of the Roland. It is, moreover, in many cases such a close translation of the version contained in the Digby manuscript (O) that it may throw light on doubtful or difficult readings. Before coming to details, however, the difference in tendency between the two versions must be noted.

In the German poem the religious element has been greatly developed. The *Chanson de Roland* has a religious background, it is true, but the contest between Christianity and heathendom is raised on to a higher level and has become a struggle between right and wrong:

> Ferez i Francs, nostre est li premers colps.
> Nos avum dreit, mais cist glutun unt tort.

In the *Chanson*, moreover, love of country, of the emperor, of glory for its own sake, are very strong rivals for the love of God. Not that the piety of the Frenchman can be questioned. It starts from the top, for the emperor never misses Mass or Matins and the archbishop, fighter though he is, has a keen eye for a heretic and many a promise of bliss for those of the true faith:

> Clamez vos culpes, si preiez Deu merci,
> ... Si vos morez esterez seinz martirs
> Sieges avrez el greignor pareis (ll. 1132-4, 5).

The prayers are fairly brief and rather conventional in character, but God does answer them, and even on rare occasions intervenes on behalf of the Christians when they are sore beset. But religion does not obtrude itself and we are not more conscious of it than we are of the intrusions of gods and goddesses into the framework of the *Æneid*.

It is otherwise in the *Rolandslied*. Here love of country, of emperor, and of kith and kin takes a back place. The author seems obsessed with a desire to parade his piety and to edify, in consequence of which it becomes sickly and often trivial. The archbishop, in his first prayer of any length, desires that God should make a little door (*ein turlîn*) through which his mouth should speak suitable words[1]; the knights are not to be like those who go into God's vineyard (*wingarten*) and come out before the evening—they are to fight throughout the day so as to become comrades of St. Lawrence, whom the heathen burned on a grid[2]; when Roland, Turpin, and Walther are left alone on the battlefield, they go forth representing the Trinity:

> Thar huoben sih tho thie thri
> ... in then thrin namen unseres Herren (l. 6581 f.).[3]

When the battle was very fierce and the Christians were suffering from thirst, God sent down a shower of dew to refresh them:

> Tho wolt ther himelisce herre
> thie sine wole gefristen.
> Ja kam uber die cristenen
> ein tror von theme himel touwe,
> ein kuole unter then ougen:
> thaz gescah an there none zit.
> sih erjungte aller ire lip:
> sie wurthen stark unt veste (ll. 4452 f.).

On another occasion a refreshing wind was sent to revive their weary bodies and drooping spirits. These few examples may be taken as typical of the moralizing nature of the German translation; many more could be cited. Nevertheless, this tendency of the poem must not be exaggerated. There is nobility in the archbishop's reply to the

---

[1] l. 968 f.   [2] ll. 6189-90.
[3] Accents have been omitted in the German quotations in order to avoid complications.

despairing cry of Roland when he sees that only Turpin and himself remain alive. Roland has just exclaimed that he is accursed, that God has forgotten him and that he has no one to whom to turn. 'Now you are helping the heathen', replied the bishop; 'Hope in my Lord; give praise to the heavenly King; nothing should dismay a good vassal'.[1] Nor does Turpin at all approve of a man who does not fight his hardest. As in the French original, he says: 'Let him go and be a monk unless he strikes well with the sword'. He himself fights to the bitter end and (again as in the *Chanson*) his four hundred victims are found around him after his death. When he fell, angels carried their loved one (*then ire lieben*) straight into the choir of martyrs on the topmost throne and (now the monkish touch) our Lord received him with the words: 'procede et regna'.[2] Such unnecessary additions as this have caused the religious tendency of the poem to be slightly overstressed.

Other considerations are not entirely lacking. There are many references to 'suozze Karlinge' (*douce France*) and friendship occupies a notable place in the poem. It is true we might have expected to find more direct emphasis laid on the idea of 'compagnonnage' which has often been claimed as a German conception. Yet such appellations as 'ther aller libeste geselle' occur frequently, and a lament such as that uttered by Roland for his friend Walther shows how the idea of friendship permeated the relationship of the knights to each other. Weeping bitterly he exclaimed:

> Scol ih nu scheithen
> Vone theme alle liebesten gesellen?
> thin groz ellen
> muoz ih iemer mere clagen.
> Ze wem scol ih nu trost haben?
> thin suozze Karlinge
> nemah thih niemer uberwinden.

He was so overwhelmed with grief that he collapsed in his saddle:

> von theme leithe unt von theme grimme
> so erkracte Ruolant inne
> thaz er sih geneihte uf then satelpogen (ll. 6442–5).

Oliver, too, in his prayer just before his death, prays not only for his own soul's salvation but for 'Karlen minen herren', for sweet France, for the Christians slain in battle ('thie hie ze then heithenen sint beliben'), but most of all for his dear friend Roland, who was ever a champion ('rorekemphe') of the true faith. After further petitions

[1] ll. 6618–32.　　[2] str. 235.

he reverts again to his anxiety for Roland and prays earnestly that God will watch over him, both as to his body and his soul.[1]

Such passages as these are very reminiscent of the spirit of our oldest known version of the *Chanson*. That this was known to the author can hardly be doubted, for many of the translations seem almost verbal. It is, of course, not impossible that the Pfaffe knew a version very nearly related to the Oxford one, but allowing for lapses of memory, the discrepancies inevitable in a double translation (first from French to Latin, then from Latin to French), the urge to give an edifying and orthodoxical religious bias to the poem, there hardly seems need to search for a nearer source than the one we possess. We might find many examples to illustrate the literalness of the translation, but one or two will suffice for our purpose. Oliver, badly wounded, cannot see for blood and strikes his comrade Roland by accident; the two corresponding passages are as follows:

Chanson de Roland: 'Sire compain, faites le vos de gred?
　　　　　　　　　　　Ja est ço Rollanz ki tant vos suelt amer,
　　　　　　　　　　　Par nule guise ne m'aviez desfiet'.
　　　　　　　　　　　Dist Oliver: 'or vos oi jo parler,
　　　　　　　　　　　Jo ne vos vei. . . .
　　　　　　　　　　　Ferut vos ai, car le me pardunez (ll. 2000–6).

Ruolanteslied:　　　'Er sprah: ia thu tiuerlicher thegen
　　　　　　　　　　　hastuz gerne getan?
　　　　　　　　　　　Warum woltestu mih erslan?'
　　　　　　　　　　　Sprah ther helet Olivier,
　　　　　　　　　　　'helet, nu antlaze thu mir,
　　　　　　　　　　　thaz min sele iht prinne.
　　　　　　　　　　　ih hore thine stimme
　　　　　　　　　　　anders ih niemen erkenne'.

In the French poem Roland replied: 'Jo n'ai nient de mal', and pardons him freely. The German poet is a little more diffuse; he makes Oliver tell the dearest friend he ever had in the world: 'ne hast thu mir niht getan'.[2] Then in both versions they leaned towards each other before they parted. 'Thuruh not muosen sie sih sceithen', says the Pfaffe, which perhaps represents a more reliable reading than the French 'Par tel amur as les vos desevré'.[3] Many other such parallel passages could be cited—such as the account of the heathen trying to snatch the dying Roland's horn and sword and the result of his daring attempt; or of Roland's description of Charlemagne's conquests; including England, which he used 'zu einer Kamere';[4] or the simile:

---

[1] ll. 3618–19.　　[2] l. 6487.　　[3] l. 2009.　　[4] l. 6805.

R

'sam der hirz vare den hunden', all familiar to us from the Digby
version (O) of the *Chanson*.

It cannot be denied, however, that the German poem is over-
weighed with religiosity. When Charles starts on his revenge
expedition the whole army in its desire for martyrdom sets out as if
for a wedding. Death to them was only the introduction to a better
life, like the corn of wheat going into the ground to die.[1] The fight
between Charlemagne and Baligant follows much the same course
as in the *Chanson*. Charles hears a voice from heaven telling him it is
time to kill the heathen, and renewed strength is given him with that
in view. He was enabled to smash the pagan's head into four pieces.
Divine strength was given to the army also and soon the heathen
fled. When they arrived at Saragossa, Bramimunde opened the gates
to them and offered of her own free will to receive baptism. She even
told the Christians not to mourn over their dead for they were
assured of heaven; the emperor was quite surprised at her intelligent
remarks. Alda's death corresponds to the account in the *Chanson* and
it is followed by the trial of Ganelon. The 'Karlinge', to whose race
he belonged, wished to spare him as nothing had been proved against
him. Ganelon, however, was honest and admitted that he had
planned the death of the twelve peers. His relations still pleaded for
him though the emperor swore in his wrath that he would make an
example of him. Roland's cause seemed lost, however, when Tirrih
(Thierry), one of Roland's kinsmen, stepped forward and offered
himself as champion on Roland's behalf. Tirrih was small and weak,
whereas Pinabel was big and strong. We are more conscious in the
German poem that we are faced with another version of the David
and Goliath 'motif'. Many prayers went up for Tirrih and, in spite
of the physical inequality of the champions, he was, of course,
victorious in the end. The men of good will rejoiced and Ganelon
was bound to the tails of wild horses which dragged him through
thorns and thickets so that he perished miserably.

It will be seen from the above that in the main the Old French
version has been faithfully followed by the German poem. Pruned
of its religious accretions the story moves steadily forward and the
author is not entirely lacking in descriptive ability. Even when it
follows the original closely the translation is not slavish. Many of the
names are hard to identify, especially those of the heathen in regard
of whom the author allows himself a good deal of liberty. Having
just described the unity and 'brotherliness'[2] of the Christians, who all

[1] l. 7885.   [2] l. 3456.

rejoice in *one* belief, *one* hope, *one* faith, and *one* truth, he turns to the heathen and describes their pride and boastfulness. They raised seven hundred idols on a tower and honoured them with horn-blowing and bonfires. So loud was the noise that the birds fell down dead to the earth just as they did in the Karlamagnus-saga and the Ronzasvallas when Roland blew the blast on his horn. Then the individual princes came with their requests and their vaunts (another version of the *gab* motif) to Marsile. Their courage sank a little when they saw Roland's army so skilfully marshalled that even Alexander would have had difficulty in breaking through. They were slain at the rate of six thousand a minute, but still their battalions pressed on to their death. No healing dew came from on high to them as it did to the Christians; they lay like dead dogs in the way, for no doctor could heal them. What pillars of the kingdom they might have been, remarks the author, had they only been Christians, but they joined the ranks of wicked Herod so their fate was deserved and our pity is enlisted only on behalf of the Christians.

It is characteristic partly of the early date and partly of the religious bias of the *Rolandslied* that the heathen appear in such an unmitigatedly unfavourable light. No good qualities are assigned to them, no help of any kind comes to them, there is no sign of any repentance anywhere—except in the Queen Brechmunda (Bramimunde), and that was, perhaps, for rather special reasons which seemed to interest the emperor. If we can believe the epilogue quoted above, the excellent story (*materia . . . scone*) was handed over to the author to translate into German by a noble lady, a king's daughter, thereby to add lustre to the kingdom[1] and merit to her own soul. He ends the work with a prayer that everyone who hears shall sing a *Pater Noster* on behalf of his Lord and that all believers should be rich in good works and certain of heaven. The *Chanson de Roland* rings deeper and truer than its copy.

Completely different in character is the other poem to which we must now turn our attention—the *Willehalm* of Wolfram von Eschenbach. This remarkable poem by a really great poet was composed some 100 years later than the original on which it was based. It differs both from its model and from the poems of an earlier period in more ways than can be accounted for by a mere passage of time. One's first thought would be that it would be an almost impossible task to transform a *chanson-de-geste* into a poem in which *Frauenkult* and *Minne* play a very considerable part. Certainly Guillaum and

[1] l. 9034.

Guibourg were the only couple who lent themselves in any measure to such a development and, even in these, the faithful devotion of the pair to each other in the French poems does not bear the slightest resemblance to 'hohe Minne'. But it must be remembered that Guibourg had a past. She was not the 'femme honnête qui n'a pas d'histoire'. She had at some time previous to the events described in any of the extant legends been abducted from her lawful husband by Guillaume d'Orange and had herself been accessory to the deed. Here, then, was the romance and the illicit love which were among the fundamental conditions for courtly poetry.

In *Aliscans*, on which, as most critics are agreed, the German poem is mainly based, Guibourg plays (it is true) a prominent part, but it is as the devoted wife of a war-weary husband whom she encourages, cares for or chides, according to the circumstances. Guillaume, too, is the loyal spouse, although he has to be bolstered up by a solemn vow when he leaves his wife to go to the French court where temptations might be too great. But Guillaume has other loyalties besides his wife in the French poem, as we can see from his prayer before the great battle:

> Si com c'est voirs, aidies vostre vasal
> K'encor revoie Guiborc au cuer loyal,
> Et Loeis, l'empereor roial,
> Et Aimeri mon chier pere carnal
> Et Ermenjart, ma mere natural
> Et mes chiers freres, ki sont emperial (ll. 553 f.).

Guillaume is the most natural and human man that ever lived. It is true that his great function is to kill as many heathen dogs as possible. But he only has to see a fine horse, a handsome boy, or a pretty niece to forget all his antagonisms and his principles. This makes *Aliscans*, in spite of the monotony inherent in the heroic epic, a very entertaining poem and an excellent study in human psychology. The triumph of humanity over religious fanaticism or blood-relationship is worked out subtly in the minds and actions of individuals without the necessity of hammering the point. Guibourg's love for her husband's nephew Vivien, Guillaume's love for his wife's brother Rainouart, give us the key to the situation, and the scene towards the end of the poem where Rainouart (the converted heathen) and Bauduc (his young, still unconverted cousin) sit side by side and look affectionately at each other after trying savagely to kill one another, is as attractive as the distress of Rainouart when he thinks that Guillaume, whom he loves more than anyone else in the world, has forgotten him. But although this welding together of heathen and Christian is, as we have said, inherent in *Aliscans*, this does not alter the fact that the heathen are utterly evil and must be destroyed like vermin:

> Puisque li hom n'aimme crestienté
> Et que il het deu et despit carité
> N'a droit en vie, je le di par verté
> Et ki l'ocist, s'a destruit un malfé (ll. 1058–62).

It is otherwise in the German poem. The *Willehalm* has been called a 'Klage'—a lament, and so to a certain extent it is, for the whole poem seems dominated by *jâmer* and *nôt*. But the lament is not only for the death and unhappiness of Christians only—it is almost equally for that of the heathen who are God's creatures too. As was natural when the first flush of the crusades was over, the poet was capable of being more objective. Guiburg[1] herself says: 'Alas, I am the ruin of His creatures, both Christian and heathen'. Guiburg was, of course, the best qualified to look on both sides. In spite of her faithful devotion to her new lord and her new faith she never completely lost all her sympathy for her family and the rest of her former co-religionists. The poet himself echoes Guiburg's words: 'Was it not a great sin?' he asks, 'to slaughter like cattle people who had never heard of Christianity and were all God's handiwork ('hantgetat')—men of the seventy-two kingdoms which He had created?'[2] At one point he almost blames Guiburg, the woman of the two names, whose life and love were so interwoven with sorrow. She has brought so much misery on her own people that his heart will turn against her unless God prevents it. But no, he concludes, the queen who abandoned her name of Arabella at the baptismal font was innocent through the One who was born of the word and gave His life for us without hesitation. There follows a little dissertation on the joys of martyrdom for the one who can keep so close to the angels as to miss no note of their heavenly song[3]—a conclusion reminiscent of many such pious passages in the *Rolandslied*.

In spite of his conclusion, however, the fact remains fixed in the author's mind that 'durch Giburge al diu not geschach',[4] and in a long, pathetic speech to the princes when they arrive at Orange to rescue her from her father and his army she herself admits that she bears the guilt on account of her desire to obtain God's grace, but

---

[1] The German form Guiburg has been used in preference to the French form Guibourg in the section dealing with the German poem.
[2] *Willehalm* 450, 15–20.
[3] 30, 21–31, 20.   [4] 306, 1.

partly ('ein teil') on account of her love for the warrior Willehalm.[1] She exonerates her former husband, Tibalt, entirely, declaring that he had never wronged her since she became his queen and that in leaving him she gave up her first love, much riches and beautiful children in order to become a poor man's wife. She admits that her love for Willehalm had been the cause of much sorrow and loss of life, that 'jâmer' filled her breast and her joy was dead. She begs the Christian knights to use their victory honourably should they triumph over the heathen, for were not all men heathens before Christ came, and did not many a woman, even after being regenerated through baptism, bring forth a heathen child?[2]

The whole tenor of the poem is completely different from that of *Aliscans*, the model on which it was constructed. Sometimes we hardly realize that the cause of Christianity was at stake. A completely new element has crept in, for it is *Frauendienst* that has brought sorrow into the hearts of heathen and Christians alike—Vivien or Arofel, it does not matter who the victim was, by their death *Frauendienst* had become the poorer and Guiburg had bewitched the hearts of both heathen and Christian alike. Possibly this bewitching quality is a faint reminiscence of the fact that she had once been an enchantress. 'Je cuit Guibors nos vuet toz enchanter', says Aïmer in *Aliscans*[3] when he sees the effect she had on Rainouart. She certainly possessed a magic power over men. This is constantly stressed in the German poem until it reaches its climax in the words of her husband: 'I observe, lady, that your shining beauty does not let the heathen have any rest; they cannot resist its beams'.[4] Immediately before this, Bernart of Brubant (Willehalm's brother) had declared that he would rather let strips be cut out of his own kinsmen's (of whom one is his own son) skin than let Tibalt get possession of Guiburg.[5] Guiburg is, in fact, a kind of vision of beauty, a Helen of Troy 'who launched a thousand ships' and became a bone of contention to leaders of rival armies, thus causing death and destruction to many. During all the laments which fill the first half of the poem, and the grief for the death of Vivien, she had been somewhat in the background of the picture. But when the weary time of waiting was over and the relief of Orange was at hand, the author brings her forth at the right moment and she fills the stage. As usual in this balanced poem, joy and sorrow were mixed. During a pause in the battle, Desramé, her father, laments bitterly over her action and beseeches her to return

---

[1] 310, 19–20. [2] 307, 21. [3] l. 4282.
[4] 260, 24–5. [5] 260, 18.

to her former husband. He is pathetic and generous in his grief—he begs and threatens in turn. But Guiburg was adamant and the baffled heathen set fire to the palace and retreated to their ships at the approach of Willehalm and his army. The rescuing force is composed of all Willehalm's kith and kin, each with their respective band of followers, and the army that the Emperor Louis, after some hesitation, has sent to his aid. Guiburg with her maidens had been holding out in Orange till Willehalm should arrive with reinforcements. As the French army approaches she stood on the battlements, fully armed with outstretched sword, a symbol of courage and faithfulness. Then Willehalm's anxiety was turned momentarily to joy for he had feared the worst. But, as the other contingents approached, he wished that all should share his joy, so a great feast was prepared as soon as his father and brothers arrived. Then Guiburg laid aside her armour, decked herself in her most beautiful clothes, and bade her maidens do the same. In 'strahlender schönheit' the countess went forward to meet the advancing army. She was so lovely that only God could have created anything so beautiful. Her very appearance won the hearts of all, and if anyone could have seen what lay beneath her garments he would have had a glimpse of paradise.[1] She was the cynosure of all eyes—a symbol of beauty. Old Aymeri (Heimrich) sat beside Guiburg during the repast, and although there were many other beautiful women there he had no eyes for any one except his daughter-in-law.[2] But they neither forgot the serious occasion of their being together and ate but little in spite of the fact that there was reason to rejoice.

In what might be called the second half of the poem Guiburg again takes a back place. We return to the battle scenes and Rainouart is in the foreground as in *Aliscans*. The battle was long and bloody, but at last the heathen fled to their ships and their emir (*amiral*) Desramé escaped with a band of followers after a gallant duel with Willehalm which the author compares to the combat between Charlemagne and Baligant. The Christian army (as in the *Chançun de Willame*) found a wonderful spread of provisions which the heathens had abandoned in their hasty flight. Many a soldier drowned his grief and forgot his wounds in wine, for theirs was not the wisdom of Solomon.[3] Master and servant enjoyed 'guot gemach', which the poet tells us was *aise* in French ('en franzois heten si *eise*'),[4] and which was equally appreciated by 'der kurteise' and the 'ungehovete man', for everyone, both 'herre' and 'knecht', had as much of the spoils as

[1] 249, 15.   [2] 265, 21.   [3] 448, 13.   [4] 449, 9.

he wished. So the Christians rejoiced over the booty the heathens had left behind and the pagan gods, Apollo, Mahmete, Tervagant, and Kahun fell into disrepute for their reputation was gone for ever.

Whilst these rejoicings were going on, however, and Willehalm was receiving some consolation for his past defeats in the possession of the land and the wife that he was destined not to lose again, another cause of sorrow poisoned his joy. During the final battle, in some mysterious way, Rainouart had disappeared. Here was fresh fuel for Willehalm's grief:

> der vürste uz Provenzalen lant
> Klagete sere, daz er niht vant
> sinen vriunt Rennewart.
> im was leit diu dannenvart (452, 15 f.).

All his grief for Vivien was now transferred to his foster-son who, ever since his adoption into the count's entourage, had been his right hand ('min zeswin hant'), had guided his ship and acted like a good wind to bring him and all his kith and kin into port. Here the *Willehalm* parts company with *Aliscans*, for we do not hear of Rainouart again, but are regaled with another long lament of Guillaume for his second great loss. We are immersed again in *jâmer und nôt* as torrents of tears flow from the count's eyes. His brother Bertrand takes him to task severely for giving way to such grief:

> du bist niht Heimriches sun,
> wiltu nach wibes siten tuon.
> ... wiltu hie selbe weinen
> als ein kint nach der brust? (457, 33 f.).

Willehalm pulls himself together for a short spell after these wise words and decides that he must pretend to be happy, even if he is not, for:

> Ez ist des houbetmannes sin,
> daz er genendecliche lebe
> und sinem volke troesten gebe (460, 18–20).

His good resolution did not last long, however, for on the third day after the final battle he began to enlarge again on his grief and had again to be reminded that a man to whom God had entrusted an army ought not to behave as he was doing. ... Here the fragment ends and we shall never know what happened to Rainouart. We cannot doubt, however, that he was found and that he was destined, as in *Aliscans*, to marry the emperor's daughter and inherit the heathen's land, after his father's death.

The poem ends on a note of reconciliation, for Willehalm has the bodies of the slain heathen kings collected to be sent back to their native land and sends the message of admiration and almost of gratitude to Desramé, whose family had been a source of blessing to him although it brought sadness as well as joy in its train. So, to the end of the story, the balance is held between joy and sorrow, gain and loss, sweet and bitter. As Bernard reminds Willehalm when he reproaches him for his unmanly grief which will depress the Frenchmen: 'Joy without sorrow is unthinkable and not meant for mere mortals':

> sueze vinden, manege sure vlust,
> niht anders erbes muge wir han (457, 10–11).

This is, perhaps, the most important lesson which the poem has to teach. Resignation, tolerance, pity for humanity—these are the imponderables that make life possible and enable us to take an objective view of things. Of course, right is on the side of the Christians, but again and again the author reflects that such a slaughter of heathen could not have been the will of the Creator. The *Klage* embraces both sides alike:

> die heiden scheden dolten
> und die getauften holten
> flust unde kummer.

It was grievous that Tervagant should have had the power to send so many souls to hell, when many of them have such good qualities in spite of their beliefs. This element of broad tolerance is present in *Aliscans* but it is much more developed in *Willehalm*. In the Old French poem we have the same conflict of loyalties—most clearly expressed in the character of Rainouart. The devotion of the heathen boy for Guillaume whom he loves more than anyone else in the world overrules his loyalty to his own family, even his own father. Guibourg's loyalty to her new husband and new faith overrides all previous attachments and reliefs. But it must be admitted that the human element is not so strong in *Aliscans*. The heathen are devils, created to be destroyed. The author does not grieve for them. There is a more merciful outlook in *Willehalm*—perhaps partly due to feminine influence on the knights, for 'Frauendienst' and 'Minneethos' are much to the fore. The heathen have their 'amies' as well as the Christians and this fact caused them to be regarded in a less hostile light. Arofel was a lady-killer; Paufameiz has an 'amie' of whom we hear no word in *Aliscans*. There are two rewards for those who observe knightly honour—heaven and the favour of noble women.[1] So spoke Willehalm when he called upon all his relations to take pity on him, the 'freuden-armen'. They all replied as one man to his request, for their hearts were all united. The strong family feeling reigned in all their hearts. It is true that at his first appeal the queen, his sister, had been very reluctant to risk her own kingdom to save that of her sister-in-law, and who can blame her? But after her conversion to the family cause, although this was brought about by brutal methods, she spoke nobly on Willehalm's behalf, reminding her brothers of the oneness of the family members, body and soul, whether they be male or female:

> Mine bruoder, die hie sin,
> gedenket, daz wir sin ein lip.
> ir heizet man, ich bin ein wip:
> da enist niht underscheiden,
> niht wan ein verh uns beiden (168, 12–16).

The idea of universal brotherhood inevitably weakened somewhat the theme of family solidarity in the German poem. The word *geselleschaft* is used in a looser sense than its equivalent *compagnie* in the Old French original. But the idea is there and keeps breaking through. It is consistent with the rest of the poem that Willehalm insists on the existence of 'geselleschaft' between himself and a merchant. The poet is not class-conscious, for he reminds us that though the deeds of the great are recorded they are no more worthy of remembrance than those of the multitude which remain unsung:

> Swa man des vil von Künegen saget,
> da wirt arm manner tat verdaget (428, 3–4).

These words are entirely characteristic of the objectivity which marks the whole work.

As regards the individual characters in the *Willehalm*, they correspond in the main to the traditional portraits in the Old French epic. Guillaume was always a man with a grievance, whether in *Aliscans* or the *Couronnement de Louis*—in spite of his loyalty and his unequalled reputation for valour. In *Willehalm* this sombre side of his character is even more emphasized. He absolutely wallows in grief. His lamentations for Vivien and Rainouart are extravagant and tend to become maudlin, somewhat in the same way as those of Charlemagne for Roland in the various versions of that legend. Even at a period when the lack of ability to weep was looked upon as a misfortune, it

[1] 'der himel und werder wibe gruoz', 299, 27.

surely verged on the grotesque when the poet declared that two carts and a waggon could not have carried all the liquid that gushed from his eyes. But everything concerning Willehalm was on a large scale —not only his bodily form and courage, but his indulgence in *jâmer*, his outbursts of wrath and indignation, his capacity for love and his ability to keep a vow. Even his language is exaggerated in expression, for in his lament over Vivien he declares that his nephew's sweetness was so great that had his toe been cast into the sea it would have made the ocean 'zuckersüzz':

> solh süezze an dinem libe lac:
> des breiten mers salzes smac
> müeste al zucker maezec sin,
> der din ein zehen würfe drin (62, 12–14).

Such language is, to a certain extent, characteristic of the author's style, but it seems to reach its height when it is placed in the mouth of the greatest of warriors. It is Guiburg whose personality has gained most in depth. Her address to the members of her husband's family is noble. She is just as heartbroken as Willehalm at the death of her nephews, but she does not give way as he does. She can rise to an occasion and forget her personal losses just as she can in the *Chançun de Willame*. Her appearance is never described, but we are skilfully left to judge of it by the effect it has on those who see her. Her faithfulness to Willehalm is never in question, although she has never completely lost her feeling for her own kith and kin. King Louis has, perhaps, of all the characters gained most in prestige, but it is some time before it can be said of him that he is acting like his father Charlemagne.[1]

III. *IN SOUTHERN FRANCE*

It might reasonably have been expected that the south as well as the north of France would have produced a crop of epic poems during the lengthened period of epic production. But in spite of the fact that Guillaume d'Orange was the hero of the Midi and that much of the geography and the landscape is evocative of the south rather than the north, this is not the case. Perhaps the language had something to do with it. A Provençal poet—Raimon Vidal—tells us in his treatise or composition (*Las razos di trobar*) that the language of Lemozi ('le Limousin', roughly what we now call *provençal*) is best

---

[1] *dicke Karle wart genant*, 182, 16.

adapted to the writing of lyric poetry (*far vers et cansons et serventes*), whereas the 'parladura francesca' is more suited for poems of a more narrative character (*romanz et pasturellas*). This does not mean, of course, that epic poetry was completely neglected in the south of France, but it certainly did not flourish there to the extent to which it did in the north. The well-known romance *Flamenca* does not fall into our category of epic poems, but it is noteworthy that the author, when enumerating the tales of kings, counts and other heroes which the 'jongleurs' vied with each other in reciting—incidentally making such a noise that it was hard to distinguish anything—tells us that one related how Charlemagne held Germany until he divided it between his sons, and another related the whole history of Chlodovech and Pepin.

The legend of Charlemagne was, of course, known in the Midi, and the names of Roland and Oliver are often cited in Provençal poems as models of courage. But the hero who has the honour of a whole poem to himself (if not in Provençal, in a mixture of French and Provençal) is that mysterious old warrior, Girard de Roussillon, whom we find in Old French sometimes fighting on the side of Charlemagne and sometimes in active rebellion against him. He undoubtedly had a historical prototype in the figure of a certain Gerardus who was frequently in conflict with the emperor, generally alluded to in the poems as Charles Martel, or simply Charles. His name was celebrated in ecclesiastical legends, and the French-Provençal poem was preceded by a *Vita Girardi* in which the pious side of Girard was celebrated. It is generally admitted that both the *Vita* and the poem proceeded from an earlier version which has not come down to us, and the whole legend provides one of the best examples of the interplay between the clerical and the lay element. 'Légende épique, légende hagiographique sont ici et furent de tout temps une seule et même légende',[1] and the question as to which came first is one which must be left on one side for the moment. In any case we have to do with an old epic tradition. 'Girart de Russilun li vielz' is mentioned in the *Chanson de Roland*[2] as one of the twelve peers fighting on the emperor's side, whereas several references in *Garin le Lorrain* and elsewhere allude to his rebellious activity and the havoc he had wrought in the land. Guillaume's 'joglere' in the *Chançun de Willame* sings of 'Girart de Viane' amongst other of Charlemagne's knights. From early time there was confusion between the different heroes of the name of Girard; the epithet 'de Roussillon' remains a mystery in

[1] Bédier, *Les légendes Epiques*, II, p. 9⁵   [2] l. 798, etc.

spite of its celebrity and proves nothing in respect of a Provençal origin.

The Franco-Provençal poem will be chiefly remembered for the loyalty and devotion of the good wife Berte which has been described in a previous chapter. Without her support Girard would have succumbed to his misfortunes when, like Tristan and Iseut, the pair wander miserably about in exile:

> Entre lo dol e l'ire e le mautraire
> Si non fus sa muller, non visquest gaire,
> El' est savie e corteise e de bone aire
> Que ne paraula melz nus predicaire.[1]

Much the same might have been said of Guibourg, Guillaume's faithful spouse, but Berte was even nobler, for she was not the wife chosen by him. She had come from Constantinople expecting to marry the king, but Charles had preferred her younger sister, so Berte had to be contented with Girard.

The extant poem of *Girard de Roussillon* can be roughly assigned to the middle of the thirteenth century, but a somewhat later date must be postulated for a poem narrating the Roncevaux story in Provençal. We possess only a fragment of the epic poem *Ronzasvals* (published by Mario Roques in *Romania* LVIII, 1932), but it lends a certain *gravitas* to what has survived of Provençal literature, the mention of which evokes an image of courtly lyrics and 'fin amor' rather than of epic grandeur. It proves, moreover, the existence of an epic tradition in the Midi, for personages and episodes are mentioned which are unknown to the more northerly versions. The main features of the story, however, are the same as in the Old French poem known to us from the Digby manuscript (O).[2] Roland's pride is much insisted upon as the cause of the disaster, though he is still the idol of his men, to whom he is equally devoted. As each of his companions gets killed he sends a message after them to say that he has got delayed but will soon join them. Charlemagne's piety is as much in evidence as it is in the *Chanson* and he has to be severely reproached by Naimes for his extravagant expressions of grief. His laments are even more drawn out and are extended to the sword Durendal which he removes from the dead Roland's hand and throws into a lake. The episode of Alda's death is somewhat expanded and she dies, like Iseut, embracing her dead lover's body. The archbishop

---

[1] See Ch. III, p. 52.
[2] Verbal correspondences have been noted in Mortier's Translation—cf. Mortier, *Les Textes de la Chanson de Roland*, Tom. III, p. 118 f.

Turpin is just as efficient in killing the heathen in spite of being a priest, as in the Old French version. Besides these characters so well known to the Old French epic, other personages are introduced who represent a different set of traditions and are little known in the north, though familiarly referred to in the Franco-Italian verse and prose romances to which we shall turn our attention in a moment. The most prominent of these personages is Galien, the son of Oliver, who had been engendered on the occasion of Oliver's fulfilment of his daring *gab* in the palace of the Emperor of Constantinople. Galien arrives on the battlefield, rides up to the emperor, discloses his identity, and demands to be knighted. His request granted, he rides straight off to find his father Oliver. Meanwhile things have reached a terrible pitch. Oliver, wounded and blinded by blood, had just struck Roland by mistake. Roland, in a line which reproduces almost exactly the Old French Oxford MS., exclaimed: 'You ought to have challenged me',[1] whereupon Oliver begged forgiveness for his mistake. At this point Galien rode up to Roland and asked to be led to Oliver. He announces himself to his father, who just has time to embrace him and commend him to God before he receives from a heathen the fatal blow to which he succumbs. Galien avenges his father with such a powerful stroke that Roland remarks: 'If only you had come before!' Galien fights bravely, but he, too, is fatally wounded and found lying on the grass by Gandelbuon, who now appears on the scene. Galien was scarcely known except inside Italy, where he became eventually a popular figure. The Italian prose versions may have been based on a Franco-Italian poem, which in its turn may have had a French original. But neither have come down to us and his fame was not great in France. The same may be said of Gandelbuon le Frison, who also has a considerable part to play in the Provençal poem though he gets hardly more than a brief mention in the French poems. Besides being 'seigneur des Frisons', he introduces himself on one occasion as 'Gandelbuon de la vaillante Afrique', and he is employed on two missions for Roland in each of which he is a bringer of evil tidings. On the second one both he and his horse are grievously wounded and, having delivered his message, he asks to be given Holy Communion as he has no further use for knighthood. Another figure much more familiar to Italian than to French hearers must have been that of Estout de Langres, who, as we shall see, has quite a special rôle to play in the *Entrée d'Espagne* and subsequent Italian works. A note of tolerance is introduced into this account of

---

[1] Cf. 'par nule guise ne m'aviez desfiet', *Ch. de R.*, l. 2002.

the 'douloureuse' battle of Roncevaux by the episode in which the heathen Falseron (Falsaron of the *Chanson de Roland*), after having killed many a noble Christian and escaped death himself, emerges as un 'Sarrasin courtois'. He could not resist a tribute of admiration for Roland. He seated himself beside the count as he lay dying, raised his head and stroked his face, and called down God's benediction on such a noble foe. There is nothing corresponding to this in the *Chanson*, where Falsaron is the most 'encrismé felun' under the sky and hurls abuses at the French.[1] He is killed by Oliver, whom his outrageous insults had driven to fury. Nor is there any redeeming feature in his character in the Franco-Italian poem *L'Entrée d'Espagne*. He plays a considerable part as the father of Feragu whose death he is most anxious to avenge. He is boastful and vindictive and professes to have one ambition—viz. to get at grips with Roland. Thus, as the epic poems were dying a natural death in France and the well-known heroes were being replaced by heroes of a different type (whose fame eclipsed temporarily that of Roland and Oliver and their fellow peers), in the south and particularly on the further side of the Alps, the older traditions of Charlemagne and his knights were destined to have a revival, but fresh characters were introduced and a different turn was given to the old stories which in the end completely changed their character.

IV. *ITALY*

It would be quite impossible in a study of the Old French epic to give any detailed account of the very varied treatment the French poems received on Italian soil during the thirteenth and fourteenth centuries. It is clear from the chaotic state of the epic tradition in Italy up to the time of Dante that it had received no national literary form or language. And yet there was much activity in the 'scriptoria', for there are manuscripts and groups of manuscripts and compilations in verse and prose which suggest many hands and much industry. Perhaps these undertakings were financed by the wealthy families who were springing up in the prosperous Italian cities. There is a case of one family in Padua who, in search of a pedigree, even dared to assert that they were descended from some of the Carolingian heroes. It would seem that French, or at any rate an Italianized form

---

[1] 'Envers Franceis est mult cuntrarius' (l. 1222).

of French, was at one period the literary language of educated people in Northern Italy. From whatever cause, we find abundant evidence of the knowledge and popularity of the Carolingian heroes. There are poems of which we have the original transformed by Italian scribes, as, for instance, the well-known manuscript in assonances of the *Chanson de Roland*[1], in which the original French is often only thinly disguised by its Italian overlay. Sometimes the Franco-Italian poem is obviously based on a French original which has not come down to us, as in the case of the poem *Machario* analysed in a previous chapter. Yet another phenomenon is a poem which does not seem to be based on a French model at all, though it celebrates French heroes, and to a certain extent rekindles the old poetic fire. This is the long poem known as the *Entrée d'Espagne* in the form of Italianized French used by Italian writers whose culture was largely drawn from French models. It would seem that a considerable number of Italians wrote in French at this time. No two wrote alike, and we may notice the analogy between these and the Anglo-Norman poets in England whose individual treatment of French makes them difficult to classify. It must have been these Franco-Italian versions of the Carolingian epics which formed the basis for such a compilation as 'Les Royaux de France' (*Reali di Francia*) about the middle of the fourteenth century, which, beginning with a genealogy of the French kings, proceeds to relate in prose various well-known French legends such as *Aspramonte*, *Ogier le Danois*, *Les Quatre Filz Aimon*, and *L'Espagne* —this last being based on the poem mentioned above (*L'Entrée d'Espagne*) which relates Charlemagne's adventures in Spain before the defeat of Roncevaux. The same poem seems to have provided a base also for two works generally known as the *Spagna en vers* and the *Spagna en prose* which went even further than the *Entrée* and carried the story of Charlemagne's activity in Spain right up to the final catastrophe. These later Italian developments, which have been studied in such detail by Pio Rajna in his numerous works on the subject, pass beyond the limits of the present study and must be left out of the picture in spite of their importance for later developments in Italy when the themes were adopted and metamorphosed by Italian poets. But the intensive production in Northern Italy is an intriguing phenomenon. Not only the heroes of the Charlemagne cycle had each his special treatment, but the Aymeri family (*Nerbonesi*) also came in for their share of attention, and the traitor family

[1] Ms. V. 4.

had an important development of its own. The race of traitors
which, as we know, was a numerous one, is generally referred to in
the Old French poems as 'les parents Ganelon', or 'le lignage Hardré',
and we are told in *Aiol* that they 'foisonent'. Then when the cyclic
idea was at its height a specific family was invented and, as we have
seen in an earlier chapter, an ancestor, Doon de Mayence, was created,
one branch of whose family formed the traitor group. It was left to
the Italian, or Franco-Italian poems to develop the idea of a *maganzi*
or *mayençais* faction. Macaire, the well-known traitor, is 'Macaire de
Losane' in the *Chanson d'Aiol*, but he has been re-christened 'un de
qui de Magance' in the Italianized poem *Machario* (Macaire). We
still hear of the 'parenti Ganelon', but the other epithet is obviously
preferred by the author:

> Co fu qui de Magance e de ses parentors.
> Que senpre fe a K. onta e desonors.[1]

So much did the party idea attract the Italian writers, used to the
faction spirit, that the family of Clermont to which Roland belonged
through his ancestor Bernart de Clermont was augmented as a make-
weight to the traitor clan. It was not till later that the Italian poems
developed this idea more fully, but Roland is already the 'Sire de
Clermont', just as Ganelon is the 'Sire de Maganze' in the poem
L'Entrée d'Espagne, of which a brief account must now be given.

The first 'laisse' of the *Chanson de Roland*, which alluded to the
seven years which Charlemagne had already spent in Spain, was an
obvious invitation to later poets to fill in the gap. The author of
L'Entrée d'Espagne, who tells us he was a native of Padua but does not
disclose his name, has made a gallant attempt to do so. In spite of
the hybrid nature of the language, the poem is an interesting and
entertaining document, intended to be 'read or sung'.[2] The author
himself is very widely-read and possesses an unusual fund of Latin
and French literature on which to draw. But although he represents
the rather bourgeois encyclopaedic culture of the end of the fourteenth century in Italy, he has often succeeded in evoking the spirit
and atmosphere of an earlier period. He claims to have been actually
commissioned by the Archbishop Turpin to undertake this work of
popularizing his famous chronicle by turning it from Latin into
French. He constantly refers to his alleged source, though obviously
these allusions are often only a concession to the epic fashion of
quoting an authority. The early part, however, he really has based

---

[1] Ed. Guessard, p. 204, l. 1451. [2] Cf. l. 56.

on Turpin—namely the battle between Roland and Feragu—though he has greatly lengthened and elaborated his source. After a short pious prologue, the poem opens with the description of the parallel counsels of war held respectively by Charlemagne and Marsilie with their barons. The knights have distinct individual characters, some of which deserve special mention. One point is noticeable: Roland is adored by them all. He is the *nonper* of virtues. No one raises an objection to Charles' intention of making him emperor of Spain. When the emperor treats him badly, not a knight but speaks in his defence—though they know that Roland's pride is a source of peril to them all. During the single combat of Roland and Feragu, which occupies all the early part of the poem, Charlemagne himself is in an agony of fear for his nephew, but when Roland, after his defeat of the giant and tired of the slow progress of the battle, goes off on his own without leave to conquer Noples,[1] leaving his uncle and the rest of the army in a rather ignominious position, he is not unnaturally very angry. It is when Roland comes back full of confidence after his successful campaign, that the well-known episode takes place in which Charlemagne strikes his nephew with his mailed glove and gives him a bloody nose.

It may be remembered that in *Fierabras* a different reason for this assault was given. It was evidently a favourite theme. Roland in *Fierabras* merely sulks like Achilles in his tent. In the *Entrée* he leaves the French army and starts out on a solitary journey which brings him eventually to the kingdom of Persia. Here he assumes the curious function of an 'arbiter elegantiae' to the court. He is particularly shocked by their table manners. It was the custom, in true Eastern style, for everyone to dip their hands into the same dish. Roland, at all events, reduced the number of co-dippers to two. There were doubtless other reforms, but a *lacuna* in the manuscript here leaves us in ignorance as to what they were. Roland won great favour at the Sultan of Persia's court; he defeated the king's enemies and rescued his daughter from an unwelcome suitor; he was given a position of trust and even commissioned to make a tour of the country to gather recruits for the royal army. When at last he leaves and, after many adventures, including conversations with a hermit, clashes with robbers, etc., arrives back in Spain, he is received with transports of joy by all his fellow-knights and we are told that his uncle, 'le bon roi Karle', 'desired him more than does a wife her errant husband'.

---

[1] Cf. *Chanson de Roland*, 'Noples a il pris, sans le vostre commant'.

He wept on his neck and uttered such moving words that all the Frenchmen wept with him.

So ends the part of the poem that may be safely attributed to the Paduan author. There is much that is of extreme interest in the work. It has been called a 'second *Chanson de Roland*',[1] and certainly both the rôle and character of Roland dwarf those of all the other characters in the poem. He is consistently charming. He cannot even look unpleasant when he sees a pagan,[2] as did the Roland of the Old French *Chanson* who reserved his kind looks for his own men and frowned on the heathen. He was courteous alike to friend and foe. The worst that could be said about him was that his ambition was so great that 'il veult contrafere le filz roi Filipon (=Alexander)'. But he is not merely a boastful swashbuckler—he is 'lo senator roman'[3] and as such he was full of good sense and knew how to spare himself when necessary. He is very patient and understanding when trying to convert Feragu and adds several cogent arguments to those adduced by Turpin in explanation of the Trinity.

Another outstanding figure in the poem is that of Estout de Langres about whom the Old French poems tell us extremely little. Estout is the 'rampogneur' who mocks at everyone and everything. Although the author tells us that his *gloriose cançons* does not resemble the 'fables of Arthur', there is a striking resemblance between Estout of the *Entrée* and Key the Seneschal (with his mocking tongue) of the Arthurian romances. Even the moderate Oliver (so like Gauvain in many ways) says of him: 'Anch de maudir un jor ne fust taisant.'[4] He is physically brave and, like Vivien in the *Chançun de Willame*, refuses indignantly to go out as a scout and 'surveer' the enemy forces, for this so often resulted in flight and a lowering of morale. Indeed, he fears no one, not even the emperor, and, like the others, he adores Roland. He developed later into a favourite character of Italian romance under the name of Astolfo.

The general attitude towards the heathen in the poem is one of broad tolerance. It is true that Roland and Feragu were fighting each for their faith:

Il (=Feragn) le feit por Machon e je (=Roland) por Jesu Cris (l. 2129).

but their attitude towards one another is by no means wholly inimical, for each admits that the other is a worthy foe. The conception of the

[1] Introduction to Thomas' edition, p. lix. S.d.A.T.
[2] ll. 4317–18.
[3] l. 2250 and elsewhere.
[4] l. 2331.

noble heathen had developed by this time and we might mistake it for an account of Sultan Saladin when we read of Feragu:

> N'oit plus biax home en tote Paienie,
> Ne mielz cortois ni plus sans villanie.
> Largece fu par lui maintenue e sanplie
> Avarice destruite e de son cor bandie
> Jamais de son nemi non dist outreguidie
> Mais envers tote gient grant bien e cortesie. . . . (ll. 831–6).

Except for the misfortune of his faith there was nothing that could be urged against Feragu and he lost the battle with Roland, not through lack of valour, but through too great simplicity in admitting his weak spot, of which Roland was quick to take advantage. Indeed, Roland, in spite of his many virtues, does not always come out too well for, at the Persian court, he is so anxious to emulate his heathen friends that he almost compromises his own faith.

Another attractive heathen is the young Isoré who, when conquered by Oliver, refuses to give up his sword to anyone but Roland, for whom he had the greatest admiration. When brought as a prisoner to the emperor who threatened to hang him, he replied proudly:

> Roi, vos devez savoir che je sui gentils hon (l. 5539).

By the laws of war he ought to be ransomed, and he is eventually exchanged for Estout who had been taken prisoner at the same time by the heathen. Isoré's honourable conduct throughout stands in striking contrast to the vindictive attitude of Charlemagne towards his foes. When, back at the pagan court, he sends a beautiful Arab steed by the returning Estout to Roland, 'the best of barons' (*le baron soveran*) who, on receiving the gift, declares:

> Anc i porterai bien honor e reverance,
> Car n'est tiel Saracin de la soe creance (ll. 6634–5).

This is, of course, another version of the noble heathen 'motif' which we have met already in *Aspremont* where Balan sends the gift of a steed to Charlemagne. Two other pagan characters stand out though the reference to them is brief. Landrais and Folquenoi (otherwise unknown) are devoted friends and, strangely enough, one of the few references we have to a sort of *compagnonnage* is to be found in the account of these two pagans. The episode is strongly reminiscent of the story of Nisus and Euryalus in Virgil (Bk. IX), when one

friend, on reluctantly parting from the other, makes a touching
speech:

> Senpres avons esté amis et bien voilant,
> Le uns a serviz l'autre et d'avoire et de giant;
> Qi con son buen amis a jois leemant
> Ou besoigne de lui, quant il le voit angrant
> Doit estre compeignons a peine et a tormant (ll. 10570–4).

Elsewhere it is said of Roland and Oliver that they bore each other
'companie tant com il furent vis'.[1] Such sentiments as these taken in
conjunction with the loyalty to Roland, the attitude of the knights
to Charlemagne, and the 'bonhomie' which breaks through between
pagan and Christian, tend to bring our poem into line, not with the
earliest series of epic poems, but with those such as *Aspremont* or
Girard de Viane, in which the grimness of the older stories is tempered
by more romantic elements.

The above-mentioned *chansons-de-geste* have not been cited at
random, for it is evident that both *Aspremont* and *Girard* were known
to the Paduan. Other *chansons*, too he knew, probably in their Franco-
Italian dress. But besides the old epic legends with which he is so
familiar, he was clearly conversant with other forms of French
literature. He speaks somewhat disdainfully of 'les fables d'Artu', but
he had evidently read and quite possibly enjoyed some of them. It
has been already suggested that Estout has every appearance of being
modelled on the evil-tongued Key the seneschal; he expressly mentions, moreover, both Galahad's quest for the Grail[2] and Tristran's
fight with the Morholt.[3] Nor does this come anywhere near to
exhausting his reading, for he knows the classical heroes and mentions
them constantly. His references to Alexander (to whom Roland is
often compared) are numerous, and on the walls of the palace at
Nobles (Noples) are depicted all the battles of Alexander and:

> E comant il oncist li suen meistre endivin
> (Naptanabus oit non, sajes d'art e d'engin)
> E comant il tua o buen brant açerin
> Nicolas de Cesaire, . . .

and so on, ending with the line:

> E com il corona les .xii. palatin (!)

Did he know of all these exploits from the text of an Old French
poem or from the paintings which existed of these legends, for the
iconography of the Alexander legend was widespread? The Latin

---

[1] l. 4336.   [3] l. 9230.   [a] l. 9712.

language would have been no obstacle to him for he knew it well. He was probably acquainted with Lucan's *Pharsalia*—a favourite work in the Middle Ages—and perhaps other classics. But there is another branch of learning in which the author of this poem was well-versed: viz., the side which consists of common-sense apophthegms (*sententiæ*), of fables with morals, of homely proverbs, of rustic similes. One textbook of secular education he knew well— viz., the *Disticha Catonis*, that collection of moral sayings by the so-called Dionysius Cato, which dates back to the fourth century and was a source of wisdom in the Middle Ages, almost vying with the Bible. The Paduan quotes Cato frequently, not always even mentioning the source of his wise saws. He mentions him as an educational textbook in conjunction with the Psalter when speaking of Roland's extreme youth:

> Mais au tamps qe il estoit meschins e valeton
> Ains q'il aüst apris ni sauter ni Caton (ll. 11301–2).

On another occasion Roland humorously tells Estout that he did not know his Caton.[1] Sometimes he quotes him in Latin,[2] at other times he gives the French equivalent,[3] not always troubling to mention his source. In addition to these his reflections frequently express themselves in the form of a proverb obviously drawn from daily life— e.g., 'Un panse le buef e l'autre le vilans',[4] or 'Qui tot veult, trestot perd, ce savez, maintes fois',[5] or:

> Si com le fols que croit prandre la bise.
> Avec la palme, dunt autrui s'en fait rise (ll. 1837–8).

Some of these sayings come from classical sources, others are merely drawn from the stock of the 'proverbes au vilain'. Similarly his animal stories (such as the lion awaking his dead cubs to life with his roar) belong to a stock of medieval lore which was common property at that period. But the effect is to obliterate all trace of an aristocratic origin or outlook in the poem and to give it a distinctly bourgeois ring. This is increased by his several references to children which strike us because they are so rare in a period when poetry was mainly for an aristocratic audience. He compares Feragu's dismay when he has broken his club to that of a child whose bird has escaped and will not return at his call,[6] or he makes the rather shrewd comparison between Roland bowing to the stroke of Feragu's club to lessen the impact and the small child who cunningly flatters his mother

[1] l. 15678.   [2] E.g. l. 15563.   [3] E.g. ll. 1827–8; 5877.
[4] l.6913.   [5] l. 123.   [6] l. 2489.

to soften her anger;[1] or he tells us that Feragu picks up a knight as easily as a mother lifts her child out of the bath.[2] Such similes as these are conspicuously absent from the Old French epic where children are rarely mentioned. They support the idea that the Paduan was a man of good middle-class breeding, who was widely read in contemporary literature and was familiar to a certain extent with classical subjects. Perhaps he was a lawyer—for he makes several references to legal proceedings and there was a flourishing school of jurists at this time in Padua. But this must remain a matter of pure conjecture.

V. EPIC LEGENDS IN SCANDINAVIA

The treatment of the Old French epic legends in the north is such a vast subject that only the briefest sketch can be given here. There is much evidence of their popularity—not, for the most part, in poetic form, but in the form of prose sagas. It seems probable that the means by which the Old French stories reached their destination in the far north were supplied by English and Anglo-Norman versions of the legends. The chief activity is to be noted in Iceland. In the twelfth century Latin learning flourished in Iceland. Lucan's *Pharsalia* (a popular work all through the Middle Ages) was adapted into a saga, together with works of English origin such as Brunne's *Handlyng Synne* and a *Life of Thomas-à-Becket*. In the thirteenth century there were intimate relations between the court of Haakon (V) and that of Henry (III) of England, and this was the period of the great popularity of French romances in Iceland. Iceland has been called 'the treasure-house of medieval romance in the north'.[3] In Denmark romantic history flourished in the hands of Saxo-Grammaticus. Geoffrey of Monmouth also was known and exploited. In Norway Charlemagne was so popular that the second part of his name was borrowed, and no less than seven kings were christened *Magnus*. The Norwegian lord, Bjarni Erlingsson, was a frequent visitor to England and Scotland. So it is not surprising when we come to an extensive *saga* of Charlemagne to find that some of the chapters are based on English rather than continental models.

Carolingian epic in the north is preserved in a great collection of stories relating to Charlemagne—the whole called the *Karlamagnus-saga*. It embraces the whole history of Charles from Pippin's death

---

[1] ll. 3404–5.   [2] l. 1188.
[3] See Leach (A. G.), *Angevin Britain and Scandinavia* (Harvard Studies in Comparative Literature, Vol. VI).

to his own burial in ten chapters or branches. King Haakon V (1217-63) seems to have wished to replace the old heathen songs of Norway by substituting for them the more edifying works of the new western chivalry. The compiler of the *Karlamagnus-Saga* has translated his models so faithfully that his version, which is based on poems of the best epoch, can sometimes be used as an aid to a critical reconstruction of French texts. Of one branch (Dame Olive et Landri) the original is not extant, but the author tells us that he found the story (in English) in Scotland. Another branch relates of the Aspremont story under the title of *King Agolant*; this is an adaptation of the Pseudo-Turpin version. A translation of the first part of the *Ogier legend* follows the French original closely. The poem of *Otuel* (French *Otinel*), which was well known in England, appears with the English form of the name (*Af Otuel*) and there is a version of the Guitelin legend (from the Saxon War) based on a version anterior to that of Jean Bodel. But the section of the greatest interest and importance for a study of the Old French epic is the chapter devoted to the battle of Roncevaux (*Af Runzival Bardaga*). The account here bears such a close resemblance to the version contained in the Oxford manuscript of the *Roland* that it has been possible to use it in places for textual criticism. The most noticeable discrepancy between the two versions is caused by the omission in the *Saga* of the whole account of Baligant's expedition to avenge Marsilie—a strange divergence, as this section of the poem contains so much that is of interest as regards the characters, and of importance as regards the triumph of Christianity. There are other omissions, however—in fact, the *Saga* abbreviates the old poem very considerably. The account of Ganelon's trial is much shorter and less dramatic than in the *Chanson*. There is no single combat to decide his fate. After some hesitation on the part of the barons, Duke Nayme gives as his opinion that Ganelon ought to die by the most horrible death possible. This advice was taken and the traitor was attached to two wild horses and torn literally bone from bone.

To balance these omissions the *Karlamagnus-saga* supplies some details which explain mysterious allusions in the *Chanson de Roland*. One of these occurs in the well-known passage referring to the taking of Noples by Roland without the emperor's permission:

> Ja prist il Noples sanz le vostre comant;
> Fors s'en eissirent li Sarrazins dedenz,
> Si-s cumbatirent al bon vassal Rollant.
> Puis od les ewes lavat les prez del sanc.
> Pur cel le fist, ne fust (apar) issant (ll. 1775-9).

In the *Saga*, Charlemagne had commissioned Oliver and Roland to go and besiege Nobles, but had expressly forbidden them to kill the heathen King Fourré. This order was disobeyed: Fourré was killed and the spot was washed and cleaned up afterwards so that the emperor should not see the blood. When Charlemagne arrived on the scene and heard what had happened, he was very angry and struck Roland on the nose with his gauntlet so violently that the blood gushed out. This was how he avenged Fourré's death, and this represents, perhaps, the original version of Charles' brutal action which we have met with in somewhat divergent forms in *Fierabras* and the *Entrée d'Espagne*.

Another episode of some importance for reconstructing the Charlemagne legend is contained in a Danish chronicle of later date which has preserved other branches of the original *saga*. The *Kaiser Karl Magnus Kronike*, which enjoyed great popularity in the fifteenth century, terminates its account of Charlemagne's wars by an account of his campaign against the heathen Gealver. In the course of this war Ogier, the Dane, performed many feats of valour, and the emperor gained a great victory which delivered the country of the King Iven. It will be remembered that the Oxford version of the *Chanson de Roland* terminates abruptly with a hint of further campaigns awaiting the weary emperor ('Reis Vivien si succuras en Imphe'), the thought of which caused him a moment of deep depression. Perhaps Turoldus, who had 'decliné la geste' so far, could not face the thought of another campaign either.

It is hoped that this very brief account of some of the contents of the *Karlamagnus-saga*, as they bear on the history of the Old French epic, will give a notion of its value and import. The Charlemagne legends occupy by far the largest part of its bulk. It is regrettable that the only chapter dealing with any portion of the Guillaume legend is devoted to the monkish account of Guillaume's 'moniage'. One would have preferred to see what the author would have made of the *Bataille d'Aliscans* or the *Couronnement de Louis*, which do not seem to have formed a part of the Scandinavian repertory. Outside the *Karlamagnus-saga* there is evidence of the popularity in the north of other epic poems such as *Les Quatre filz Aymon*, *Elie de Saint Giles* and *Floovent*, the heroes of which were perpetuated in ballad and rhyme. Amis and Amiles became popular heroes and found their place in Iceland amongst the songs, or so-called *rimur*, of that country. Any detailed account of these sagas and poems of the north would belong to the history of literature of those regions. The importance, from our point of view, lies in the existence of such a wealth of literature in the north, all deriving from the one source. The French epic legends of the eleventh and twelfth centuries, whether monkish or warlike in character, swept the whole of Western Europe from Iceland to Italy. The ball which started rolling in the north of France gained momentum rapidly. It was brought to a rather rapid stop in its own country by the appearance of a rival hero to the great king and a sudden growth of new ideals. But its repercussions, though in a form often differing from the original one, were felt for many a long year and proved the innate productiveness of the elemental stock.

CHAPTER XII

EPIC TRADITIONS

(1) CHARACTERS

AN attempt has been made in the foregoing pages to bring into relief the psychological skill with which the main characters of the Old French poems are drawn. Yet it is in the nature of epic poetry that many of the characteristics of the heroes should be typical and traditional; that stock qualities should appear with only slight variation in many of the characters. We have seen how the character of the converted heathen appears again and again in our poems. Strangely enough, however, it is in the figure of the Christian king—in fact, of Charlemagne himself—that some of these fixed features can be most readily discerned. In the *Chanson de Roland*, where royalty still plays a distinguished part, the great king appears in his noblest and most authoritative rôle. He receives the embassy from a rival sovereign with dignity; he is autocratic in his relations with his barons; he valiantly leads the avenging expedition after the defeat of his rearguard, and does not shun the single combat with the formidable pagan leader, Baligant. And yet, except perhaps in his moments of dejection, Charlemagne, even in the *Chanson de Roland*, is never completely human. There is a strong tradition of royalty, and Charles is, to a certain extent, a symbolic figure of kingship. This, like many other traditions, is biblical in character. There are certain traits which must mark a king from the time of Solomon onwards. He must be an object of great reverence; he must be generous, for giving is a royal prerogative (*roial mestier*); he must not be hasty in his speech, for his words partake of the divine.[1] This is expressed clearly in the *Chanson de Roland*:

> De sa parole ne fut mie hastifs,
> Sa custume est qu'il parolet a leisir (ll. 140–1).

Many are the occasions when the poet tells us that Charlemagne sat with bowed head (*chef enclin, chef enbrunc*[2]), wrapped in thought and guarding a silence on which his knights were too respectful to intrude. When the envoys arrived from King Marsilie and delivered their message, he gave no reply, but bent his head and began to think

---

[1] Prov. xvi. 16, etc.   [2] Cf. the provençal *cab cle*.

('Baisset sun chief, si cumencet a penser'). Nor did he even consider their proposals the same day but, having had them suitably accommodated, he arose early the next morning, attended Mass and Matins, and only then did he take counsel of his barons. This tradition of deliberation and slowness of thought runs all through the Old French epic. In *Renaut de Montauban* we find:

> Et qant li roi l'oï, si se va embronchant.
> D'une grande loée n'ala un mot sonant (37, 27-8).

It is noteworthy that when Charlemagne acts quickly he is generally in the wrong, as when he struck Roland on the nose in anger and brought about unforeseen and dire results. Combined with this deliberateness, and not in the least clashing with it, is the capacity in the king to be terrible in his wrath when once his anger is roused. When Charlemagne rides forth against the enemy 'par grant irur' and caracoles ('fait son eslais') calling upon God and the apostle of Rome, he strikes terror into their hearts. 'The King's wrath is the roaring of a lion', says Solomon; it is 'a messenger of death',[1] and so it proved to the Saracen army. The monk of St. Gall tells us how Charlemagne almost annihilated a man on one occasion with his flashing glance. He is alarming in the Old French poems, too, when he rolls his eyes in anger.

There is another side, however, to this accepted semi-divine nature of a king which brings us down to earth and which is also reflected clearly in the Old French poems. The pensive attitude, the slowness of speech and decision might easily degenerate into a regrettable hesitancy and weakness. This inactivity had become traditional amongst the merowingian kings—the 'fainéants'—who were eventually replaced by the more energetic mayors of the palace. We have in Eginhard's *Life* a rather comic description of King Hildericus (Chilperic) being conveyed, with flowing hair and beard, to the annual council (of which he was a useless member) on a cart drawn by oxen.[2] The impression of this static side of the king's character forces itself upon us in the French poems, as time goes on. In the later poems it has become traditional and, strange to say, this aspect of royalty was passed on to Charlemagne's poetic successor, King Arthur, whom some of the earliest romances depict as the pensive monarch, slow to move or undertake active operations. Sometimes he acts as a brake on the adventurous propensities of his knights. Was he not indulging in a nap in Chrétien's *Erec* when the knights

[1] Prov. xvi. 14 and 19.   [2] Ch. II.

were holding an animated discussion about their future plans? In the *Perceval* of the same author the young hero, on arrival at the court, finds the king in an attitude of 'pensiveness' caused by the depredations of a hostile neighbour: 'Li rois panse et mot ne li sone'.[1] The ill-mannered youth turned his horse round and rode so near the king that he actually knocked off his 'chapel de bonet' before an answer to his request could be obtained. Only then did the king arouse himself:

> Li rois torne vers le vaslet
> Le chief que il tenoit beissié,
> Si a tot son pense leissié. . . .[2]

It is again the tradition of the thinking king with bowed head which only occurs occasionally in Charles' natural descendants. When his feeble son, Louis, replied, 'I will think about it', to an urgent request from his brother-in-law for help, Guillaume was furious because the answer was dictated by fear, not by a commendable desire to give a just decision. The 'fainéant' side of the royal character is the one that emerges in all the *chansons* constituting the Guillaume cycle and many of those included in the feudal group. It was a sad end to the original tradition of royalty and magnanimity.

It is more difficult to speak of an epic tradition in the case of the multitude of knights who composed the armies of pagan and Christian, or of rival factions. Valour is obviously the main ingredient of a warrior's character, especially in the earlier poems which are not yet tinged with the ideas of a chivalrous code of honour. It is often the exterior aspect of the knight which assumes a certain epic character. He is not, as a rule, particularly large in size (*ingens*), for courage was more important than stature. More often than not it is the heathen who is gigantic, and he found to his cost that a 'petit home' could fight well.[3] We are reminded again of Virgil's description of the bees, whose small bodies can scarcely contain their mighty spirits—a passage actually quoted, as we have seen, by Paulus Diaconus when describing a plucky boy who proved a match for his full-grown assailants. The idea emerges again in the famous phrase of Guillaume d'Orange, applied to his young nephew: 'Cors as d'enfant mais raison as de ber'. In the short epic interlude introduced by Jean Bodel into his *Jeu de Saint Nicolas*, the same sentiment is expressed by the valiant young Christian knight who, when faced by the odds of a hundred

---

[1] *Li Contes del Graal*, 926. [2] Ibid., 638–40.
[3] Cf. *Couronnement*, 1. 923.

to one in the battle against the pagans, begs his comrades not to despise him on account of his youth for, says he:

> On a veü souvent grant cuer en cors petit.[1]

But although actual bulk was not considered a necessary characteristic of a good fighter, yet a well-formed body with certain definite features was admired and these features were soon crystallized into an accepted formula. Already in the *Chanson de Roland* we find them in the description of the heathen Baligant, whose knightly appearance is much insisted upon:

> La forcheüre ad assez grant le ber,
> Graisles les flancs et larges les costez.
> Gros ad le piz, belement est mollez.
> Lees les espalles et le vis ad mult cler.

We notice the wide (*lees*) shoulders, the ample chest (*piz*), the slender hips beneath the well-formed ribs and the frank countenance. Similar descriptions to this can be found in most of the *chansons-de-geste*. Garin le Lorrain has the same contours ('gros ot les bras et les membres fornis / Larges espaules et si ot gros le pis').[2] It is a heathen again in Aliscans who has the 'espaules lees, les bras gros, les poins carrés en som'. The author of the fragmentary *Roman d'Alexandre* enumerates the traits in his strange mixed dialect:

> Ample lo peys et aformas
> lo bu subtil non trop delcad
> lo corp daval beyn enforcad. . . .

The description of Roland in the *Entrée d'Espagne* gathers up nearly all the scattered traits:

> La jambe ot loinge et grose, li pie chanbres agu,
> Les cuises plates, et dougies por le bu,
> Anples le spaules et par le piz gros fu,
> Les mains longues et blances, le bras gros e nervu
> Le cols et loing et gros bien demi pie et plu.

It must have been a widespread tradition and it is interesting to find that these physical features are almost identical with those required in a recruit according to the Treatise on War (*De Re Militare*) of Vegetius in the fourth century. Here again we find the *lato pectore*, the *humeris musculosis*, the *longioribus brachiis*, the *ventre modicus* and *exilior cruribus* (the change of construction in the original accounts for the apparently disorderly syntax). Vegetius himself takes us even further back, for he quotes Virgil's description of the two kinds of

---

[1] *Jeu de S. N.*, l. 409.   [2] ll. 153–4.

bees[1]—the one kind alert and fighting-fit, the others slothful and dull, and dragging ingloriously an ample paunch (*latamque alvum*).

Another traditional feature of the well-trained knight in the early epics is the change of face he can adopt according to the persons he is addressing. He must have one face for the friend, another for the foe. He must encourage his own men by his kindly looks but strike terror into the heart of the enemy by his fierce aspect. This, too, was a biblical idea, for God would 'cause His face to shine' on those who pleased Him but 'scatter away evil with His eyes' when He acted as judge.[2] In the earliest French poems this change of countenance is described. We read of Roland:

> Vers Sarrazins reguardet fierement
> E vers Franceis humele(s) et dulcement.[3]

In *Garin le Lorrain* Bègue is described by his brother Garin in the 'regret' for his untimely death:

> Frans chevaliers, corageus et hardis!
> Fel et angris contre vos anemis,
> Et dols et simples a trestoz vos amis.[4]

In the *Entrée d'Espagne* it is remarked as a striking proof of the sweetness of Roland's disposition that he was incapable of changing his expression even to his foes:

> Cun un dulz vis qe muer non savoit
> Se treit Rollant la o li paiens voit (ll. 4317–18).

It was, of course, merely a concrete way of showing one's feelings, just as the shedding of tears was the accepted evidence of grief and was no disgrace even to the stoutest warrior. Indeed, the absence of an ability to weep might be misinterpreted and to obtain the 'grace of tears' sometimes became a subject of prayer. The heroes, though individuals themselves, had certain typical conventional ways of expressing their feelings for epic personalities must have epic characteristics.

One of the legacies inherited from a much earlier period was, as we have seen, that of a special bond between two men which produced such an identity of interests that one would sacrifice anything for the other. This sort of blood-brotherhood (*compagnonnage* or *compagnie*) brought a mutual advantage to the participants which sometimes caused envy in others who could not share this advantage

[1] 'Nam duo sunt genera . . .', *Georgics* IV, 88 f.
[2] Quoted by the Monk of St. Gall, Ch. xi.
[3] *Chanson de Roland*, ll. 1162–3.　　　　[4] Ed. P. Paris, II, p. 263.

—as in the case of the senechal in *Amis et Amiles*. This hatred, caused by jealousy or the rankling of wounded pride, gave rise to a class of traitors who carried on a sort of personal vendetta against those they wished to ruin. These so-called 'traitors' were often cited as belonging to the kith and kin of Ganelon whose genealogy was thus swelled out to vast proportions. This was not fair to Ganelon for he was not a typical *traitor*. He was an outstanding personality, not a type, and the author of the *Chanson de Roland* has succeeded in rendering him an object of pity and fear. His treachery was on a grand scale. He played for high stakes and although his gamble did not succeed he brought about the downfall of a whole army by his treachery. The traditional traitor-type is completely different from this. He is generally a steward, or some sort of functionary who stands high in the royal confidence. He has the king's ear, he is a flatterer, a whisperer, a spy, a tale-bearer who knows how to 'servir de langue';[1] he hates to see anyone in a position which might rival his own. The idea of the false steward is a very ancient one which lived through the centuries. The Middle English *Book of Curtesye* says of them: 'Few are trew but fele ar fals'. In the monastery this sycophant would be the bishop's 'amicus auricularis' who indulged in back-biting (*dorsiloquia*) and tale-bearing out of jealousy and hatred of his fellows. The story of the three inseparable friends who suffered from this in the monastery of St. Gall is known from Ekkehard's *De Casibus Monasterii S. Galli*. The traitor in this case was the 'refectarius' who had wormed himself into the bishop's favour. We do not meet with this type in the earliest French poems. There is no hint of such a character in the *Roland*, the *Chançun*, or in *Gormont et Isembard*. But already in the *Couronnement de Louis* he rears his ugly head, though even here his designs are less personal than imperial, for the traitor hopes to step into the shoes of royalty. But as a rule his aims are less exalted. He merely wants to ruin a personal enemy of whom he is jealous and whom he watches with an evil eye,[2] or a woman who has inspired in him an unrequited passion. The first example we have of this type is the 'aulicus' in the Latin poem of Rudolfus Tortarius which, as we have seen, is the earliest known version of the *Amicus et Amelius* legend. Here the traitor already has the traditional name of Ardericus (Old French *Hardré*). It was jealousy which made him denounce one of the two friends to the king in the hope of ruining

---

[1] Cf. *Garin le Lorrain*.

[2] Cf. 'Drances infensus, quem gloria Turni / obliqua invidia stimulisque agitabat amaris'. Verg. *Æneid* XI, 335–6.

him because he would not become his 'blood-brother'. In the *Vita*[1] he is called the 'delator'. The Hardré of *Garin le Lorrain* has the same characteristics. He belongs to a little group of conspirators who give dishonourable advice to the king with a view to advancing their own ends. When the king, in his traditional attitude, bows his head in thought ('bronche le vis') they draw to one side ('a une part se sunt trait') and it is Hardré who actually makes to the king the mean proposal which he adopts. In *Renaut de Montauban* the typical traitor again belongs to a little group (all relations of Ganelon) who go privately to the king and ask permission to pursue and kill Renaut in order to avenge the emperor's nephew and thus gain his favour. They are promised a good reward (*gent don*) if they will do so. Alas, Charlemagne does not shine in this poem.

Another stock traitor of this contemptible kind is Macaire, whom we have met as Machario in the Franco-Italian poem of that name. He had wormed himself into the king's confidence by means of gifts and had made himself powerful by distributing bribes. Unrequited passion for the emperor's wife made him behave in the most despicable fashion. Having once gained his point he even sacrificed his accomplice, the dwarf who had risked everything for him. In the end he was defeated by a dog and died a traitor's death. The contemptible method of trying to compromise the queen by employing someone else to creep into her bed while the emperor was at Mass, became popular in legend and ballad. We meet it again in the English ballad *Sir Aldingar*, where the dog of the Old French poem is replaced by a mysterious stranger. Makaire is the name of the traitor in *Aiol* who had caused the hero's father to be exiled:

> Il fu cachiés de France par poesté
> Par le conseil Makaire le deffaé (ll. 1109–10).

He has just the same character of meanness. He is 'un mavais losengier', 'un quivert de put lin'. He had committed many treacherous acts (not one big one like Ganelon); he had ruined many noble men but always managed to get the law on his own side.[2] He is the 'souduiant', 'li mal-parliers', who serves the king with flatteries. He is absolutely true to type for he draws the king aside into a corner,[3] and tells him how foolish he is to trust and reward Aiol.

It is unnecessary to discuss further the type of the traitor, but a word must be said about the dwarf. These little creatures (unlike Virgil's

---

[1] Cf. Ch. X, p. 221. [2] l. 2297.
[3] A une part le trait a i. recoi (l. 3546).

T

bees) have mean souls in mean bodies. The dwarf who has been pampered and caressed by the queen in *Macliario* is easily induced by promises of large sums of money to betray her. In the Anglo-Norman version of *Fierabras* a dwarf tries to insinuate himself into Floripas' bed when he is sent by her father to retrieve the magic 'ceinture' she has stolen. The rôle of the dwarf in Béroul's *Tristan* will be remembered as conforming to the same type of untrustworthy and corruptible agent. A similar type, which plays a rather unhappy part, is that of 'portier' or 'huissier' (*doorkeeper*). He, however, often comes to a bad end as a direct result of doing his duty. His lot was not a happy one, for an active, warlike spirit was not likely to be deterred either from escaping from a fortress (like Roland in *Aspremont*) or entering a town (like Guillaume in many a poem) by a helpless watchman or doorkeeper. An exception to this was the porter in the *Couronnement* who, after angrily refusing to admit Guillaume, changed his mind on hearing who he was and called forth Guillaume's remark to his nephew Bertrand: 'Oïstes mais si bien parler portier'.[1] The porter was actually rewarded by being knighted on the spot—an unheard-of honour. It would seem that the doorkeeper was often a sort of pensioner who had been wounded and was unfit for more active service. Raoul brutally tells the wounded Rocoul that, having lost a leg, he can become a 'portier', and Ernaut (who has lost an arm) may take on the job of a watchman ('gaite'). Similar grim jokes were made by Guillaume and, with slight variations, by Hagen and Walter in the *Waltharius*. In the later decadent poems types became more numerous. We have the hermit, the conjuror, the love-sick princess—but these do not form an integral part of our epic material. They are necessary figures introduced to fill out the framework of the poem when the old 'magnanimous' heroes could no longer carry the action along by their own weight.

(2) Epic Episodes

Besides these traditional figures there were certain episodes which recur so often, especially in the later poems, that we almost miss them if they are not there. The scenes, based on the close relationship between uncle and nephew, have been noticed and are too well known to need special treatment here. But what would seem a more natural relationship, that between father and son, strangely enough appears in a somewhat ambiguous light. It is interesting that affection

[1] l. 1645.

between father and son, and vice-versa, is more often a characteristic
of heathen family life than of Christian in the Old French epic.
Charlemagne is completely crushed by the death of his nephew—
and for him are the lamentations which come so naturally from the
mouth of father and mother for their son in the *Chanson de S. Alexis.*
Marsilie and Baligant, on the other hand, are both deeply and
genuinely afflicted by the death of their sons.[1] It is not uncommon
among the Christian army, on the other hand, for father and son to
be actually fighting on opposite sides and to meet in the midst of
battle. This undoubtedly represented an old tradition—perhaps
Germanic in origin, for the most outstanding example we have of it
occurs in the well-known Old High German poem, the *Hildebrants-
lied.* The issue here remains doubtful owing to the fragmentary state
of the poem. It is, perhaps, left intentionally so in similar circumstances by the artistic sense of the French authors. The earliest
example we have of this curious episode is in *Gormont et Isembart,*
where Isembart the renegade meets his father (known by various
names in the different versions) who is fighting on the royalist side
against the invaders. The father and son did not recognize each other,
otherwise as the author remarks, it would have been most unnatural,
for they would have had other things to talk about. Isembart unhorses his father and rides off with his horse, but otherwise the
outcome was not serious. Aymon de Dordon, the father of the four
famous 'fils d'Aymon', who is on the side of the royalists, meets his
sons in the battle. Renaut (de Montauban) was mad with anger (*'le
sens cuide derver'*) when he saw his father; he began at once to abuse
him. Family relationships were out of place at such a time: 'Ja n'est
il mie tans com doie parenter',[2] and his father answered him with
angry threats. But the fighting passed them by and neither suffered
hurt. Later in the same poem Aymon speaks with the utmost
brutality when his sons return in rags to the house and crave to see
their mother. He is in the curious position of having 'forsworn'
(forjuré) his sons when they had rebelled against the emperor. It is
true that he softens somewhat at the close, but his insults and taunts
when he tells them to leave the house (Issiez fors de ma sale, widies
moi mon donjon) must be read to be believed.[3] Rainouart, in
Aliscans, after his conversion to Christianity, when he was fighting
on Guillaume's side, met his father Desramé in the battle and wasted

---

[1] The heathen Borrel with his twelve sons was evidently a well-known character. We find
him already in the *Fragment de la Haye,* in the *Chançun de Willame,* in *Aliscans,* and his numerous
sons were always his title to distinction in the epic tradition.
[2] p. 64, p. 9.   [3] p. 93, l. 5 f.

no time on parental feelings. But he, too, refrained from killing him. It was always a rather difficult situation when the antagonists both had a claim to the sympathy of the audience. An ingenious device was employed by the 'jongleurs'. The long-drawn-out single combat between Roland and Oliver (whose sister Roland admired) must inevitably have ended with the death of one of the heroes,[1] had not a cloud miraculously descended between them and an angel appeared who forbade them to fight any longer. Thus the battle was brought to a draw. In *Renaut de Montauban* there is a fierce duel between Roland and Renaut, Charlemagne is in agony for his nephew and prays God for a miracle to save him; Renaut's brothers were just as insistent in prayer for the safety of their kith and kin. What could the Almighty do when besieged thus from both sides, but separate them by a miracle? Once again He sent a cloud which spread over the meadow and hid them from each other, thus effectively bringing the battle to a standstill:

> Tel vertu i fist Dex por Renaut l'aduré,
> Et por Karle de France, le fort roi coroné.
> Une niule (*mist, cloud*) leva qui espant par le pré.
> L'uns ne pot veoir l'autre, tant i ot oscurté.
> Entrequerant se vont contreval par le pré.[2]

In *La Chevalerie Ogier*, when the implacable fury of Ogier against Charlemagne's son Charlot for having killed his own son urges him to the very point of cutting off the head of the poor repentant lad, once again a natural obstacle intervenes in the shape of a lightning flash which descended from the clouds and came between the combatants like a burning fire. Ogier, having relieved his feelings by giving Charlot a monstrous 'soufflet' which hurled him to the ground, the two combatants parted with relief on both sides. The skill and artistic sense which restrained the authors from bringing these unnatural battles between near relations or friends to a tragic end is admirable.

This intervention of a cloud (or some similar natural phenomenon) for putting an end to an embarrassing situation was a clever device and clearly one that the audience appreciated. The beginnings of a quarrel also had their accepted tradition. The game of chess, still a novelty in the West in the eleventh century, provided an excellent and reasonable starting point for a quarrel. In the *Chanson de Roland*

---

[1] 'Ja lor bataille ne fust mes departie / Einz en ëust li uns perdu la vie' (*G. de V.* 3874–5) (une nue, l. 5891).

[2] *R. de M.* 322, 27–31. Reminiscent of similar scenes in the *Iliad*.

it is the older, more prudent men who play at chess while the younger knights have a more active diversion:

> Et as eschecs li plus saive et li veill.
> Et escremissent cil bacheler leger (ll. 112–13).

In *Raoul de Cambrai* a quiet game of chess was not forbidden on Good Friday, and Raoul sat down to it gloomily when, having forgotten it was Lent, he had just been refused the plenteous meal for which he had asked. He was a practised player[1] and he had just got his castle in a good position, taken a knight with a pawn, and had almost checkmated his rival, when he wearied of the game, leapt to his feet, and called for wine.[2] So the game ended without any dire results, for his opponent had discreetly played a losing game. In the later poems, however, the appearance of a chess-board generally boded ill. It was a game of chess between the respective sons of Charlemagne and Ogier in the *Chevalerie Ogier* which gave rise to all the horrible wars between the two fathers in which appalling scenes of massacre took place. Ogier's son Baudouinet, who had probably inherited some of the character of his father, was indiscreet enough to render the emperor's son Charlot 'échec et mat' in a few moves. The young prince was so furious at this impudence that he seized the chess-board and gave his opponent a fearful blow on the head which killed him on the spot.[3] Ogier so completely lost his self-control that he killed the emperor's nephew, knocked down Charlemagne himself, and would have killed him had he not been prevented; he then fled and offered his services to the King of the Lombards. As we have just seen, Ogier's wrath was only appeased by a miracle, which was as much a part of the jongleur's stock-in-trade as the beginning of the enmity. The episode was much exploited. The lengthy, though often grandiose poem of *Renaut de Montauban*, a mine of wealth for epic traditions and scenes, makes use of the chess episode at least twice. On the first occasion Renaut, the eldest of the four famous sons of Aymon, sat down to a very enjoyable game of chess with the emperor's nephew Bertolai.[4] But they went on playing so long that at last they quarrelled and Bertolai called Renaut names and gave him a 'bufe'. The blood flowed and Renaut went and complained to Charlemagne. The emperor, however, gave him no satisfaction, and when Renaut answered him back rudely he struck him with his gauntlet and the blood flowed afresh. This was too much for Renaut.

---

[1] l. 1586.   [2] l. 1593.   [3] ll. 3156–80.
[4] 'As esches vont jouer u se sunt delitié', 51, 18.

On meeting Bertolai again he picked up the heavy chess-board, struck him on the head with it and killed him. Then the fat was in the fire and the author remarks: 'La commence meslee, de cou ne dotes mie.'[1] 'O quot millia animorum Orco transmissa sunt', exclaims Alexander Neckam, referring to the same incident, 'occasione illius ludi quo Reginaldus filius Eymundi, in calculis ludens, militem generosum cum illo ludentem, in palatio Karoli Magni, cum uno scaccorum interemit'.[2]

The theme of chess is exploited again and again in the decadent period when 'clichés' and hackneyed phrases formed the chief stock-in-trade of the jongleurs. In the *Enfances Garin*, Garin plays Charlemagne for his kingdom and actually wins. But his loyalty is too great to let him take advantage of his victory. It would be tedious to cite other examples of this motif which was popular enough to pass into the more romantic literature. In Chrétien's *Perceval*, Gauvain and his lady-love keep a whole township at bay with chess-board and pieces, the board acting as a shield and the figures as missiles. It is interesting, too, to find a quarrel over chess adduced as the cause of a mortal quarrel between Fouke and Johan, son of King Henry in the prose romance of *Fouke-Fitz-Warin* which, incidentally, has every appearance of being based on an earlier poem. In this case it was the king's son who snatched up the chess-board and gave Fouke a great blow: 'Johan prist l'eschelker, si fery Fouke grant coupe'. Fouke replied by a kick in the chest which sent Johan crashing against a wall and made him lose his senses. Johan went and complained to his father, who told him it served him right, but Fouke was never forgiven: 'unque pus ne le poeit amer de cuer'. Once again a game of chess was the cause of much bloodshed and misery. The constant use of the word 'mater' in Old French tells its own tale, for *mater* came to be used as an equivalent of 'kill', 'destroy'.

More characteristic of the early, more exclusively warlike poems, and hence more epic in character, is the tradition of the favourite sword, the much valued personal property of the warrior. In spite of being inanimate the sword was looked upon almost as a person, an individual, as for example in *Waltharius*, where the sword fears the helmet on account of its strength. The case of Roland addressing his sword three times in his farewell lament[3] is not an isolated one. There is an invocation to all the pieces of armour in the *Chançun de Willame*;

[1] 52, 15.
[2] *De Naturis Rerum*, Ed. Wright, p. 326. (Cf. *Romania* IV, 474.)
[3] E. Durendal, bone, si mare fustes, etc., l. 2304 f.; E. Durendal, cum es bele et clere et blance, etc., 2316 f.; E. Durendal, cum es bele et seintisme, etc., l. 2344 f.

Ogier addresses and threatens his sword when it fails to kill his opponent in *Renaut de Montauban,* and other examples could be given from later works. Durendal was, of course, the most renowned of all the epic swords of legend. From the *Chanson de Roland* we learn that Charlemagne had been commanded by an angel to give it to a noble leader and the emperor had obeyed by girding it on Roland's side. In *Aspremont* the story is varied. Eaumont, the king's son, handed it to the youthful Roland before he died so that it might not fall into the possession of a coward. Most of the celebrated swords had a history of this sort. Oliver's sword Halteclere[1] had belonged to a Roman emperor (according to the account in *Girard de Viane,* 5540 f.). When the emperor was killed it got lost in the grass on the field of battle. It was found by mowers when one of their scythes ran against it, handed over to the pope who deciphered its name (Halteclere) in the lettering inscribed on it, kept amongst the treasures of S. Pierre in Rome, taken possession of by Pepin of France, given as a feudal gift to Duke Bueve, sold to a Jew, who kept it carefully hidden for a hundred years until he handed it finally over to Oliver, 'fiz Renier de Genvres'. It was no wonder that Olivier treasured a sword with such a past. To return to the *Chanson de Roland,* in which sword-names abound; besides Roland and Oliver, Turpin has his renowned sword Almace,[2] Ganelon his weapon with a more sinister-sounding name, 'Murglies', the emperor proudly wields the flashing 'Joyeuse'—'l'épée de France'.[3] The Emir Baligant also has his special sword 'Precieuse' to which the heathen rally as to a battle-cry corresponding to the French cry of Montjoie. Many of the names are significant in meaning, but the name of Ogier's sword 'Cortain', of which the origin is not so obvious, is explained as having been given to it by Ogier when it broke on the testing-stone in front of the palace at Aix, and he had it pointed afresh because he was loth to lose it:

> Por votre grant bonté vos fis je apointer,
> Por cou aves nom *corte*[4], nel vos quier a noier.[5]

an episode explained by a passage in the *Karlamagnus Saga,* Chapter I.

The legend of the blacksmith, forger of most of the famous swords, was well known and occurs frequently. His name in French was Galant, the romance form of the Old German *Welant* and the earlier

[1] *Chanson de Roland*, 1952, etc.
[2] l. 2089.
[3] l. 3615. Called Joyeuse on account of the holy relic it contained, l. 2506.
[4] Nom-form: Acc. cortain; cf. nonne, nonnain, etc.
[5] *Ren. de Mont.* 210, 12.

old Norse form *Varlundr* celebrated in the Edda. In some of the later poems he is replaced by a legendary Jew, skilful in metal work. This 'good jew', 'li bons Juis' (an uncommon figure in the Middle Ages), appears under various names. In the *Prise d'Orange*[1] he is Ysaac de Barceloigne. In *Girard de Viane* it was, as we have seen, a Jew who had guarded the sword, but the workman (fevre) who had made and engraved it went by the name of Manificans.[2] Later poems give other names to the Jewish fabricator. The three ominous-sounding swords of the giant Loquifer (Isdose, Recuite and Dolerose) in the *Ch. de Jerusalem* are attributed to a certain Mathusalem. The three swords of Fierabras (also of Jewish origin) in one of the Old French versions are equally impressive, being: Bautisme, Plourance, and Garbain. These names were probably added to the original poem as a concession to the popular taste for significant names.

It may have been noticed that Guillaume d'Orange has not figured so far as the owner of a noted sword. He became, however, the proud possessor of the incomparable sword Joieuse, the emperor's sword, with which Charlemagne presented him[3] and which was the best sword in the world next to Durendal—'Fors Durendal sous ciel milleur n'en a'.[4] It kept up its reputation in spite of the fact that Guillaume did not have it all his own way in the combat with Aerofle and at one point cursed it and nearly threw it away. The next blow, however, was so successful that Guillaume was full of praise and gratitude to it. There are many references to this gift of Charlemagne to Guillaume which seems to give a kind of lineage to the sword and a link between the two famous defenders of the faith. In the *Couronnement* we read on several occasions that Guillaume girded on the celebrated sword:

> Et ceint Joiose a son senestre flanc,
> Que li dona Charles li combatanz (ll. 2501–2).

Its efficacy was proved on many occasions, but Guillaume, although attached to it and appreciating its qualities, had a more absorbing object for his affections—viz. his horse—and that brings us to another important set of epic traditions.

There is no need to insist on the poetic value of the horse in epic literature. From the warrior-horse of Job which smells the battle from afar and greets it with a loud neigh,[5] we have a long line of famous steeds which probably come to an end as regards their martial

---

[1] l. 968. [2] l. 5558. [3] *Aliscans*, 1277.
[4] *Aliscans*, 1266. [5] Ha, ha! cf. Job xxxix. 25.

value with the appearance of the internal combustion engine. Speed and strength were the two main qualities needed in a battle-horse. Good training, moreover, as Xenophon insisted long ago in his book on cavalry, was necessary to bring out the best in a horse and kindness had better results than harshness. The taming of the fierce man-eating Bucephalus by Alexander was a constant feature of a legend which was widespread in the Middle Ages,[1] and the grief of a devoted horse following the corpse of Pallas, its cheeks wet with big tears, was probably familiar to generations brought up on Virgil. The outburst of epic poems in France in the eleventh and twelfth centuries was accompanied by a spate of horses which were as indispensable to the knights as the swords they wielded. Contact with the Arabs and the Moors of Spain had brought the horse back to its true level, and the *equus* which had become a *caballus* was reinstated as a *destrier* or *cheval*. In fact, the faithful horse became a personality to a greater extent than the favourite sword, which was only natural since the horse was an animate creature and could respond to its master's feelings. This it did often in unmistakable manner. The famous horse Bayard—to which further reference will be made—sensed its master's grief at the loss of a friend, refused its food and did not expect the usual playful signs to which it was accustomed while being saddled: 'Why can you not talk?' said his master—'you would have comforted me in my grief'. But the horse's silent homage to Renaut's sorrow was perhaps even more affecting than words would have been. A similar dumb show of grief was the tribute paid to its murdered master by Bègue's horse in *Garin le Lorrain*. It showed its teeth ('Li dent li saillent de la goule plain pie'),[2] neighed, snorted, and pawed the ground so fiercely that it was impossible to saddle it. It was a sight to behold, and even the 'belles dames' and the 'clerc du mostier' came to have a look at it from a discreet distance. Just as terrifying was the horse that was presented to Roland by the sultan in the *Entrée d'Espagne*, which 'brayed' like a lion and allowed no one to approach. Here the inspiration of Bucephalus is obvious, for the sultan declares that not even Bocifal in the days of Candace[3] could equal him in worth. Roland mounted him with the greatest ease, and the author, loyal to his French models, remarks: 'Jameis ne l'oit meilor, *for Velaintif*.'[4]

The mention of Veillantif brings us back to the *Chanson de Roland* where we already find many notable horses with significant names, but not yet the 'cheval faé' of the later poems. Even here, however,

---

[1] Cf. *Entree d'Espagne.*   [2] p. 241, Bk. II.
[3] l. 12603.   [4] l. 2614.

they are capable of amazing speed and acrobatics—particularly the horses of the heathen. It is noteworthy and a tribute to the fundamental veracity of the author that few fabulous feats are attributed to the Frankish steeds. Veillantif, Roland's horse—so celebrated in later fiction—is merely 'sun bon cheval curant'. Charlemagne's horse Tencendur, which he had conquered from Malpalin de Nerbone,[1] is completely left to our imagination, though we do know that the emperor was riding him when he made his *eslais* (prance) before a hundred thousand men. Tencendur, moreover, gave four leaps—presumably as an affirmative reply—when Charlemagne, at sight of the emir with his huge army of Arabs, pronounced his stimulating challenge to his own men:

> S'il unt grant gent, d'iço, seigneurs, qui calt?
> Ki errer voelt a mei venir s'en alt! (ll. 3338–9).

From this we may gather that horse and rider were animated by the same feelings. The archbishop's horse Grossaille also had a history, for he had been captured from a king whom Turpin had killed in Denmark,[2] and no beast could compete with him. The description given of this animal is conventional: 'gambes . . . plates', 'quise curte', 'crupe . . . large', 'costez lungs', 'l'eschine . . . halte', 'cue blanche', 'crignete jalne', 'oreilles petites', and 'teste falve . . .'; we come across it with slight variation frequently in later poems, and we would perhaps prefer to have been spared it here, but it was probably a concession to the popular demand for something concrete.

A more epic phraseology is applied to the Arab steeds ridden and skilfully handled by the pagan warriors. Barbamusche, the horse of Climborin, is 'plus . . . isnels que espervier ne aronde'; the description of Valdbrun's horse Gramimunde is varied in the second half-line by 'que nun est uns falcuns';[3] of Malcuiant's steed Saltperdut (how significant are their names!) we are told: 'Beste nen est nuls Ki puisset curre a lui';[4] of Grandoine's horse Marmorie: 'Plus est isnels que n'est oisel ki volet'.[5] Of the feeble King Marsilie's horse Gaignun we learn nothing, but the eager steed of Baligant the Emir, jumps fifty feet across a ditch as his master makes his *eslais*, and not unnaturally calls forth the acclamations of the watching army.

But the real lover and judge of horses in the Old French poems is Guillaume d'Orange. He could tackle a fierce horse like the one (Alion by name) that he captured from the heathen Corsolt (*Couronnement*). He would risk his own life so as not to injure the

[1] l. 2995.   [2] l. 1489.   [3] l. 1522.   [4] l. 1554.   [5] l. 1572.

coveted horse of an opponent, as he did in the battle with Aerofle (*Aliscans*). He was devoted to his own horse Baucent in this latter poem, spared it when possible, promised it rewards if it helped in the fight or the pursuit, and thanked God cordially for it when the issue was successful. And Baucent, who had the sense of a man,[1] answered him with appropriate sounds and actions—snorting, neighing, pawing the ground, rolling its eyes, etc. Guillaume abandoned it for Volatille, the coveted Arab mount captured from Aerofle, but not until he had released it from its harness to give it a better chance of escape from the pagans. But alas, the faithful Baucent was found and cut to pieces. It is noticeable that Baucent is properly a generic name for a piebald horse. The first horse of that name we meet was Guiburg's horse in the *Chançun de Willame* which she lent to the little Gui to enable him to follow the army.

The tradition of the faithful horse who thought and fought for his master became very popular. We have seen how the horse in *Aiol* with the pleasant name of *Marchegai* dealt with Aiol's enemies.[2] Ogier's horse, Brojefort, was of the same breed. In fact, on the occasion of a fight between Ogier and Renaut (the owner of Bayard) the two horses joined in the battle and bit and kicked each other like mad when they saw their masters fighting so furiously: 'Autresi se conbatent com dui chevalier', says the author.[3] Ogier feared for his horse as Bayard was the stronger. He had good reason, for Bayard was a 'cheval faé' who recognized his master after a separation more quickly than a wife does her husband, and actually went down on his knees to him in the sand.[4] During a single combat between Renaut and Roland he attacked Roland's horse by giving it a kick on the left ear, breaking its reins ('u il vosist u non') and chased it over the river. Bayard, too, like Marchegai, took part in a horse race, the stakes for which were very high, being no less than the emperor's crown. The object of the race was to obtain a horse for Roland, in exchange for the crown and a large sum of money. Needless to say, Bayard won the race and Renaut, who had come to the course in disguise, rode off with both the horse and the crown. No wonder Charlemagne hated the horse as much as its rider, and when at last he had it in his power, tried to drown it with a weight round its neck. Bayard, however, freed itself and escaped to the Ardennes, where it

---

[1] 'Ausi l'entent con s'il fust hom senez, 526'.
[2] Cf. supra, Ch. X, p. 205.
[3] *Renaut de Montauban*, p. 209, l. 18.
[4] Ibid., 205, 31 f.

lived on, avoiding all human contact and rushing about more like a devil than a horse:

Que bien samble annemi qui de Dex ne n'a cure.[1]

Charlemagne closed both his eyes in grief and anger when Bayard escaped, but his men were glad and praised God. We are in the realm of romance, but there is an epic quality about both Bayard and its master which explains why the tradition has lived on through the centuries.

(3) Epic Sentiments

It would be easy, but pointless, to multiply the number of epic characters and episodes. For the light they throw on the manners of the times and on the society for which the poems were composed, it is even more illuminating to review some of the sentiments which recur often enough to prove that they were received with approval, or perhaps amusement, by the audience. Starting from the most important relationships—namely, those of man to man or man to woman—it is obvious from the start that the poems were composed for a warrior-class. The close friendship between two men bound by loyalty to stand together (which was expressed, as we have seen, by the idea of *compagnonnage* or *compagnie*) is a prominent feature in the earliest known poems. It plays a conspicuous part in *Roland* in the *Willame*, in *Raoul de Cambrai*, as well as in many later poems. The relationship between uncle and nephew (sister's son), which was observed by Tacitus amongst the German tribes,[2] pervades most of the Old French poems. One has only to think of Guillaume and his many nephews, or Charlemagne's affection for Roland to realize the truth of the Latin author's words: 'Quidam sanctiorem artioremque hunc nexum sanguinis arbitrantur'. The more the better, for a man's honour and strength consisted partly in the number of relations and friends (often expressed by the same word: *ami*) he possessed. It was the depth of anguish for a man to think he had no friend but God! 'Suz ciel ne quid aveir ami un sul', laments Charlemagne as he gazes on the corpse of his nephew; 'se tu lui perz, n'avras ami fors Deu', Guibourg tells Guillaume in the *Chançun de Willame*, when warning him of the risk he runs in abandoning his nephew. Over and over again the sentiment is expressed that friends are more precious than wealth—or rather that they are the true form of wealth. 'Tant buer

[1] Ibid., 403, 7.   [2] Cf. Germania XX.

fu nez (= how fortunate is the man) qui plenté a d'amis' recurs almost like a refrain. In *Garin le Lorrain* the sentiment is expressed in so many words:

> N'est pas richoise ne de vair ne de gris
> Ne de deniers, de murs (=mules) ne de roncins
> Mais est richoise de parens et d'amis.
> Le cuers d'un homme vaut tout l'or d'un païs.[1]

The value of a man's heart (i.e. of true friendship) is beautifully expressed in the last line quoted. The sentiment became deservedly popular: 'Li cuers n'est mie en dras envelopés / N'en vair n'en gris m'en ermin golés / Ainz est el ventre dedans bien reposés', says the author of *Aliscans*, and practically the same idea clothed in somewhat different words has already been referred to in Girart de Viane. 'A friend in need is a friend indeed' (*Au grant besoing voit-on bien son ami*) and a loyal heart will never let anyone down (*Fins cuers ne puet mentir*), whereas money is of no avail when one is in a tight corner. Moreover, the aristocratic outlook of the knightly class was reflected in its scornful attitude towards money and trade. 'Ne sui pas marchëans qu'aie borsée' cries Aiol angrily when the king offers him a reward of money and the same scornful words—with slight variation in detail—come from the lips of many a proud scion of noble family. A horse, on the other hand (one of the most costly items of the knight's equipment) was highly valued, but could often be obtained from a fallen foe. Rainouart was sharply reprimanded by Bertrand for his method of fighting with his huge pole because he killed both horse and rider. Armour could be stripped from a man's corpse but a dead horse was useless. Rainouart was an apt pupil for, having followed Bertrand's instructions to 'push' (*bouter*) rather than strike with his formidable weapon, he rapidly secured quite a number of costly Arab steeds for those who needed them. The epic value of the horse in poetry has already been indicated, but in fact it had a monetary value as well, or rather the still greater value of being a friend in need. Even a horse, however, could not compete with a human being for 'ce est grant chose d'un ami conquester'.[2]

The prominence given to the sentimental relationship between man and man in the early epic inevitably affected that between the sexes in a somewhat adverse manner. There is, as has been mentioned, very little in the way of amorous manifestations—in Roland they are conspicuously absent; in Charlemagne completely so; they are non-

---

[1] *Garin le Lorrain*, II, 218.   [2] *Girart de Viane*, 6123.

existent in the youthful Vivien. The exception which proves the rule is in the case of Guillaume d'Orange, and even his attitude towards Guibourg is not exactly that of a passionate lover. This is, perhaps, the reason why what is often called 'là nouvelle conception de l'amour' in the romantic literature, both epic and lyric, swept in eventually on a full tide, to submerge the cruder, more realistic *chansons-de-geste* and replace the code of chivalry by that of 'galanterie'. This latter quality is indeed completely absent, as has been noticed in a previous chapter, even in the case of the otherwise courteous knights Bernier and Aïol. No dallying that might weaken the warlike spirit was to be allowed. It was a disgrace for a knight to allow himself to be swayed in warlike matters by feminine influence or advice. Aymeri knocked his wife down when she attempted to restrain his ruthless method of sending forth all his sons on perilous adventures. Raoul was extremely rude to his mother when she tried to check his obstinate determination to rush into a most ill-advised war. How different from Perceval's attitude in Chrétien's romance where the young hero had to be gently remonstrated with for quoting his mother too often. Beuve d'Aigremont, uncle of the four sons of Aymon, was equally unpleasant to his wife when she wished to prevent him from making war on the emperor. 'Go to your painted chambers, lady; look after your maidens and think about dyeing your silken thread. *My* job is to wield the sword and joust against the knights':

> Mal dahé ait (=cursed be) la barbe a nobile princier
> Ki en chambre de dame vait por lui conseiller[1]

More insulting still were the taunts hurled by Hernaut (in the *Narbonnais*) at his old father and by Guiberg d'Andrenas in the poem of that name. Guibert told his father, the renowned Aymeri (who actually was still fighting fit), to go and take a sleeping draught and get fat resting on four cushions for his greater ease.

This determination on the part of the knight not to allow anything to deflect him from his warlike aims is illustrated equally clearly by his attitude towards undue grieving for those who have been slain. Charlemagne had to be sharply reprimanded for his knights (including his trusted counsellor Naimes) for those exaggerated expressions of grief for his nephew, which remind us so vividly of the father's lament for his son Alexis in the poem relating the life of that saint. This form of funeral dirge is biblical in character and had doubtless come down through the ages, but it did not survive the earlier

---

[1] *Renaut de Montauban*, 14, 37 f.

chansons-de-geste in its full pathos. A more realistic note crept in. Of what use is it to mourn for the dead if we cannot bring them back? 'Desqu'ele est morte n'i a nul recovrier', sasy Bernier, speaking of his mother's death in *Raoul de Cambrai*. The same sentiment is expressed several times in this poem. The author of *Girart de Viane* is just as explicit:

> Seignor barons, assez l'avez oï,
> Puis c'omme est morz et alez a sa fin,
> C'est une chose molt tost mise en obli.

It was callous, perhaps, but merely a way of expressing the words of Christ: 'Let the dead bury their dead'. In medieval times it was, in fact, an item of the general belief in the necessity for moderation in all things. Grief, like other emotions, was in danger of being displayed to excess and the exhortations as to the need for *mesure* are numerous for 'hom senz mesure ne vaut un alier'.[1] A strong strain of common sense marks the literature of the epoch represented by the somewhat later *chansons-de-geste*. The warriors of the more heroic period, a Roland, a Vivien, were characterized by such religious fervour and such exalted patriotism that a certain degree of *démesure* was an almost inevitable part of their make-up. The danger of this was distinctly indicated in the *Chanson de Roland* and reached its logical conclusion in the description of the tragic life and death of Raoul de Cambrai, though here it had no worthier cause than pig-headed ambition. Bernier, on the other hand, the antagonist of Raoul, presents this common-sense side when protesting against the futility of indiscriminate slaughter as vengeance for the past: 'Laissiez les mors, n'i a nul recovrier', he cries in a pathetic appeal to Raoul's better self. But he cries to deaf ears. In *Girart de Viane* and *Garin le Lorrain* there is constant recurrence to the same theme, for human nature cannot stand excess of grief:

> 'En nom Dieu', dame, 'ce dit li dux Hervis,
> En grant duel faire onques gaigner ne vis.
> Duel sor dolor, ne joie sor joir,
> Home ne fame ne le doit maintenir.[2]

In *Girart de Viane* the Duchess of Borgoigne is even more practical as regards her dead husband. She comes to the king to ask him to sanction an immediate second marriage and to supply a suitable 'remplaçant'. The emperor grieves for the loss of his friend but pulls himself together quickly 'car en duel fere ne puet riens recovrer'.[3]

---

[1] *Raoul*, l. 2103.   [2] *Garin le Lorrain*, 45, 5f.   [3] l. 1231.

He expresses sympathy with the widow, who promptly replies that she also grieves for her husband but that grieving is useless, so would he kindly provide her with another:

> Sire, fet ele, ce pois(s)e moi formant,
> Mes en duel fere n'a nul recovrement.
> Se il vos plest, autre mari demant.

It shocks our modern sensibilities, but is less revolting than the thinly-disguised eagerness of Laudine to espouse Yvain in Chrétien's romance of that name. The pretence and face-saving which the artificiality of the romances necessitated gave rise to much casuistical pleading, but they readily adopted both the matter and the form of the expression which became proverbial: 'li vif aux vis, li mort aux morz' (or the singular form: 'li vix au vif, li morz au mort').

If the death of a friend or relation was not to cause excessive grief, how much less should the loss of a personal possession or even a part of oneself. The loss of a horse was hard to bear, it is true, and we have many examples of grief on this score—but to lose a limb or a piece of one's body could be borne with equanimity. The badly-wounded Bernier, in *Raoul de Cambrai*, when taunted by his enemy, replies that he feels lighter on the damaged side, that he has no use for superfluous flesh of which one can have too much: 'De povre char se puet on trop charchier'.[1] This identical line occurs in the *Couronnement de Louis* when Gui d'Alemaigne scorns to be intimidated by a blow from Guillaume which has cut off more than a foot of his flesh.[2] Thus we find the same ideas expressed in much the same words in the various poems, and it is difficult to say which borrowed from which or whether the expressions had become merely proverbial. In any case the proverbs had to be adapted to the metrical form and it is interesting to see how this process was effected. Proverbs became more and more popular as the epic period advanced. They are practically absent from the earliest of our poems. In the *Chanson de Roland* and the *Chançun de Willame* repetitions abound, but they are used to enforce a statement or mark a progression of thought—not merely to express some accepted idea. In the poems of second rank, however, they become very frequent and denote a falling-off of poetic invention. *Raoul de Cambrai* is rich in them; the same is true of *Garin le Lorrain*, which has its own particular favourite (it occurs at least three times): 'Qui son nes coupe, il deserte son vis'. An expression conveyed in proverbial form may have dire consequences, as when Raoul (de Cambrai) exclaims in his arrogant pride:

[1] *Raoul de Cambrai*, 4534 f.　　　[2] l. 2583.

'Ne Diex ne hom ne t'en puet garanter'.[1] His mother had already warned him: 'Se Diex te heit, tu seras tost finez', and his doom was sealed directly he uttered such blasphemy. The same words are just as ominous in other poems (e.g. *Couronnement, Garin le Lorrain*). It is clear that it was a well-known formula of defiance. On the other hand, no harm can possibly come to a man who enjoys God's favour ('*Ja n'iert honis cui Diex vuet bien aidier*) is a conviction expressed in the same three poems and many others. We have seen the importance attached to the possession of a good friend or a good neighbour; the proximity of a bad neighbour was correspondingly undesirable. Eginhart, in his *Life of Charlemagne*, quotes a well-known Greek proverb to the effect that 'the Frank is a good friend but a bad neighbour'; the dread of a bad neighbour is an oft-repeated thought in those days of territorial disputes represented by the Old French poems. 'Bien dure guerre deit rendre a sun veisin', remarks Guibourg of Guillaume after he has consumed a gargantuan meal; Raoul, on receiving a marvellous helmet from the emperor assures the giver that he accepts it with the intention of making good use of it: 'Vostre anemi i aront mal voisin'. Examples of this idea could be multiplied, summed up in the proverb: 'Au besoin conuit on l'ami'. The poetic form of an idea sometimes improved on the original. An old proverb said: 'Hardi a l'escuelle et couart au baston' (a descendant, perhaps, of Jove's taunt against the 'semper inertes', Tyrrhenians).[2] Raoul's mother, in her unaccountable contempt for the Arrouais, harps on the same theme:

> Trop par sont bon por vuidier escuele
> Mais au combatre, tex en est la novele,
> Ne valent mie .i. fromaje en fissele.

One would like to know the original version of *Raoul de Cambrai*. It is so full of archaic details and ancient customs in the version we possess. But it also abounds in the tags and locutions which became a hall-mark of later poems when rhyme had replaced assonance. These stock formulae were almost like the 'bouts rimés' of a later date. They exist for all moods and for all rhymes. In the earlier poems the stereotyped phrases were largely confined to descriptions of battles. We cannot assume from the similarity of those we find in *Roland*, in *Willame*, and in *Gormont et Isembart*, that any one of these poems had consciously imitated the other. But they do prove the existence of a regular pool of phrases from which the 'jongleur-'

---

[1] l. 3018.
[2] Virgil XI, 736 f.: 'exspectate dapes et plenae mensae / hic amor, hoc studium', etc.

U

poet could draw. The set expressions used in the 'regret' for a dead knight existed already, as has often been pointed out, in the *Vie de St. Alexis*, which was composed, moreover, in the decasyllabic metre common to most of the *chansons-de-geste*. The three *chansons* mentioned above all use the hackneyed battle-descriptions such as: *Pleine sa hanste, raide sa lance, parmi l'eschine* . . ., *l'escut li frait* . . . and many another of the same kind to describe the course of the numerous single combats. They are, indeed, used to satiety, but it must have been difficult to vary them. Here again, as with the proverbial expressions, certain poems have a predilection for one or another of the formulae. The author of *Aliscans* is particularly fond of describing terrible wounds by the phrase: 'De la menor morust uns amires' (or 'uns fors roncins'). The extraordinary popularity of the formula: 'Cui il consuit ne puet de mort garir' in its many adaptations according to metre, has been noticed. The ingenuity of the 'jongleur' in inventing a variation in the second half-line must have been considerably taxed. In *Girart de Rossillon*, owing to the fact that the pause occurs after the sixth syllable, the formula appears as: 'cui esconsec a coup/, pois ne vit goute'; the author of *Renaut de Montauban* gives a refreshing touch of variety by putting into the mouth of the hero (speaking in alexandrines): 'Se je l'ataing a cop, jeté a ambesas' (*If I catch him a blow he has thrown a double ace*). There are six variations in the second half of the formula employed by the heathen in the *Chanson* to describe Roland's fate. One will suffice to show the form: 'Se truis Rolant, ne lerrai ne le mat'. It is like the recurrent theme in a piece of music and is not to be confused with the tiresome tags (chevilles) which stamp the later poems. The *Chanson de Roland* has its own favourite locutions, but they are not the hackneyed ones. *Par amur et par feid* was a feudal formula which occurs frequently, but the author (Turoldus?) specializes generally in those with a somewhat fatalistic ring. 'Que fereient il el?' (What other (*el*) could they do?) is an oft-repeated remark. 'De ço cui calt)' (= *cui bono*) is another favourite; 'vueillet o non' (= willy-nilly), 'ne puet muer' (followed by subj.), 'qui qu'en peist u qui nun' or its equivalent in meaning 'qui qu'en plurt u ki'n riet' (= *whether one likes it or not*), each occur in their place to give a sense of the inevitable. But there is not the sickening repetition of phrases found in the decadent poems which actually turned 'cui qu'en poist' into a proper name (*Quicampoix*) through its constant repetition. The author of the *Chançun de Willame*, like Turoldus, has his pet expressions. Such is the oft-repeated deprecatory reply of the youthful Gui: 'unc mais n'en oï tel' (*I never heard of such a thing*), or the more elaborate response of his uncle: 'Cors as d'enfant mais raison as de ber'. Otherwise the phrases in the *Chançun* belong to the same category as those in *Roland* and *Gormont et Isembart*, including the simple exclamatory ones such as: 'Ki dunc veïst', 'si veïssez', etc.

Antoine Thomas, in his edition of *Raoul de Cambrai*, has listed the phrases which disfigure that poem in its present form—e.g. 'por tot l'or de Milan, Tudele, Montpelier', etc.; to describe beauty, 'o le cler vis'; anger: 'n'i ot que correcier' or 'le sens cuide desver', etc. etc.—all of which are employed 'ad nauseam'. References to God are many and varied. 'Si Dex n'en pense' is a prelude to almost certain death; 'nes (= not even) Dieu tonant' strengthens a description of deafening sound; 'Dieu qui haut siet et loing voit' gives an impression of God's majesty and is much affected by the author of *Renaut de Montauban*. As we advance in time and decadence the number of these devices to fill up a line increases and they become more and more trivial in character. One has only to glance at any of the late twelfth or early thirteenth-century poems to realize how completely stereotyped the style has become and how the padding increased as the inspiration diminished. By the time this stage was reached the period of epic poetry in France may be said to be over. Romances with their love-intrigues, their often pointless adventures, and their exploitation of the 'merveilleux' had already taken their place. Had they not been revived in other lands under a completely different guise, most of the heroes would have died a natural death, but they lived on in their strange new forms for many years, and even the horse of Renaud de Montauban, the famous Bayard, can still be heard neighing in the Forest of Ardennes by those who have ears to hear.

EDITIONS OF TEXTS CITED

AIMERI DE NARBONNE. Ed. M. L. Demaison. S.A.T.F. 1887.

AIOL (CH. D'). Ed. J. Normand et G. Raynaud. S.A.T.F. 1877.

ALEXANDER-FRAGMENT. Ed.W. Förster. *Altfranzösisches Uebungsbuch*, 1915.

ALEXIS (VIE DE ST.). (1) Ed. Gaston Paris (Large Edition). Paris. 1872. (2) Ed. Gaston Paris. C.F.M.A. 1925. (3) Ed. C. Storey. Publ. E. Droz. Paris 1934.

ALISCANS (CH. D'). Ed.Wienbeck, Hartnacke, Rasch. Halle 1903. Ed. G. Rolin (*Altfr. Bibl.*). 1894.

AMIS ET AMILES (CH. D' and VITA). Ed. Konrad Hoffmann. Erlangen 1882.

AMIS AND AMILOUN. Ed. MacEdw. Leach. E.E.T.S. 1937.

ASPREMONT (CH. D'). Ed. Louis Brandin. C.F.M.A. 1919–21.

AUDIGIER. Ed. Barbazon et Méon. *Fabliaux et Contes*. Vol. IV.

BARBASTRE (SIÈGE DE). Ed. J. L. Perrier. C.F.M.A. 1926.

BELLA PARISIACAE URBIS. See *Monumenta Germaniae Historica Poetae Lat. Aev. Carol.* 4, 72 ff.

CHARROI DE NÎMES. (1) Ed. J. L. Perrier. C.F.M.A. 1931. (2) Ed. E. Lange-Kowal. Berlin 1934.

CHEVALERIE OGIER. Ed. J. Barrois. Paris 1842.

CHEVY-CHASE. *Oxford Book of Ballads*. No. 128.

CHRONICON WALCIODORENSE. See *Romania*, Nos. 37, 38.

COURONNEMENT DE LOUIS. Ed. E. Langlois. C.F.M.A. 1920.

COVENANT VIVIEN (or CHEVALERIE VIVIEN). Ed. A.-L. Terracher. Paris 1909.

DESTRUCTION DE ROME. Ed. Louis Brandin. *Romania*. 1938.

DOON DE MAYENCE (CH. DE). Ed. A. Pey. Paris 1859.

ENFANCES GARIN. (1) Analysis in *Histoire Littéraire*, tome xxii, pp. 438–40. (2) L. Gautier, *Les Epopées Françaises*, tome iv.

ENFANCES VIVIEN. Ed. H. Zorn (Diss). Leipzig 1908.

ENTRÉE D'ESPAGNE. Ed. A. Thomas (2 vol.). S.A.T.F. 1913.

EREC (Chrétien de Troyes). Ed. W. Förster. 1899. Small ed. (2nd) 1909.

FIERABRAS. (1) Ed. A. Kröber et G. Servois. A.P.F. 1860. (2) L. Brandin, *Romania* 1938.

FLOOVENT. (1) Ed. Michelant et Guessard. A.P.F. 1858. (2) Ed. F. H. Bateson, 1938.

FOUQUE-FITZ-WARIN. Ed. L. Brandin. C.F.M.A. 1930.

FRAGMENT-DE-LA-HAYE. (1) See Introduction to *Les Narbonnois*. Ed. H. Suchier. (2) Ed. Koschwitz und Förster. *Altfr. Uebungsbuch*.

GARIN LE LORRAIN. Ed. Paulin Paris, 2 vols. R.D.P. II and III. 1833–5 (not complete).

GESTA FRANCORUM (ANONYMI). (1) Ed. H. Hagenmeyer. 1890. (2) Ed. B. A. Lees. Oxford 1924.

GIRARD DE ROUSSILLON. Selections in (1) Appel: *Chrestomathie Provençale*. (2) Paul Meyer, *Recueil des plus Anciens Textes*, Vol. I.

GORMONT ET ISEMBART. Ed. A. Bayot. C.F.M.A. 1931.

GUIBERT D'ANDRENAS. (1) Ed. J. Crosland. Manch. Univ. Press 1923. (2) Ed. J. Melander. Paris 1922.

GUILLAUME (CH. DE). See Willame.

KARLAMAGNUS-SAGA. (1) Ed. C. R. Unger. Christiania 1860. (2) Selections (translated). Gaston Paris. See *Bibl. Ec. Chartres*, Vᵉ Serie, t.v. (3) German translation by E. Koschwitz. *Romanische Studien*, 1878.

LOHIER UND MALLARD. Translation by K. Simrock. 1868.

LUDWIGSLIED. Ed. C. Braune. *Althochdeutsches Uebungsbuch.*

MACAIRE (MACHARIO). Ed. F. Guessard. A.P.F. 1866.

NARBONNAIS (LES). Ed. H. Suchier. S.A.T.F. 2 vols. 1898.

OGIER LE DANOIS. Ed. J. Barrois. R.D.P. 1842.

OTINEL. Ed. F. Guessard et H. Michelant. A.P.F. 1859.

PÈLERINAGE DE CHARLEMAGNE. (1) Ed. E. Koschwitz, 5th ed. Leipzig 1932. (2) Ed. A. J. Cooper. Paris 1925.

PERCY REED. *Oxford Book of Ballads*. No. 146.

PRISE DE CORDOUE. Ed. O. Densusianu. S.A.T.F. 1896.

PRISE D'ORANGE. Ed. B. Katz. New York 1947.

PSEUDO-TURPIN (CHRONICLE OF TURPIN). (1) Ed. F. Castets. 1880. (2) Ed. R. Mortier. *Chanson de Roland*, Vol. 3. 1941.

QUATRE FILZ AYMON (RENAUT DE MONTAUBAN). (1) Ed. E. Tarbé. 1861. (2) Ed. E. Castets. Montpelier 1909.

RADULPHUS TORTARIUS. Ed. De Certain. *Archives des Missions Scientifiques*, V, Iʳᵉ Série. 118f.

ROLAND (CHANSON DE). (1) L. Gautier. Many editions from 1872 onwards. (2) Ed. Stengel. *Das Altfranzösische Rolandslied*, Tome 1. 1900. (3) J. Bédier (d'apres le manuscrit d'Oxford) 1921. Commentaire 1927. (4) T. A. Jenkins. Boston 1924. (5) R. Mortier. *Chanson de Roland*, Tomes 1 and 2. 1945. (6) Song of, Ed. T. Herrtage. E.E.T.S. Extra Series XXXIX (1880).

RONZASVALS. (1) Ed. M. Roques. *Romania*, LVII, 1932. (2) Ed. R. Mortier. *Chanson de Roland*, Tome 3.

RUOLANDESLIED. Ed. K. Bartsch. *Deutsche Dichtungen des Mittelalters*, III. 1874.

SAISNES (CH. DES). Ed. Fr. Michel. R.D.P. 1839.

SIR ALDINGAR. *Oxford Book of Ballads*. No. 4.

SIR FERUMBRAS. Ed. S. J. Herrtage. E.E.T.S. Ex. Ser. XXXIV.

TURPIN (HISTORIA CAROLI MAGNI ET ROTHOLANDI). See Pseudo-Turpin.

VITA CAROLI MAGNI (Eginhard). Ed. L. Halphen (*Cl. de l'Histoire de France*). 1923.

WALTHARIUS MANU FORTIS. Ed. K. Strecker. 2 Aufl. 1924.

WILLAME (CHANÇUN DE) (1) Ed. Suchier. Halle 1911. (2) Ed. E. S. Tyler. New York 1919.

INDEX OF PROPER NAMES